CW00554551

THE WATERFORD LIMERICK & WESTERN RAILWAY

Ernie Shepherd

Ian Allan
PUBLISHING

This book is dedicated to my wife Joy, who had to endure many absences
and lonely evenings as researches continued.

The WL&WR crest

The WL&WR shield is divided into three parts, which is unusual, and at the same time includes an escutcheon. On the left is Waterford — three lions and three ships (the latter displayed vertically, whereas they are horizontal on the D&SER crest). On the right is part of the arms of Limerick by a structure markedly different from that of the GS&WR. At the base is represented Clonmel, with a stag pursued by greyhounds across a three-arched bridge (which should consist of five arches) with three fishes naiant (swimming) in the base. The escutcheon portrays a tolerably good representation of the company's 4-4-0 express engine *Jubilee*, unexpectedly finished in a green livery.

First published 2006

ISBN (10) 0 7110 3147 9
ISBN (13) 978 0 7110 3147 0

All rights reserved.
No part of this book may be reproduced or
transmitted in any form or by any means,
electronic or mechanical, including photocopying,
recording or by any information storage
and retrieval system, without permission
from the Publisher in writing.

© Ernie Shepherd 2006

Published by Ian Allan Publishing

an imprint of Ian Allan Publishing Ltd,
Hersham, Surrey KT12 4RG.
Printed in England by Ian Allan Printing Ltd,
Hersham, Surrey KT12 4RG.

Code: 0603/B
_____

Visit the Ian Allan Publishing website at
www.ianallanpublishing.com

CONTENTS

Title page: **Limerick station on 12 June 1953, showing to good effect the overall roof over a portion of the platforms. The main station buildings and concourse are at the inner end of the platforms, which are numbered 1 to 4 from the right-hand side. In platform 4 an enthusiasts' special has arrived from Tralee behind 'J15' 0-6-0 No 156, while an unidentified ex WL&WR 4-4-0 stands at the head of a train in platform 1.** D. G. Coakham

Above: **View taken about 1900 of engine No 54 *Killemnee* and a train of assorted carriages approaching Clonmel.**
Photographer unknown, G. Beesley collection

ACKNOWLEDGEMENTS

This, the fourth in the series of illustrated histories of Irish railways, could not have been written without the usual unstinting assistance from many quarters. The official statutory records of all Irish railways which became a part of the Great Southern Railways in January 1925 are held by Córas Iompair Éireann at Heuston station in Dublin. These records were kindly made available through the good offices of the company secretary and staff. It would be remiss of the author not to specifically mention the present Secretarial Services Manager, Marcella Doyle and her predecessors, Mary Oliver and Dympna Kelledy, for allowing free access to this material over a period of many years.

Tim Moriarty, Joseph Leckey and Brendan Pender, respectively librarian, past archivist and current archivist, of the Irish Railway Record Society (IRRS), made a vast amount of material in the care of the Society freely available for research, and to them the author is extremely grateful. Other members of the IRRS also helped in many and varied ways, including Gerry Beesley, the late Bob Clements, Desmond Coakham, Eugene Field, Clifton Flewitt, Séan Kennedy, the late Norman McAdams, Ken Manto, Herbert Richards and Peter Rowledge. Peter had carried out quite considerable research into the Waterford & Limerick Railway over a number of years, and made this material available to the present author. He also read the finished manuscript and made some helpful and useful suggestions.

Bob Clements's notebooks on the company's locomotives provided the bulk of the material for the relevant chapter. Just as the author was putting the final touches to the locomotive and rolling stock chapters, Barry Carse very kindly loaned an official WL&WR stock register which had recently come into his possession. This proved invaluable in finally correcting some previous misconceptions and inaccuracies. It also enabled the author to piece together a virtually complete history of the company's locomotives and rolling stock. Gerry Beesley was a great support at a time when the author had grave reservations about continuing with the research, following the publication of another work on the W&LR in the year 2000. Subsequently, and despite his frequent overseas travels, Gerry read through the various drafts of the manuscript and made many constructive comments. He also assisted in the researches into the locomotive and rolling stock chapters.

Séan Kennedy is responsible for many of the excellent photographic illustrations, some reproduced from his own vast collection. Desmond Coakham kindly provided the author with carriage and wagon photographs as well as some of the station views, reproduced to his usual high standard. The IRRS also made available photographic material in its collection; in this regard, thanks are again due to Séan Kennedy for reproducing these images. I would also like to thank Ian Allan Publishing and the Stephenson Locomotive Society for assistance with photographs.

Outside of the IRRS, the author must mention the assistance and encouragement received from Bill Irish of Waterford. Bill first came to the author's attention in late 2001 with the publication of his book entitled *Shipbuilding in Waterford 1820-1882*. This book included several photographs showing the W&LR quay extension at Waterford. Since that time, Bill has kept a watching eye for items of railway interest on behalf of the author.

The author would also mention the assistance provided by the National Archives at Kew (the former Public Record Office), which holds the records of the Board of Trade, including reports of line inspections and accidents. Also worthy of mention are the National Archives and the National Library in Dublin. Finally, I make an unreserved apology for any omissions from the list of people who assisted, but it is purely unintentional.

AUTHOR'S NOTE

At the time of its demise in January 1901 the Waterford Limerick & Western Railway ranked fourth in terms of size among the railway companies of Ireland, after the GNR(I), GS&WR and the MGWR. The total route mileage was in excess of 342 miles; total train miles worked in the last six months of the company's independent existence amounted to 593,538, of which 417,661 were passenger train miles. Authorised capital was £2,624,443, while rolling stock consisted of 58 locomotives, 179 coaches and 1,350 goods vehicles. These figures are quoted to show that the WL&WR was no small enterprise. On the other hand, it has received scant attention from historians, apart from one or two articles in *The Railway Magazine* and a pocket history of the line published in 2000. Perhaps this is because it has for too long been regarded simply as an arm of the GS&WR, or is due to its departure from the scene more than a century ago. The line however had a fascinating and tortuous history, relying for much of its existence on rebates and other assistance from the Great Western Railway. The present author feels this fascinating story is worthy of recording in full.

Whilst the total mileage exceeded 340, the original W&LR line was only 77 miles in length. The remainder consisted of various lines absorbed or worked in the intervening years. Among these was the grandiosely titled Southern Railway, with a line only 25 miles in length. This line retained its independence until 1925 when it became the last company absorbed into the newly formed Great Southern Railways in November. This resulted from the fact that advertisements seeking shareholders failed to produce any claimants and this obviously delayed the vesting of the line. The foregoing examples only give the merest flavour of a line which eventually stretched from Sligo to Waterford and from Limerick to Fenit in Kerry.

As in the companion volumes, the 24-hour clock has been used throughout, except in direct quotations from other sources. Once again, monetary values have been expressed in the currency of the period. Prior to 1970, both the Irish and British pounds (£) consisted of 20 shillings, each of 12 pennies, there being thus 240 pennies to the pound. The abbreviations used were 's' for shillings and 'd' for pence, as for example £324,225 10s 0d. Mention might also be made of the guinea, now a thing of the past except in horse-racing circles; the guinea consisted of 21 shillings. Sterling and Irish currencies diverged in 1970, the Irish punt, introduced in that year, consisting of 100 new pennies, making a conversion of 2.4 old pence to the later 1p. In turn, the punt was superseded by the euro as from 1 January 2002, this latter being worth IR£0.787564; the euro floats on a daily basis against sterling. Imperial weights and measures have likewise been overtaken by metric equivalents. One imperial ton weight consisted of 20 hundredweights (cwt), the latter being comprised of 112 pounds (lb). An imperial ton equates to 1.016 metric tonnes; one pound to 0.4536kg. Finally, a linear mile is made up of 1,760 yards or 5,280 feet, and equals 1.609 kilometres. The reader is referred to tables of weights and measures, found in any good diary, for further details if required.

It should be mentioned that the classification of engines shown in Chapter Fifteen and in the relevant appendices is one of the author's choosing. It was in no way an official classification, but has been used to simplify the description of different groupings of engines.

Any omissions or errors are the sole responsibility of the author.

BIBLIOGRAPHY

As in all research, it has been necessary to consult many different records. In relation to official records, once again the board, traffic and works minute books of the company and its subsidiaries have been extensively researched with a view to forming the basic structure of the line's history. In addition, it has been necessary to go through similar records for other companies which had relations or disputes with the WL&WR. These include the minute books of the GS&WR and the MGWR. Some additional material is still extant, including finance committee minute books and officers' committee minute books for the W&LR. Sufficient timetables exist to enable a good summary of services to be recorded.

In addition to the company's own minute books, Acts of Parliament, Parliamentary plans, etc proved useful, along with the Board of Trade files and reports on both inspections and accidents, the latter documents held in the National Archives at Kew. A few stray copies of Books of Reference still survive, also Ordnance Survey maps, reports of arbitration proceedings and the transcripts of Parliamentary hearings. Station layout diagrams date mainly from the GS&WR era or later, likewise signal cabin diagrams.

Newspapers referred to include:
Freemans Journal, Irish Independent, Irish Press, Irish Times, Saunders Newsletter and *Waterford News*.

Railway periodicals include:
Engineering, Herepath's Railway Journal, Irish Railfans' News, Irish Railway Gazette, Journal of the Irish Railway Record Society, The Locomotive, Railway Gazette, Railway News and *Railway Times*.

Other printed sources referred to:
A History of Railways in Ireland: Conroy, J. C.; Longmans Green & Co Ltd 1928.
Claremorris to Collooney Railway The Burma Road: Swinford Historical Society, 1996.
Dublin & South Eastern Railway: Beesley, G. & Shepherd, E.; Midland Publishing Ltd, 1998.
Great Southern & Western Railway: Murray, K. A. & McNeill, D. B.; IRRS, 1976.
History of the Great Western Railway: MacDermot, E. T.; GWR Co, 1927.
Ireland since the Famine: Lyons, F. S. L.; Fontana Press, 1985.
Irish Railways Today: Pender, B. & Richards, H.; Transport Research Associates, 1967.
J.G. Robinson, A Lifetime's Work: Jackson, David; Oakwood Press, 1996.
Johnson's Atlas & Gazetteer of the Railways of Ireland: Johnson, S.; Midland Publishing Ltd, 1997.
Journal of Commerce & Shipping Telegraph: 13th November 1901.
Locomotive & Train Working in the latter part of the Nineteenth Century Vol. 6: Ahrons, E. L.; Heffer, 1954.
Midland Great Western Railway of Ireland: Shepherd, E.; Midland Publishing Ltd, 1994.
On the Move CIE 1945-95: Ó Riain, Mícheál; Gill & Macmillan, Dublin, 1995.
Portlaw, A Local History: ICA Local History Group.
Portlaw, Co. Waterford 1825-1876: Hunt, Tom; Irish Academic Press, 2000.
Railway Lines of CIE & NIR: Doyle, O. & Hirsch, S.; Signal Press, 1985.
Reflections on Munster Railways: Limerick Museum, 1984.

Robinson Locomotives: Haresnape, Brian & Rowledge, Peter; Ian Allan Ltd, London, 1981.
Shipbuilding in Waterford, 1820-1882: Irish, Bill; Wordwell Ltd, 2001.
Sligo Leitrim & Northern Counties Railway: Sprinks, N. W.; IRRS London Area, 1970.
Some Industrial Railways of Ireland: McGrath, Walter; Cork, 1959.
Southern Railway: White, Walton; an unpublished manuscript, New Zealand, 1997.
The Dingle Tram: Rowlands, D., McGrath, W. & Francis, T.; Plateway Press, 1996.
The Lartigue – Listowel & Ballybunion Railway: Guerin, M; Lartigue Centenary Committee, 1988.
The Listowel & Ballybunion Railway: Newham, A. T.; Oakwood Press.
The Life & Times of a Railwayman, Limerick Junction 150 years on: Slattery, P. J.; The Author.
The Malcomsons & the Economic Development of the Lower Suir Valley, 1782-1877: Fogarty, Margaret in an Essay presented for a Degree of Master of Economic Science of NUI.
The Malcomsons of Portlaw: Morley, John; The Winkle Market, 1989.
The North Pembroke & Fishguard Railway: Morris, J. P.; The Oakwood Press, 1969.
The Railways of Kerry: O'Connor, Michael; Country Watch, 1988.
The Shannon Scheme: ed Bielenberg, Andy; Lilliput Press, Dublin, 2002.
The West Clare Railway: Taylor, Patrick; Plateway Press, 1994.

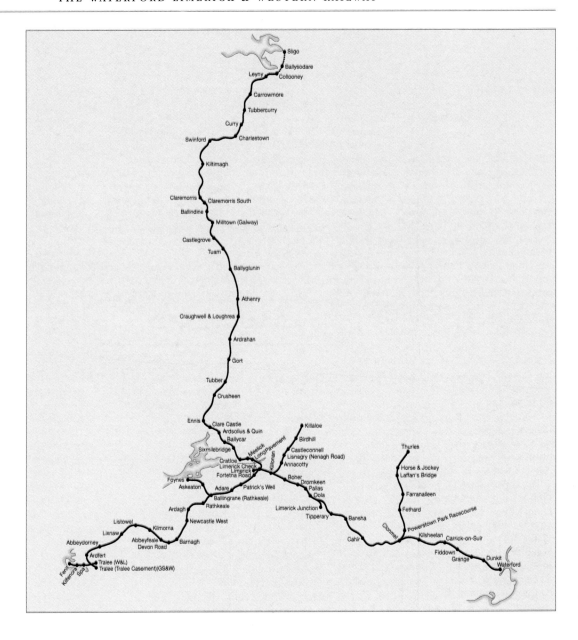

ABBREVIATIONS

A&EJR	Athenry & Ennis Junction Railway	
A&TR	Athenry & Tuam Railway	
A&TECLR	Athenry & Tuam Extension to Claremorris Light Railway	
B&CLR	Ballinrobe & Claremorris Light Railway	
BoT	Board of Trade	
BoW	Board of Works	
C&CR	Claremorris & Collooney Railway	
CIE	Córas Iompair Éireann	
C&LDR	Cork & Limerick Direct Railway	
C&TR	Clonmel & Thurles Railway	
CoDSP	City of Dublin Steam Packet Co	
D&SER	Dublin & South Eastern Railway	
DW&WR	Dublin Wicklow & Wexford Railway	
ESB	Electricity Supply Board	
F&RR&H	Fishguard & Rosslare Railways & Harbours Co	
GN&WR	Great Northern & Western Railway	
GNR(I)	Great Northern Railway (Ireland)	

GS&WR	Great Southern & Western Railway	
GSR	Great Southern Railways	
GWR	Great Western Railway	
ISER	Irish South Eastern Railway	
KJR	Kilkenny Junction Railway	
L&BR	Listowel & Ballybunion Railway	
L&CR	Limerick & Castleconnell Railway	
L&ER	Limerick & Ennis Railway	
L&FR	Limerick & Foynes Railway	
L&KR	Limerick & Kerry Railway	
L&NKJR	Limerick & North Kerry Junction Railway	
L&NWR	London & North Western Railway	
MGWR	Midland Great Western of Ireland Railway	
P&PBR	Parsonstown & Portumna Bridge Railway	
PWLC	Public Works Loan Commissioners	
R&NJR	Rathkeale & Newcastle Junction Railway	

RIC	Royal Irish Constabulary	
SL&NCR	Sligo Leitrim & Northern Counties Railway	
SR	Southern Railway of Ireland	
SWR	South Wales Railway	
T&DR	Tralee & Dingle Railway	
T&FP&HC	Tralee & Fenit Pier & Harbour Commissioners	
T&FR	Tralee & Fenit Railway	
W&CIR	Waterford & Central Ireland Railway	
W&KR	Waterford & Kilkenny Railway	
W&LR	Waterford & Limerick Railway	
WCR	West Clare Railway	
WD&LR	Waterford Dungarvan & Lismore Railway	
WL&WR	Waterford Limerick & Western Railway	
WWW&DR	Waterford Wexford Wicklow & Dublin Railway	

Chapter One

EARLY DAYS — LIMERICK TO WATERFORD

The first public railway, the Stockton & Darlington Railway, was opened for traffic on Tuesday, 27 September 1825. Within months of this event, the secretary of the Hibernian Railway Company received a report from a Mr Alexander Nimmo on a proposed railway between Limerick and Waterford. Nimmo's main line was to run from Limerick to Carrick-on-Suir, with a continuation line to Waterford and a branch into north Tipperary to serve the coalfields at Killenaule. The promoters, who included the Earl of Glengall and the Earl of Belfast, were sufficiently impressed with Nimmo's findings to persuade them to go to Parliament, success being achieved for the Limerick & Waterford Railway Act which received Royal Assent on 31 May 1826, the only Act passed for an Irish railway in the reign of George IV.

The proposed main line was to commence at the Canal Lock in Clare Street in Limerick and would have passed through, among other places, Singland, Killowen (Killonan), Grainge, Oolagh (also spelt Ulla), Solahidmore, Bansa (Bansha), Cahir, Clonmell (sic) and Kilsheelin (sic) to a terminus 'at or near to a certain place called or known by the Name of the Ozier Beds in the Town of Carrick'. There were to be three branches, one from Prior's Town in the parish of Kilsheelan to a terminus at Strangman's Stores in Waterford, and passing through Kilmacow, Granny (Grannagh), Grace Dieu and Bilberry Rock. The second branch was to run from Cappagh through Cashel and Ballytarsna and to terminate at Thomas Dwyer's Lot in the Townfields of Thurles. The third line was to be a branch out of the second line to serve the coalfields of Killenaule and Ballingarry.

Powers were granted for the making of inclined planes, presumably in connection with the collieries, and the erection of docks, basins, quays and wharves at Carrick, Clonmel and Waterford. It was ordained that the works might be commenced immediately. Nimmo estimated the cost of the entire works at £324,225 10s 0d, the capital being fixed at £350,000. Steam engines, if used, were to be capable of 'consuming their own smoke'. Whilst provision was made in the Act for the company to carry goods, it is clear that it

was envisaged that owners could run their own wagons, carriages, etc. Section 126 stipulated that owners were to put their names on the outside of their wagons, which were to be constructed to the designs of the company's engineer. There were one or two strange provisions in the Act which would certainly not have been acceptable to the Board of Trade (BoT) in later years. Section 143 allowed for owners of adjoining land to lay down 'collateral branches from their respective lands to communicate with the Railway'; they were also empowered to make roads across the railway.

Whilst the Act passed into law, it was not possible to raise the necessary finances despite an offer from the Board of Public Works to make available a loan of £100,000 once a similar amount was subscribed locally. The Limerick & Waterford suffered a slow lingering existence as further surveys were carried out, including one by George Stephenson in 1828. The scheme was briefly revived in 1836 under the title of the Suir & Shannon Junction Railroad, a line promoted by the Great Western Railway, which saw potential in Limerick as a future transatlantic port.

In 1831 the Dublin & Kingstown Railway Act was passed, the line being opened from Westland Row, Dublin, to Kingstown (now Dun Laoghaire) on 17 December 1834; it was the first railway to open in Ireland. Various schemes now emerged and with the rapid expansion in proposals, Parliament decided in October 1836 to set up a Royal Commission to consider and report on the most favourable system of railways for Ireland. The Commission's final report was issued in July 1838 and after providing a review of the country's economy and existing traffic by canal and road, looked at likely railway schemes.

The Great Leinster & Munster Railway which had proposed a line from Dublin through Sallins and Athy to Kilkenny, with possible extensions to Cork, Clonmel, Waterford and Limerick, was set aside. The Commissioners proposed a trunk route from Dublin through or near Portarlington, Maryborough (now Portlaoise), Mountrath, Thurles, Cashel, Cahir, Mitchelstown and Mallow to Cork. Kilkenny was to be served by a branch leaving the main line near Mountrath, following much of the route of the later Kilkenny Junction Railway. Charles

Vignoles, who carried out the surveys for the southern lines, proposed a line leaving the Cork route at Holycross, a few miles south of Thurles, to run through Cappagh, five miles north of Tipperary, to Limerick, where a terminus would be provided near the Lunatic Asylum on the Cork road. From Limerick the line was to continue through Pallaskenry and Askeaton to Tarbert, thought to be another likely contender as a transatlantic port. From Donaghill (close to Cappagh) another line would run southeastwards through Golden Bridge, crossing the Cork line between Cashel and Cahir, at a point 104½ miles from Dublin and 36 miles from Limerick, to Clonmel. This was as far as Vignoles surveyed, as he considered Nimmo's earlier line sufficient to bring the railway on into Waterford.

On 6 August 1844 the Great Southern & Western Railway Company obtained an Act for a railway from Dublin to Cashel with a branch to Carlow. Cashel was chosen as a terminus pending a final decision on the choice of route onwards to Cork. In any event, the decision was taken to proceed first with a branch to Carlow, this being opened on 4 August 1846.

Revised plans and an Act is obtained

Meanwhile, the *Irish Railway Gazette* of 11 November 1844 reported on a meeting of the Provisional Committee of the Waterford & Limerick Railway Company held in the Town Hall at Waterford for the purpose of hearing a report from its consulting engineer, none other than Charles Vignoles. There was reported to be a large attendance at the meeting, which was chaired by Thomas Meagher, Mayor of Waterford. Vignoles reported favourably on the proposed line, estimating the cost of construction at not more than £750,000. Vignoles again considered two routes from Carrick, one, and the most feasible, being via Fiddown and Ballytarsna with a crossing of the River Suir at Grannagh; the bridge there would cost about £50,000. From Grannagh, the line would proceed by Bilberry Rock into Waterford, passing to the south side of the Barrack, along the north side of the Roman Catholic College, across the Manor and John Street to the terminus beside the river at the Neptune Foundry.

At the Limerick end the line would commence on the east side of Nelson Street, crossing the old road about a mile from Limerick. It was unanimously agreed at the meeting that the necessary notice for application to Parliament should be served.

Another scheme briefly came to the fore about this time, namely the Great Munster Railway of Ireland, for a line leaving the GS&WR near Mountrath and passing through Limerick and Tarbert to Tralee, but this scheme was short-lived. It should be mentioned that the GS&WR also had plans for a Limerick extension at this time, powers being granted under its Act for a branch diverging from its main line in the townland of Kyle and terminating 'in a field adjoining the Lunatic Asylum near the city of Limerick, and at or near the Junction of the Mail Coach Roads to Tipperary and Cork in the townland of Spittalland'. Representatives from the two companies met on 11 February 1845, as evidenced by a GS&WR Board minute, and it was agreed that the W&LR should proceed with the construction of the line into Limerick. Failure by the latter company to purchase land or to construct the line within a period of time to be set by Parliament would leave the GS&WR free to proceed with construction.

Success was achieved on 21 July 1845 when Royal Assent was given to *An Act for making and maintaining a Railway from the City of Waterford to the City of Limerick, with Branches*. Included among the subscribers were Thomas Meagher, William J. Geary (Mayor of Limerick), Charles Bianconi (Mayor of Clonmel and operator of stage coach services), Henry Denny and three members of the important business family of Malcomson from Waterford. Capital was £750,000 comprising 15,000 shares, each of £50. The Act made provision for a branch from Grace Dieu East to or near the premises of Messrs Strangman & Davis' Brewery in Waterford.

Section XXVII of the Act laid down that the portion of line from the south bank of the River Suir below Grannagh Castle to Carrick-on-Suir should not be commenced or even contracted for until the BoT should

determine the correct course for the line, north or south of the river. Section XLII recognised the GS&WR interests and stipulated that the line from its point of intersection with the GS&WR to Limerick was to be common to both companies, although the GS&WR was to be at liberty to construct its own station at Limerick. The latter company was further safeguarded in that the W&LR line into Limerick was to be completed by 1 May 1847, failure to do so leaving the GS&WR free to take over and complete the works. Furthermore, if the W&LR failed to commence work within three months of the passing of the Act, or at any time failed to proceed with the formation of that portion of line for a period of three months, then the powers would transfer to the GS&WR.

With its Act passed, the first meeting of W&LR shareholders was held in Waterford on Thursday, 21 August, Thomas Meagher, chairman of the company, presiding. William Septimus Saunders had been appointed secretary to the new company at a salary of £600 per annum. Saunders was the brother of Charles Saunders, Brunel's finance cornerstone, the company secretary, general manager and superintendent of the line of the GWR. This appointment represented the close alliance between the two companies which was to remain almost to the end of the W&LR's independent existence. It was resolved that the directors from Limerick should provide accommodation at Limerick for the engineering staff while their Waterford colleagues should rent a house, at a maximum rent of £50 per annum, for use as the company's offices. Vignoles was authorised to proceed at once with the Limerick to Tipperary section, work on which was of course required to commence within three months. The requirement that the BoT decide on the course of the line beyond Carrick-on-Suir, arising from the opposition of the Suir Navigation Company, led to the decision to leave the southern portion of the line *pro tem*.

A month later, at a meeting held in Cruise's Hotel in Limerick, it was reported that the entire line to Tipperary had been

marked out and 10 miles surveyed. Notices had been served on landowners and the secretary was requested to seek tenders for construction. Discussions were opened with the governors of the Lunatic Asylum in Limerick for the purchase of land, payment for which amounting to £1,100 was made in October; the company also agreed to erect two walls. Tenders were received from a number of contractors in October, that of William Dargan being in due course accepted.

Turning the first sod

Wednesday, 15 October 1846 was an important day for the new company. During the morning, the board members visited the proposed site of the new Limerick terminus. Then, at 1 o'clock, a procession of cars and carriages left the city for a certain field at Boher some seven miles away, the property of the Rt Hon the Earl of Clare. This latter gentleman performed the ceremony of turning the first sod 'in capital style.' The ceremony was repeated by various personages including William Dargan, Charles Vignoles and Richard Osborne. It was reported that Dargan distributed a large sum of money to the several country people present and £5 to James McCormack, tenant of the field, so that he might entertain his neighbours. The dignitaries then returned to Limerick for a splendid dinner in Cruise's Hotel, the party numbering 40.

Mention has been made above of Richard Osborne. Born in London in 1815, he emigrated to Canada at the age of 19, shortly afterwards moving to the United States where he became involved with railways, becoming chief engineer to the Philadelphia & Reading Railroad in 1842. While in its employ he became friendly with a gentleman by the name of Howe who had invented a new form of girder bridge. Osborne returned to England in May 1845 and made early contact with Vignoles to whom he explained his interest in bridges. Vignoles was at this time considering the bridging of the River Suir at Grannagh, and the upshot of the meeting with Osborne was that the latter was offered the post of

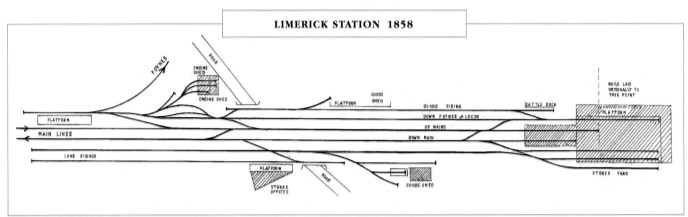

LIMERICK STATION 1858

The famous Keane's Points at Limerick Junction looking towards Limerick. The line diverging to the left provides access to Limerick Junction station. The two houses on the right were occupied by signalmen. Note the water pump between the two lines. W. A. Camwell/IRRS collection

resident engineer to the W&LR under Vignoles at Waterford. The latter, who was required to attend eight times annually, for a minimum of a week on each occasion, was receiving £1,000 per annum, while Osborne was to receive £800 a year plus travelling expenses.

Difficulties were encountered in relation to the purchase of land. Whilst the company believed it had made fair offers of compensation, which were 'liberal in the extreme', these did not meet with the approval of the landowners. An example was given in January 1846 of a Mr Dixon from whom the company required about 32 acres on which stood 16 cabins yielding a rental of £94 per annum. Dickson himself was only a lessee as the land belonged to the Earl of Limerick. He demanded a figure of £16,000 in compensation; the case went to arbitration before a jury where he was awarded £3,222 15s 0d, apparently a fraction of the sum offered by the company. Even the jury jumped on the bandwagon, demanding an attendance fee before handing down its award. Another case was that of William Roche who claimed £1,800, was offered £260 and finally accepted £85. Such awards soon brought a halt to exorbitant claims. In contrast, the case of Dr Henry White is worthy of mention. Dr White was the landlord of a cottage required by the company. He readily agreed to forgo compensation for himself, instead handing it over to the tenant of his property, one by the name of Morrison, who had lost an arm in an accident.

At the half-yearly meeting of shareholders held in February 1846 it was reported that several cargoes of rails had been delivered at Limerick. Vignoles reported that difficulties had been encountered in obtaining land which had delayed the contractor. Of the 25 miles to Tipperary, about one-third was well advanced, with 1,200 men employed. This number was expected to increase considerably in the ensuing months. In view of the distress from want of employment and the failure of the potato crop, application had been made to Parliament for a loan which had, however, been unsuccessful. In view of the fact that the line to Tipperary was to be completed by 1 May 1847, it was decided to seek tenders for locomotives and rolling stock. In addition, tenders were to be obtained for the section from Tipperary to Waterford and for 50,000 sleepers.

Captain Moorsom, engineer to the Waterford & Kilkenny Railway (W&KR), attended the board meeting on 18 February 1846 in relation to the terms for passage of traffic from Grannagh to the Waterford terminus over the section of the W&LR on which the W&KR sought to have running powers. The W&KR was an unfortunate company with most of its directorate based in Bristol and holding its board meetings in London. Remote control did little for the company and it spent much of its time in dispute with its neighbours, including the W&LR. Discussions took place in relation to the proposed approach to Waterford; apart from the W&KR, the Waterford Wexford Wicklow & Dublin Railway (the 3Ws), another company with GWR connections, also had an interest in Waterford. The 3Ws terminus in Waterford was to be situated at Grannagh, where it was to form a junction with the W&LR, 'if such last-mentioned Railway shall be authorised to cross the said River at or near the said Ferry' (of Grannagh), and it was also seeking running powers over the W&LR line from Grannagh into the city.

Another company associated with the W&KR was the Irish South Eastern Railway (ISER), which was to exercise running powers over the line from Lavistown into Kilkenny and joint use of the station there. The ISER was born out of an amalgamation of two earlier enterprises in 1846, viz the Great Leinster & Munster Railway and the Wexford Carlow & Dublin Junction Railway. The ISER line connected the GS&WR at Carlow with the W&KR at Lavistown. Later, as we shall see, this company tendered unsuccessfully for the leasing of the W&KR.

Some labour problems surfaced at that time with a report from Mr Geoghegan, the superintendent of works, to the effect that a labourer by the name of John Cavanagh was inciting the workmen to leave their employment for an advance of wages. When the case came before the magistrates, the chairman of the Bench said he regretted that a body of men should be so unmindful of their families as to commit such illegal and wanton conduct as to deprive them of means of support. Furthermore, the railway company was being put to considerable trouble. On conviction for such an offence, the penalty was transportation, but the fate of Cavanagh is unknown.

Despite no agreement on the course of the line between Carrick-on-Suir and Waterford, the engineer and secretary were instructed in February 1846 to prepare advertisements for tenders for execution of the works 'along the entire line from Waterford to Tipperary'. Later, in July, the board agreed that no time be lost in taking all necessary steps to obtain possession of the land from Grannagh to Clonmel 'with a view to commence the works thereon'.

Exit an engineer

In March, the directors decided that, whilst they had undiminished confidence in him, they regretted that Vignoles was unable to exercise the constant attention required. They found it necessary, therefore, to vest full control in Osborne. The latter had tendered his resignation but had been persuaded to withdraw it. At the second half-yearly meeting in August 1846, some of the shareholders expressed disquiet at the amount of money expended on lands as well as Parliamentary expenses which appeared to be excessive. The chairman agreed that the latter were high but there was little option but to expend the sum involved. As regards Osborne, the board decided in May 1848 that with the line then open, the 'engagement with (him) has ceased'. Arrangements were made to finalise his account, but eventually this matter had to be referred to arbitration by Thomas White Jacob of Waterford. Osborne returned to the USA in 1850, where he died in 1899 at the age of 84.

A shareholder, the Rev John Medlycott, inquired at the August 1846 meeting as to where finances would come from for the extension to Waterford, bearing in mind that

Limerick Junction station.
The GS&WR main Dublin to Cork lines are to the left of the North Signal Cabin. The Limerick Bay platform is directly beneath the left-hand of the three signals, while the line to the Waterford Bay is to its right and runs behind the station buildings. On the left is Limerick Junction engine shed.
W. A. Camwell / IRRS collection

£250,000 of the capital had already been expended on the line as far as Tipperary. The chairman in reply stated that the price of land had to some degree been dictated by the obligation placed on the company to finish the line to the point of junction with the GS&WR within the time limit specified in the Act. Some discussion took place regarding the construction of the bridge at Grannagh, the reverend gentleman commenting that he hoped it would not be constructed on the same principle as the metal bridge near Limerick, as there was every likelihood of it being 'precipitated into the Suir'. This was a reference to the Roxboro' Road bridge, then known as Meagher's Viaduct, which had collapsed. Osborne explained that the collapse was due to the negligence of some parties.

At the board meeting on 23 December 1846, Messrs Riall and Bianconi were appointed a sub-committee to decide on the location of the station at Cahir. In addition, the Limerick committee was instructed to obtain sufficient land outside Limerick terminus for a 'Y-track' for the turning of engines and carriages without the necessity of a turntable. Seven months later the decision was taken to order a turntable at a cost of £150.

The Rev Medlycott and several other shareholders returned to the question of legal and construction costs at the March 1847 shareholders' meeting, without any more detailed explanation being forthcoming. Some hints of disagreement between Osborne and the directors also surfaced. The latter hinted that the government had

consented to an advance of monies for the Waterford extension with work about to commence. Osborne on the other hand talked of practical difficulties in carrying out the proposed works; Medlycott suggested that the directors would be wrong to sanction the construction of a bridge at Grannagh and the viaduct at Ballybricken in the then depressed state of the company. Two directors, Messrs Strangman and Russell, announced their resignations at this meeting and the decision was taken not to fill the vacancies thus created.

Early in March a distinguished party, including the Earl and Countess of Glengall, attended the ceremony of turning the first sod of the Clonmel extension at Cahir. The Earl performed the ceremony after which he addressed the gathered labourers, urging them to co-operate hand-in-hand with the engineers, letting no discord creep between them. Immediately after the ceremony, Osborne placed 120 labourers to work at a wage of 9s per week, a good sum at that time. Another ceremony reported on in April was the trial of the company's first engine, *Glengall*. The *Irish Railway Gazette* reported that 'this splendid piece of railway architecture had been built in Bristol, its cylinders and condensing apparatus being on an entirely new principle . . . at 10 o'clock she commenced to whiz and hiss and snort to the no small surprise of those who did not expect to see the *Flying Dutchman*'. A Mr Rollings reported to the press that she had once or twice reached 70mph and the reporter himself claimed that he personally travelled no fewer than 60 miles in 60 minutes. 'The wonder was how easy it was to stop the engine at her full speed . . . the break (sic) of the tender is a most powerful one.'

On the same day that these tests were being reported on, the directors were giving consideration to a request from Osborne for an increase in salary. Whilst they had considerable confidence in him, they could not accede to this request until the works were

completed; furthermore they were also surprised that he should request an absence from his duties at this time. Osborne was not satisfied with this response and corresponded further on the matter, bringing forth the comment that he did not show the same liberality to the company as he expected it to show him. Instead, he was urged to make every effort to have the line as far as the junction ready for traffic by 1 May. This was to be wishful thinking as it did not open for a further 12 months.

A deviation at Clonmel and a difficult financial period

As originally envisaged, the line was to pass to the south of Clonmel. It would have deviated from the line's present route near milepost 43 in the townland of Lisnamuck and turned southeast, crossing the River Suir at Knocklofty, then headed eastwards to the south of the town through the townland of Monacallee. It would then have turned east-northeast to recross the river between the townlands of Tikincor and Killaloan, to rejoin the present route of the line at Priorstown, close to milepost 55. The W&LR Act of 22 July 1847 sanctioned the diversion of the line to the route by which it was actually constructed. Two other minor deviations were also sanctioned under this Act. In the case of one of these, near Bansha, Section XI of the Act obliged the company to construct a wall 6ft high through the demesne of Hugh Baker; this wall was to be completed prior to the commencement of works on the deviation.

Financial difficulties were by now besetting the company and the directors met in April to consider 'making reductions necessary in the present straightened [sic] circumstances of the company'. Reductions were to be made in staff and letters were sent to contractors stating that the company was unable to accept delivery of rails. In July, the secretary was instructed to write to Dargan remonstrating at the line not being ready on time and also drawing attention to a recent accident and the use of the company's engine without sufficient guards. Osborne received a number of instructions in July, viz he was to furnish plans of Pallas bridge to the contractor and to examine the country on the south side of the Suir; this he did in due course, but a decision was postponed.

Discussions took place regarding stations — the houses at Tipperary and Killonan were to be finished, temporary arrangements to be completed at Pallas while a goods shed and a box were to be provided at Oola. Wooden bridges were to be constructed at Downey's, Dromkeen, Roxboro and Tipperary, with iron bridges at Pallas and Oola. As the statutory time for the completion of the line to the junction with the GS&WR had by now expired, application was made to Parliament, resulting in the

Waterford & Limerick Railway Amendment Act of July 1848, which extended the time limit and allowed for certain small deviations.

Difficulties of another kind had also been coming to light, the company threatening to suspend all works in any district where outrage or injury was threatened on its contractors or labourers. In July 1847, a notice appeared in the local press under the signature of Saunders offering a reward of £50 for information in connection with an atrocity on 20 June when an obstruction had been placed on the rails at Boher, causing the derailment of a ballast train and resulting in the death of a labourer and serious injuries to two others. A second such incident occurred six months later between Pallas and Oola, mercifully without loss of life. This time the reward was increased to £100.

Dargan wrote to the board in October 1847 suggesting that he should discontinue his contract and submit his account to date. Osborne was asked for his views, the result of which was that the company agreed to release Dargan from his contract, subject to his agreement to hand over 50 wagons and horses. The directors agreed to pay him £50,000 in four instalments. Osborne immediately contacted two friends, James Chisel, a former contractor to the Philadelphia & Reading Railroad, and Patrick O'Reilly. Within a month, O'Reilly was in a position to resume the works, so much so that notice was given to the BoT for an inspection on 20 February 1848. While all these problems were being attended to, a deputation waited on the Lord Lieutenant at the Viceregal Lodge for the purpose of submitting a memorial requesting his Excellency to use his influence with the Treasury to grant a loan to enable the completion of the line to Waterford. This matter progressed and by the time of the next shareholders' meeting in March 1848, the chairman was reported to be in London to meet the Government representatives.

Another trial trip was made on Monday, 27 March 1848, this time with the second locomotive *Bessborough*. This event was reported on at length in the *Limerick Chronicle* two days later as a train was laid on to bring patrons to the Tipperary Steeple Chase. In all, about 400 passengers travelled on the train which departed from Limerick at 10 o'clock. The train was described as consisting of three superbly furnished second class carriages 'fully equal, whether in material, manufacture or fittings, to first class on other lines, and a third class equal to others of second class. The carriages accommodated with facility and comfort 90 passengers each.' The engine was described as being 'a specimen of engineering art and skill the most perfect of its kind'. It was further stated that the company officials were most polite and attentive to the ladies and gentlemen, 'who gladly embraced the proffered compliment of a trial trip to Tipperary'. The flowery language of the period stated that the train rapidly passed over the 'nicely defined route . . . yet accurately poised with an equilibrium firmly marked to the observant eye, and a steadiness undisturbed by the celerity of its motions or the occasional change of a curve in the line, though shooting through tunnels (sic) and bridges with a rate of speed equal to 35 miles an hour'.

BoT inspection and opening
The line was inspected by Captain John L. A. Simmons on behalf of the BoT on 18 and 19 April 1848, being referred to by him as the Limerick & Waterford Railway, perhaps because he began his inspection from the Limerick end of the line. He stated that the curves were favourable, none having a radius of more than half a mile, while a large proportion of the line was perfectly straight. The ruling gradient was 1 in 170 for a little less than 1½ miles. The earthworks were generally moderate and appeared firm, but the cuttings were excavated 'to such a narrow

width that in case of slips occurring, even though very slight, traffic might be impeded'. There were 24 road bridges, 10 of timber, the remainder a combination of wrought and cast iron; spans varied from 17ft to 85ft. In addition, there were 20 bridges built of stone or timber carrying the line over roads. 'The bridges were introduced by Mr Osborne, the Engineer, from the U.S, where the principle is of common application in timber structures, known as How's (sic) Patent and are a modification of Col Long's trussed bridge. A similar construction is used in a curved form for the support of the roof of 80ft span at Limerick.'

All level crossings were provided with gates and keepers, and the principal roads with semaphore signal posts. Simmons referred to the fact that there was no gate at the public road adjoining Tipperary station. It appeared that by Parliamentary authority the company was compelled to build a bridge here, but was also required to construct a second bridge only 100 yards away. Simmons objected to the line opening past this crossing until either a bridge or gates were provided, the alternative in the interim being a temporary station for the town on the west side of the road, less than 100 yards from the present terminus. The permanent way was double to Pallas and consisted of 71lb/yd double-head rail in chairs with elm wedges. Simmons also referred to the unusual design of the carriages, based as they were on American principles, further details of which are provided in Chapter Sixteen.

An undertaking was issued by Osborne regarding the outstanding points which satisfied the BoT and the line was duly opened for traffic to Tipperary on Tuesday, 9 May 1848. There were three intermediate stations: Killonan, Pallas and Oola. Ten days after the opening, the *Limerick Chronicle* 'rejoiced to perceive (the line of railway) is daily thronged with passengers and traffic luggage'. Complimentary remarks were made with regard to the carriages, which were thought to be a model that might usefully be copied by the GS&WR, where passengers regularly complained about the rough and uncomfortable condition of the second class accommodation. Instructions were given in June for a temporary station to be provided at Boher.

Less than two months after the opening of the W&LR, the GS&WR completed its line to the point of junction, an event calling for some recognition. Lord Clarendon, the Viceroy, was invited to travel on the first train from Dublin on 1 July, which duly arrived at 'the Junction'. The event was described by one newspaper as 'a glorious success', while another report referred to a crowd of workmen being paid 1s each to applaud. They were reported to have given 'one of the most consumptive cheers we

The crossing of the two companies' lines at Limerick Junction with a train departing in the direction of Waterford. Just beyond the crossing is a set of trap points to prevent a runaway from the Tipperary direction fouling the main lines.
W. A. Camwell / IRRS collection

ever heard' for His Excellency, but 'a real Tipperary cheer' for the patriot John Mitchel. A banquet was subsequently held at Lord Hawarden's estate at Dundrum. Many compliments were again paid regarding the W&LR rolling stock. The GS&WR was opened for public traffic a week later. Arrangements were made with the latter company for the working of through traffic from the junction to Limerick, but it was not long before complaints were being made of unnecessary detention of trains at the junction, in part due to a shortage of staff.

Further financial difficulties

Financial considerations continued to occupy the attentions of the directors throughout 1848. In May the board determined to adopt the utmost economy consistent with the prudent management of the line. In this regard, some changes were made in the engineering department and Mr Martley, locomotive engineer, was advised that his services were being dispensed with; Mr Khlos, who had been foreman in the workshops, was additionally placed in charge of locomotives and carriages. Despite these economy measures, Osborne persisted in a request for an increase in his salary, a request which found little favour. Evidence of the troubled state of the company was the resignation of five directors in June, including Thomas Meagher and John Riall. New directors were elected the following month, these including the Earl of Glengall, who was appointed chairman, and the Rev John Thomas Medlycott, already alluded to in connection with earlier financial matters; he was later to be briefly elected as chairman of the board.

The Great Famine was of course affecting the country as a whole and undoubtedly contributed greatly to the company's poor financial condition. An important meeting was held at Cahir in December 1848 to consider several matters of importance in relation to the management of the company including the removal of the head office to Limerick until the line was completed through to Waterford. This led to correspondence from the accountant and his clerk intimating that they would require an increase in salary if they were to move to Limerick. The board refused to agree to this suggestion 'in the present circumstances of the company . . . but would be prepared to pay removal expenses'. Obviously unhappy with this reply, the accountant, Mr Murphy, tendered his resignation on 22 February 1849. The train service was reduced, and as the result of a saving in the use of one engine, it was placed at the disposal of the resident engineer, Andrew Stewart, who had succeeded Osborne, for ballasting. On completion of this work, one driver was to be dismissed.

At the shareholders' meeting at Waterford on 5 March 1849, the chairman reported

that it was cause of much regret that no improvement was evident in the traffic department, no doubt due to the severe distress pressing on all ranks and classes of the community, 'which was producing a complete stagnation both in trade and travelling'. Nevertheless, average receipts were £256 per week as against expenditure of £175. A shareholder, Francis O'Byrne, queried the annual charge for police at £1,836, which appeared to be high. The chairman confirmed that the item in question included guards, porters, switchmen and policemen. Medlycott, by now chairman of the board, said the company was very much at the mercy of drivers 'for no Irish are to be had in that capacity'; the rate of pay however was on a par with that paid by the GS&WR.

The doubling of the line between Pallas and Limerick Junction was completed by mid-1849 and was inspected by Captain George Wynne of the BoT on 23 May. Wynne commented that the second line had been laid in every respect similar to the existing one, the ballast consisting of broken stone to a sufficient depth. The line was duly passed for opening, subject to the removal of facing points at Pallas. Wynne did however note that fencing still required attention as it had not been in any way improved since Captain Simmons's previous inspection. He also commented that there were still only six locomotives in use.

The company's financial position was no better by September 1849. Once again the shareholders homed in on the expenditure and inquired what further reductions were in contemplation. Medlycott commented that they had dismissed the master mechanic (a reference to Khlos), which saved £400 per annum and consideration was being directed to the amalgamation of two or three other positions. The directors themselves were working gratuitously morning, noon and night and travelling in Bianconi's cars to save undue expense. There was little doubt that when times got better, the 'lowest order of people' would make use of the line more than they did at this time. Measures had again been taken to obtain a loan but the chairman commented that 'English feeling towards Ireland was improving and prospects of a good harvest had led to several propositions being put before the directors'.

The *Clonmel Chronicle* for 1 December stated that there was every prospect of the line from Tipperary to Waterford being undertaken shortly as the directors were reported to have entered into a treaty with an eminent and wealthy English contractor, who was reported to be inspecting the line in the region of Tipperary. The *Irish Railway Gazette* elaborated on this report, pointing out that the engineer who had constructed the London & Brighton Railway was in Caher (the contemporary spelling of

Cahir) with a staff of assistants surveying the unfinished portion of the W&LR previous to making a proposal for constructing the line as far as Carrick-on-Suir. This was John Urpeth Rastrick, who had been appointed resident engineer to the L&BR in 1837. Rastrick had had a distinguished career, having been one of the judges at the Rainhill Trials in 1829. Despite these credentials, the *Gazette* commented that the L&BR had been noted for the character of its most expensive works — and such an engineer was not wanted in Ireland; 'We have, we confess, little faith in English contractors, generally undertaking Irish works.'

The *Gazette* need not have concerned itself, for nothing further was heard of Rastrick in this respect. A couple of weeks later, however, the newspaper made mention of a pamphlet from a Maj J. P. Kennedy, secretary to the Devon Commission on railways and a director of the W&LR. Kennedy referred to the intelligent endeavours of the new board to retrieve the fallen fortunes of the company. The pamphlet was however used as a means of casting disparaging remarks at the previous board. He referred to the previous directors as having reduced matters to extremities, having squandered £½ million of the company's capital in making less than one-third of the line. 'The reckless extravagance which characterised the management was only equalled by the ignorance, presumption and pig-headedness of the managers who had done everything wrong.'

The Waterford extension committee presented a report to the directors at their meeting on 8 January 1850, having discussed matters at some length with Dargan. The latter, after a considerable lapse of time, had agreed to construct the line as far as Clonmel, accepting debentures in lieu of cash. The Waterford extension committee was strongly opposed to only going thus far, and urged Dargan to continue construction through to Waterford. He went to England to try to persuade others to become involved, without success.

Difficulties with the secretary

At the half-yearly shareholders' meeting on Thursday, 28 February 1850, Medlycott was able to report that although passenger revenue was down, that from goods traffic was up. The former resulted from a reduction in the number of trains; in December, the 07.00 from Limerick had been altered to the status of a slow goods train with a single composite carriage attached. The chairman went on to report that it had been hoped to announce the signing of a contract for the construction of the Waterford extension, but regrettably this was not the case.

Another matter which arose was a resolution from a Mr Nivens to reduce the

Above left: **Tipperary station looking towards Limerick. Note the single passenger platform on the Down side. The station building was a large structure, but devoid of architectural merit compared with other stations on the line.**
R. M. Casserley

Above right: **Tipperary station looking east, showing the RSC signal cabin of 1892 with a 15-lever frame. The train, headed by 'J15' 0-6-0 No 106 and 'J25' 0-6-0 No 239, is bound for Limerick.** H. C. Casserley

secretary's salary to £300 per annum. (A letter in the *Railway Times* nearly two years previously had suggested that Saunders might be about to retire.) In reply to the resolution, Saunders said that if he remained silent it might be supposed that he was in fact overpaid. He had acted not only as secretary to the company, but also as treasurer and finance manager. He would be happy to resign and leave the matter in the hands of the directors. Following Saunders' withdrawal from the meeting, another shareholder, a Mr Milward, commented on Saunders' good management of the company and said he considered a sum of £600 was not too much for the great services he had rendered. A proposal was put that the secretary's salary should be reduced to £300 from 1 January 1851, but a final decision was postponed to the following meeting. Obviously realising the inevitable, Saunders announced his resignation, and on 11 September 1850 John O'Connor's application to be appointed secretary of the company from 1 October at a salary of £300 per annum was approved. O'Connor was the late vice-chairman of Waterford Union (the unions were set up under an Act of July 1838 'for the more effectual Relief of the Destitute Poor' and were responsible for the establishment of workhouses within their areas).

There had been considerable correspondence during 1850/51 regarding the intended route of the line between Tipperary and Waterford; the original proposal was for it to have been south of the river from Knocklofty, about three miles southwest of Clonmel. This course would have involved a tunnel at Nicholastown and a viaduct at Knocklofty and, to avoid unnecessary expense, it was altered to run north of the Suir from Cahir to Fiddown, to cross the river at Grannagh. Later, it was agreed that the line would remain north of the river all the way, as later constructed, to make a junction with the W&KR. This was given effect to by an Act of 1851, further details of which are outlined below.

An estimate was in due course submitted in the sum of £349,960 for completing the line from Tipperary to Fiddown, which would be secured by the company's debentures at 5%. Following consideration of the matter, it was resolved that the Waterford extension committee be empowered to complete a contract. At the board meeting on 21 August 1850, approval was given to the contract with Dargan for the completion of the line from Tipperary to Fiddown. George Willoughby Hemans was appointed consulting engineer with Stewart as resident engineer. (Hemans, born in August 1814, the son of Captain Alfred and the famed poetess Felicia Hemans, had a distinguished railway career.)

A further reduction was made in the train service and a committee appointed to look into the expediency of this move and also investigate ways of reducing expenditure generally. It was resolved that Sunday excursion trains should continue for the present, provided they did not interfere with the hours of Divine Worship. The running of trains on Sundays was to be a contentious issue on many lines and was to surface again in later years on the W&LR.

Government loan and a haulage contract

Success in relation to a Government loan finally came in September 1850. At the board meeting held on 18 September, Hemans reported that the Public Works Loan Commissioners had passed a resolution to lend the company a sum of £120,000. The first instalment of £100,000 was to be paid to enable the company to construct the line to Fiddown with the balance to be paid only when powers were obtained to form a junction with the W&KR. The board acceded to this arrangement and Hemans was instructed to carry out a survey for forming a junction line north of the Suir, and to take the necessary steps to obtain the powers required in the next session of Parliament.

At the same meeting, Hemans submitted specifications in relation to a haulage contract, which were approved, and it was agreed to prepare and issue the necessary newspaper advertisements. In November, the secretary was requested to approach both the GS&WR and Messrs Dawson of Dublin inquiring as to the terms they would require to undertake haulage for one or two years. The GS&WR advised that any haulage contract would have to be subject to a minimum mileage of 100,000 and in addition, it would wish to have the option of appointing stationmasters. Neither of these requirements was to the liking of the W&LR, which suggested reducing the minimum mileage to 60,000. An agreement was in fact signed with William Dargan early in April 1851; the contract was for 18 months, or until the extension beyond Tipperary was completed. Including maintenance and the provision of police, the rate was to be 1s 8d per train mile for the first three months, after which he would endeavour to reduce it. There was to be no charge for shunting.

Enter the Malcomsons

The Waterford & Limerick Railway (Deviations) Act, passed on 24 July 1851, was an important one from the company's point of view. It will be recalled that the 1847 Act precluded the company from constructing or even contracting for the section of line from Grannagh to Carrick-on-Suir until such time as Parliament decided on the best route. The decision to run the line on the north bank of the Suir was incorporated in Section IV of the 1851 Act, which also made provision for the construction of a toll bridge over the River Suir at Fiddown to accommodate the inhabitants of Portlaw on

One of the earliest known photographs of a railway scene in Ireland. Probably taken in the late 1850s, we see a Limerick-bound train at Clonmel in charge of one of the Stothert & Slaughter 2-2-2 engines. Note the tall chimney and high-domed firebox. In the background can be seen the goods store. Also note the early signal. The character on the left of the picture is probably one of the early railway policemen.
Hemphill Collection / Image courtesy South Tipperary County Museum

the south side of the river. It was stipulated that no construction should be carried out on the line from Carrick-on-Suir before work commenced on the bridge, nor should the line be opened for traffic until the bridge was likewise ready for opening. The bridge itself was to be of timber construction with bays of not less than 40ft each, the soffit to be not less than 9ft above the surface of the quay at Carrick and there was to be an opening swing or draw bridge of not less than 40ft in width.

The inclusion of the bridge in the Act had its origins in the Malcomson family of Portlaw. It might be appropriate to digress at this point in the narrative to take a brief look at the origins of this most important family so far as Waterford was concerned, and who played such a defining role in the history of the railway. The family was descended from the ancient Presbyterian Scottish Malcolm family. It appears to have first settled in the north of Ireland, where Joseph (born *c*1690) married Rachel Greer, a Quaker, from the Lurgan area. From that time onwards, one branch of the family remained Quakers. One of their 11 children, David, at the age of 18, obtained a job with his cousin, Sarah Grubb of Anner Mills near Clonmel, but he was soon dismissed for keeping late hours. Another brother leased lands from the Rev J. T. Medlycott and his father, on which stood a small flour mill. The Grubbs and the Medlycotts were also Quakers and were connected with the railway.

David Malcomson was one of the promoters in 1835 of the River Suir Navigation Co, which was behind the opposition to the original plans for the extension of the railway to Waterford. David was also the founder of the family cotton business and largely responsible for the establishment of the town of Portlaw. He handed over the running of his business interests to his

seven sons in 1837. The family also founded the Neptune Ironworks in Waterford in 1844 and the Waterford Steamship Co, in addition to the Shannon Fishery Co and the Annaholty Peat Works for the manufacture of turf briquettes at Castleconnell. The cotton business took a serious downturn with the outbreak of the American Civil War, and the consequent shortage of raw cotton. The firm of Malcomson Bros finally failed in 1877 with the collapse of the London bankers, Overend Gurney & Co, the family reputedly losing some £2 million. The Steamship Co was eventually sold to the Clyde Shipping Co in 1901. The principal member of the family involved with the railway was William Malcomson (1813-1892) of whom we shall be hearing more anon. William's daughter, Susan, married into the well-known Cork family of Penrose. This latter family was also involved in shipbuilding and had railway interests, as well as being involved in the foundation of the world-famous Waterford Glass company.

The Malcomsons lived at Portlaw and travelled daily to Waterford. It was they who had the toll bridge erected at Fiddown, although the crossing was originally intended to be at Mooncoin. Returning to the railway, we find the company was authorised to erect toll gates on the bridge, a scale of maximum tolls being laid down in Section XVI of the Act. Foot passengers were to be charged ½d, as was each head of calves, swine, sheep or lambs; oxen, cows or neat cattle attracted 1d each, while the charge for horses, mules or other beasts drawing carriages, carts, cars or drays was to be 3d. There were certain exemptions — the Queen or other members of the Royal family, any vehicle conveying mail, manure or lime for improving land (remember this Act was passed not long after the disastrous famine years), and vehicles being used for

military purposes were all to be allowed to cross free of toll.

It was stipulated that vessels should not be unnecessarily detained, 'no longer than the space of time required for a carriage to approach and cross the bridge'. The penalty for such detention was to be a fine of £10. The city of Waterford is situated on the south side of the Suir and to provide access from the Kilkenny (north) side, a toll bridge was erected across the river in 1793. Section XXVII of the Act made provision for the railway company to acquire the existing bridge. If it did so, it was obliged within six months to increase the opening to 40ft, such opening to be formed into a draw or swing bridge to be approved by the Admiralty. The PWLC suggested an iron bridge, the company's response being that it did not feel justified in going to this expense unless the Loan Commissioners would contribute an additional £1,000.

The bridge at Fiddown was reported to be ready for opening by the end of January 1853 when some consideration was given to the appointment of a toll keeper. No provision had been made for the erection of either a toll house or a gate, plans for the former being approved in March. The tender of Messrs Doolan at £180 was in due course accepted, they being granted a general pass for their workmen from Clonmel while the work was in progress. In the following December it was agreed that the Fiddown stationmaster be authorised to collect the tolls in future. Prior to this, the Rev Gregory had collected these, in recognition of which he and his family were granted a free pass over the bridge. Later, complaints were made regarding the avoidance of tolls by car drivers. This was due to the fact that there was only one toll gate, situated on the Kilkenny side of the bridge; car-owners crossed the bridge and dropped passengers off just short of the toll gate before turning about and recrossing the bridge.

The remainder of the 1851 Act dealt with railway matters. Powers were granted for a deviation to commence at Granny (sic) and terminate by a junction with the line of the W&KR in Dunkitt. The company was empowered to abandon the proposed line at or near the Neptune Ironworks and the Waterford Coal Company's yard as well as the branch to the premises of Messrs Strangman & Davis' brewery (all on the south side of the river). Running powers were granted from the junction to the intended station of the W&KR. Important provisions were included in the latter portions of the Act, with Section XLVII laying down a deadline of 25 March 1853 for completion by the W&KR of the line from the junction to, and at the terminal station. Failure to meet this deadline would result in the transfer of its powers to the Limerick company, with running powers then granted to the W&KR.

The board received a letter from John Riall in June 1851 stating that the late secretary and the then directors had promised to provide a station between Cahir and Clonmel on his land at a place called Beanfield; in addition, calls on his shares were to go for compensation for the land. Having considered the matter, Riall was requested to produce any agreement he held in this regard, but there the matter appears to have rested. At a later date, a request was made by the local inhabitants for a stopping place at nearby Nicholas-town, this being declined.

Towards Dunkitt

In August 1851, Dargan put forward proposals to contract for the further extension of the line from Fiddown to a junction with the W&KR at Dunkitt on the same schedule of prices as that for the line from Tipperary. This proposal was accepted in October, subject to Dargan's agreement to accept payment in preference shares. Approval was given in October to Hemans to erect a signal station at Boher at a cost not exceeding £35. At a later stage it was confirmed that Boher should have a cattle siding and that there should be two rooms for the clerk there. At the same time, plans were submitted for the station houses and goods stores at Cahir and Clonmel, instructions being given for tenders to be obtained. These latter were submitted to the board in December, William Dargan's tender at £3,500 for the two being accepted, subject to £2,000 of this figure being in preference shares and £1,500 in cash.

Dargan offered to have the line open as far as Clonmel by 5 April 1852 provided the company agreed to pay him £250 towards 'the temporary bridge over the Suir at Cahir'. Mention was also made of penalties required by Richard Grubb in the event of the non-removal of the temporary bridge by 1 August 1853. In August 1852 the resident engineer sought instructions as to the stoppage of traffic at Cahir while rails were being laid on the bridge there. Hemans was called upon to report whether the bridge works might be carried on without inter-ference with traffic, as the directors had been led to suppose when the temporary bridge was sanctioned. There is no further reference to the temporary bridge, but we do know that traffic must have ceased as 10s was paid to each guard and engineman as a gratuity for extra services while the bridge was closed.

The line was opened as far as Clonmel on 1 May 1852. This allowed a review of Dargan's haulage contract; he now agreed to work five trains as laid down in the proposed new timetable in lieu of four trains each way daily which had been operating up until then. This had the effect

Clonmel station in July 2005 showing the ornate station building on the Up platform and the footbridge, the latter supplied by Arrol Bros of Glasgow. W. E. Shepherd

of reducing the haulage rate from 1s 8d to 1s 4d per train mile. Work proceeding on the Fiddown extension enabled the chair-man to report to the half-yearly share-holders' meeting in February 1853 that it was hoped to open to that point in April and to Dunkitt by June. Trial trips were made over the Clonmel to Fiddown section in the first week of April and the line was duly opened to the public on 11 April 1853. It was expected, pending the opening of the line to Waterford during the autumn, that a small steamer would carry passengers and goods between these points: 'a trip (which) would be most agreeable to passengers'. The W&KR was meanwhile making progress with its line towards Dunkitt, but arrange-ments were now made in accordance with Section 47 of the Act of 1851, for the powers for the extension from the latter point to the terminal to be transferred to the W&LR.

The 7m 77c Dunkitt extension was inspected by Captain Wynne on 18 August 1853. The permanent way was similar to the sections of line already opened, with sufficient ballast. However, Wynne reported that there were three public road crossings — at 69m 7c, 70m 6c and 71m 72c — which had not been authorised by the Act. In reply, the W&LR stated that the crossings in question were substituted for bridges at the request of the county surveyor and neigh-bouring inhabitants. Wynne also com-mented that the line was divided 'into certain districts for safe working and (the directors) have appointed a travelling porter to each district who is to accompany the trains in his district each way'. The company was informed that written orders should be issued nominating the travelling porters by name and that these be furnished to stationmasters and enginemen. Wynne, however, was of opinion that 'a separate staff or stick for each district', would be better than the porter; this was put forward purely as a suggestion. The company

responded in October to the effect that the recommendations for the prevention of accidents were being carried out. This section was duly opened to the public on 23 August 1853.

Considerable difficulties were encoun-tered by Dargan with the remaining 1½ miles from Dunkitt to the terminus at Newrath, where it crossed marshy ground close to the river. It was necessary to use piles driven in 40ft. This final section was inspected by Captain Wynne on 29 August 1854, at which time he found the station and permanent way in need of further works. The opening was postponed for a month, but we find Wynne back again on 5 September when he passed the line for opening; this latter took place six days later.

The terminus at Newrath, which was to remain in use until a further short extension was completed to the bridge of Waterford in 1864, was situated about ½ mile west of the present-day station, and was constructed from materials removed from one of the buildings housing the Dublin Exhibition of the previous year. This building had been designed by Sir John Benson. The local press reported that the terminus was 'beautifully decorated with evergreens and flags of all nations'. The station, which had the appearance of a double tunnel, was of course intended for the use of both the W&LR and W&KR, each having a tunnel! On the opening day, excursion trains ran from Limerick and Kilkenny, a dinner being provided for the officials of both companies and invited guests at Dobbyn's Hotel.

Chapter Two

A LEASE, A BRIDGE AND THE MARKETS

Evidence of some discontent with the directors' handling of the company's financial affairs surfaced in August 1854. A shareholder, Joseph Fisher, suggested that the directors had exceeded their borrowing powers to the extent of more than £11,000. Fisher also wrote to Richard Kane, the company's solicitor, objecting to the latter's attendance at the recent general meeting and attempting by threats to put an end to free discussion on the conduct of the company's officers. It was pointed out to Fisher that his remarks were not only untrue, but they were also injurious to the interests of the company. Probably arising from this affair, a meeting of shareholders was held in Waterford in January 1855 to consider the position of the company. It became clear that there was considerable dissatisfaction at the way in which the directors had filled vacancies within their number. For the first time, evidence was emerging of a section of the board representing the GS&WR. There seemed to be a clear impression that the GS&WR was endeavouring to draw the trade of the south of Ireland to Cork and thence to South Wales, thus depriving the port of Waterford of its legitimate traffic.

An extraordinary meeting of shareholders was held in Waterford on 14 August 1855. Whilst traffic returns had been showing a steady and continuous improvement, due in no small measure to the exertions of the secretary and the traffic manager, it was nevertheless disappointing and surprising to record that the company's shares were not going up in proportion. Once again, this was felt to be down to the directors. One good factor to emerge was that the South Wales Railway, a concern supported by the GWR and absorbed by it in 1863, was, in conjunction with the W&LR and the W&KR, about to charter steamers to ply between Waterford and Milford Haven three times weekly, which would augur well for the future prospects of the company. At the meeting, one shareholder expressed himself as being totally opposed to any further expenditure at the Limerick end of the line as it had already cost too much. The chairman, however, pointed out that such expenditure was necessary as three companies would shortly be sharing the terminus there.

Once again at the half-yearly meeting, in September 1856, the directors were accused of gross mismanagement of the company's affairs. Reference was made to the working expenses, Mr Levy proclaiming that the company would never do any good while it was under the present management. If properly managed, he believed the shareholders could confidently expect a return of 2½% or 3% on their holdings. The chairman dismissed Levy's comments but congratulated him on 'the great improvement, both in his language and manner . . . in contrast with a former period. It was pleasant to observe what a good effect the air of Waterford had upon the gentleman.'

Mutiny and a new chairman

This was little more than a stalling tactic as a special meeting was held at Waterford on 8 January 1858, following a requisition from shareholders. The purpose of the meeting was twofold, viz to remove and replace the present board of directors, and to appoint yet another committee to investigate the state of the company. The chairman said it was believed that there were interests who wished to sell the line to another company. Sir Edward M'Donnell, the chairman of the GS&WR, however pointed out that neither he nor his board of directors had ever made any offer or entered into any negotiations on the subject. Mr Levy stated that there were sufficient votes present to oust the existing board. Their sole object was to improve the property in the W&LR line and

Waterford station with a Waterford & Central Ireland Railway train in charge of an 0-4-2T, date unknown.
Photographer unknown / G. Beesley collection

to get some return for their investment. Levy then resolved that a new board of directors be appointed, including Abraham Stephens, John Connolly, John Riall and Lord Donoughmore. The chairman endeavoured to declare the resolution illegal, but on being put to the meeting it was carried unanimously 'amidst loud applause'. The *Railway Times* commented in an editorial that there had been a want of energy, and not unlikely of intelligence, in the late board.

It soon became obvious, however, that some moves were being made towards finding a suitor. In October 1858 the new chairman, Maj Massey, was authorised to treat with Sir Edward M'Donnell and the GS&WR board with a view to an amalgamation with, or a lease to, that company. The chairman reported in November that the GS&WR was willing to purchase the Waterford company, paying in the first year 1% on the ordinary share capital of the W&LR, 1½ % in the second year and 2% in the third year. On the expiration of this period the annuity was to be redeemed by giving £25 of GS&WR stock for each £50 of W&LR stock, the GS&WR to apply to Parliament for the necessary Bill. It was agreed that the interests of the port and city of Waterford would be taken into account.

When the matter was considered, it was decided to seek 1%, 2% and 3% respectively in each of the three years, to commence as from 1 July 1869, amalgamation to be at the rate of £30 GS&WR stock for each £50 of that of the W&LR. The GS&WR however stuck to its original offer; if not accepted, instructions would be given for the withdrawal of the Bill, which was in fact what happened. The *Railway Times* commented that the W&LR shareholders would be well advised to accept the offer as they had little chance of receiving any dividend under the present circumstances of the company.

The matter was raised again in November 1859 when those attending a meeting of the Dublin shareholders agreed unanimously to request the directors to open negotiations with the GS&WR and to appoint a deputation for that purpose. The directors expressed a reluctance to make any approach, believing that it should be left to the Kingsbridge directors to make the next move. Not satisfied with this suggestion, the Dublin shareholders set up their own meeting with the GS&WR board. This led to a fresh offer being made which was also, in due course, declined and a counter-offer made. The GS&WR responded intimating that the negotiations might be considered as being at an end. Despite this, it soon became obvious that it was proceeding with the Amalgamation Bill in Parliament, obviously hopeful that wiser counsel would prevail.

At this stage, John Connolly, who had only succeeded Maj Massey a year previously, resigned his position as chairman and also as a director in January 1860. The GS&WR had alleged that the Amalgamation Bill was being proceeded with at his request, an allegation which he strenuously denied. Three more directors, Messrs Elliott, Boswell and Furnell, followed Connolly's move and resigned their positions. William Malcomson

The new Waterford station of 1864, showing the toll bridge across the River Suir. Author's collection

was appointed in place of Elliott, being elected chairman at a meeting on 26 January 1860. Following this an advertisement was placed by a self-constituted committee in Dublin, calling upon shareholders to refuse their proxies to the board and to declare that it was unworthy of their confidence. Reference was made to a proposed line connecting Limerick with Cork, which would bring the latter city into direct competition with Waterford for cross-channel traffic. With the withdrawal of the Amalgamation Bill in March 1860, negotiations between the two companies were at an end and it was to be another 10 years before moves were again made in this direction.

Before taking a look at two extensions, we will briefly review a few other events following the opening of the line to Waterford. In October 1854 a memorial was received from the inhabitants of Mooncoin requesting the removal of the station at Grange to Ballincur, about a mile and a half to the east; the request was declined. At Waterford itself, it was agreed that the centre platform at the terminus be concreted. As a result of the necessity to divide trains of wagons at Clonmel it was decided, in November 1854, to make a siding beyond Patrickswell (at 46m 60c, about 2½ miles west of Clonmel). There is no evidence that a siding was actually made, but if it was its existence must have been short lived. Twelve months later, in November 1855, a committee was appointed to make arrangements for increased goods accommodation at the terminus. Another committee was appointed to meet the Waterford Bridge Commissioners for the purpose of arranging the matter of the toll for the company's traffic passing beneath the bridge in lighters. In December, the Commissioners suggested a payment of £200 per annum for working the company's boats under the bridge.

Also in December 1855, it was decided to dispense with the services of the traffic manager, Mr Lewis DeMay, as traffic had not come up to the directors' expectations. Although DeMay had been in the position for only 12 months, the board agreed to pay him three months' salary and allow him

immediately to seek other employment. John O'Connor, the secretary, agreed to also act as traffic manager at a salary of £200 per annum, but by June 1855 William Labatt Payne had been appointed traffic manager at a salary of £250 per annum. Thereafter, O'Connor's stay was not to be for very long, notice of motion for his removal being put forward at a board meeting in June 1858. It was reported that O'Connor had made complaints against Mr Davis, his assistant. The nature of these complaints is unknown as is the outcome of the investigation into the affair. Thomas Ainsworth was duly appointed secretary to the company in September 1858.

Arising from an inspection of the works in progress on the Limerick & Castleconnell Railway by Captain Tyler on behalf of the BoT, a letter was sent to the W&LR at the beginning of August 1858 noting that the section of line between the old and new termini at Limerick had been opened for traffic without BoT approval. In reply, the W&LR advised that it thought an inspection unnecessary as it regarded the new station as being 'an alteration of arrangements and not an opening of a new portion of line', the alteration in question being 540 yards in length. The BoT was unsympathetic to this argument and inquired if there was any reason why it should not request the Attorney General to issue proceedings against the company for penalties involved. The secretary replied to the effect that the original platforms had been inspected in 1847 and the mileage charged to passengers remained unaltered; furthermore, the Foynes line extension into the station had also been previously inspected.

The unauthorised extension was duly inspected by Captain Ross towards the end of August. Generally, he found everything in good order, although he suggested that a traverser be provided through the carriage shed to obviate the necessity of shunting on the main line. He also called for lamps to be provided for semaphore signals at the new terminus. At this early stage, adverse comment was passed on the practice of reversing Foynes line trains out of the terminus, something which should, if possible, be avoided.

Lease of a neighbour

Reference has previously been made to the entry of the W&KR to Waterford by means of running powers over the W&LR line from Dunkitt. The first tentative approach for a possible lease of the former line by the latter was made by G. W. Hemans in May 1855. However, before we deal with the various negotiations which led up to the lease being agreed, it would be advantageous to provide a short background history of the W&KR, which, as already noted, had many of its shareholders in Bristol, while the board met in London. These arrangements resulted in inefficient management, and the company

The original Waterford station at Newrath, just beyond the wagons on the left of this view; the extension to a new station at the north side of the wooden toll bridge was opened on 29 August 1864. Following this, goods services were concentrated at Newrath, as witnessed by this photograph. Immediately beyond the bridge can be seen the large goods store on the North Wharf.
Lawrence Collection/National Library

was almost constantly in dispute with one or more of its neighbours, the GS&WR, ISER and the W&LR.

Public meetings were held in September 1843 with a view to connecting Kilkenny and Waterford by railway. It was decided, in October 1844, to publish notice for a Bill for such a line with a branch to Kells, some miles south of Kilkenny. The decision was also taken to lay the line with Prosser's patent wooden rails. Not only were the rails unusual but the patent also included flangeless wheels with broad tyres; the wheels were held on the rails by small guide wheels. This meant that the rolling stock using this patent system could not run on conventional track, a fact commented on by the BoT. Despite this drawback, the W&KR company's engineer, Captain C. R. Moorsom, persuaded the board that there would be a considerable saving in construction costs. Some consideration was also given to the idea of using atmospheric traction on the line. The wooden-rail patent was not in fact employed and the company had to pay Prosser £15,000 to be released from the contract.

Apart from the main line, surveys were carried out in late 1845 for branches from Waterford to New Ross and from Kells to Clonmel. The first contracts were let early in the following year for the main line from Kilkenny to Bennetsbridge to Messrs Wright & O'Toole and from the latter point to Thomastown to Messrs Murray & Patterson, work commencing in April 1846. The line between Kilkenny and Bennetsbridge was inspected and passed by the BoT on 21 April 1847, but the directors decided to await the completion of the ISER as far as Lavistown before opening their line, as this would give through access from Dublin to Kilkenny. The ISER line was delayed in its completion and the W&KR opened the line between Kilkenny and Thomastown on 12 May 1848. Construction of the viaduct across the River Nore at the latter point was to delay opening of the line southwards for a further two years. The line eventually reached Dunkitt on 23 August 1853 where a temporary station was provided. Reference has already been made to the agreement with the W&LR for completing the line in to Waterford, this last section being opened by the W&LR on 11 September 1854.

As referred to above, the first overtures for a leasing of the line were made to the W&LR in May 1855, but nothing further appears to have transpired at this time. The next moves were made in the autumn of 1858, the first proposals being based on a mileage rate. Serious proposals were put forward in March 1859 when a deputation from the W&LR board met with the Kilkenny company directors in London. The lease was to be for 20 years, with a minimum annual rent, payable half-yearly, of £12,000 for the first seven years, increased by £100 per annum for the next five years, and by a further £200 per annum for the remainder of the term. There was to be a right of surrender of the lease after the first seven years with six months' notice on either side. The W&KR rolling stock was to be taken over by the W&LR after valuation, this latter to be made good at the end, or earlier determination, of the lease. Prior to handing over the line, the W&KR was to put the permanent way, bridges, including the Nore Viaduct, and station buildings in a perfect condition. Finally, there was to be a clause allowing for the W&LR to purchase the Kilkenny company if the lease was still in existence after 10 years.

At the same time as these proposals were put forward, it was announced that Messrs Charles Nixon & Co of London had offered a ten-year lease, agreeing to pay £12,500 per annum by weekly instalments, plus 60% of traffic receipts in excess of £22,000 per annum. They also agreed to deposit the necessary parliamentary plans for the proposed extension to Abbeyleix (the Kilkenny Junction Railway). About this time, the ISER also stated its interest in leasing the line, but the price asked proved to be too high. The English shareholders preferred to lease the line to Nixon, whereas the Irish shareholders favoured the W&LR. Following some further meetings and correspondence, it was to the W&LR that the line was leased, the latter company taking up the working as from 1 July 1860, although the agreement was not formally signed until 28 January 1861. The agreement as finalised allowed for a payment of 45% of gross receipts for working the Kilkenny Junction Railway section when opened throughout, or in sections from Kilkenny to Ballyragget or Abbeyleix. The term was to be for five years with monthly payments. A service of four trains each way daily was provided initially, later reduced to three, for which the W&LR received 43% of the gross receipts. The locomotives, rolling stock and machinery, consisting of six locomotives, 23 carriages and 102 wagons, all in very run-down condition, were taken over at a valuation of £13,418 9s 6d; passenger brake van No 1, valued at £50, was later added.

Hardly had the W&LR taken over the working of the Kilkenny line than Pim, the locomotive superintendent of the former railway, reported on the very bad state of the locomotives and rolling stock and the necessity for extra boilermakers, fitters and helpers, in addition to carpenters. Further details of the W&KR locomotives and rolling stock can be found in Chapters Fifteen and Sixteen. There were further complaints at this time, namely the poor state of the roof at Kilkenny station and the bad water supply for locomotives, the latter causing leakage of tubes etc. Consideration was given to the supply of river or stream water to alleviate the problem. When approached, the GS&WR, which had been working the ISER since its opening in 1848, refused to contribute to the cost of providing a proper supply and the subject was deferred. This matter was still causing problems as late as February 1862.

Another cause of complaint was the unpunctuality of train services, which Martin Atock (Pim's successor as locomotive superintendent on the W&LR) attributed to the poor state of the rolling stock. August 1861 saw the first request for a station at Knockmoylan Park, between Ballyhale and Mullinavat, a decision being deferred. The matter was again raised at the end of 1861 when the Rev Mr Walsh asked for the stopping of at least one train each way daily, or at least on the two market days — Wednesdays and Saturdays. He was politely informed of the company's objections, viz the adverse gradients, the poor district and the cost of providing the necessary platform. This reply appears to have brought an end to the requests, although additional goods accommodation was provided at Ballyhale in November 1861.

Two unusual fatal accidents occurred in the early years of working. On 27 December 1861, a man by the name of Dean was killed, we are told, because of 'a gush of steam from the engine due to a tube being displaced and he jumped off through fright'. It is not clear whether Dean was the fireman, but we are told that the driver, Dunn, was injured in the incident. The inquest attributed no blame to the railway. A second accident occurred in April 1863 when an old man, Newman, was killed by the 17.00 up train. The minute states that it was not possible to say whether he had been killed by the engine or by falling, once more, through fright! Again, the inquest found his death to be accidental, with no blame attached to the company. Complaints were made in April 1862 regarding the facilities at Thomastown station and, on investigation, it was discovered that liquor was being sold at the station and that discipline was lax. It was ordered that the stationmaster be removed to another station, but following receipt of 'influential memorials from the district' he was retained for a further trial period.

Improvements were proposed at Kilkenny station in April 1864, Tighe, the W&LR engineer, being requested to produce the relevant plans. These were submitted and approved in May and it was agreed that the cost of the alterations would be divided three ways. The turntable at Kilkenny was a major cause of concern, it being reported in the following December that it had taken 80 minutes to turn a GS&WR engine. Instructions were issued in February 1865 for its replacement at a cost of £345, of which £300 was for the new one and the balance for the removal of the old one.

Kilkenny Junction Railway
In 1845, the Galway & Kilkenny Railway Company brought forward plans for a line of railway from Ballinasloe via Parsonstown (later known as Birr), Roscrea and Abbeyleix to Kilkenny, shortly afterwards cut back to run from Cuddagh on the GS&WR main line. Powers were obtained in 1846 under the title of the Kilkenny & Great Southern & Western Railway, but were allowed to lapse. The Kilkenny Junction Railway, largely promoted by James Delahunty, MP for the county of Waterford, was incorporated in 1860 to connect Kilkenny with Mountrath. Delahunty was later to become closely involved with the W&KR. The Kilkenny Junction line was vigorously opposed by the ISER, which feared a diversion of its traffic via Carlow. This opposition was overcome by offering a reduction of £300 per annum in the rent payable by the ISER for the use of Kilkenny station. The plans were altered in 1861 to make the connection with the GS&WR at Maryborough (known today as Portlaoise), rather than Mountrath, with a branch to Ballybrophy.

Delahunty reported to the joint committee meeting on 17 November 1864 that the KJR line should be ready for opening as far as Abbeyleix by 1 December. It was agreed that it be opened for goods traffic immediately it was passed by the BoT inspector, and for passengers as soon as possible, and not later than 15 December, 'if the line is passed next week'. This did not prove possible and it was duly announced early in the following February that it would open on Monday, 22 February with a service of three trains each way daily. The W&LR was asked to commence the formal working as from 1 March, 'running a few unannounced trains earlier if found desirable in settling staff, etc'. A Mr McEvoy announced his intention of running a 'two-horse buss' (sic) between Abbeyleix and Mountrath in connection with the trains.

The line from Kilkenny to Abbeyleix was inspected by Col Frederick H. Rich in December 1864, this section being opened for traffic on 1 March 1865 and worked by the W&LR. With the new line barely open, the GS&WR, which had taken over the ISER in July 1863, remonstrated that it had been opened without prior consultation and demanded the provision of booking offices and waiting rooms. The GS&WR also referred to the dangers to passengers of its company using the Kilkenny station. Initially, a service of three trains daily was provided, but this was reduced to two shortly afterwards.

The KJR board soon sought to find another company which would work its line on more equitable terms, but there were no takers. As a result of this move, the W&LR quickly intimated that it could not be expected to continue working the line temporarily 'at the present serious loss', and therefore gave notice that it would work it only on the usual mileage basis in force with other companies, viz 2s 3d per train mile for a two-train service and 1s 11d for three trains from the date of opening up to the end of the following July. This was provided the proposition was put to a special meeting of KJR shareholders without delay, otherwise the working arrangement would have ceased on 31 May. It was, however, to be June before the latter company responded to the effect that it was now prepared to enter into an agreement with the W&LR for working between Kilkenny and Abbeyleix for any period to 28 January 1866 (the date when the agreement with the W&KR was due to expire, unless renewed), on any terms it deemed proper, but not to exceed receipts. The service was suspended completely as from 31 August 1866 due to poor returns. The line was opened throughout to Maryborough on 1 May 1867 and worked by the W&KR, with running powers granted to the W&LR.

Negotiations opened in September 1865 regarding the proposed arrangements for working the W&KR after January 1866. A

proposition was handed in by Delahunty that the W&LR should continue the working, but at rates similar to that mentioned for the KJR, ie 2s 3d and 1s 11d per train mile respectively for a two- or three-train service. No decision was arrived at and the W&LR decided to inquire as to what rolling stock and plant the W&KR would require to be returned on termination of the lease on 28 January 1866. When January came, however, it was agreed to continue working the W&KR at 45% of receipts and the KJR at 2s 3d or 1s 11d as referred to above. The revised heads of agreement were not finally approved until 24 November. Finally, it was agreed that the W&LR would cease working the Kilkenny line as from the evening of Friday, 31 May 1867. So came to an end a lease which had been of little benefit to the W&LR.

Extension to bridge end
Erecting a permanent station at Newrath could never have been a serious long-term proposition, situated as it was more than half a mile from the toll bridge, and it was not long before an omnibus service was commenced to connect the station with the city of Waterford. Despite this, plans for new offices and a board room at the Newrath terminus were approved in April 1858, John Challoner Smith, the company's engineer since December 1853, being requested to invite tenders. At the same time he was also requested to prepare plans for a bridge across the River Suir for the purpose of the railway and the public. Clearly, the board had in mind constructing a bridge in a location which would absolve them from having to pay ongoing tolls to the Bridge Commissioners. However, when the plans were submitted in May, the directors had a change of heart, bearing in mind the estimated cost of construction of nearly £50,000, apart from any compensation which might be awarded to the Commissioners. In the meantime, the tender of John Connor at £700 18s 0d was accepted in June for the erection of offices.

Powers were taken under the company's Act of July 1860 for an extension of the line from near the Newrath terminus to terminate at the north end of the wooden (toll) bridge in the townland of Mount Misery, along with a pier or wharf running westwards from the bridge for a distance of about 1,600 yards. At the Limerick end, powers were obtained for the construction of a tramway from near the Limerick station to the Market Place in the townland of Irishtown. (We shall take a look at the tramway in more detail a little later in our narrative.) Section XXI of the Act, in referring to the period of four years allowed by the previous section for the completion of the works, was unusual in that it stipulated that if the railway was not completed and opened for traffic within that period, no dividend was to be paid on the company's ordinary capital until it was completed. The normal course was for powers to lapse at the expiry of the period other than for any portion of the works already completed. Section XXI was clearly intended as a penalty to ensure the completion of the tramway.

Provision was made under Section XXIX for the use of the extension railway and the pier by the W&KR, they being provided with all necessary accommodation. This section also allowed for the payment of an annual rent of 5% on half the cost of construction of the works and half of all sums properly expended on maintenance, repairs and support. As we shall see shortly, this section of the Act was to assume some importance when the W&KR again undertook the working of its own line in June 1867. The remaining piece of this legislation of note is to be found in Sections XXX and XXXII. These allowed for the transfer of the bridge at Fiddown to the Grand Juries of either counties, Waterford or Kilkenny, if either could be persuaded to take responsibility for it. On completion of the transfer, the bridge was to be made free of tolls, mainten-ance and repairs henceforth becoming the responsibility of the Grand Jury in question.

Reporting in August 1860, the engineer suggested the propriety of at once pur-chasing the necessary land for the extension to bridge end at Waterford, he being requested to advise on what accommo-dation might be made available 'in the event of the Board at any time inclining to give passenger accommodation there'. This would seem to imply that its initial intention was to use it purely for goods traffic. Admiralty approval was given to the relevant plans in December, at which time the Harbour Commissioners agreed to supply mud from dredging works to provide landfill. An arbitrator was called in in January 1862 to value all lands and houses between the river and the roadway right up to the bridge. Work was well under way by the close of 1862 when it was reported that mud was piling up at the Upper Jetty front, effectively putting a stop to activities. When this matter was referred to the Harbour Commissioners, they stated that they would not be in a position to provide a 'dredge vessel' for some two months. In the meantime, they offered the use of hand dredge plant at 6d per ton for mud raised, this option soon proving impracticable.

Tenders were submitted in July 1863 for the booking and general offices, that of John Connor, the lowest of four at £1,698, being accepted subject to the engineer's satisfaction with his proposed security and of the joiners' work. A tender was also received from Messrs McClellan of Glasgow for the roof of the passenger station in a sum of £820, this also being accepted. By the end of 1863 it

was reported that almost £10,000 had been paid out for the purchase of land and property. In February 1863, James Tighe, who had become the company's engineer following Smith's departure in June 1861, had been requested by the company solicitor to take possession of Thomas Cosgrave's holding and then return it to him at a yearly rent of £5 from 25 March. Tighe, uncertain how to actually go about this, inquired whether he should have Cosgrave turn everything out of his house. The solicitor however was rather more understanding and suggested that Cosgrave should simply turn the key in the door and then hand it to Tighe, thus acknowledging his new role as a tenant of the W&LR. The largest property owner was one Robert Leckey who received in excess of £2,100 in compensation.

Col Rich inspected the extension, which was about 19½ chains in length, on 9 August 1864. Regarding the permanent way, Rich confirmed that it consisted of a double line laid with double-headed 72lb/yd rail, fixed with wooden keys and chairs to 9ft long sleepers situated about 3ft apart. The signals and points at the junction of the W&LR and W&KR lines, near to which the extension commenced, were installed by Messrs Courtney & Stephens of Dublin, being worked by a locking frame manufactured to W. Anderson's patent of 1864, which they manufactured. Rich gives a brief description of this type of interlocking, which had also been adopted by the Newry & Armagh Railway. 'The lever handle (moving on a segment notched and marked for the several lines) governs and locks the whole of the signals and points at the Junction except those for the trains which it is intended to admit. The heels of one set of points at the Junction are not properly fixed and the trenail fastenings are unsafe.'

A few minor requirements were in due course attended to and the line was opened for traffic on the day of the half-yearly shareholders' meeting, 29 August. The local press referred to the new station building, which remained in use until 1969, as being of red and white Irish bricks faced with English bricks and quoins of Scottish brick. The timber and iron roof had been provided by Messrs McClellan and was reportedly covered with Messrs Malcomson's patent waterproof canvas supplied from their factory at Portlaw. The station was partly built over the River Suir on beech piling driven to a depth of 25ft. There were two platforms, each 479ft in length and 14ft wide.

The Battle of Newrath

At this period, the W&KR traffic was still being worked by the W&LR but, when the former company resumed the working of its own line as from 1 June 1867, problems immediately arose over the new section of line. The old Newrath station had, in the

interim, been used for goods traffic and the passenger facilities there had been some-what neglected. The W&KR initially availed of its right under Section XXIX of the 1860 Act to the use of the extension and the new station. It chose, however, to ignore any reference to payment of a rent, intimating that its use was only temporary and did not therefore constitute a 'user' in the strict legal sense. It was hardly surprising that the W&LR objected to this interpretation of the Act and it sought to claim a rent. The W&KR wrote late in September 1867 to the effect that it proposed to commence working its own traffic from the old station as from 1 October, claiming to be 50% owners of the premises.

The W&LR endeavoured, unsuccessfully, to prevent the departure of the first two trains from Newrath station on that morning. Shortly before the departure of the 16.00 mail for Kilkenny, the W&LR placed a train of wagons and two locomotives so as to effectively block the mail. It would appear that there was some verbal, and probably physical, altercation between the two com-panies' staff, as a result of which some of the passengers on the mail 'became frightened'. Eventually, the W&KR solicitor arrived and a temporary truce was arranged. The matter was referred to the BoT for the appointment of an arbitrator, it being reported in mid-November that Seymour Clarke of the (English) Great Northern Railway had been appointed.

In an attempt to capture traffic, the W&LR announced that it would issue tickets to Dublin via Limerick Junction at the same fares as the W&KR were charging. The latter company, now deprived of the use of Newrath station, erected a temporary platform and buildings about ¾ mile further west at Newrath Commons. It was reported on 29 October that this temporary platform had collapsed. Nobody seems to have con-sidered the plight of intending passengers as, on the one hand, they had to endure a road journey out to the Commons, on the other, they were faced with a considerably longer train journey to get to Dublin.

The W&KR issued a notice in November 1867 of a Bill to grant it ownership, or at least the use, of the old station. The Bill also sought to change the name of the company to the Waterford & Central Ireland Railway. Clarke held an arbitration meeting in Waterford on 5 December and recommen-ded provision for equal use on half the cost of the new station to each company, the staff to be common. The old station was to be divided in part, the rest common, while the river frontage was also to be divided. Lastly, he suggested a joint committee of two from each board to control the common premises. The W&LR agreed to the heads of the agree-ment, the W&KR understandably declining.

Once again the W&KR wrote advising its intention to run its trains to and from the old terminus, as from 1 April 1868, and it called on the W&LR to carry out any necessary works 'to put an end to (the) serious loss to them (the W&KR) and inconvenience to the public'. Tighe was instructed to restore the passenger offices, making the northern half of the station suitable for use by the W&KR for the accommodation of its trains. It was even agreed to put timber paling down the centre of the platform. The Kilkenny company served a Common Plea writ in May 1868 for loss and expense incurred by the W&LR's refusal to allow it earlier use of Newrath station. Three months later the W&CIR, as the W&KR had become on 13 July, complained that the buildings were in a dilapidated and dangerous state, Tighe being instructed to effect repairs.

Eventually, in June 1869, an agreement was reached in regard to the extension line and the new station. Ownership and occupation were to be on equal terms, except for some of the upstairs offices; in this latter context the W&CIR was to be allowed £50 annually for the provision of alternative office accommodation. The W&CIR agreed to pay 5% on one-quarter of the outlay etc for five years, one-third for the next five years and one-half in perpetuity thereafter. The station was to be worked by a joint committee with joint staff at joint equal expense. So came to an end the 'Battle of Newrath'. W&CIR trains began using the new station on a permanent basis as from 1 July, following which the old station was restricted to goods traffic. There was a minor disagreement later, in July, when the W&CIR objected to paying joint wages of signalmen and switchmen, who it was reported were 'clamorous for their pay'. The W&LR agreed to pay them in full, debiting the Central Ireland company half of the figure.

A tramway at Limerick
The first moves towards a tramway into the markets area at Limerick came from the Markets Trustees themselves when they approached the board in September 1859. The engineer, having been requested to prepare a plan and estimate, submitted these to the board showing an estimated cost of £450. Smith suggested that the company might bear this outlay subject to Limerick Corporation granting the company powers to cross two streets, Roxboro Road and Mulgrave Street, on the level, and in addition purchasing the right-of-way. As already stated earlier in the chapter, powers were taken under the company's Act of 1860 for the construction of a tramway commencing out of the main line at a point 385 yards east of the terminus and terminating at or near the Market Place. Not more than two lines of tramway were to cross the aforementioned roads. Section XII of the Act precluded the company from using steam or atmospheric traction or carriages, or wagons drawn by ropes worked from a stationary steam engine.

As early as October 1860, the Markets Trustees were pressing for the early completion of the works and in reply, the directors expressed their willingness to proceed 'on getting the land and free passage secured', to them. It was not however until June 1863 that John Long, district engineer in Limerick, reported a requirement for 45 tons of rails for the tramway; 17 tons of old Kilkenny rails were already on hand, orders being given for advertisements to be placed for the balance and also for rails required at the Waterford end of the line. Long also referred to a requirement for four wagon turntables, these being supplied by a Mr Graham at £70 each, fixed at Limerick. Rails weighing 42lb per yard were obtained in September from the

Cork & Youghal Railway at a cost of £4 15s 0d per ton. The tramway was completed and opened for traffic on 2 January 1864, at which time it was queried whether it would be worth incurring the necessary outlay for the laying of a second line of rails. This latter matter was deferred until traffic prospects improved.

In April 1870, Messrs Matterson & Sons, bacon curers, offered to pay half the cost of putting in an extension from the tramway to their premises, also agreeing to give the company all their traffic, amounting to about £100 per week. The work in this connection appears to have been completed by January 1871. In December of that year, a tracing was submitted for a further extension of the tramway into the premises of Messrs Denny & Sons at an estimated cost of £212 10s 0d. Permission was duly granted by the Markets Trustees with certain stipulations. The tramway was not to be worked during the hours of business in the corn or pig markets. Any sheds in the markets which might be interfered with or removed were to be re-erected as laid down by the Trustees, a nominal rent of £1 per annum to be payable.

Messrs Shaw & Sons were also customers of the tramway, but they appeared reluctant to pay tolls to the company, being threatened with a withdrawal of the service to them. Later, in 1875, however, when an amount of £5 odd was outstanding, it was decided not to press for payment 'as these people refused to pay quietly'. The traffic manager submitted complaints in 1874 to the effect that Messrs Denny were in the habit of ordering wagons down the tramway and then keeping them idle all day, while their traffic was forwarded via a competitor, the Cork & Limerick Direct Railway. This matter was referred to Mr Denny himself for his intervention.

WATERFORD STATION 1858

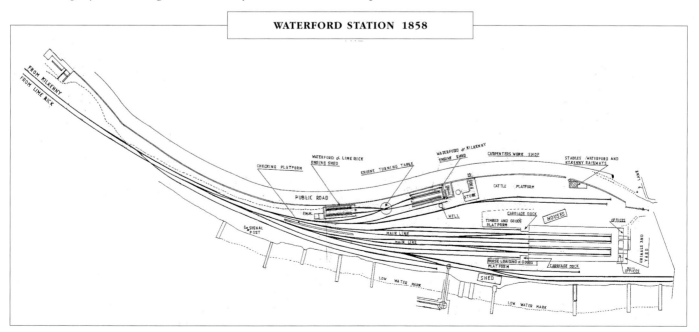

Chapter Three

TOWARDS FOYNES AND NEWCASTLE

We must, however, return to September 1852 when a deputation of interested parties had an interview with the board of the W&LR to promote a proposed line from Limerick to Foynes on the Shannon Estuary. Arising out of this meeting, Hemans was requested to inspect the proposed route and report back to the board. He looked at two possible routes, one 23 miles long, remaining close to the Shannon through Kildimo and Askeaton, the other two miles longer via Adare, Rathkeale and Askeaton. This second route was similar in direction to that proposed by the promoters and would give reasonable levels without heavy work. Hemans also suggested a branch to Newcastle, 'an important town in a very central position about seven statute miles from Rathkeale'. The branch would 'greatly conduce to the profits of the scheme by bringing produce from all parts of the county', and it was felt that it might also induce the whole county to consent to a guarantee on the necessary capital. Hemans also reported that William Dargan had offered to undertake the construction work on very advantageous terms.

Arising out of Hemans' report, the board approved of making a subscription to the proposed undertaking. The Limerick & Foynes Railway Act received Royal Assent on 4 August 1853; subscribers included the Earl of Dunraven, Lord Monteagle of Brandon, William Monsell and William Dargan. Powers were granted to the GS&WR to subscribe £15,000 and to nominate three directors; the W&LR £17,500 and four directors. Powers were also granted for the W&LR to work the new line. As regards the latter company, Messrs Robert Shaw, Richard Sargint, John Mackesy MP, and Henry William Massy (sic) were appointed directors of the new company to look after the W&LR interests.

The first meeting of the directors was held at the Chamber of Commerce in Limerick on 31 August 1853. The Earl of Dunraven was elected chairman, S. A. Dickson as vice-chairman, while William Carroll was appointed secretary. At the same meeting, William LeFanu, engineer to the company, sought a fee of £4,020 for past and future services and expenses. The directors considered this to be excessive and offered

LeFanu a sum of £3,500, from which was to be deducted a penalty of £500 if the Valuator's plans were not completed by 8 November. This offer was accepted by LeFanu, who was requested to prepare the necessary plans and specifications.

The ceremony of turning the first sod of the new line was undertaken by the Lord Lieutenant, the Earl of St Germans, at Foynes on 29 September. LeFanu wrote to the board in March 1854, stating that Dargan had informed him that his tender was for the building of single bridges similar to those on the Killarney line. He would however be prepared, for an additional £2,000, to make the over-bridges double and the embankments 18ft wide. LeFanu recommended this course of action which was accepted by the board, which now stressed the necessity of commencing the works as soon as possible. By this time, most of the land valuations had been agreed and about 10 miles had actually been paid for. The board was happily anticipating the establishment of Foynes as a transatlantic packet station following an announcement that the Limerick Steamship Co had arranged to dispatch its steamer *Brandon* to New York. Apart from this, the trade of the district was continuing to improve, with increased prosperity in the agricultural sector. Ideas were also forming in relation to a steamer service between Foynes and Kilrush. (Steamer services are dealt with more fully in Chapter Nineteen.)

Limerick station photographed in 1930 showing the Station Signal Cabin. No 4 platform on the left is the old C&LDR terminal. The station was remodelled to allow Tralee and C&LDR trains to arrive and depart from platforms 2 and 3 as shown in this view. To the right is the 'Top Yard' goods area. This area also provided access to the Markets Tramway.
Ian Allan Library

The engineer reported in July 1854 that about 1,100 yards of the line had been formed, but there were only 110 men at work. Dargan was requested to have the work prosecuted with more energy during the summer months. Two months later, the board was pleased to hear that Dargan was at work on six miles of line, half of the total actually in his possession. Some 22,000 cubic yards of clay and 4,000 yards of rock had been excavated and two miles of line were then up to formation level. He had taken delivery of a considerable quantity of additional plant and anticipated a large increase in the number of men employed as soon as the harvest was in. Expectations were that the line would be opened as far as Rathkeale in the summer of 1855 and, as the works were of a light character from there to Foynes, the remainder would be completed shortly afterwards. The *Railway Times* reported in December 1854 that masons employed by Dargan had gone on strike on a recent Saturday as they were dissatisfied at

An unidentified WL&WR 0-6-0 crossing the lattice bridge over the River Maigue near Adare. Photographer unknown

the time allowed them for breakfast and dinner. In addition, it had been necessary to provide protection for men working at the Limerick end of the line following the perpetration 'of a brutal outrage'.

It would appear that William Carroll had not received any remuneration since taking up office. As he had been actively engaged in the formation of the company since 1851, it was agreed to pay him a sum of £150 for past services and to fix his salary at £100 per annum. Arrangements were made for the renting of accommodation for offices at the School of Art house in George's Street, Limerick, for one year at a rent of £25.

Plans for stations
September 1854 also saw attention being given to the provision of stations on the line. The directors visited Patrickswell on the 23rd and decided that the station there should be near the Attyflynn Gate. It was also decided to employ an architect, Joshua Hargrave, to furnish designs and to superintend the erection of the various station houses. Hargrave was requested to produce drawings of stations on the Killarney and Tullamore lines for inspection. These drawings were submitted in October, and the directors agreed to pay Hargrave £200 to cover the various plans and for superintending the works. Plans were approved for the stations at Adare and Patrickswell, the secretary being requested to seek tenders for their construction. Six tenders were submitted to the board at its meeting on 16 December, that of Edward Nagle and George Hunt being accepted at a figure of £1,300, exclusive of goods stores. A plan for the station at Rathkeale was approved in the following February, Messrs Nagle and Hunt initially tendering at £1,340, later reduced to £1,260, but also to include a goods store. In the following July the contractors agreed 'to the removal of the Rathkeale station building to the new site at Ballingrane recommended by Mr LeFanu on condition of the company paying them £100 extra for

additional cartage of materials'. Mrs Anne Shire was paid £50 for the purchase of her land required and £15 compensation for crops growing thereon.

As far as permanent way was concerned, an order had been placed with Messrs Crutwell Allies & Co in November 1854 for 1,312 tons of rails and chairs, to be delivered at Limerick at £8 5s 0d per ton. Messrs John Martin & Son of Dublin had agreed to supply sleepers. Five sets of points and crossings were later ordered from Messrs Courtney & Stephens of Dublin. In June 1855 LeFanu wrote to the board with an agreement from Dargan to the effect that if level crossings were substituted for the proposed bridges on the Adare Road and at Attyflynn, a saving of £2,101 15s 8d would accrue to the company. This alteration was approved of — they being rather strangely referred to at the time as 'level bridges'. LeFanu advised in May 1856 that the BoT would not allow the public roads at Attyflynn and Mount Earl to be crossed on the level, but would require over-bridges. The board expressed its disappointment that the opening of the line must be deferred and LeFanu was instructed to attend at Limerick to explain matters. It is not clear why an engineer of LeFanu's experience had not raised this matter previously. Another matter of concern was the fact that a large quantity of rails had been found to be defective. In the interim, LeFanu was ordered to proceed with the erection of mileposts and also signals at level crossings. Attention was also directed to the provision of 'policemen's cottages' at level crossings, it being agreed that four were required.

Opening to Rathkeale
Agreement was reached with the W&LR in May 1856 in connection with the working of the line by the latter company. The rate was agreed at 2s 3d per train mile, the Waterford company to be responsible for the appointment of all stationmasters, policemen and

clerks. It was agreed that the service to be provided would consist of three trains each way on weekdays and two on Sundays. The W&LR secretary was requested to order the necessary tickets, stamping presses and stationery for each station. In addition, he was requested to prepare a draft timetable for the approval of the Foynes board.

Towards the end of June, with an opening of the line as far as Rathkeale expected within days, the chairman invited the Lord Lieutenant, the Earl of Carlisle, to inaugurate the opening on 10 July. It was arranged that a *déjeuner*, to be supplied by Mr T. A. Polson, would be held at Adare after the opening ceremony in a marquee supplied by Mr Hynes. It was decided that all the shareholders be invited, along with other guests as agreed. The several bills for this event, amounting to £128 1s 5d, were paid in August. Captain Henry W. Tyler inspected the line and reported to the BoT on 8 July. The line was 16¾ miles long, 'running into a siding on the W&LR and from thence on an independent line into Limerick'. Tyler requested the provision of a signal at Limerick, to be worked from the station platform, for the control of trains running from the siding into the station. The permanent way consisted of 80lb per yard bridge rails on transverse sleepers with stone ballast; Tyler required the latter to be increased in quantity and broken into smaller pieces. He referred to the works generally as being light. There were 13 over-bridges on the line, and eight under-bridges, all of masonry, and four further viaducts, these consisting of wrought-iron lattice girders. A turntable at Rathkeale was 'not quite complete', while two over-bridges were to be substituted for level crossings (already referred to); the crossings had apparently been retained at the request of the Grand Jury and some local mill owners.

The BoT wrote on 10 July directing that the opening of the line be deferred for a month. The company replied the next day advising that the signal at Limerick had been erected, the turntable would be completed in a few days, and the two over-bridges in four months. The directors agreed to work the line on the 'one-engine-in-steam principle', a tank engine to be used at a speed not exceeding 15mph. The BoT relented and confirmed on 15 July that the line might be opened. The company had however beaten it to it with the opening having taken place three days earlier!

An announcement in the local press showed trains leaving Limerick on weekdays at 08.00, 14.00 and 19.00, with Sunday departures at 09.00 and 15.00. Journey time was 45 minutes (50min on Sundays) and, with one exception, all trains returned from Rathkeale an hour after leaving Limerick. All three classes were provided for, although no fares are shown for third class returns. In addition to the three classes of travel, the company was progressive in that return tickets issued on Saturdays and Sundays were available for return on the following Monday. Intermediate stations were provided at Patrick's Well (sic) and Adare. Within a month of the opening the timetable was altered to better suit traffic arrangements, in addition to which market tickets were issued in the up direction on Wednesdays and Saturdays.

Edward Green of Rathkeale wrote to the company in August requesting that a flag station be opened 'at the village of Patrickswell at the place originally intended as the site of the station house'. The request was declined in view of the close proximity of the site and the existing station. Green later waited on the board and presented a memorial from residents of the village for the establishment of a flag station near Fort Etna gate, consideration being deferred. Such a station was subsequently opened at Fort Etna on 23 July 1861. Only nine months later, it was reported that receipts averaged only £1 10s 9d per week, but it was agreed to keep it open a little longer. By November 1864, receipts had not improved, the figure for the previous 12 months being only £79. Instructions were given for its closure, but the L&FR, who paid 10s per week to keep it open, objected and it was agreed to keep it open 'for the present'. The agent there applied for better office accommodation in June 1866, the W&LR agreeing to provide a sentry box if the L&FR would pay for it. This it apparently declined to do as a Mr White wrote in February of the following year complaining of the want of shelter. These complaints, allied to continuing poor receipts, led to the halt being finally closed towards the end of 1867.

The line is completed

Attention now turned to completing the next section of line as far as Askeaton. Plans were furnished by Hargrave in August 1856 for a station at the latter point, but they were considered to be too elaborate and expensive, and he was requested to modify his ideas and furnish an estimate for the work. Meanwhile, William Payne, the traffic superintendent, stated that the platform at Adare station was too short and should be lengthened; he also recommended that accommodation be provided for the loading of carriages, these matters being referred to LeFanu. The lengthening of the platform at a cost of £70 5s 0d was approved in September and a ticket platform was ordered to be erected at Rathkeale. Revised plans for Askeaton were submitted by Hargrave and approved. John Condon tendered in

The 4.15pm Foynes to Limerick mixed train is seen shunting at Adare on 22 April 1955. This station, which opened in 1856, was just over 11 miles from Limerick and in its heyday was served by trains off the North Kerry line as well as by those on the Foynes branch.
R. M. Casserley

November for the station building at £682 plus £520 for a goods store. He was offered £1,150, which he declined. Richard Brash of Cork tendered in December for all building works at Askeaton at £1,300. Plans were now also furnished for the terminal station at Foynes, the tender of Michael Walsh being accepted at £3,400 on the understanding that he complete the booking office, passenger shed and goods store within four months.

Reference has already been made to the BoT requirement for the building of bridges at Attyflynn and Mount Earl in substitution for unauthorised level crossings. William Barrington, the resident engineer, reported that the former bridge had fallen on 12 March 1857, delaying the first up train. LeFanu was ordered to come down and inspect the second of these bridges and report urgently to the board as to its security.

Captain Tyler returned to Limerick on 11 May 1857 to inspect the next section of line, that from Rathkeale as far as Askeaton, a distance of 3½ miles. The only adverse comment was that the ballast of broken stone once again required to be more finely broken. The only important feature noted on this section was the three-span viaduct over the River Deal. Here, the railway was carried on timber planks resting on iron lattice girders, in turn supported on masonry piers and abutments; each span was of 32ft. Permission was verbally given for opening, this taking place on the next day. Tyler had commented that there was a gravel hill near the line, which he strongly recommended the directors to purchase. Instructions were therefore given to LeFanu to treat for the purchase of the land required at Ballinacahera between Adare and Rathkeale. It is not clear whether or not this purchase fell through as a board minute of 19 December refers to the purchase for £100 of a ballast hill on the lands of Mr Eyre

Lloyd at Clonoul. The company also owned a quarry near Carey's Road at this time, this being let to a Mr John Fogerty between September 1859 and June 1862.

Notice was given to the BoT in October 1857 of the completion of the remaining section of line to the terminus at Foynes, but this was withdrawn six days later following the sinking of part of the embankment at Robertstown. This took several months to put right, further notice being given early in April of the following year in the hope that the line would be opened in time for the Great Munster Fair on 29/30 April. It was a close shave — the line was in fact opened on the 28th with a service of two trains each way daily on weekdays with a third on Saturdays, and two on Sundays, following the customary inspection by Captain Tyler. He referred to the ground at the Foynes end of the line as being of 'a treacherous character', with the permanent way on piles for some distance between Robertstown Viaduct and firm ground. The viaduct itself was quoted as being 315ft long, consisting of 15 21ft timber spans, each including 12 wooden piles.

The W&LR engineer proposed having a ballast train on the line between passenger trains under a requirement that it be moved to a siding quarter of an hour before a passenger train was due. Tyler, rightly, was of the opinion that this proposal had an element of serious risk and recommended that the ballast trains be run at night. This was agreed to, as was the requirement for an undertaking that the line be worked on the basis of 'one engine in steam'. It would appear that no goods accommodation was initially provided at Foynes, as in July a goods siding was ordered to be erected as soon as possible. Permission was given in August for the extension of a line of rails along the quay at Foynes, the company

Top right: **The 4.15pm Foynes to Limerick mixed train shunting at Askeaton on 22 April 1955. There is much in this picture to explain why so many railway enthusiasts made their way to the remote corners of the CIE system in the 1950s. Apart from the locomotive, octogenarian 'J15' No 106, mixed trains were still to be found on a few branch lines in Ireland.** H. C. Casserley

Lower right: **'J15' class 0-6-0 No 106 is seen beside the engine shed at Foynes on 22 April 1955. This 1874-built locomotive was rebuilt with a superheated boiler in 1937 and was converted to burn oil for a few years in the late 1940s. Withdrawn in 1965, No 106 was one of CIE's last steam locomotives. Members of this 118-strong class worked on both passenger and goods services all over the former WL&WR system.** H. C. Casserley

undertaking to remove these on receiving due notice from the BoW. Meanwhile in November 1857, Pim, the W&LR locomotive superintendent, reported that the L&FR had removed the turntable from Askeaton to Foynes, notice being served that the Waterford company would not be liable for any accidents to trains between Askeaton and Limerick, which now had 'to run end foremost on a line badly and insufficiently ballasted'.

An intruder
Notice was published in December 1858 of intention to apply to Parliament for the construction of a line from Charleville on the GS&WR Cork main line to a junction with the L&FR at or near Patrickswell, the decision being taken by the L&FR to oppose the new line. Another project announced at that time was the Kilrush & Kilkee Railway & Poulnasherry Reclamation, which sought a subscription from the L&FR, this being declined. Whilst the Act for this line received the Royal Assent on 23 July 1860, nothing further was done towards construction. The scheme was later resurrected as the narrow-gauge West Clare Railway Co, which we will come across later.

With regard to the proposed line from Charleville, the *Railway Times*, reporting on the W&LR half-yearly meeting of shareholders held on 27 August 1859, quoted the chairman as stating his belief that there was no prospect of such a line being built, it being introduced solely to frighten them. He wondered if the GS&WR would support a line which would have the effect of forcing the W&LR 'into the arms of the Midland and thus divert traffic from Tipperary, Carlow and Clonmel'. The W&LR had in fact written to the GS&WR pointing out that Cork and Dublin traffic would be diverted via the Killaloe line and the Shannon steamers of the Midland Great Western Railway — the 'Midland' — and asking it to join in opposing the Bill. What the W&LR does not appear to have appreciated is that the

scheme was being actively supported by the GS&WR! The *Cork Herald* was rather more optimistic of success, pointing out that it would reduce the distance between Cork and Limerick by 20 miles.

The proposals foundered in 1859 but by November of that year the scheme for the Cork & Limerick Direct Railway was again being promoted, this time with the addition of an independent station at Limerick. Correspondence had been exchanged between Sir John Benson, consulting engineer to the C&LDR, and the L&FR board, requesting running powers over the latter's line, powers (if necessary) for the laying of a second line of rails between Patrickswell and Limerick, and a subscription of £10,000. A petition was lodged against the Bill in December as a precautionary measure to protect the company's interests.

A deputation from the provisional committee of the C&LDR comprising Ebenezer Pike, Francis Lyons MP, and William Shaw, merchants of Cork, met with the Foynes board late in February 1860, resulting in the signing of an agreement dated 5 March. This provided for the C&LDR to use, with its own engines and carriages (in actual fact those of the GS&WR), the section between the proposed junction and Patrickswell station,

provided its trains were run by arrangement so as not to interfere with Foynes line trains. In return for these powers, the C&LDR was to pay a rent from the date of the opening of the line equivalent to 5% per annum on half the cost of that portion of line, it being agreed that the cost was not to exceed £10,000 per mile. If a second line of rails was deemed necessary, it too was to be subject to the same rent, viz 5% per annum on half the cost. The C&LDR was in addition to pay half the cost of maintenance of the line(s). It was not allowed to take up local traffic between Patrickswell and Limerick or any stations on that section of line. Following the passing of the C&LDR Act, the agreement was incorporated in an indenture dated 6 August 1860. Correspondence with the W&LR regarding accommodation at the terminus at Limerick led, in due course, to an award being made by Thomas Harrison, engineer to the North Eastern Railway (of England) in May 1862.

The *Limerick Chronicle* reported in September 1860 that Mr Roddy, resident engineer to the C&LDR, had spent some three weeks laying out the line, work on which was expected to commence at once. The contract for the construction of the 17-mile-long branch was awarded in January

1861 to Messrs J. Trowsdale & Son of Stockton-on-Tees, but it is clear that work had been ongoing for some time prior to this. In the following June, John Long, the L&FR resident engineer, was requested to report on the cost of track doubling between the junction and Patrickswell station, this being estimated at £1,900. Initially it was proposed to tender for these works, but as it was realised that it could not be executed without engine power, the W&LR was requested to carry out the necessary works. The new line was completed by July 1862 and was opened for passenger traffic as from 1 August following a BoT inspection by Col Rich. He had ordered the extension of the double line to the Limerick side of Patrickswell station, the construction of a separate platform for the use of C&LDR trains, and the erection of signals on both sides of the station.

The question of paying for the maintenance of the line arose in March 1863, when the C&LDR declined to pay for sleepers under this head, and also the gatemen's wages. It referred the matter to Mr Ilberry of the GS&WR for an opinion, the L&FR in the interim requesting payment of undisputed items as per accounts furnished. It is not clear what Ilberry reported, but the matter was further referred in January 1865 for Counsel's Opinion, following which it was conceded that sleepers should be paid for, but not the wages. Arbitration was suggested, the matter dragging on for a further three years, when an award was made in July 1868, this ruling that gatemen's wages be charged to the Waterford company. The C&LDR however refused to accept sections of the award and requested that any further reference to the arbitrator should involve the participation of lawyers. The matter appears to have been finally settled in January 1872 when the Foynes board reluctantly accepted a payment of £400 in lieu of its claim for £493 odd, 'without admitting the principle of any deductions claimed by them' (the C&LDR). In the intervening years, a number of complaints were made regarding disruptions to Cork line trains resulting from the W&LR changing the times of trains without prior notice.

Working the line
The Foynes board wrote to the W&LR in January 1859 requesting a reduction in the charge for haulage to a fixed sum of £3,500 per annum for two trains each way on weekdays and one on Sundays, extra and special trains to be charged at 2s 3d per train mile. The W&LR declined to consider this request 'as the current rate of 2s 3d entails a serious loss'. Further correspondence led to an offer of £5,000 per annum for one year as from 1 May 1861, all specials etc to be charged at 2s 0d per train mile, this offer being accepted. A year later,

Foynes station looking towards Limerick on 22 April 1950. The line diverging to the left ran to a siding on the pier.
H. C. Casserley

the W&LR agreed to reduce the sum to £4,300 on the understanding that the third train ran only to Rathkeale, this in turn being accepted by the L&FR. Further reductions were made in 1863 when the service was cut to two trains each way during the six winter months. Complaints were, however, made of inconvenience to passengers. Various agreements were made over the next 10 years and by October 1872 the Waterford company was seeking a figure of 2s 6d per train mile, or the actual cost of working. This was turned down by the Foynes board, which refused to pay any increased charge. By this time, negotiations had been ongoing for the purchase by the W&LR of the L&FR, and the former agreed not to seek any alteration in rates pending the finalisation of these negotiations.

As early as June 1871, the W&LR had been engaged in discussions with the GWR in relation to the amalgamation of various branch lines. Arising from these discussions the Foynes board wrote in July offering two L&FR £25 shares for one W&LR £50 share. No reply having been received from the Waterford company, the L&FR wrote again in October assuming that any arrangement was now at an end. Various other meetings took place at Paddington and it was announced in November 1872 that the W&LR had agreed to take up the liabilities of the Foynes company, amounting to £6,810, and also to pay a sum of £800 as compensation to William Carroll for loss of his position. The Act giving effect to the transfer of the L&FR to the W&LR received Royal Assent on 21 July 1873, Section 7 allowing for the dissolution of the former company as from 1 July.

Extension to Newcastle
Reference has already been made to suggestions made by Hemans to the effect that the L&FR should consider an extension to the important west Limerick town of

Newcastle. This idea was not to be pursued by the Foynes company. Instead, parliamentary notice under the title of the Rathkeale & Newcastle Junction Railway (R&NJR) appeared in November 1860 for the construction of a line of railway from a junction with the L&FR at Rathkeale and terminating at Newcastle West. Powers were to be granted to the C&LDR and the L&FR to subscribe to the new undertaking and for the latter company to work the line. Brief reference is made to the notice in the W&LR board minutes under the revised title of the Newcastle & Rathkeale Junction Railway, the vice-chairman being authorised 'to treat for getting control of this line'. However, it was not until October 1863 that the expediency of subscribing to the line was considered by the directors of the W&LR.

In the meantime, a meeting of the provisional directors of the R&NJR was held at No 29 South Mall, Cork on 2 January 1861, with Col Samuel Dickson MP, in the chair. Those in attendance included H. Williams Wood (secretary, not only to this company but also to the Cork & Kinsale Junction and the Cork & Limerick Direct companies), Michael Leahy (solicitor), William Barrington and Sir John Benson (engineers), Edward Curling and W. J. Shaw. Barrington reported that he had been in negotiation with Mr Hall of Messrs James Trowsdale & Son who had agreed to execute the works on the line, including permanent way, for the sum of £38,493. They had also agreed to accept one-quarter of this amount in the company's shares. Messrs Trowsdale had already been appointed contractors to the Cork & Kinsale Junction Railway and the Cork & Limerick Direct Railway.

It was decided to accept Messrs Trowsdale's offer, conditional on their providing a sum of £3,000 towards the parliamentary deposit, the company finding the balance of £1,000. In the event, the contractors refused

Newcastle West station on 14 July 1934 showing 'J15' 0-6-0 No 106 on the 17.30 Tralee to Limerick train. Note the second coach in GSR two-tone livery and the station nameboard referring simply to 'Newcastle'. H. C. Casserley

to contribute more than £2,000 and this led to negotiations being conducted with Messrs Joshua Hargreave of Cork, who offered to complete the works for the reduced sum of £36,991; they also agreed to the conditions regarding the deposit and method of payment. They were awarded the contract in February, even though the Act of Incorporation had yet to be obtained.

The secretary reported that the Bill received Royal Assent on 22 July 1861, the engineers now being instructed to prepare the necessary working plans and drawings. Capital was £50,000 with subscriptions of £5,000 each authorised from the C&LDR and the L&FR. In August, the Earl of Devon was elected a director and was quickly persuaded to take the position of chairman, with Col Dickson as vice-chairman. Some discussion took place regarding the remuneration of the engineers, a figure of £2,000 being agreed on. Mr Wood also made a proposal for his services between October 1859 and August 1861 in respect of the promotion of the railway. He suggested a figure of £650 plus an additional £150 as travelling and accommodation expenses to and from Ireland. He was offered £550 in cash and the balance in paid-up shares, which he declined. The matter was referred to the arbitration of Sir Cusack Roney, chairman of the Cork & Youghal Railway, Wood in the interim being offered the secretaryship of the company at a salary of £100 for one year from 1 September. When

the award was made, Wood accepted £500 in cash and £250 in shares.

The ceremonial turning of the first sod for the R&NJR was performed by the Earl of Devon on 10 August 1861 'in the presence of a vast concourse of people (estimated at some 3,000 people)', at Courtenay Castle near Newcastle West. The procession was led by a band playing *Garryowen.* A plank was laid for 10 yards on a grassy slope, and a wheelbarrow of polished walnut was provided, along with a 'handsomely finished spade', this latter being duly presented to the Earl. The local press reported that Newcastle was 'the chief depot of produce and business of the West Limerick area', and would connect the great plain of the north with Limerick and Cork (via the C&LDR). Work progressed slowly, and by the time of the second half-yearly shareholders' meeting in August 1862, possession had been taken of about 3½ miles at the Newcastle end. Two miles of line had been completed, including bridges and culverts, with the exception of the bridge over the River Deal, work on this latter not commencing until May 1864. Financial matters were however pressing on the directors. Whilst a sum of £23,520 of the capital had been subscribed for, only £7,549 had been received. It was hinted that even if the calls on shares were paid, there would only be sufficient monies to continue the works to the end of the year.

Working agreement

Twelve months later, almost five miles of line had been brought to formation level. Work had however slowed, in part due to the calls on shares not being paid up, but also difficulties with works across the bog near Rathkeale. In fact, land in the immediate Rathkeale area had not even been acquired. It was in this context that approaches were made to the W&LR in

October seeking a subscription of £10,000. An agreement was concluded between the two companies on 19 December 1863, under which the W&LR agreed to subscribe a sum of £5,000. The agreement stipulated that the line should be completed during 1864 'unless prevented by Causes beyond their Control', the works to be undertaken to the satisfaction of the W&LR engineer. From the date of completion and sanctioning for public traffic by the BoT, the W&LR would, for a term of 20 years, provide plant and rolling stock for the working of the line, and it was also to be responsible for the appointment and removal of staff. In return, the R&NJR was obliged to pay a sum of 2s 3d per train mile for a service of two trains each way daily, or 1s 11d for a three-train service. If however in any year during the term of the agreement, gross receipts amounted to £5,200, the payment was to be altered to 45% of such receipts for the remainder of the term.

Notice was to be given to the Waterford company at least two months prior to the completion of the line, when a joint committee consisting of three directors from each company was to be formed to oversee the management and working of the line. The terms of the agreement were given effect to by the Waterford & Limerick, Limerick & Foynes and Rathkeale & Newcastle Junction Railways Companies Act, which received Royal Assent on 25 July 1864. The Act also gave power to the W&LR to appoint some person to vote on its behalf at meetings of the R&NJR, William Malcomson joining the board of the latter company. Provision was made in the Act for the Waterford company to raise additional capital in respect of its subscription and also for the provision of the necessary rolling stock.

Reporting to the shareholders of the R&NJR in February 1864, the chairman

Newcastle West station on 12 June 1953
with ex GS&WR 'J15' 0-6-0 No 156 en route
to Tralee on an enthusiasts' special.
The goods shed is on left; the overall roof
was later removed. D. G. Coakham

stated that eight out of the ten miles of land required had been obtained, with six of these completed and ready to receive permanent way. Arrangements were being made for the more vigorous prosecution of the works, which 'will ensure the opening of the line for traffic this Autumn'. A letter to the *Limerick Chronicle* in June however seemed to tell a different story, the writer commenting that the line was fast becoming the laughing stock of the whole country. He went on to say that no station houses had been commenced, nor had any progress been made with the swampy ground at Rathkeale Workhouse, which 'swallows much'. In addition, it was stated that the contractor was seldom present.

In August, once again short of funds, the directors made application to 'big brother' for finance to purchase rails. The W&LR refused but offered, on its own behalf and that of the L&FR, to give £1,000 for every £2,000 worth of rails put on the ground. The secretary was instructed to borrow, if necessary, 1,100 tons of rails lying idle on the ground of the West Cork Railway as that company would not require them for the next 18 months. Plans were submitted at this time for Rathkeale station, some two miles from the Rathkeale station of the L&FR — the latter being later renamed Ballingrane Junction to avoid confusion. A contract was entered into in January 1865 for the supply of 1,100 tons of rails at £8 10s 0d per ton delivered free on board at Cardiff or Newport, while 6,000 rectangular sleepers were ordered in February at 4s 9d each, delivered on the line. The W&LR agreed to carry permanent way materials between Waterford and Rathkeale for 7s per ton, including loading and unloading.

At the August 1865 shareholders' meeting, the chairman referred to unexpected diffi-culties, entirely beyond the control of the board, which had considerably retarded the progress of the works, namely the deferred delivery of rails and the fact that the L&FR had not yet paid any portion of its £5,000 subscription. This had led to a virtual suspension of the works and an application being made to the Public Works Loan Commissioners (PWLC) for a loan to enable the line to be completed and opened for traffic. Success in this latter regard was reported towards the end of the year. By now the station at Rathkeale was complete, with that at Newcastle in a forward state.

Financial difficulties were evident in other areas also. Messrs T. & C. Martin of Dublin had obtained a judgment in April 1865 for an outstanding debt on sleepers delivered, while Messrs Hargreave served writs against the Earl of Devon in respect of three overdue promissory notes. The contractors were persuaded to renew these for three months, renewable if required for a further similar period, the company issuing Lloyd's Bonds as collateral security. Lloyd's Bonds were instruments under the seal of a railway company, admitting the indebtedness of the company to the obligee to a specified amount for work done or goods supplied, with a covenant to pay him such amount, with interest, on a future day. They were a device by which railway companies were enabled to increase their indebtedness without technically violating their charter. The name is derived from the Counsel who settled the form of the bond.

Opening to Newcastle

By January of the following year, the works were at last nearing completion, and an approach was made to the W&LR for permission to lay a turnout at the point of connection with the L&FR. This was agreed to on condition that the R&NJR indemnified the Waterford company against accidents and paid a man to mind the points. It was suggested that the line might be opened for traffic on 10 May 1866, but Tighe found matters wanting and it was not until 23 October that Col Rich inspected the line on behalf of the BoT, he duly authorising its opening. Tighe however was still not satisfied and requested the provision of engine and carriage sheds, and a water column at Newcastle. One of the local directors, Edward Curling, offered to put up the estimated £400 to £500 required if the Earl of Devon did not do so.

The outstanding matters were finally attended to in December 1866 and at length the long-awaited opening to traffic took place on 1 January 1867 with a service of three trains each way daily. The W&LR traffic manager submitted an account of expenses connected with the opening amounting to £10 7s 9d, a figure of £4 10s 0d for the hiring of a band being debited to the Newcastle company.

The line was not long open before complaints were being made in respect of the train service. To be fair to the W&LR, some of the problem related to contamin-ated water at Newcastle and the want of a water tank at Ballingrane, this latter on occasions necessitating engines having to go to Askeaton to obtain water. In July 1867 the service was reduced to two trains each way. The working company contemplated an increase in the rates for haulage, figures of

Newcastle West station, the nameboards simply referring to it as 'Newcastle'. The diesel railcar set has as its leading vehicle No 2661, one of six railcars with bodies designed by O. V. S. Bulleid on AEC underframes and built at CIE's Inchicore Works. Late Rev John Parker/Hugh Davies

2s 6d for a two-train service and 2s 2d for a three-train service being suggested. This probably led in part to the Newcastle board stating its desire to negotiate the sale of the line. Negotiations took place in 1873/74 and a purchase price of £60,000 was suggested by the W&LR. A meeting chaired by the Earl of Devon was held at Newcastle in June 1873 to consider the matter further. The Earl referred to the company's heavy debts, amounting to a figure in excess of £63,000, mainly owed to the Earl himself. The offer from the W&LR would in normal circumstances have been regarded as a poor deal, but considered against the precarious state of the company and the ever-present possibility of one of the creditors foreclosing, it was little better than could be expected. A sale to the W&LR was recommended and approved, but nothing further transpired in this regard.

The chairman sues for a debt

Later, in April 1877, the Earl of Devon sued the company in the Court of Common Pleas for a sum of £55,014 5s 9d, being monies lent to it; an additional sum of £8,404 was subsequently claimed by the Earl. However, neither of these judgments was enforced and under an Act of 1879 the company obtained power for the issue of 'Postponed Debenture Stock' bearing accumulated interest at 5% per annum. When William Malcomson resigned as a director in February 1884 he suggested that the Earl should purchase his shareholding in the company. The secretary replied to the effect that this was unlikely due to the Earl being 'a heavy loser by the line'. The PWLC had called in its advance in December 1876, necessitating the company borrowing a further £16,000 odd to pay off this debt.

Approaches were made to the company in 1867 by Messrs Enright of Castle Matrix Mills near Rathkeale for a siding, authority being given in December for such a facility capable of holding six wagons, subject to Enright's traffic being offered to the railway. The siding was brought into use towards the end of 1868. Its removal was suggested in 1884 by Tighe on the grounds that it was dangerous to work in one direction without proper signalling. It remained in use, however, into GSR days.

The original working agreement with the W&LR was for a term of 20 years from the date of opening, but with provision for it to be made perpetual. This made sense in the context of the Waterford company preparing to work the extension from Newcastle to Tralee, the agreement being finalised in August 1879. Five years later, when the Limerick & Kerry Railway lodged a Bill to give effect to a proposed merger with the Rathkeale company, the W&LR found it necessary to oppose it on the grounds that it would be most objectionable and injurious to its interests. Bearing in mind that it was now leasing the line in perpetuity, it was prepared to pay a fair cash price. Once again, no purchase was made and the amalgamation Bill was defeated in the House of Commons.

Following on the opening of the L&KR line it soon became obvious that the station layout at Newcastle West was far from ideal for the through working of trains. Lt-Col Hutchinson, when he inspected the line in November 1880, stated that the provision of an additional crossover road and two signals would enable the station to be used as a crossing place. Plans were in fact drawn up by Tighe in 1881 for what in effect would have been almost a new station. This would have involved the removal and rebuilding of the passenger shed and goods store and the construction of new platforms, sidings and a carriage shed, alterations which would have adequately provided for Kerry line trains. The cost of this work was estimated at about £4,000, which, in addition to the difficulties likely in obtaining additional land, made it impracticable. William Barrington therefore drew up plans involving only one platform with additional siding accommodation and other facilities at the back of it. These plans were approved by the W&LR and the works were completed in 1883 and passed by Gen Hutchinson following an inspection in January 1884. This left the station basically as it was at the time of its closure.

A traffic inspector is appointed

Reference is made in Chapter Nine to the appointment of Edmond Cooke as traffic inspector to the L&KR. He was at the same time appointed to a similar post on the R&NJR in September 1884. In August 1885 he was appointed to the position of

Examining Director, which was to cause considerable friction with the W&LR board. At an adjourned half-yearly shareholders' meeting in April 1886, Anthony O'Connor put forward a motion striking out Cooke's name as a director on the ground that he could not legally serve as such as he was already a salaried servant of the company. This motion was defeated but at future meetings of the joint committee, the Waterford company's representatives attended, objected to Cooke's presence and then withdrew. The animosity existed on both sides. When the W&LR insisted on the implementation of certain BoT requirements, imposed following the passing of the Regulation of Railways Act of 1889, Cooke commented that it 'seems pretty clear . . . that they (the W&LR) are disposed to go out of their way unnecessarily to embarrass and throw upon the Rathkeale company if possible, the burden of a vast expense in connection with the interlocking of signals, points, etc'.

Little of note occurred in the remaining years of the R&NJR's independent existence. The Earl of Devon died in November 1888, a sad loss to a company to which he had been such a munificent benefactor. He was replaced as chairman by Falkiner Collis Sandes of London, who only remained until May 1892 when he resigned to take up an appointment in India. William Barrington was informed in December 1885 that as his duties were now effectively restricted to the preparation of the half-year certificate, his fee would be reduced to £5 per half-year in future. Barrington reluctantly accepted this figure, but not before he had informed the board that the Ilen Valley Railway paid him 10 guineas per half-year for a similar duty!

In the months preceding the amalgamation of the WL&WR with the GS&WR, consideration was given to the future of certain of the salaried staff. The GS&WR informed the R&NJR that it would not require the services of Mr Cooke after 1 January 1901. Cooke was in due course awarded compensation of £198. Henry Holmes, who had been secretary of the company since January 1878, was awarded a sum of £300.

Chapter Four

TO DEEP WATER ON THE SHANNON

In 1854 proposals were put forward for the construction of a line from the W&LR at Killonan and terminating at Castleconnell. The prospectus issued towards the end of the year extolled the virtues of the district to be served and added that construction of such a line would result in 'handsome villas springing up on the route'; a return of 10% was confidently expected on the capital. At a meeting of the provisional committee held at Limerick on 19 July 1855, Sir Richard DeBurgh of Castleconnell was elected chairman, other members of the provisional committee including John Brown, John Quin and Michael Furnell, all of Limerick, and Henry William Massey of Rosanna, Tipperary. The latter gentleman was of course already connected with the W&LR. E. William Maunsell was appointed secretary to the new company at a salary of £100 per annum. Arrangements were approved with John Challoner Smith, whereby he proposed to make a subscription of £4,500 in return for a guarantee of a return of his deposit in the event of the line not proceeding, otherwise he was to be awarded the contract for construction on equitable terms.

William LeFanu declined to tender for the engineering of the line, as did William Barrington of Limerick, so long as Charles Cheyne was connected with it. We know nothing about this latter gentleman, but presumably he was originally to have taken charge of engineering matters. The secretary was instructed to advertise in the *Limerick Chronicle* for tenders for the engineering of the line, the total length of which was quoted as 5m 6f 22y. Various tenders were received in October 1855, that of James B. Pratt at £200 being accepted; Pratt was already engineer to the Limerick & Ennis Railway, a company that we will meet in the next chapter. Cheyne, who had also tendered, objected to the appointment and considered he had been unfairly treated and went on to say that he had been 'unceremoniously sacrificed'. A cheque was sent to Cheyne in respect of the parliamentary expenses incurred to that date, whereupon he requested the return of his account for amendment, a request which was refused. Pratt now made some minor alterations in the original plans. He

mentioned that there were two important bridges on the line, viz those over the River Mulkear and the Dublin Mail Road; this latter would be expensive, it being necessary to raise the existing road by 14ft to cross the railway and he suggested an application to the BoT for a level crossing instead.

A contract is signed and work commences

The Act of Incorporation for the Limerick & Castleconnell Railway (L&CR) received Royal Assent on 26 June 1855 empowering the construction of the 5¾-mile line, capital being set at £25,000 with borrowing up to £8,000, subject to the usual requirement as regards paid-up capital. Messrs John Bagnell and J. C. Smith submitted an estimate in February 1856 for the construction of the line at a figure of £11,500, excluding rails and station buildings, a proposal which was accepted. Possession was taken of Mr Browne's land at Lisnagry on 16 April 1856 and the contractors commenced work there. However, even before any construction got under way, the secretary was instructed to call on the W&LR board and seek its approval for an extension of the line to Nenagh. The latter company had no objections provided the L&CR applied for the Bill and inserted a clause agreeing to lease or sell the complete undertaking to the W&LR.

Within months, rumours began circulating about the financial state of the new company, rumours which the chairman stated were groundless and based on unfounded suspicions. Various shareholders complained of waste and unnecessary expenditure, lengthy discussions taking place at a special meeting of shareholders at Cruise's Hotel in Limerick on 16 July 1856. A Mr Anglim seriously doubted whether the line could be constructed within the capital as the L&FR was reputed to be costing £6,000 per mile.

In January 1857 the engineer complained that the contractors were making up embankments from side cutting on the company's ground. He was instructed not to certify any accounts until the contractors complied with his directions. Smith attended the board in January and advised that the W&KR had for sale second-hand rails at £6 per ton. Pratt however was of

opinion that these would be an uneconomic buy, even at that price, and it was decided to wait until tenders were accepted by the L&ER for rails, when a contract would be placed. By the following month, some 2½ miles of earthworks had been executed and the line was expected to be ready for the receipt of rails in June and to be opened in August. Rails, however, were not delivered from Wales until July, these being carried free over the W&LR from Limerick to Killonan, the L&CR agreeing to load them themselves. Adverse weather and a shortage of men and horses had also conspired to delay work on the line.

Bridges or level crossings?

In July, the company sought to dispense with two bridges, at Grange and Nenagh Road (later respectively Annacotty and Lisnagry). Following an inspection by Col Wynne, this request was turned down, although Captain Tyler did re-inspect at the beginning of August, it being reported that a Mr J. Watson was paid £4 11s 5d for luncheon and James Barry £6 6s 0d for wine on the occasion of the Captain's visit. It was later agreed that a *déjeuner* would be given to the shareholders at a cost not exceeding £100, on the occasion of the line being opened for traffic. Various memorials had been received from the Grand Jury, residents and hackney car proprietors, praying that the BoT would not enforce construction of the bridges. There was a general feeling against the bridges due to the comparatively unimportant traffic on the roads in question and the lightness of the proposed train service. Tyler recommended dispensing with the requirement for bridges. On the other hand, Caleb Powell MP (a supporter of the repeal of the Act of Union) wrote to the BoT totally opposing level crossings, which 'will obviously become most dangerous to passengers'. Nevertheless, permission was granted for level crossings at these points, subject to the company agreeing to erect bridges within 12 months or obtain the sanction of Parliament to dispense with them. The latter course was adopted.

In August, further consideration was given to the question of a Nenagh extension, it being reported that the MGWR was prepared to subscribe either to such an extension or one to Killaloe. Following completion of the normal business, the shareholders' half-yearly meeting on 21 August was made special to consider an extension of the line and to sanction a proposed traffic arrangement with the W&LR. The latter, which was to operate for a period of five years at a rate of 2s 3d per train mile for a three-train per day service, was approved. The question of an extension to Nenagh was also approved. However, when the Notice for a Bill was published in November it was for an extension northwards to Killaloe. As the MGWR was operating vessels on the River Shannon between Killaloe and Athlone, and such an extension would be of benefit to it, it was decided to seek a subscription of £10,000 from that company, the L&CR putting up a similar amount and Messrs Smith & Bagnell £8,000.

This apparently insignificant alliance with the MGWR has, however, to be viewed in a wider context. Between 1852 and 1860, the GS&WR and the MGWR had been in a state of war. The difficulties began in the former year following the signing of a rates agreement between the GS&WR and the Grand Canal Company. In November 1852, the boards of the two railway companies met, ostensibly to discuss the possibility of the GS&WR constructing a line from Tullamore to connect with the Midland. During the course of these discussions, it was agreed that any arrangements with the Grand Canal Co should be regarded as being on behalf of the two railway companies. Only a month later, however, it was announced that the MGWR had made an offer for the purchase of the canal. The Bill giving effect to this was defeated in Parliament and the Midland directors had to resign themselves to taking a seven-year lease. This move was to lead to action and counter-action, relations becoming ever more bitter. Finally, in August 1860 an award was made, basically precluding each company from trespassing on the other's territory. Under this award, the Midland found itself in difficulties over the proposed subscription to the L&CR. Further details of the dispute between the two big companies can be found in the companion volume on the history of the MGWR (*The Midland Great Western Railway of Ireland* — Midland Publishing Ltd, 1994).

Extension to Killaloe
Work was sufficiently advanced for an engine to run over the line on Monday, 28 December 1857, although the opening was still some months away. In fact, the chairman, in his half-yearly report in the following February, stated that the opening would take place in a few days. This also proved to be rather optimistic. In addition, he referred to financial problems facing the

company, pointing out that the directors had made themselves personally responsible. The Killaloe Extension Bill received Royal Assent on 2 August 1858, and included powers to dispense with the requirement for the two bridges alluded to earlier. The Bill had been opposed by two landowners, referred to as 'stooges of the GS&WR'. The extension line was to be maintained separately from the main undertaking, and known as the Limerick Castleconnell & Killaloe Railway. Reference was made to the possible construction of a tramway over the lands of the Shannon Improvement Commissioners to the riverside. It was announced in September that Pratt, the engineer, was unable to devote the constant time and attention needed to the Killaloe extension line and it was decided to look for the assistance of another engineer. Pratt was presented with a gratuity of £100 and a piece of plate suitably inscribed. His position was taken by William Barrington of Limerick. At the MGWR half-yearly shareholders' meeting, their chairman, John Ennis, said that 'arising out of the Grand Canal contest, a contest that I shall ever deplore, has been our subscription to the L&CR. I quite admit that this line is not in our district, but we were hurried into the circumstances of the subscription as part and parcel of the general principle of offence and defence into which we were plunged.' The purpose of the subscription had of course been to bring Limerick nearer to Athlone and thus carry the Limerick traffic over the Midland line via the Shannon steamers. Ennis announced that they would be quite willing, subject to satisfactory agreement with the GS&WR, to place their shares in the Killaloe extension in the hands of the latter company.

A BoT inspection was carried out at the beginning of July by Captain Tyler. The only important work on the line referred to by him was the wrought-iron lattice bridge over the River Mulkear, consisting of two spans, each of 55ft. The bridge was described as being 'strong and rigid', but requiring a parapet. Permanent way consisted of 75lb/yd flat-bottomed rail with sleepers at 3ft intervals. Other requirements were the provision of bolts in fishplates, red signals and gatesmen's boxes at level crossings, and a signal and turntable at Castleconnell. The line was re-inspected by Captain George Ross on 26 August and passed for opening, this latter taking place two days later. The initial train service consisted of two trains each way daily, from Limerick at 11.00 and 16.30 and from Castleconnell at 09.45 and 13.00; journey time was 30 minutes each way. There were also two trains each way on Sundays. Stations were at Killonan (4½ miles), Grange (6½) and Nenagh Road (8). It was reported that the opening had been delayed due to 'a real obstacle, a technical

objection by the BoT to a matter beyond the company's control'. This referred to the unauthorised extension of the W&LR from the old to the new stations at Limerick.

It was decided in October to rename two of the intermediate stations. Grange was to be henceforth called Annacotty while Nenagh Road was to become Nenagh Road & Newport. This latter station later became Lisnagry, a name which it retained until eventual closure. Advertisements were placed in various publications, in January 1859 including the *Railway Times*, seeking tenders for the construction of the Killaloe extension; that of John J. Bagnell at £11,700 was accepted in February. It was confidently hoped that the line as far as Birdhill would be opened for traffic by the summer, and for that station Messrs Courtney & Stephens supplied a turntable of 16ft diameter at a cost of £206. At the half-yearly meeting in August 1859 it was announced that passenger numbers were 19,219 for the six months. The directors had endeavoured to induce more people to travel by putting on fireworks displays and other forms of entertainment. In addition, return tickets were being offered at single-fare prices on Sundays. Work on the Killaloe extension had commenced on 2 March, and of the 4¾ miles, 4½ were up to formation level and ready for rails. The heavy rock cutting at the Killaloe end had also been commenced. It was reported that some of the landowners had not acted fairly, although this could not be said of the Shannon Improvement Commissioners.

Opening to Birdhill
It was reported in February 1860 that the opening of the line to Birdhill had been delayed by bad weather, although rails had by then been laid. Application was made to the PWLC for a Government loan of £12,000 to enable the company to complete the works and pay off its debts. The loan was refused on the grounds of insufficient security. The Birdhill extension was finally opened for traffic on 23 July 1860. Whilst the station at Birdhill was reported to be complete, there was only a temporary wooden goods shed there measuring 50ft by 20ft. As already mentioned, the turntable was of only 16ft diameter and complaints were soon being made of the time involved in turning engines, causing delays and danger of disablement (to engines or staff?). It was reported that it took six men 17 minutes to uncouple an engine and tender and to turn both. Later, the locomotive superintendent Martin Atock reported that engines were travelling from Limerick tender first, which he regarded as dangerous. In addition, there was no water supply for engines, and later still, when the Killaloe extension was opened, engines had to run there to take water. The GS&WR,

**Killaloe engine shed with 'J15' 0-6-0
No 106 on the turntable. The running line
is to the right.** W. A. Camwell/IRRS collection

following the opening of its line from
Nenagh, with its usual obstinacy, refused to
allow the W&LR engines to take water from
its column at Birdhill.

The W&LR called for the provision of a
ballast pit to serve the line, this being
provided about 1861 at Coolnadorney,
north of Birdhill. An agreement was
concluded with Mrs Hill of Nenagh for her
to run a coach service between Birdhill and
Nenagh in connection with the trains. The
company had itself purchased an omnibus
in February 1859, this being sold to a Mr
Patrick Lynch for £15 in January 1865. As
already referred to, the L&CR had expressed
an interest in extending to Nenagh, and it
was decided to promote a Bill to this effect
in the 1861 Session of Parliament, along
with a separate Bill for an extension to
Roscrea. The former line was planned to
deviate from the Birdhill to Killaloe line
about 1,100 yards north of Birdhill. About
this time, the L&CR inquired of the W&LR
whether, if it worked its own line, the W&LR
would attach carriages to its trains at
Killonan. The W&LR declined this suggestion on the grounds that it would cause
delay and disarrange the traffic. A new
agreement was concluded with the W&LR,
whereby it would work the line for six years,
running three trains a day, for 1s 10d per
train per mile. In an attempt to encourage
traffic, the L&CR board agreed to grant free
passes between Limerick and Castleconnell
for people who constructed houses worth
£300 or more. It was a stipulation that the
parties concerned reside in the houses and
the passes, which were non-transferable,
were given only to heads of families.

The long-running dispute between the
MGWR and the GS&WR had finally come to
an end in February 1860 with the publication of the award by Messrs Huish and
Watkin. As far as the L&CR was concerned, it
was stipulated that the shares of the Castleconnell line held by the MGWR were, within
a month of the passing of an Act authorising
such transfer, to be transferred to the
GS&WR. In addition, the Shannon steamer
traffic operated by the MGWR between
Athlone and Killaloe was to be in future
worked by the two companies under the
direction of a joint committee. The L&CR
directors expressed some concern at these
moves, which they felt might 'spell the doom
of Killaloe as a river/railway exchange point
even before the opening of the line to
Killaloe'. Consideration was nevertheless given
to the sale of the Castleconnell undertaking

to the GS&WR at par, although a sale to the
W&LR, 'even for worse terms', would have
been more acceptable. The latter asked for
time to consider the matter, but the L&CR
directors panicked and agreed a sale to the
GS&WR for a price reported at £65,000.

The Killaloe extension was inspected by
Captain Rich on behalf of the BoT on
24 March 1861, and being duly passed, was
opened for traffic on 12 April. One of two
engines provided by the W&LR for the BoT
inspection ran short of steam and the
charge of £10 for the use of the engine was
duly halved. Atock called for the provision
of a water tank and engine pit at Killaloe. It
was agreed to give the landlord an annual
sum of £5 for a water supply, the company
to lay down the necessary pipes. It was also
stated that a strong stop-block was
absolutely essential in view of the adverse
gradient there.

When the L&CR published Notice of a Bill
for the purchase of its line by the GS&WR, it
was opposed by the W&LR. It was stated
that Sir Richard DeBurgh, in the course of a
meeting with his opposite number on the
GS&WR, had settled on the proposed
purchase within 10 minutes and signed an
agreement of intent. Mr Quin, a director of
the L&CR, had then met with Malcomson,
advising him of what had transpired and he
agreed to approach the W&LR board. In the
meantime, the L&CR directors had ratified
the agreement to sell to the GS&WR. When
the bill came before the Parliamentary
Committee, Ilberry, on behalf of the
GS&WR, stated that the Nenagh route to
Limerick was not competitive, it being
single track from Ballybrophy. An extension
to Roscrea by the L&CR, at the behest of the
W&LR, would be injurious to GS&WR
traffic, in addition to which it (the GS&WR)
was considering a line from Nenagh to
Banagher. Various witnesses testified to the

carving up of the district by the two big
companies, which was disastrous to the
development of the area. After consideration of the matter, the Parliamentary
Committee rejected the Bill, 'desiring to
record their unanimous and strong dis-
approbation of the course pursued in the
negotiations for the sale of the L&CR'.

Resignations and closures

Maunsell and Payne, respectively secretary
and traffic manager of the L&CR, both resigned
their positions in October 1862, much regret
being expressed by the directors. They
attested to Maunsell's unsurpassed ability,
zeal and integrity over the past eight years.
Thomas Naan was appointed to replace
him, while Payne's position was left vacant
pro tem. In the following February, it was
announced that Messrs Malcomson and
Stephens were prepared to take transfers of
all securities under borrowing powers and
all unissued shares of the company, the
securities amounting to £20,333 and the
unissued shares to £33,860, a total commitment of £54,193, and to discharge all
liabilities of the company. Reference in the
W&LR board minutes makes it clear that it
recognised the great importance of not
allowing the L&CR to fall into the hands of
those whose interests were hostile to the
W&LR. Messrs Malcomson and Stephens
were duly placed on the board as directors
and were elected respectively to the posts of
chairman and vice-chairman.

As late as July 1863, it would appear that
no gatehouses had been provided on the
line, as John Long reported a possible
annual saving of £91 if five such houses
were provided at an estimated cost of £200.
In the following February it was announced
that four gatehouses had been built at a cost
of £200 and were producing a saving of
£104 per annum. A conference was held

with the GS&WR in July 1863 in relation to the opening of the line from Nenagh to Birdhill and arrangements for working into Limerick. No agreement was reached at this conference. In October, the Waterford company stated it was willing to run a two-train service for 1s 10d per mile and, in return, the L&CR agreed to the closure of Annacotty station as an economy measure with effect from 1 November 1863. Brief consideration was given to the leasing of the line to Nenagh and obtaining Parliamentary powers to work it, but the company solicitor was stated to be against the idea and it was allowed to drop.

Proposals were received for the removal of Nenagh Road station to the Newport road crossing and the erection of a station there. Mr Bourke, the lessee in possession, agreed to give 1 rood 11 perches (Irish) free of charge to build a station house and platform and to lay down a siding for coal and manure traffic of the vicinity. Instructions were given for the conveyance of the land, the W&LR to carry out the necessary works. Nenagh Road station was to be closed when the new station was opened. The W&LR traffic manager recommended that a large station house with a long siding and small warehouse be provided. A decision was deferred, but arrangements were made for the closing of Nenagh Road as from 31 May,

Killaloe Pier with a 'J15' 0-6-0 and train. It is obvious from this photograph that a visit by the weed-spraying train is overdue! The vessel alongside the pier is unidentified. W. A. Camwell/IRRS collection

receipts for which were reported to be less than £1 per week. Long was requested to prepare a plan and estimate in May 1864. In the following month, a complaint was received from the residents of the district stating that as from 1 June all trains to and from Limerick were to run to Castleconnell, the intention of the board being to exclude them from accommodation previously afforded by Nenagh Road station. There were acknowledged to be special grounds for complaint since the opening of the line from Nenagh, which gave direct communication with Dublin, and they requested a reconsideration of the decision to close the station. It was agreed to have one train each way daily stop at Nenagh Road. A siding was laid in there by September 1877, when it was inspected by Gen Charles S. Hutchinson on behalf of the BoT, and from this event it would appear that the site of the station remained at Nenagh Road.

Birdhill becomes a junction

In May 1864, Long was requested to provide an estimate of the expenditure required for the extension of the line to deep water at Killaloe, along with a plan and estimate for a station house and goods store there. At Killaloe itself, a temporary wooden engine shed was to be provided adjoining the temporary station. Long submitted a report in August, having declined to supply a plan and estimate (most likely at the instigation of the W&LR), which he considered was the duty of the engineer who originally laid out the line. Consideration was given to Long's position 'with a view to retrenchment of

salaries'. Meanwhile, the Nenagh to Birdhill line was opened for traffic by the GS&WR on 17 May. Outlay at Birdhill, now an end-on junction, was reported to be £228 11s 1d and this figure was approved by the GS&WR engineer. The Ballybrophy to Roscrea section had been opened as far back as 19 October 1857, the intermediate section from Roscrea to Nenagh on 5 October 1863, so that a new alternative route to Limerick now existed. The rolling stock for use between Birdhill and Limerick was provided on alternate weeks by the GS&WR and the W&LR, this being changed to monthly from October 1867.

In October 1864, the W&LR announced that it was working the Birdhill to Killaloe section at a loss and the traffic manager inquired whether traffic at the former would be much affected if the 2½-mile line, now effectively a branch since the opening of the line from Nenagh, were cut off. It was suggested that the solicitor be requested to consider the legality of such a closure. A Captain King communicated with the Waterford board in November inquiring whether a shed or store might be erected at Waterford in connection with ore traffic from Birdhill. The company considered the cost was hardly justified, particularly as King was also seeking a reduction in the rate for the carriage of the ore from 6s 3d to 4s 6d — it had in fact been increased from 5s 6d to the former figure only in the previous January. In response, the company inquired what traffic might be guaranteed by the company, based at Shallee on the GS&WR Nenagh to Birdhill line, if the shed were built and a special rate granted for fire clay only.

Attention once again turned to the Killaloe extension in 1865. The Grand Canal Co proposed to terminate its River Shannon services at Killaloe and forward the traffic, estimated at 400 tons per week, by land. This brought a certain urgency to the completion of the extension. Work commenced in September, but had to stop two months later as the Board of Works (BoW) refused to sell land necessary for the construction. It was therefore decided to go to Parliament for a Bill in the 1866 Session to obtain powers for the line and the necessary wharves etc. The Act was duly obtained on 6 August 1866 enabling work to recommence. Meanwhile, the Grand Jury of Co Tipperary was approached to grant liberty to span the roadway at the foot of Killaloe bridge for the purpose of carrying the extension to deepwater, this being granted in August 1865. Additional capital of £7,500 was granted along with borrowing powers up to one-third of that amount. Powers were also granted to enter into traffic arrangements with a number of companies, including the Grand Canal Co the GS&WR, Midland Counties & Shannon Junction Railway, and the Parsonstown & Portumna Bridge Railway

Two sidings for peat

Tighe applied in February 1866 for permission to install a siding into a peat works near Birdhill, which had been set up by Malcomson, who agreed to pay the necessary outlay. It is not entirely clear whether this siding was at Thornhill near MP7 or that at Annaholty, some six miles further north. The former was supposed to have opened about 1866, Annaholty about 1869. *Johnson's Atlas & Gazetteer of the Railways of Ireland* (Midland Publishing Ltd, 1997) shows Malcomson's line near Birdhill, peat being collected by a system of 2ft 6in gauge portable lines. Johnson states Malcomson started the factory about 1869. Two local history projects in Waterford County Library dealing with the Malcomson family state also that the factory was at Annaholty, and that it was sold following the bankruptcy of the family business (about 1877). It seems more likely that the 1866 siding refers to the Castleconnell Tramway Co about which we know nothing. Perhaps Malcomson was at one stage involved in both projects. A W&LR traffic minute dated 19 January 1871 refers to rates for peat from a bog siding at Birdhill (Annaholty?), mention being made of Captain King. An interesting aside referred to in August 1867 concerns a consignment of whiskey which arrived at Birdhill from the GS&WR line. On opening the casks at their Killaloe destination, it transpired that they did not contain whiskey, but water!

In October 1867, the engineer was instructed to resume work on the 65-chain-long deep-water extension, the BoW having

KILLALOE BRANCH.

Miles frm Killaloe.	DOWN TRAINS TO LIMERICK.	WEEK DAYS.						SUNDAYS.			
		1 1, 2, 3 Class. a.m.		2 1, 2, 3 Class. p.m.		3 1, 2, 3 Class. p.m.		1 1, 2, 3 Class. p.m.		2 1, 2, 3 Class. p.m.	
		Arr.	Dep.	Arr.	Dep.	Arr.	Dep.	Arr.	Dep.	Arr.	Dep.
...	KILLALOE	...	8 30	...	1 15	...	5 55	...	...	...	...
2¾	Birdhill	8 36	8 39	1 23	1 30	6 3	6 5	...	...	...	...
7½	Castleconnell	8 50	8 52	1 43	1 45	6 20	6 22	...	...	...	...
9¼	Lisnagry	8 56	8 57	1 49	1 50	6 26	6 27	...	...	...	...
13	Killonan	9 6	9 7	1 58	2 0	6 37	6 38	...	...	...	...
17¼	LIMERICK	9 22	...	2 15	...	6 50	...	...	...	...	...

Miles frm Limerick.	UP TRAINS TO KILLALOE.	WEEK DAYS.						SUNDAYS.			
		1 1, 2, 3 Class. a.m.		2 1, 2, 3 Class. p.m.		3 1, 2, 3 Class. p.m.		1 1, 2, 3 Class. a.m.		2 1, 2, 3 Class. p.m.	
		Arr.	Dep.	Arr.	Dep.	Arr.	Dep.	Arr.	Dep.	Arr.	Dep.
...	LIMERICK	...	10 40	...	3 40	...	7 25	...	...	...	...
4¼	Killonan	10 50	10 51	3 50	3 51	7 34	7 35	...	...	...	...
8	Lisnagry	11 0	11 1	4 2	4 3	7 43	7 45	...	...	...	...
9¾	Castleconnell	11 6	11 8	4 10	4 12	7 50	7 52	...	...	...	...
14½	Birdhill	11 20	11 32	4 25	4 35	8 5	8 15	...	...	...	...
17¼	KILLALOE	11 40	...	4 45	...	8 25	...	...	...	...	...

GREAT SOUTHERN AND WESTERN TRAINS.

		a.m.	p.m.	p.m.			a.m.	p.m.	p.m.
Nenagh	Dep.	8 0	12 45	5 30	Birdhill	Dep.	11 25	4 28	8 10
Birdhill	Arr.	8 33	1 23	6 3	Nenagh	Arr.	11 55	5 0	8 40
Patrick's Well	Dep.	8 52	12 50	8 42	Limerick	Dep.	6 40	10 35	5 15
Limerick	Arr.	9 11	1 9	9 1	Patrick's Well	Arr.	6 56	10 51	5 31
Patrick's Well	Dep.	6 3	} Gds {	9 39 ℗	Limerick	Dep.	☰7 30	} Gds {	9 30
Limerick	Arr.	6 25		10 1 ☰	Patrick's Well	Arr.	☰7 51		9 51

A page from an 1890 timetable depicting services on the Killaloe branch.
Author's collection

finally consented to give the necessary land. The tender of William Barrington for the construction of a bridge over the railway at Killaloe for £359 was duly accepted.

It is not entirely clear as to when the deep-water extension actually opened for traffic. A report in the *Limerick Reporter* for 10 September 1867 states that the line 'to the deep water of the Shannon opposite Ballborough was opened (yesterday) by the running of trains to that point'. Yet a report to the half-yearly meeting of shareholders in August of the following year stated that the cuttings and embankments were nearly complete and at the end of the year, expenditure of £1,500 was required to be incurred. However, in May 1870 a notice appeared advertising for Killaloe Fair, which commented that 'as the railway is now open to deep water, residents in the upper Shannon district have facilities for landing and embarking stock'. Special trains to Killaloe Fair were stopped in June 1870 on the grounds of economy. It was reported that for the April fair only thirteen passengers and eight wagons of pigs had been carried, while in the following month, only two and a half wagons of stock were carried, but the engine of the special had been in steam for ten hours. On the other hand, no fewer than 575 passengers were carried in connection with Limerick Races in October.

Parliamentary notice was issued by the L&CR in November 1871 for a Bill with various provisions. Powers were to be taken to sell the railway, and also for the purchase of rolling stock. The name of the company was to be altered to the Limerick Nenagh & Lough Derg Railway, and working arrange-

ments entered into with the GS&WR. Running powers were also sought to Limerick, via the W&LR, and to Nenagh over the GS&WR. Strenuous opposition was mounted by the Waterford company which led to negotiations taking place. Malcomson, who had purchased the company to prevent it falling into the hands of the GS&WR, sought compensation as he had not received any return on his investment, no dividend ever having been declared. In course of time, Malcomson agreed to accept £10,000 and the Bill was altered so as to authorise the dissolution of the L&CR and its vesting in the W&LR, as from 1 January 1873. The Bill, so amended, received the Royal Assent on 6 August 1872. So came to an end a small company which had played an important role in the history of railways in the area to the northeast of Limerick.

In July 1873 the W&LR traffic manager urged the necessity of constructing a new station at Killaloe, memorials having been submitted from local residents requesting a more convenient location. In fact, it was not until 9 July 1894 that a new station, 34 chains north of the old station, was opened on the same date the old station was closed. As we shall later see, the passenger service on the Killaloe line ceased on 17 July 1931, goods traffic being suspended as from 24 April 1944 due to the fuel crisis, and never reinstated.

Chapter Five

NORTHWEST TO ENNIS

The first scheme for a line to the north of Limerick was the ambitious Irish West Coast Railway, incorporated in 1845 for a line from Limerick through Clare, Galway, Mayo and Sligo to a junction with the proposed Sligo & Enniskillen Railway. The company was, however, reported in August 1850 to have been wound up with liabilities estimated at £20,000. This was to be the end of the notion of a single company building a line right through from Limerick to Sligo, but the line was eventually constructed piecemeal, being finally completed in 1895.

The next proposal was for the Limerick Ennis & Killaloe Railway incorporated in July 1846, a line from Limerick to Ennis, with branches to Clare and Killaloe. At this time the GS&WR still contemplated constructing a line into Limerick and it was intended to make a connection with the proposed line to Ennis. Included among the promoters were Francis Spaight, the Rt Hon William Monsell, Richard Russell and Sir David Roche, all of whom were to be associated with the line in later years. Nothing further was done towards forwarding the project, mainly as the promoters had hoped for a Government loan which was not forthcoming. Two Acts were passed in 1853, one giving powers to Messrs Richard William Johnson & Thomas William Kinder of Worcester to lease the line for a term of 21 years. These gentlemen had recently agreed to undertake the haulage on the MGWR. They also agreed to provide engines and rolling stock and work the Ennis line, and to invest a sum of £50,000 in the project. The second Act altered the title to the better-known Limerick & Ennis Railway (L&ER), abandoning the various branches.

Messrs Johnson & Kinder started work in 1853. The local press reported early in March 1854 that workmen employed in the construction had unearthed at Ballykilty a collection of ancient gold ornaments, armlets, bracelets and collars, which at the time constituted the largest number of gold ornaments associated with the Bronze Age found in Western Europe. Regrettably many of these were dispersed and lost, but 13 of them ended up in the National Museum in Dublin. In April 1855 a deputation from the directors waited on the Lord Lieutenant to ask his help in obtaining an advance of £50,000 from the PWLC. It was reported that His Excellency had 'risen to the occasion nobly and promised to do his best'. By the end of the year, it was reported that the embankment between Clarecastle and Ballykilty had been completed as well as a cutting at the latter point, while iron bridges were in course of construction over the Shannon and Owenagarvey rivers.

An acute shortage of money led to the suspension of the works in 1856 and Messrs Johnson & Kinder agreed to forgo their rights and obligations and not to claim the balance of monies due to them until the line had been open for 12 months. A fresh contract was entered into with William Dargan for the completion of the outstanding works in a sum of £53,000. Dargan commenced the works on 22 November 1856, at which time some 11 of the 23¾ miles had been completed. Tenders for rails were considered in February 1857, that of Frederick Levick & Co of London being accepted for 2,000 to 3,000 tons of flange rails in 18ft, 24ft and 27ft lengths at £9 per ton, delivered at Limerick. At the same meeting a contract for sleepers was awarded to John McDonnell of Limerick to supply whatever quantity might be required of Baltic red pine at 3s 3d each. A fortnight later, McDonnell Senior wrote declining to accept his son's tender and an alternative source was found.

A letter from the PWLC was read in April 1857 expressing the view that it considered it inexpedient for the company to renew its application until a very large proportion of the call on shares had actually been paid. About the same time, a letter was received from Limerick Town Council recommending that the terminus at Limerick be removed to the head of Glentworth Street instead of at Boherbuoy 'as at present contemplated'. At the half-yearly meeting of shareholders in May 1857, the chairman congratulated them on the improved prospects of the company since Dargan had taken over the construction works. By this time, 21 miles had been fenced in, with 14 miles of earthworks completed to formation level.

In the following month, success was achieved with the PWLC when it was announced that the Treasury had agreed to grant a loan of £40,000 in four equal instalments, bearing interest at 5%, repayable in 18 annual instalments commencing three years from the date of each advance. Also in June, Thomas Edwards attended the board on behalf of Dargan seeking a payment on account of works done. The response was to urge him to use more exertions to have the line completed and ready for opening. Edwards offered to have this done as far as Newmarket-on-Fergus by 1 November, the W&LR being asked if it would work this section of line, but it postponed any decision on the matter. It would appear that a similar request was made to the GS&WR. Having given due consideration to the question, the W&LR came up with an offer in September to work the line at 2s 4d per train mile, including provision of staff and keeping the permanent way in repair. It was stipulated that no passenger train was to exceed seven vehicles, and no goods train to have more than 25 vehicles.

A defective bridge

Notice was given to the BoT in July that it was the company's intention to open the line to the far side of the Shannon Bridge on 1 September. Col Wynne carried out what was to be the first of a number of inspections on behalf of the BoT on 11 September 1857. A train consisting of an engine and three wagons of rails was provided by the W&LR and was driven by the locomotive superintendent, Jonathan Pim. Wynne was unhappy with the state of the Shannon Viaduct and expressed the opinion that a further inspection would be required before he could give a full report. The bridge had already been the subject of adverse comments in the local press, the *Munster Express* on the other hand, commenting that the doubts were 'not rational'. It went on to state that the critics were 'associating bulk with strength' and gave its opinion that the viaduct was 'a skilful and graceful piece of mechanism'.

When he did inspect the bridge again, Col Wynne said that it was one of the worst bridges on record. From a perusal of the plans supplied by the company's engineer, he considered it unsafe. The late contractors

Ardsollus & Quin station as viewed from a passing train on 22 April 1955. Note the bilingual enamel station nameboards introduced by the GSR. H. C. Casserley

stated that the bridge had in fact been constructed to a different specification, one which provided for greater strength. It was clear, however, that the bridge had not been constructed to either plan. The report shows that the bridge consisted of six spans, each 73ft long, with cast- and wrought-iron girders supported on piers consisting of four hollow cast-iron pillars. There were insufficient piles under the piers, and the entire weight of the bridge came on the joints between the two sections of the pillars. Furthermore, the workmanship generally was defective and rivets imperfectly filled holes, some of them being bent with split heads. Col Wynne, reporting in October 1857, stated that an entire reconstruction of the bridge would be required.

The board immediately contacted Messrs Johnson & Kinder who promised that Mr Kinnard, who had been responsible for the work on the bridge, would give his serious and immediate attention to the matter. Col William Yolland tested the bridge again in July 1858 at the request of the directors so that any additional alterations required might be carried out before the line was otherwise ready for opening. Yolland, who was later to be involved with investigations into the collapse of the Tay Bridge in Scotland, was not entirely satisfied with the lateral rigidity of the bridge and the board therefore at once undertook to add more piles. The board minutes state that a Mr Terence Flanagan, engineer to the Blackburn Railway, inspected the bridge at this time at the directors' request and had totally condemned it. Robert Stephenson was also approached but declined to undertake an inspection.

Despite the earlier condemnation of the structure, permission was granted on 22 November for the opening of the line, 'the Shannon bridge being considered sufficiently propped for the conveyance of traffic until a stronger one can be built alongside it'. This time, the inspection was carried out by Captain Tyler. In fact, an advertisement had appeared in the *Railway Times* for 30 October seeking a contract for a new bridge. What followed next is not entirely clear. Whilst the *Clare Journal* for 31 January 1859 stated that 'the bridge over the Shannon is complete and presents a specimen of architecture of the most massive and durable description', the short timescale means that this did not refer to the new

bridge. This is borne out by an entry in the board minutes referring to correspondence with the BoT in relation to piles both to the original piers and the intermediate trestles, as well as references to additional bracing. An item worthy of note in the unfortunate saga of the bridge was that the company quickly took steps to recover the costs of alterations and strengthening; these works had been carried out by Messrs Courtney & Stephens of Dublin. The action however dragged on for some time and in due course had to be referred to arbitration. A payment of £1,260 8s 2d, exclusive of costs, was finally received in February 1860.

Attention was called in 1867 to the decayed state of the timber sheeting and also indications of decay in some of the piles. Tighe estimated that repairs would cost about £250 but he intended spending only £100. The board instructed him to do what was needful as cheaply as possible. It was also suggested that a speed restriction be placed on traffic over the bridge. Repairs were again mentioned in July 1870 when it was agreed that these be carried out at a cost of £200. Fire damage was sustained in May 1877 as the result of clinker being dropped from an engine crossing the bridge, instructions being given for engine dampers to be closed in this situation. Finally, following the collapse of the Tay Bridge in Scotland in December 1879, and obviously mindful of earlier reports on this bridge, the BoT was requested to carry out an inspection of the Shannon Bridge. A thorough examination was carried out by Col Rich, particular attention being paid to the piers in the deepest part of the river and any others showing signs of decay. Rich found the bridge's condition better than expected and as safe for trains as when opened. His report in fact confirms that the new bridge sought in 1859 was never constructed. His

only suggestion was that guard rails be placed on the bridge, and he confirmed the advisability of maintaining a speed limit. The bridge was eventually replaced by the GS&WR in 1909.

Stations and an opening

We must now return to September 1857 when plans for station houses were submitted to the board at an estimated cost of £409 each. These were approved, three such buildings to be provided with two additional smaller stations at £150 each. The former were for Sixmilebridge, Newmarket and Clarecastle, the two second-class stations being at Quin and Cratloe. The tenders received were considerably in excess of the engineer's estimated figures and thus fresh advertisements were placed. Plans for Ennis station were ordered to be prepared in August 1858. This was a much more elaborate affair and was estimated to cost in the region of £2,500. The tender of Mr William Carroll of Ennis at £2,700, being the lowest, was accepted in October. Meanwhile, with BoT approval having been obtained, the line was opened between Longpavement and Clarecastle on 17 January 1859, followed on 26 March by the section from the former station across the Shannon Bridge into Limerick. The final four-mile section from Clarecastle to Ennis was inspected in June 1859 by Col Yolland and passed for opening. This section included a 249ft-long iron-girder bridge across the River Fergus. The final stretch was opened for traffic on 20 June with a service of three trains each way daily.

An item of note, as early as February 1859, was a report of flooding at Ballycar. In May 1860, the engineer was instructed to proceed with raising the embankment, at an estimated cost of £600, so as to guard against future flooding. This item is noteworthy as this section of line has regularly been a problem

area right up to the present day. As recently as 1995 the line was closed for more than three months, with water at one stage reported to be more than 5ft above rail level. Initially, the W&LR agreed to work the new line but despite ongoing negotiations, it was not possible to reach a final agreement on terms. As a consequence, a letter was sent to the railway at the end of February thanking it for its assistance and requesting its continued aid until alternative haulage arrangements could be made. By mid-March it was reported that a contract had been concluded with Messrs Rogerson Dawson & Russell of Dublin for the supply of passenger and goods stock, 'equal to the best in Ireland'. Also in March an engine was ordered from Messrs Fairbairn and Robert Cruise was appointed locomotive super-intendent on the 26th at a salary of £100 per annum. James B. Pratt, who had held the post of resident engineer since 1853, resigned his position in June 1859 and, despite objections from certain of the directors to his replacement, John Long was appointed, at a salary of £150 per annum.

Some difficulties arose in relation to the rent to be paid for the use of the terminus at Limerick. Initially, a figure of £300 per annum was offered, but the W&LR demanded twice this amount. The Ennis board informed the W&LR in April that it would pay £450 a year, to include all clerks, porters and the use of the goods shed, turntable and water tanks. The W&LR responded by agreeing to accept this figure for one year, after which it would increase to £600. The matter was finally resolved in June when a figure of £1,050 was agreed for the period to 31 December 1861. For this, the L&ER was to have an office jointly with the L&CR, use of the general waiting room, turntable and watering facilities for engines, and siding accommodation for its engines,

carriages and wagons. The L&ER staff were to be under the full and entire control of the W&L company's officers, and the latter company was to appoint a signalman at Ennis Junction.

In May 1859, it was ordered that a timber platform be erected at the level crossing at Meelick and that one train each way would stop there on Wednesdays and Saturdays. Five months later, the engineer was instructed to prepare an estimate for enclosing the station at Ardsollus and provide a siding there, this work being completed by May 1860. It would appear that there was some delay in completing the arrangements at Meelick, as it was not until October 1861 that instructions were given for the new station to be opened for three months on trial, 'but to be closed again unless the receipts amount to £2 per week'. Within that period complaints were being made of the high fares charged to and from this station. These were reduced but the station was closed as from 30 April 1862, receipts having averaged only 13s 7d per week. A recommendation was made by the traffic manager in April 1861 for the provision of a platform for the loading of timber at Ennis, but a decision was postponed. However, in the following August, Long was instructed to construct a 40ft-long platform at a cost not exceeding £60, this to be divided equally between the L&ER and the W&LR.

The rolling stock necessary to allow the directors to operate their own line was delivered at the end of October 1859, the company proceeding to work the line as from 11 November. Within a week, however, the three-train service previously provided by the W&LR was reduced to two trains each way, with a third on Saturdays only, with a journey time of 80 minutes each way. At the half-yearly shareholders' meeting in March 1860, Long reported that the line was in a

Ennis station looking towards Limerick, with the station buildings on the right, opposite which is the goods store. The roof of the South Signal Cabin can just be seen below the footbridge. On the right is a narrow-gauge West Clare train.
Ian Allan Library

bad state following the severe winter. Ballycar had once again been flooded for several weeks in the spring. He was ordered to seek tenders for six additional ballast wagons, making a total of ten. However, finding it impossible to either purchase or hire any, Cruise was instructed to build them in the company's workshops at Ennis, at £62 17s 6d each. Long was also instructed to erect a carriage shed at Ennis capable of holding about six carriages.

A working agreement, resignations and finances
Having worked their own line since November 1859, we find the L&ER directors once again in negotiations with the W&LR in December 1860 in connection with a working agreement. It is probable that the initiative came from the latter company which was reportedly fearful that the L&ER might slip out of its 'sphere of influence'. The negotiations concluded in February 1861 with an agreement whereby the W&LR would work the line for 45% of gross receipts for a term of 20 years. The Ennis company's rolling stock was to be handed over and paid for at cost, less a fair allowance for depreciation. The rent for the terminus at Limerick was agreed at £250 per annum. The management of the line was to be vested in a joint committee of four directors from each board, and the W&LR was to pay all wages and salaries, except that in the case of the secretary, it would pay half only. A service of three trains each way was

to be provided, good and sufficient engines to be provided for haulage of the line.

In February 1862, E. W. Maunsell, the company secretary, tendered his resignation on his appointment to a similar position with the Dublin Wicklow & Wexford Railway (DW&WR). Maunsell had by then served the company as secretary since 1853, and whilst congratulating him on his new appointment, the directors regretted the loss of his valuable services and testified to his energy, zeal and fidelity in carrying out the arduous duties of his office. Thomas Naan, who already held the posts of cashier and accountant, was additionally given the responsibility of the secretaryship, his salary being increased to £200 per annum accordingly. Later, in April 1868, Naan's salary was reduced to £150, apparently following a prolonged absence due to ill health. The directors were paying the clerk, Burns, to carry out Naan's duties and found themselves unable to grant full pay to both officers. Leave of absence was granted to Naan in July 'to go to the seaside and Blarney for the recovery of his health'. He was apparently back at work at the beginning of August when he was censured for allowing leave of absence to Burns. In April 1872, Naan applied to be refunded the amount deducted on account of illness from his salary for the period 1 May 1868 to 31 December 1870, it being ordered that he be allowed a sum of £125 in lieu.

William Payne, the traffic manager since July 1858, quickly followed Maunsell, as he announced his resignation in December 1862, joining the DW&WR as traffic manager. In October 1867, the W&LR wrote declining to pay half of John Long's salary as engineer to the L&ER. The latter board considered the matter and proposed reducing his salary by two-thirds to £50 per annum as from 1 January 1868. It is hardly surprising that Long contested this decision. In fact, by May 1868 he had refused to accept his reduced salary over the previous three months and instructions were given for it to be relodged in the bank to the credit of the company. Long now issued a civil bill for recovery of what he believed was owed to him, and he obtained a decree in July. The chairman of the Quarter Sessions held that the company should have given Long 12 months' notice of its intentions as from 11 June, the anniversary of his appointment, and further declared that the notice given him in October 1867 was illegal. An appeal was considered, but in August, it was decided to issue notice of dismissal to Long in consequence of his having neglected to carry out his duties over the preceding six months, or to accept the salary fixed by the board. However, following further discussions with Long, he agreed to accept the reduced salary as from the previous January.

Financial matters were discussed in September 1863, it having been stated that a number of banks had refused to grant the company a loan of £20,000. The Bank of Ireland had agreed to loan such a figure, but at a rate of interest of 6%, a figure considered excessive. Fifteen months later, in December 1864, following a memorial, the Treasury agreed to commute the company's loan of £40,000 into an annuity for 22 years. This liberal concession was gratefully acknowledged and accepted. However, the board now sent a second memorial seeking a further loan of £74,000 to pay off its existing debts, other than the annuity, this including £20,000 borrowed from the Bank of Ireland. The board was now in a desperate situation; this included increasing arrears due on traffic receipts to the W&LR, which was threatening to take the traffic receipts. Approaches were made to the latter company suggesting an amalgamation, but the terms offered were considered unacceptable.

Some small measure of relief came in April 1865 when William Malcomson agreed to discount his bills on the company amounting to £11,000. Further approaches were made to the Government praying for a loan at reasonable interest to pay off the company's debts. The Government finally agreed in 1868 to extend the time limit for repayment of loans, this representing 'the extreme limits of concession to which they (the Loan Commissioners) would feel it right to go', but the rate of interest was increased accordingly. In April 1871 approaches were made by the W&LR proposing to purchase the Ennis company on the basis of exchanging two ordinary £25 shares of the L&ER for one ordinary £50 W&LR share, an offer which was declined. Final agreement was achieved in February 1873, one 5% preference share of the W&LR being exchanged for two ordinary Ennis line shares. The Act giving effect to the amalgamation, not only of the L&ER but also of the L&FR, received the Royal Assent on 21 July 1873, and so came to an end the independent existence of the L&ER.

This chapter concludes with some other minor matters. Trouble was reported at Ennis station in July 1864 when a group of emigrants leaving by the afternoon train were being seen off by a large group of friends and relatives. Some of the latter clung to the carriages as the train moved off and Head Porter Blood pushed one man, he in return receiving a violent blow to his head and being forced against the moving carriage by the man's brother. Two constables had to come to Blood's rescue, after drawing their swords.

In April 1871 it was decided to provide goods stores at Sixmilebridge and Ardsollus, the company agreeing to contribute half the cost of each. The carriage shed at Ennis, which was described as being dangerous to the safety of passengers, was removed in November 1872, the W&LR agreeing to purchase the materials of the building.

As early as June 1860, the company's support was sought for a projected line from Ennis to Kilrush, a tramway as far as Ennistymon being mentioned the following October. Long was requested to make some inquiries as to the probable cost of such a tramway, he stating, however, that the country was difficult; as a consequence, instructions were given for Long's report to be filed. The matter refused to go away, and by July 1862 the board was considering that such a line would be most useful and would assist in developing traffic returns, provided the owners and occupiers of land could be induced to aid by giving the land free of charge. A meeting with the W&LR board in June 1863 led to the unanimous opinion that it was advisable to promote such a line, provided a county guarantee could be obtained. Plans were duly prepared for a line from Ennis via Corofin and Willbrook Valley to Ennistymon, but by now the company was, as already indicated, beset with major financial difficulties, and there the matter rested. In later years the connection was made by means of the narrow-gauge West Clare Railway.

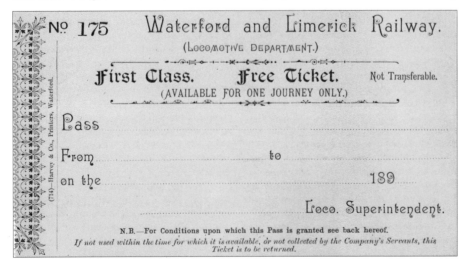

No. 175   Waterford and Limerick Railway.
(Locomotive Department.)

First Class.   Free Ticket.   Not Transferable.
(AVAILABLE FOR ONE JOURNEY ONLY.)

Pass

From   to

on the   189

(714)—Harvey & Co., Printers, Waterford.

Loco. Superintendent.

N.B.—For Conditions upon which this Pass is granted see back hereof.
If not used within the time for which it is available, or not collected by the Company's Servants, this Ticket is to be returned.

Chapter Six

NORTH AND SOUTH FROM ATHENRY

The Midland Great Western Railway of Ireland was incorporated by Act of Parliament dated July 1845. The line was constructed and opened in stages, reaching Mullingar on 2 October 1848 and was completed through to Galway, via Athlone and Athenry, on 1 August 1851. The company had a difficult gestation period, stemming from a rival project backed by its southern neighbour, the GS&WR. The important market and post town of Tuam, about 15 miles north of Athenry, had a population of 4,927 in the 1851 Census and was served by road coaches from Athenry, Galway, Claremorris and Westport. Athenry (Ath-na-Riagh or the King's ford), with a population of 1,487, was the nearest point by rail at this time. However, as early as October 1845 Martin Blake, MP for Galway, was threatening strong opposition to the new company due to its failure to serve the large northern area of counties Galway and Mayo. As a result, the MGWR engineer was instructed to carry out a preliminary survey for a line from Athenry to Tuam, with the eventual intention of extending to Castlebar and Westport. Nothing further transpired in this regard at that time.

In April 1853, the *Warden of Galway* reported on rumours that the MGWR intended to construct a single line of railway from Athenry to Tuam and that the directors were preparing to go to Parliament for the necessary powers. Two months later, the same newspaper was reporting the company's willingness to proceed if the Mayo people would give an undertaking to continue the line on to Westport; it also stated that the Government was prepared to make available a loan for the purpose. In September, the *Galway Packet* reported that meetings were about to be held to urge upon the railway directors the importance of the Tuam branch. A large meeting was in fact held in Galway on Wednesday, 28 September, chaired by the Rev Peter Daly, parish priest of Tuam. It was reported that the MGWR had two extensions in contemplation at this time, one to connect its proposed Longford branch with Belfast and the second to connect Athlone with Mayo. The latter in particular, would be damaging to the counties of Galway and Roscommon, which had agreed to guarantee the Government loan of £500,000 already provided to the company. Adverse comment was made on the fact that a sum of £30,000 from this loan had been expended on a hotel at Galway.

Arising from this meeting, George Hemans, the company's engineer, made a preliminary survey for a line from Athenry to Tuam. Other competing lines were however in contemplation, in particular the Grand Junction Railway of Ireland, which was proposing a line from Tullamore through Athlone and Roscommon to Sligo, Castlebar, Westport and Ballina. This line had the backing of the GS&WR and it was hoped to have the various counties involved guarantee the capital. June 1854 saw two schemes being put forward by the Midland: the Tuam branch and a branch from Longford to Strokestown in County Roscommon. *Saunders Newsletter* reported in September 1854 on a meeting between the Galway Grand Jury and a deputation from the MGWR, the latter consisting of John Ennis, the chairman, and Martin Blake MP. Ennis stated that the company was anxious to have 'a great and stupendous line of railway through the west of Ireland' and proposed to make a line from Athenry to Tuam at its own expense, only wanting in return the goodwill of the county. He went on to say that the line would be a great facility to Galway, an extension into Mayo being dependent on co-operation and assistance from the counties concerned. Another meeting was held in Tuam on 21 October, chaired by Lord Dunsandle, again with a view to adopting measures for a Tuam extension, following which the company decided to publish notices of a Bill for extensions to Tuam and Strokestown. The former line as proposed by the Bill was to commence by a junction 167 yards to the east of Athenry station and terminate in Tuam at the Old Road leading from that town to Athenry.

The Mayo Grand Jury communicated with the company in December to the effect that it could not consider any guarantees unless both Ballina and Westport were to be served by the extension. January 1855 brought a change of policy when an extraordinary general meeting of shareholders was called to consider the Bill for the two proposed extensions. The Galway Grand Jury now felt that any extension to Ballina or Castlebar would be to the detriment of the Galway

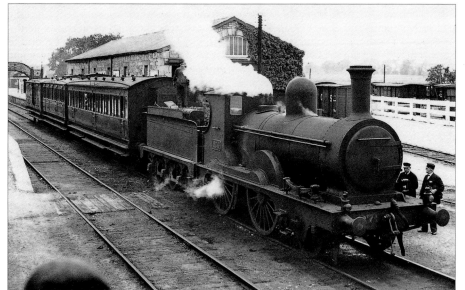

GSR Class G3 2-4-0 No 276 — ex WL&WR No 23 *Slievenamon* — is seen at Ennis on the 09.25 Claremorris to Limerick on 21 June 1939.
H. C. Casserley / SLS collection

Ballingrane station looking west with the station buildings on the down platform. The two lines to Rathkeale and Foynes diverge just beyond the level crossing.
Late Rev John Parker/Hugh Davies

people, particularly bearing in mind its guarantee on the company's loan. A shareholder, Mr McBirney, moved that in the current state of the money market and the present circumstances of the country it would be unwise to proceed with any extensions. Having considered the matter at some length, the shareholders agreed and the matter was dropped *pro tem*.

A new company

By September 1855, the *Railway Times* was reporting that the idea of an extension to Mayo was again being agitated, two plans having been put before the MGWR for its consideration, one of which contemplated a branch from Athenry through Tuam to Castlebar, 'and thence at some period in the indefinite future to Ballina, etc'. The Mayo people now agreed to pledge their support for such a line, as did a meeting of the landed proprietors and cesspayers of Galway, who offered a guarantee of 4% on an outlay of £6,000 per mile. The Midland directors therefore called another EGM for 10 January 1856 to enable shareholders to reconsider the matter. The chairman said he was 'as hostile to extensions as ever I was' but circumstances had now changed in that both counties were now prepared to support the scheme financially. The matter dragged on, however, and by November it had become clear that the line was then being promoted independently of the Midland. A meeting was held in Castlebar comprising the members of the provisional committee of the Athenry & Tuam Railway Company (A&TR), Captain Bellew being appointed chairman and Denis Kirwan as deputy-chairman. These two gentlemen were appointed a deputation to meet with the MGWR board to see if it could be persuaded to take half the shares of the new company.

The Midland directors agreed to take one-third of the required capital, subject to the promoters finding *bona fide* parties to subscribe the other two-thirds. This latter proved to be unattainable and after further

discussions the Midland announced that it could not alter its stance. Despite this setback the promoters decided to proceed with a Bill in the 1858 session. They sought powers for the Midland to subscribe one-third of the capital and, more importantly, sought running powers over the MGWR between Galway and Athlone, with use of both the MGWR and the GS&WR stations at the latter point. Another company had now entered the arena, namely the Great Northern & Western Railway, which had been incorporated in July 1857, with Lord Lucan as its chairman. This company envisaged a line northwestwards from Athlone into County Mayo.

Suffice to say that the GN&WR wrote to the Midland in February seeking its opinion on the A&TR Bill then before Parliament. The reply was read, 'with much surprise', as it seemed to the GN&WR that rather than being the line's most determined opponents, the MGWR directors were being very supportive. It was felt that the Midland was placing itself in a position 'altogether inconsistent with the amicable relations which this board had hoped would have existed between the two companies'. When the A&TR Bill came before the House of Commons Committee in June 1858, it became clear that both the GN&WR and the MGWR had petitioned against it. The latter company objected to the running powers and the compulsory accommodation and facilities sought, which it considered in-expedient and unnecessary. The MGWR stated that, in its opinion, the proposed line was defective from an engineering point of view, was not calculated for the public advantage, would not be remunerative and could not be constructed within the estimate. The GN&WR petition was similar, but in addition stated that the proposed line would abstract traffic from its line. Having examined the various points, the committee decided to restrict the running powers to the portion of line between the junction of the proposed railway and Athenry station,

including the use of the latter. The Act of Incorporation for the A&TR received Royal Assent on 23 July 1858.

A contract is signed

No time was lost in advertising for a secretary, a salary of £200 per annum being offered to a suitable candidate. In due course, John Fowler Nicoll, was appointed to the post. Negotiations had been ongoing with the Midland and a lease of the line was finalised for a period of 10 years at an annual rent of £4,000. An agreement had also been concluded with the GN&WR, whereby no line was to be promoted or assisted by the MGWR to the northwest of Tuam for a period of at least 10 years, unless the GN&WR failed within that period to complete its line to Castlebar. The A&TR also agreed not to extend its line during the same period of time. It was announced in November 1858, that a contract had been entered into with William Dargan for the construction of the line, 15m 3f 5c in length, for a sum of £67,000, and it was to be ready for traffic by 1 January 1860.

At the new company's half-yearly meeting held in the New Town Hall in Tuam on 30 April, it was announced that the commencement of work had been delayed by the bad winter weather, but that the works were now being carried on 'with vigour'. Plans of stations at Tuam and Brook Lodge (Ballyglunin) had been prepared and the contract for their construction was awarded to a local contractor, Mr Andrew Egan. Some of the shareholders had sought a change in the location of the station at the former point. The Act specified that it was to be at the Old Barrack, but suggestions had been made to alter the site to a point beyond the workhouse on the Dublin road, a mile from the town. Such a location would be inconvenient for travellers and act as a barrier to any future extension of the line. At the next half-yearly meeting in October, the chairman was able to report good progress, the ground being nearly ready to receive sleepers and rails; a cargo of sleepers had recently arrived at Galway with rails expected soon. On completion of the ordinary business, the meeting was made special to consider the proposed line from Athenry southwards to Ennis with a view to giving support to that company.

Open for business

January 1860 proved to be an over-optimistic date for the opening of the line. Nevertheless, it was completed by September enabling the *Tuam Herald* to announce

Crusheen station looking towards Athenry on 22 September 1955. R. M. Casserley

the arrival, on 20 September at Athenry, of Captain George Ross on behalf of the BoT in the company of George Hemans and William Forbes, engineer and traffic manager respectively of the MGWR, and the Tuam company's secretary, Nicoll. On the following day a thorough inspection of the new line was carried out, following which the party retired to the spacious waiting room at the new Tuam station for a magnificent luncheon. Captain Ross expressed himself quite satisfied with the state of the works and gave permission for the opening of the line the following week. It was duly opened for passenger traffic on Thursday, 27 September, the first train leaving Tuam at 06.15. It returned to Tuam at 13.00 to a tumultuous reception and was met by Mr John Browne, chairman of the Town Commissioners, who, on the part of the townspeople, congratulated the board of directors and the company officials 'on the happy and successful consummation of their persevering and united exertions'.

The line was opened for cattle traffic in connection with a fair on Saturday, 20 October and for goods traffic on 13 November. At the half-yearly meeting held on 27 October, it was stated that the portion of the line which passed through a bog was not in as satisfactory a state as the remainder, 'but when it would be subjected to the pressure of the goods traffic, it would be solidified'. Presumably this is what transpired, for no further complaints were made in this regard. In November, and despite the agreement with the GN&WR, it was stated in the *Railway Times* that it was proposed to extend the line north to Claremorris and Ballina, thus opening up the entire western seaboard from Cork, via Limerick to Ballina when the connection southward to Ennis would be completed. This proposal was, however, somewhat premature as we shall see shortly.

Approaches were made to the Midland in February 1861 inquiring if it would consider purchasing the new line. When a deputation visited the MGWR at Broadstone and suggested a figure of £80,000, the Midland directors summoned a special board to consider the matter further. Their reply was short and to the point, viz 'inasmuch as the ideas entertained by this board of the value of the line so widely differ from the sum the directors of the A&TR have asked for it, the board think it better to decline making any proposal'. It is not clear what sort of figure they had in mind, but the Midland obviously expected to get it for a knockdown price.

It was not long before complaints were being made of a shortage of wagons in use on the A&TR. One correspondent to the *Galway Vindicator* referred to the great dissatisfaction at the manner in which the traffic of goods and seaweed was carried on by the MGWR. He also complained of the high charges between Galway and Tuam for passenger traffic, which was causing a high proportion of this traffic to be still carried by car. Arising from this, the Midland reported a loss of £1,000 for the first half-year's working of the line. It was reported that livestock was even being driven from Tuam to Athenry for the want of wagons. Reporting at the half-yearly meeting of the A&TR shareholders, the chairman made it clear that the company had done everything to make matters smooth and agreeable to the Midland, but it never experienced the same feeling in return. The Midland people never consulted it or acceded to its wishes in the arrangement of trains, or anything for that matter! The losses continued, and a Midland shareholder suggested the closure of the line. Expenditure for the second half of 1862 exceeded receipts by £1,728, a situation which the Tuam directors hoped was the lowest point in their fortunes. Eighteen months later, the Midland directors reported that the A&TR was 'almost in *status quo* and was still being worked at a loss'.

In an attempt to reduce expenditure, Sunday trains were withdrawn in February 1866. In the following November, the A&TR chairman reported that the prospects of the company were never in a better or more prosperous condition. Much of this 'prosperity' (it could hardly be described accurately in such terms) was due to the untiring zeal of the company secretary, John Fowler Nicoll; he was applying himself with

untiring energy, ability and business habits to the affairs of the company. Traffic had increased, and it was then stated that the most amicable and friendly relations existed between the two companies. Despite these cordial relations, complaints were made regarding the unsatisfactory condition of the permanent way. The Midland replied forwarding a copy of its engineer's report which stated that the ballast was better than on any other Irish railway!

With the end of the ten-year lease in the offing, consideration was once again turned to the possible purchase of the line by the MGWR. At a Midland board meeting on 4 August 1869 a resolution was moved to the effect that if the Tuam company undertook to legalise the transaction, the directors would recommend the shareholders to accept 20,000 ordinary shares as payment. An amendment to the effect that the time was not yet right for such a move was in due course adopted. Sir Ralph Cusack, the Midland chairman, stressed that the line should belong to its system and said it would be happy to enter into further negotiations. There was an added problem, however, in that the A&TR had received a Government loan of £30,000, and this was to prove a stumbling block in the negotiations.

A final offer and an approach to the W&LR

Notices appeared in the local and county newspapers in October 1870 to the effect that the MGWR would cease to work the line after the expiry of the lease on 27 October. Negotiations were by now already in hand regarding a further lease or purchase. The A&TR had offered to lease the line for 999 years at £1,250 per annum (less than 2% of

'D17' 4-4-0 No 16 takes water on the 09.00 Galway to Limerick train at Gort station on 22 April 1955. R. M. Casserley

Dunmore Light Railway, again commencing by a junction with the A&TR near Tuam and terminating at Dunmore, a small town about eight miles northeast of Tuam. Neither scheme progressed beyond the initial plans. As we shall see shortly, an extension of the A&TR northwards, and running roughly midway between the two earlier schemes, was soon to be announced.

Sale to the Midland?
Despite the working agreement with the W&LR, a proposal was put forward in October 1886 for a sale of the line to the MGWR. An offer was made whereby the Midland was to pay £6 5s 0d per share to the Tuam shareholders payable in cash or shares, and to take over and discharge the Government loan. The Midland responded by offering the following terms, viz it would accept responsibility for the Government loan, and would purchase the 6,177 paid-up ordinary £10 shares of the A&TR at £6 each. Matters proceeded sufficiently for consideration to be given to the issue of notice of a bill for the purchase of both the A&EJR and the A&TR, but in the final event, the lines went to the W&LR. In November 1892, the W&LR agreed to recommend to its shareholders acceptance of the sale of the A&TR for a figure equal to £75,000 of 4% W&LR debenture stock. The final figure agreed was £79,000 in 4% debenture stock at £110%, the W&LR agreeing to execute works under the Regulation of Railways Act of 1889. Messrs Percy Bernard, Martin Murphy and Anthony O'Connor were appointed three joint directors to represent the W&LR. Payment was finally made in September 1893 and the independent A&TR ceased to exist.

Ennis to Athenry
A deputation waited on the board of the MGWR in October 1858 in connection with a proposed line of railway from Athenry to Gort, requesting that company's aid in forwarding the project. Nothing further transpired at that time, but early in April of the following year the L&ER board received a letter from G. W. Hemans to the effect that he had been employed to lay out a connecting line between Ennis and the Galway line of the MGWR. Hemans suggested alterations in the terminus at Ennis to better accommodate the proposed extension. Drawings of the station there were sent to him so that he might mark his proposals on them. Hemans, along with a deputation from the provisional committee

the capital) or to take a sum of £25,000, the Midland to take care of the Government debt. This offer was to be considered final, a strange move; the MGWR replied early in October declining to agree to the terms proposed and expressing regret that the offer was final as it was prepared to propose referring the matter to arbitration. It went on to ask the A&TR to name a rent for the use of the Athenry station.

It is clear that the Tuam directors quickly retracted the finality of their offer as Denis Kirwan was dispatched to the Broadstone to make another offer and seek the loan of some rolling stock. As regards the latter, he came away with an engine, a carriage and an agreement on through goods and cattle rates. Further offers were made but declined by the Midland; an offer of £125 per annum for the use of Athenry station was turned down, the Midland agreeing to take £200 to avoid arbitration, provided it was arranged with a Mr Irwin to permit a supply of water to the Tuam company for £5 per annum. The A&TR began to work its own line as from 28 October, receipts for the 21 weeks from then until 25 March being reported at £1,849, equal to £6 per mile per week; at least it was making some money, as the expenditure for the same period amounted to £1,237.

Further proposals were made to the Midland which were declined. By January 1872 it became clear that negotiations had been opened with the W&LR for a possible leasing of the line. These negotiations soon came to the notice of the MGWR, Lord Gough stressing that traffic from the Tuam and Athenry & Ennis Junction Railway lines should not go to the Waterford company. Despite these remarks, it was with the W&LR that the company finally made an

agreement in December 1872. The terms were that the W&LR should receive all earnings, paying out of gross receipts to the Tuam company the sum of £2,600 per annum, retaining the residue up to £5,000. If the gross receipts should exceed the latter figure, the surplus was to be divided equally between the two companies. The agreement was for 20 years from 1 November 1872, with power to renew. A minimum service of three trains per day each way was to be provided, Sundays excepted, such trains to run through between Tuam and Limerick. At least one of the trains was to provide a good connection to the steamer service from Waterford.

Despite the apparently promising figures quoted by the A&TR, losses were still reported, the line having shown a deficit of £221 11s 6d for the months of November and December 1872. Complaints were soon made regarding the unsatisfactory state of the rolling stock used on the line. In fairness, it cannot have been any worse than the company's own stock, which was described by Mark Wardle, the W&LR's locomotive superintendent at the time, as being sadly neglected and 'a bad bargain to us altogether'. Various works were carried out at Athenry by the MGWR, the cost of which, at £1,071 19s 3d, was referred to the Tuam company for payment.

Two lines were proposed in 1885/6, one being the Tuam & Mayo Junction Light Railway, commencing by a junction with the A&TR near Tuam and terminating at 'the river dividing the townland of Urracly in Co Galway from the townland of Garrymore in Co Mayo'. Powers were sought for working arrangements with the SL&NCR, MGWR, W&LR and the A&TR companies. The second scheme was for the Tuam &

of the Athenry & Ennis Junction Railway, attended a board meeting of the L&ER in May and submitted a report with surveys and estimates for a 17-mile extension to Gort, estimated to cost £92,000. After some discussion, the L&ER directors refused to commit themselves, stating the matter would have to be considered by the shareholders.

In due course, Sir Colman O'Loghlen, one of the leading promoters of the new line, advised his colleagues that no decision had been arrived at by the L&ER shareholders, and it was decided therefore to remove the names of two of that company's directors from the prospectus, namely Col Vandaleur and Austin Butler. It should be mentioned that Vandaleur was later to appear as a subscriber and director in the Athenry company's Act of Incorporation. There were also plans to include the town of Loughrea in railway accommodation and the residents of that town were urged to give their backing to a branch from there to Craughwell. Consideration was also given to forming a branch to Oranmore so as to shorten the route to Galway; this latter was already being considered as a terminus for a line via Loughrea, Parsonstown (more familiarly known today as Birr), and Kilkenny to Waterford.

It soon became clear that the GS&WR would mount a strong opposition to the projected line and it was therefore regarded as essential to procure the assistance of its rival, the MGWR. When a deputation attended the Midland board at the beginning of September, it was pleased to come away with that company's approval of the scheme. A little more detail came to light at this stage. The line was to commence by a junction with the L&ER at or near Ennis, pass through Gort and form a junction with the MGWR and the A&TR at Athenry. It was to include the towns of Ardrahan and Craughwell, the exact route of the line between these points to be left in the hands of Hemans, who had been appointed consulting engineer to the company. A 'most numerous and influential meeting of the Gentry and Landed Proprietors', was held at the Courthouse in Gort on Tuesday, 6 September 1859, the attendance including Captain Gough and Sir Colman O'Loghlen. J. F. Nicoll, secretary to the A&TR, also attended as did Hemans. It was reported that in the short space of half an hour, no less than £13,080 worth of shares had been subscribed. Hemans advised that the 35-mile-long line could be constructed for £6,000 per mile and would return £10 per mile per week, allowing of a dividend of at least 5½%.

At the half-yearly meeting of shareholders held at the end of September, the Midland board recommended a subscription of £100,000 towards the construction of the new line, this sum to be paid in proportion as the local subscribers contributed. The W&LR expressed no opinion on the project at this stage. When the notice of application to Parliament was issued in November, it provided for arrangements or agreements with the A&TR, GS&WR, L&ER, MGWR, South Wales Railway and the W&LR, or any of them, as regards interchange, accommodation, etc. At this stage, the Midland directors came back and advised that they 'regret that they are not in a position to give any assistance to the project in question'. It was clear that the company did not wish to prejudice the arbitration hearing in the long-running dispute with the GS&WR, a fact which was later admitted had decided these views on the project. Capital was to be £200,000, plus borrowing of up to £66,000. It was hoped that the A&TR, GS&WR, L&ER, MGWR and the W&LR would all subscribe to the line.

It was also reported that a rival project, the Ennis & Galway Junction Railway, was going to Parliament seeking powers for a line from Ennis to Gort, then to Oranmore with running powers over the Midland, and a line from Lough Atalia to Fair Hill, and the laying of rails along the pier and breakwater to be constructed by the Galway Harbour Commissioners. The *Railway Times* for 14 January 1860, reported in an editorial that the A&EJR capital 'may now be considered fully subscribed', local promoters undertaking to put up half the required capital. It was stated that the GS&WR was backing the Ennis & Galway Junction project, although the editorial went on to say that it was convinced that it would not be further heard of, and that the A&EJR would obtain an Act. It was to be proved correct in its views and in fact, when the arbitrators' award was issued in February, the GS&WR withdrew both support for the Ennis & Galway Junction Railway and opposition to the Athenry line.

A petition was lodged against the Bill by the L&ER, although it advised that this was 'not to be considered of a factious nature, but simply lodged to acquire a *locus standi* for the L&ER'. It dissented to a clause in the Bill empowering it to subscribe £25,000, this clause being struck out and the opposition was then withdrawn. At the following half-yearly meeting of the MGWR in April 1860, some doubts were cast on the enterprise, a shareholder commenting that he disputed that the A&EJR would ever pay 1%. He also thought it was a monstrous thing to give so much as £100,000, although he might give £20,000 or £30,000 as an encouragement.

The promoters were obviously in confident mood as the decision was taken in June, two months before the Act was passed, to issue letters to possible railway contractors. Hemans estimated the cost of construction at £180,000, the works were of a light nature and the line would open up the whole of the west and northwest of the country to the ports of Cork and Waterford. The railway distance between Galway and Cork would be reduced from 211 to 132 miles by the opening of the new line, while Waterford would be 57 miles closer to Galway. It was expected that the contractor would take up to at least one-third by way of paid-up shares. The contract was to be let in two sections, viz Ennis to Gort and Gort to Athenry, the company to decide which was to be constructed first. On completion of either section, either party would be at liberty to end the contract.

Act of Incorporation

At a meeting on 11 September 1860, J. F. Nicoll was appointed secretary to the A&EJR at a salary for the time being of £100 per annum. It was reported that the Act of Incorporation had received Royal Assent on 20 August, the chairman going on to say that the establishment of Galway as a transatlantic packet station rendered the junction line a matter of pubic necessity. The directors had unabated confidence in the line, Hemans commenting that it was the most important line yet to be carried out in Ireland, as Galway was now next in importance to Belfast. However, it is worth noting that virtually every railway line projected at that time was regarded in a similar light! Anyhow, it was anticipated that the completion of the A&TR would also justify the promoters in their selection of Athenry as the point of junction between the south and west of Ireland.

Despite the issuing of letters, nothing further was done towards commencing construction. Then, in February 1861, the Midland board passed a resolution to the effect that on condition of the A&EJR agreeing to abandon the portion of line between Gort and Athenry and obtaining a Bill for a line from Gort via Loughrea to a point on the Midland line between Attymon and Woodlawn, and finding half the capital for the entire undertaking, the MGWR would subscribe the other moiety, it being equally represented on the directorate. In addition, the line was to be opened simultaneously throughout. This was a clear departure from the original agreement and the Athenry directors suggested Ardrahan as the point of deviation rather than Gort. They also referred to a much talked-about rival line making a junction with the A&EJR at Craughwell and running via Loughrea and Portumna to Parsonstown, although this was the last to be heard of this scheme.

In October, William Munro wrote offering to make the line from Ennis to Gort for £127,000. He was offered a cash payment of £17,000, to be paid *pari passu* with £25,000 debentures and £85,000 in shares, the latter

Tuam station looking towards Athenry on 20 April 1955. The locomotives are 'J15' 0-6-0 Nos 187 (on the turntable) and 123. Note the elevated signal cabin supplied by the Railway Signal Co in 1893.
H. C. Casserley

at par. On 27 October it was agreed that the contract be awarded to Munro for the entire line for £250,000, payments now to be £20,000 in cash, £100,000 in Lloyd's Bonds, £50,000 in debentures and £80,000 in shares at par. The resolution was however conditional on the security offered by Munro proving satisfactory to the board.

The *Railway Times* for 24 January 1863 referred to two pieces of legislation being put forward by the company. The first sought an additional two years for completion of the works, postponing the earliest opening to August 1867, a subscription by the W&LR, and traffic arrangements with that company to fully develop the A&EJR. The second piece of legislation was sought in the event of the first one being rejected in Parliament, and was for the abandonment of the undertaking. Failure, if it occurred, would be ascribed to the disappointment at Galway not becoming the great packet station for transatlantic mails and passengers, and the subsequent failure of the Midland to subscribe to the undertaking.

Messrs Malcomson and Stephens, respectively chairman and vice-chairman of the W&LR, were introduced to the board in February, and it was agreed that a majority on the board should be secured to that company. The W&LR now undertook to subscribe £6,000 on the contract from Ennis to Gort, and a further minimum of £3,000 upon the works being completed to Athenry. A clause was to be inserted in the A&EJR Bill confirming a working agreement for 20 years at 1s 9d per mile for more than three trains each way daily, 1s 10d for three, 2s 0d for two and 2s 6d for one train daily. Col Vandaleur, Mr Calcutt and Gen Hatt resigned their positions as directors to allow Malcomson, Stephens and others to join the board. It was also decided to withdraw powers given by the original Act to enable the Midland to work the line 'if such would not interfere with the progress of the Bill now before Parliament for an extension of time'. The Bill passed through unopposed and received Royal Assent on 20 August 1863.

The directors held with their original notion of locating the junction at Athenry, it forming the most advantageous and desirable point of junction and the only one authorised by the Act of Incorporation. A letter was received from the BoT in June 1863 in relation to the projected bridge over the River Fergus, reminding the company that under clause 31 of the 1860 Act, the bridge was to have an opening span,

whereas the plans as submitted showed a fixed bridge. It was stipulated that one span was to be made 32ft wide in the clear initially so as to correspond with the nearby L&ER bridge. The company was obliged to give an undertaking to make the span an opening one within a year of being called to do so by the BoT, on a plan to be approved by that body. In November the L&ER confirmed its agreement to the A&EJR being allowed to store rails and sleepers on spare ground adjoining Ennis station for a nominal rent of 1s per year. Tighe, the W&LR engineer, raised objections to sleepers in December, reporting that rectangular sleepers from Dantzic (sic) and other Baltic ports were adequate, but while 65% of the round sleepers, presumably native, were good, 20% were extra sappy and porous, while 15% were still more inferior.

Problems with the contractor
By July 1864, the directors were able to announce that about five-sixths of the total earthworks between Ennis and Gort had been executed, along with more than half of the masonry work. In addition, three miles of permanent way had been laid and the River Fergus bridge nearly completed. Plans for stations at Crusheen, Tubber and Gort had been furnished to the contractor. Between Gort and Athenry about one-quarter of the fencing and one-fifth of the earthworks had been executed. Munro suggested that the opening of the line to Gort should be deferred to May 1865, when he expected the whole line would then be ready for opening. By October 1864, matters had, however, taken a turn for the worse. Hemans had signed a certificate for works to 30 September, and the board having failed to meet this certificate, had stopped work on 6 October. Having taken legal opinion on the matter, Munro advised that the company was clearly in breach of its contract and he refused to resume the

works unless his conditions of payment were bettered. He insisted on £10,000 additional cash in lieu of shares. Hemans advised the company that if it broke the contract with Munro, it might well find it difficult to obtain the services of another contractor on such good terms. Munro's work had, in his view, been first class and he deserved every assistance. In response, the chairman stated that the contractor was in breach of his contract in that the section from Ennis to Gort was not ready for opening by 1 October and a penalty of £50 per week was due.

Following further discussions between Hemans and Munro, the latter agreed to accept the sum of £3,000 due from the W&LR and £7,000 more in debentures. The fact was that the company was endeavouring to pay the contractor one month in arrears, eg work done in September was certified by Hemans in October and the company sought to pay this in November. Counsel totally disagreed with the company's interpretation of the contract. Even with this adverse opinion, the company sought to stall matters by refusing to accept Munro's security. The matter was finally resolved in January 1865, when the board agreed to accept his amended terms.

The *Railway Times* for 4 March 1865 referred to the company's half-yearly shareholders' meeting at which calls were made for the setting up of a shareholders' committee to investigate the affairs of the company and report back. Gough had resigned his position in protest at the appointment of the W&LR directors to the board, which he considered to be in contravention of the company's agreement with the W&LR. When the shareholders' meeting was resumed in March, Thomas Greene, one of those appointed to the committee, read the report on their deliberations. In the main, it dealt with the terms of the contract with Munro and the events which had led up to the stoppage of works. The directors were criticised for their lack of action in dealing adequately with Munro. Regarding the appointment of the W&LR directors to the board, the committee felt that this move was 'adverse to the general interests of the Shareholders, and not likely to facilitate the making of the line'. The shareholders had not in fact been consulted and felt they had an undoubted right to appoint whomsoever they wished as board members.

Hemans reported to the board in May that about 200 men were again at work and suggested an application to Government for a loan of £50,000 to ensure the continuation of the works. The secretary was authorised to make application for the full amount which the company was entitled to raise (£66,000). It was a difficult period for raising money for railway projects generally, but nowhere more so than in Ireland. In July, Munro asked the directors to advance the necessary wages to keep the works in progress and gave them full powers to retain all debentures coming to him as security for such advances until the loan was obtained from Government. The board however declined to assent to this request and it is therefore hardly surprising to hear that work had stopped by 4 August and that the sheriff, at the suit of Messrs Leech & Son in Ennis, had seized plant for debts. Despite a sworn declaration and a letter from Munro stating that the plant was the property of the company, the sheriff said the sale would go ahead. There was also an action at Gort by one of the sub-contractors. One of the directors, William F. Clarke, resigned and was replaced by Sir Colman O'Loghlen, who was elected chairman. At the half-yearly meeting, the chairman said he hoped the stoppage would be short-lived.

Search for a fresh contractor

Despite the chairman's hopes expressed in August 1865, work was still at a standstill in the following June when the L&ER reported that an amount due on freight at Ennis remained unpaid and instructions were given for all goods at the station for either the A&EJR or its contractor to be held there. In September Hemans inspected the works and reported to the board, he being authorised to communicate with prospective contractors to have the works resumed. The directors themselves decided to speak to Munro and see if he would make an offer, 'entirely independent of his previous connection, the previous contract being now altogether void', to complete the entire line and works, subject to solvent security. It was also decided to go for a new Bill for an extension of time for completion, a rearrangement of the capital and, if possible, to effect working or other arrangements with various companies.

Munro sought more cash and the board found itself unable to accede to this and realised it must look for a new contractor. In November 1866 it was reported that the chairman had held talks with his opposite number on the MGWR, Ralph (later Sir Ralph) Cusack with a view to obtaining that company's assistance in completing the line. It was suggested that the Midland might subscribe £36,000, of which sum £6,000 would require to be repaid to the W&LR. In return, the MGWR would receive 'B' preference stock. The outlay on the line would be subject to the approval of the Midland engineer, the entire line to be opened simultaneously. A 20-year working agreement was offered at the same rates as set out in the company's agreement with the W&LR, traffic to be worked under the supervision of a joint committee of seven, four of whom would be appointed by the Midland. The latter company however stated it would not feel justified in subscribing such a large sum. A further approach was made in December seeking £10,000 in cash and £20,000 in original stock, a request which was also turned down.

Various tenders were opened at the board meeting in December, including one from Munro. Also included amongst those received was one from Charles Chambers of Westminster, who offered to complete the works, including supplying and laying of permanent way. The tender also included station houses at Crusheen, Ardrahan, Gort and Craughwell, repairs to the Fergus bridge, goods stores at four stations at £200 each, a tankhouse, water columns and a turntable (£250) at Gort. Ennis to Gort was to be completed in nine months and from the latter to Athenry in 24 months, weather permitting. This tender was accepted, but was then rescinded at the next board meeting as it was found impossible to obtain the required signatures to the bond required by the PWLC. This bond required the directors to have the line completed within a specified time, one of the conditions being put on the advance of £59,000 from the Treasury. The obtaining of the loan was described as being 'the very foundation of any agreement between the board and a contractor'.

Chambers saw it differently however, responding that there was no condition in his contract referring to a bond, and he must therefore hold the company to the contract. The board wrote to the PWLC in the hope that it would agree to divide the loan as follows: £24,000 in respect of Ennis to Gort and the balance for the remainder of the line, but it refused. Messrs Edgeworth & Stanford wrote to the board in April 1867 suggesting, 'on account of the stagnation in which the affairs of the company seem plunged', that some of the stations be left incomplete and omit the telegraph line. If this were done, they believed the line could be completed for £57,000 cash. If vested with the superintendence of the works, they would agree to complete the line for this figure. Hemans, who was closely connected with Messrs Edgeworth & Stanford, advised that the company would be unable to enter into other arrangements, otherwise it would give Chambers grounds for proceeding against it. The only course open seemed to be to complete the line itself through its engineer, with Edgeworth & Stanford as his assistants, advising Chambers accordingly. If this course were adopted, the line could probably be completed and ready for opening by June 1868.

Work finally resumes

The board now decided to go along with Hemans' idea. The first instalment of £20,000 of the Government loan was paid on 13 June 1867. At the same meeting, Hemans advised that there was a consignment of 1,300 tons of rails available on the Cork & Bandon Railway at £6 10s 0d per ton on rail at or near Bandon. Unable to agree on a method of payment for these rails, Stanford was authorised to obtain 1,078 tons of 68-69lb/yd flange rails, free on board at Cardiff for £5 a ton, half in cash and half in bills. These rails were in fact the property of Standish Motte, who became involved in the Bagenalstown & Wexford Railway. About 700 tons of these rails were in fact stored at Letterkenny, a further 40 tons at Belfast and the remainder at Newport. An engine was obtained for the contractor from the MGWR (No 11).

The L&ER was approached in October requesting permission for the formation of a junction with its line at Ennis, that company now seeking a rent of £250 per annum for the use of its station. Hemans submitted plans of the alterations proposed at Ennis, plans which were then submitted to the W&LR for its approval. Plans were also submitted to the board for the station at Gort, including a stone goods store with crane, passenger shed, booking office, a temporary engine shed, turntable and water tank, all for £1,300. Having first adopted these plans, the board then decided to seek fresh plans and specification for erections in both stone and wood. Hemans was able to report in December that an engine was running 'at a fair speed' between Ennis and Crusheen. However, the section to Gort would not be completed at least until March, and Hemans pressed for the completion of the whole line instead of opening this section first. Despite this suggestion, the board expressed the strongest intention of opening as far as Gort and exhorted Hemans accordingly.

In March 1868, Hemans reported that he had met a deputation from the Midland inquiring on what terms it might be granted

the working of the line. The board stated that the lowest terms would be the payment of £9,000 to the W&LR and about £6,000 for the completion of stations etc. Cusack did not demur at this, but objected to a clause in the company's forthcoming bill for compulsory powers for the Midland to subscribe. In any event the board decided not to pursue the matter at this stage. The W&LR also contacted the directors at this time stating that it was agreeable to cancel the working agreement of 27 May 1863 on condition of being repaid £6,000 plus interest at 5% per annum, and relieving them from the additional subscription of £3,000. The A&EJR was to pay a rent of £250 for Ennis station as well as paying half the staff wages and expenses there. The board considered the claim for interest as well as the rent and half the working expenses excessive. A request for the £3,000 was made to the W&LR in November 1868 but the latter company advised that it was only payable when the line was completed and actually opened for traffic. Instead, the company obtained a loan from the Hibernian Bank by way of an overdraft.

Plans for the junction at Athenry were submitted to the MGWR in June 1868, the finalisation of these being left to the decision of Lt-Col Rich of the BoT. About this time, a Mr Gregory requested a flag station at Kiltartan, about three miles north of Gort at a road crossing. Edgeworth advised that this could be provided for an outlay of about £60-70, and the directors inquired whether it might be used for public purposes, but in any event, a station was never provided here.

Tighe inspected the works in December but found various matters wanting, even to the extent that no junction had yet been created at Ennis. While this was going on, the A&EJR directors were once again meeting with the Midland board seeking a transfer of the working agreement from the W&LR. The latter in fact proposed such a

Above left: **The engine shed at Tuam on 30 June 1938 with GSR 'D19' 4-4-0 No 6 (ex GS&WR).** H. C. Casserley

Above right: **Tuam station in CIE days on 21 April 1955 showing 'J15' 0-6-0 No 123 on the 15.10 to Galway.** R. M. Casserley

transfer if the Midland agreed to pay the £6,000 with interest at 5% and £3,000 compensation. Whilst the MGWR expressed an interest in entering into a working agreement, it could not agree to the terms proposed, as it was not in a position to advance money to the W&LR.

First of various Government inspections
March 1869 saw the first of a series of Government inspections of the line. Lt-Col Rich spent three days at the beginning of the month carrying out a close inspection of the line, which he described as single through-out with sidings and a short crossing at Gort, although land had been taken for a double line. The ruling gradient was 1 in 70 and the sharpest curve of 15 chains radius. Permanent way consisted of Vignoles pattern rail weighing 70lb per yard, laid in 21ft lengths. Sleepers were generally half round, about 3ft 1in apart, rails being fixed with fang bolts. Ballast consisted of large stones with a top surface of gravel. There were intermediate stations at Crusheen, Gort, Ardrahan and Craughwell. Whilst there were turntables at both terminal stations, these were owned respectively by the L&ER and the A&TR. Rich felt that the

company should see to providing its own in case of subsequent difficulties.

There were 11 under-bridges, eight of wrought iron, the remainder of stone. Sixteen over-bridges were all of stone construction. The bridge over the Main Street of Gort consisted of stone abutments with the intermediate supports consisting of cast-iron columns. These latter, Rich was of the opinion, were deficient in section although strongly anchored down into the abutments. The single cover plates on some of the iron bridges were also defective and would require strengthening, while the outside piles of the Fergus bridge required strapping to the vertical piles. The under-bridges and cattle passes required completing so that loose stones on top of the abutments would not drop off and injure persons passing under them. None of the stations and associated signalling was complete, second platforms being necessary at both Gort and Ennis. The line itself required better packing, while the rock cuttings were in need of cleaning and completion of side drains to improve the removal of water. All in all, there was a good deal of work still to be done and a further report from the BoT at the end of March added some further items for attention.

Still desperately short of funds, the board approached the A&TR which agreed to contribute a sum of £1,000. A second inspection was carried out by Rich in May, when various matters still required attention. This was followed by a third inspection on 2 July. By now the permanent way had been much improved and although in fair order, would in the future require a good deal of care and attention to keep it right. Water columns at Gort and Ennis were placed too close to the edge of the platforms and were required to be moved back at least four feet. The company was still refused permission to open the line. Contact was made with the Midland regarding the use of Athenry station as it was now confidently hoped to open the line in the first half of August. The MGWR replied that it could not accept less than £400 per annum, a figure regarded as exorbitant in the extreme.

A fourth inspection was carried out on 21 July, the line now being much improved, although still not sufficiently to allow of an opening to the public. On this occasion, the W&LR wrote inquiring whether the usual engine and carriage would be required for the inspection, the response being in the negative as the Midland had obliged this time round. The fifth and final BoT inspection was conducted by Lt-Col Rich early in August. On this occasion he passed the line for opening, although he once again referred to the necessity for careful and close attention to the future state of the permanent way.

An opening at last

The W&LR was now requested to proceed without delay to open the line. Tighe had carried out his own final inspection on Wednesday, 28 July but was unhappy with what he saw. The board was now determined to see the line opened, even if it meant doing so itself. The Waterford company's response was to the effect that it could not do so without its prior consent. Thoughts once again turned towards the Midland, which now agreed to 'a liberal exchange of carriages and wagons'. The decision was taken to open the line for passenger traffic as from Wednesday, 15 September and for goods and cattle 12 days later. Messrs Edgeworth & Stanford agreed to their engine being sent at once to work the traffic, in addition to the loan of two ballast wagons for at least one month, delivery to be at Bagenalstown. The engine in fact remained on hire for some time at £4 4s 0d per week. The Midland also granted the use of three carriages and a van for a fortnight, later augmented by one more carriage and its locomotive No 8. The W&LR, meanwhile, threatened to obtain an injunction to restrain it from proceeding.

The staff at the time of opening was confirmed as consisting of four stationmasters, one foreman, one clerk, one guard, one driver, one stoker, one cleaner, one carriage lifter, one (temporary) permanent way inspector and 32 milesmen. Thomas O'Malley, late of the W&LR, was appointed traffic superintendent for three months certain at £150 per annum. Within a month the ranks had been swollen as reference is made to dispensing with one driver, retaining Thornley with Kennedy as stoker and Dowling as cleaner. Kennedy was authorised to take out a special engine at any time required. By 2 March 1870, Dowling was the No 2 fireman, when his wages were increased from 15s to 17s 6d per week.

Agreement was reached in January 1870 for the purchase of MGWR engine No 8 at a cost of £300, £50 up front and £25 per month. At the same time it was decided to offer £100 per annum as rent for the use of Athenry station, a figure declined by the Midland. It was then decided to offer £150 for the current year, the Midland once again stating it could not accept less than £400. The matter had in due course to be referred to arbitration. Later, in August 1870 the Midland requested the company to desist from taking water at Athenry as the aforementioned Mr Irwin had threatened legal proceedings.

Reports reached the board in April 1870 of a delay to the 16.30 up train when it ran short of water between Ardrahan and Craughwell in consequence of the feed pipe between the engine and tender becoming disconnected. The driver, Fletcher, uncoupled the engine from the train and ran to Athenry for water. The result was a 74 minutes late arrival of the train. The guard stated that had he known of Fletcher's intentions, he would have sent the Galway passengers forward on the engine — no mention was made of the number involved! O'Malley, reporting on the incident, referred to this as 'being another example of the incapacity of Fletcher, it is plain that ultimately he must be got rid of, but not, I fear till he has done damage'. No punches were pulled when it came to reporting on recalcitrant staff! Fletcher was dismissed later during the month of April and replaced by Mullen, recommended as 'an experienced and steady engineman'. Various stationmasters also ran foul of the directors, mainly for their absence from duty. As an example, when the traffic superintendent was at Craughwell on the morning of 18 April he could not find any account of McCormick, who had apparently left on the previous Saturday night by mail car for Galway. An applicant for a vacancy as stationmaster at Gort in May had an inquiry made into his antecedents before being taken on.

An experienced steady mechanic by the name of James Cameron was appointed in April to supervise the engines and rolling stock. Cameron had previously worked at the Broadstone headquarters of the MGWR and had been highly recommended by Ramage, that company's locomotive superintendent. Cameron was soon called upon to inspect some engines which the Dublin & Meath Railway was offering for sale. Further details of this may be found in Chapter Fifteen.

A meeting took place with the W&LR in July 1870 when the latter company expressed an interest in cancelling the agreement of May 1863, it to be released from the payment of £3,000. It was suggested that it might take debentures bearing interest at 5% in discharge of its subscription of £6,000 as soon as the company obtained powers to create new debentures.

A train is seized by the sheriff

The secretary reported the seizure on 10 November 1870 of the whole of the company's rolling stock, including engines, by the sheriff of Co Clare, under a judgment obtained in December 1866 by the London City Bank on a sum of £3,000 of overdue Lloyd's Bonds. Traffic had been paralysed for a day, owing to a seizure also by the sheriff of Galway of the train, which had been allowed to proceed by the Clare sheriff. Arrangements were made for the trains to run as from Monday, 15 November under the charge of bailiffs. The sheriff was advised that the rolling stock was not the property of the company, the Midland withdrawing its carriages before there was any possibility of them being sold. Engines Nos 1 and 2 were advertised for sale in mid-December, being bought by the company's northern neighbour, the A&TR, from whom they were subsequently bought back, the price being in part set against monies owed by the Tuam company for locomotive coal.

A meeting of shareholders and creditors was held in June 1871 at the request of the Financial Corporation, which held shares to the extent of about one-sixth of the company's capital. Proposals were put forward for the reorganisation of the company's finances, the current position being far from satisfactory. In December details were reported of a conference with the W&LR at the Imperial Hotel in Dublin, when it was stressed that the 1863 agreement was binding on the company. It was agreed that the Waterford company would pay the £3,000 previously referred to, and would take up the A&EJR plant at an agreed valuation. At the end of the working agreement it would hand over the line in the condition in which it was found. It was also agreed to put on a three-train service. The Gort company (as it is referred to in W&LR minutes) was to be guaranteed out of the gross receipts an amount of £5,200 per annum for the purpose of paying interest on its loan and rent or tolls at both Athenry and Ennis stations; any residue was to go to the W&LR in lieu of the previously agreed mileage charge. When the gross receipts exceeded an annual figure of £11,000, any surplus was to be divided equally between the two companies. Ennis and Dublin traffic and all other competitive traffic was to be put into a common fund and divided on terms to be agreed on.

The question of the rent for Ennis station was referred to the arbitration of James S. Forbes, managing director of the London, Chatham & Dover Railway. Forbes made his award in September 1872, a total figure of £1,323 being granted up to the end of the year 1871. At one stage the Athenry company actually discussed the idea of a separate station at Athenry to force the Midland into reducing its demands.

**Class D15 4-4-0 No 298 at Athenry
on 30 June 1938.**
H. C. Casserley/SLS collection

More financial difficulties
and a proposed sale

In 1872/73, at a time when the W&LR was in the course of taking various companies under its wing, powers were taken in the Waterford company's Act of 1873 for the purchase of the A&EJR. This was at a time when the PWLC was threatening a sale of the line for arrears of principal and interest. In October 1874, the PWLC advised that, due to continued default on the part of the company, it had instructed its solicitors to prepare the necessary warrant for taking possession of the property comprised in its securities. In reply, the board stated that it had been in negotiations with the W&LR for a possible purchase; these negotiations had however been suspended due to dissensions between the directors and shareholders of the W&LR. With the recent settlement of these differences, the A&EJ board was sure a new arrangement could be arrived at and it therefore asked the Commissioners to suspend proceedings against it for, say, two or three months. In the meantime, the board offered to hand over the receipts received from the W&LR, this latter offer being turned down.

By October 1875 the company had begun to make regular payments of interest to the PWLC. Little of note happened over the next three years, but in July 1878 we once again find negotiations being entered into with the Midland, this time for a possible sale of the line. It was clear that this could only be effected either by persuading the W&LR to release it from the working agreement or by waiting until the latter expired. Nevertheless a purchase price of £145,000 was offered by the MGWR, arrangements being made for the Government loan to be provided for. These terms were considered to be totally inadequate, the A&EJR board looking for £200,000. Nevertheless, notice of a Bill was published to carry out the sale. When the W&LR came to consider the

matter, the decision was clear from a purely monetary point of view. It was costing it 4s 4d per train mile to work the line, whereas receipts amounted to only 3s 4d. However, any indirect value had to be also taken into consideration, as well as the question of whether any such benefits would be materially diminished if the line fell into the hands of an interest adverse to that of the W&LR. It was a difficult question to answer, but it was decided to petition against the Bill, which was defeated.

Attention now turned back to the W&LR, agreement having been reached in November 1880 with the GWR for purchase of the A&EJR. In the interim, however, an application had been made to the Railway Commissioners to decide on the expiry date of the 1863 agreement. The A&EJR maintained that the agreement ran for 20 years from the date on which the company opened the line in September 1869, whereas the W&LR maintained that it dated from November 1872 when it took up the working. It was also necessary to ascertain whether renewal of the agreement for another period was compulsory. In addition, the W&LR had apparently not been keeping proper accounts, and it was necessary to decide whether this could be construed as a breach of the agreement, allowing the A&EJR to walk away from it. The arguments went against the A&EJR on this occasion and it looked, therefore, as if it would have to wait another 12 years or so to be released from the agreement.

A second arbitration was held under the auspices of Sir James Allport, general manager of the Midland Railway (of England) to decide on the Ennis competitive traffic. Agreement had been reached on a figure of £145 per annum for the rent of this station. In this instance, the A&EJR was awarded a sum of £2,134 15s 6d which was paid over by the W&LR. Some further correspondence took place in 1884 regarding a possible sale of the line to the Midland and then, in the

following year, with the W&LR. By May 1886, the Waterford board said it was willing to recommend the purchase of the line to its shareholders in terms of a figure of £165,000 in 3½% debentures, but the negotiations fell through in June. July 1886 saw the MGWR once again in the frame, by which time the offer had gone up to £170,000, the transfer to take effect when the working agreement with the W&LR expired. A large majority of the Athenry company shareholders voted in favour of the sale and Nicoll was dispatched to London to assist in the framing of the Bill.

Once again, the Bill was defeated, a result which was welcomed by the Waterford Harbour Board, which was glad to observe that 'the policy of the Dublin railway monopolists sustained a signal reverse in the failure of the MGWR to obtain control of the A&EJR line'. It went on to impress on the W&LR the paramount necessity of giving every facility to the traders of Waterford. The W&LR for its part advised that it would, in the fullness of time, be seeking a renewal of the working agreement and indeed would proceed in its endeavours to purchase the line, powers for which had been granted by the 1873 Act. In October 1888, the company made an offer to the Midland to sell for £180,000, the latter company refusing to go beyond £170,000 as originally proposed. An offer to lease the line for 14 years at a net rental of £6,700 per annum was also declined by the Midland. When the W&LR matched the figure of £170,000, the Midland went to £175,000, but by now an agreement to sell to the Waterford company had already been reached. In the event, a final offer of £180,000 was made by the W&LR and it was to it that the Gort company was eventually sold.

There were many shareholders in the A&EJR who would much rather have allowed their line to be taken over by the MGWR. The latter company always regarded Ennis as the natural southern boundary of its territory. It had also hoped to procure the A&TR. One wonders what the railway map of Ireland would have looked like had these two companies gone to the Midland. It is even possible that the W&LR might not have ended up in the hands of the GS&WR, although it has to be said that the latter company's interests were always directed towards access to the port of Waterford. Events in Wales eventually decided the fate of the Waterford company and these would probably not have changed with the lack of a connection north of Ennis. In the next chapter, we return to the W&LR to consider events from 1870 onwards.

Chapter Seven

ACQUISITION, ACRIMONY AND A KEY

Reference has already been made to discussions between the W&LR company and the GS&WR towards the end of the 1850s regarding a possible merger or take-over, these talks being terminated without agreement early in 1860. Negotiations were opened with the GWR in December 1867 with a view to finalising an agreement for rebates on through traffic. Six months later, the latter company was holding back on finalising an agreement as it did not wish 'to quarrel with the L&NWR'. This was to lead to the matter in effect being sidelined. By 1870, the Waterford company's traffic and receipts were on a rising curve, and this prompted a meeting of shareholders in Dublin, prior to the holding of the half-yearly meeting of shareholders in February, to once again consider a sale to the GS&WR. The directors, however, cautioned that it was probably an inexpedient time to place a value on the company, in addition to which there had been rumours of a possible Government take-over of, or assistance for, Irish railways. Having said this, the board was prepared to consider any fair offer made by the GS&WR on the condition that the port of Waterford was fairly treated.

At the half-yearly meeting on 25 February 1870, a shareholders' committee was appointed to further consider the matter and a meeting was held at Limerick Junction a fortnight later. A set of proposals was drawn up not vastly different from those considered in 1859. When these proposals were considered at a meeting specially convened for the purpose, Malcomson moved that if a majority of shareholders wished to go down this route, then the board would accept the majority decision. However, the vice-chairman, Abraham Stephens, put forward an amendment to the effect that with increasing traffic receipts, this was an inopportune time to sell the undertaking. When the vote was taken on the amendment, it went four each way with the chairman voting against it. On putting the original motion, the voting went the same way, the chairman now voting in favour. Mr Jacob then handed in a protest on the grounds of inadequate protection for the trade of the port of Waterford; this was clearly the reason for the opposition to a

sale as the GS&WR would undoubtedly divert the port's legitimate traffic via Dublin and the L&NWR. When an amended offer was put to the shareholders at the end of May, approval was given for its acceptance by a narrow majority, but the GS&WR now refused to accept the terms offered.

More committees
The shareholders' committee was once again asked to go back to the GS&WR, leading to the latter company seeking permission in August for its officers to inquire into the state of the line. Concerned at the turn of events, Sir Daniel Gooch, by now chairman of the GWR, wrote to Stephens offering traffic rebates which would provide the W&LR shareholders with a 2% dividend for three years and then 3% for a further 18 years. This led to yet another committee being formed to confer with the GWR. This committee reported to the shareholders in November confirming the above terms, in addition to which an annual payment of £1,000 was offered to start a reserve fund against future accidents. The GS&WR now returned with a 'final' offer of a 2½% ordinary dividend in perpetuity. These various negotiations had the effect of almost trebling the value of the company's ordinary stock to £25.

A meeting was held on 20 December to decide on the two offers, opinion still being strongly divided on whether the company should be sold to the GS&WR or an arrangement made with the GWR, but in the absence of a decision, the meeting was adjourned. When reconvened in February the meeting was a lengthy one, the outcome of which was that the directors recommended that no alliance be formed at this time, which was accepted by the share-holders. Stephens and his supporters now claimed that many of the votes cast at the February meeting were invalid, further claiming that the corrected vote would have given victory to the pro-GWR faction. Arising from this, the board voted in July on accepting the Paddington offer, this being passed by a majority of one. Malcomson, who was still strongly opposed to an agreement with the GWR, now refused to hand over the key of the seal box to finalise the agreement. Counsel's Opinion was

sought, but when a further meeting was held on 15 August, the chairman once again refused to produce his key. A workman was called to the boardroom and, in the presence of the other two key holders, he opened the box despite protestation from Malcomson as to the legality of their actions. The seal was then put on the agreement in the presence of the secretary.

When the forms for obtaining BoT approval for the agreement were produced for signature in October 1871, Malcomson again obstructed matters by refusing to sign them. Further approaches were made to the GS&WR, which now guaranteed a 4% dividend, this being matched by the GWR in February 1872. This long-running saga finally came to an end when the agreement with the GWR was signed on 18 April by Malcomson. The agreement was for 21 years and came into effect on 1 July 1872. Rebates were to be allowed on through fares and rates, traffic interchange and services at Waterford and New Milford, to effectively provide the W&LR shareholders with a 4% dividend. The Waterford company was obliged in return to provide an adequate connecting rail service to and from the steamers, the GWR to put on a daily steamer service with connections to and from London. This service had just recently been taken over from Messrs Jackson & Co as related in Chapter Nineteen.

Acquisitions in the offing
While the negotiations with the GWR and the GS&WR were ongoing, other matters came up for discussion. Perhaps the most important of these was the question of amalgamating some of the worked companies with the W&LR. We have already looked in some detail at the early history of these companies, but it is useful to consider the amalgamation issue in an overall context. To recap, by the end of 1870 the W&LR was working the following companies: the L&CR, the L&ER and the L&FR out of Limerick, in addition to which the R&NJR was in effect an extension of the latter company's line. To the north, on either side of Athenry, were the A&EJR and the A&TR. The latter had been worked by the MGWR until 27 October 1870 and, despite negotiations between the two

companies extending over more than 12 months, they could not agree on terms for an extension of the working agreement or for an outright purchase. The A&EJR had concluded an agreement with the W&LR in May 1863 but had worked its own line after its opening in September 1869.

As we have already seen in Chapter Four, the L&CR was taken over as from 1 January 1873. Negotiations began in December 1871 between the W&LR and a number of the worked companies with a view to their amalgamation or sale. These discussions eventually came to an end with the passing of the Waterford & Limerick Railway Act of 1873 which made arrangements for the dissolution of both the L&FR and the L&ER as from 1 July 1873. In the case of the former, for every holding of £25 actually paid up, a certificate was to issue for W&LR perpetual preference shares for a like amount, bearing interest at 5% per annum. Ordinary shareholders were to receive a like amount of W&LR shares for their holding in the Foynes company. A sum of £800 was to be paid to the Foynes directors to enable them to provide compensation to their secretary. Similar provisions pertained as regards shareholders in the L&ER, but in this case, a sum of £2,000 was to be paid to provide compensation 'to such officials as the L&ER directors shall consider to be entitled thereto in respect of loss of office'.

Although not destined to join the fold at this time, provision was also made in the 1873 Act for the R&NJR, A&EJR and the A&TR to transfer and convey to the W&LR their respective undertakings, railways and the like for such a price as might be agreed between the companies. Maximum sums were laid down in the Act: £60,000 in the case of the R&NJR, £180,000 for the A&EJR and £75,000 for the A&TR. Powers were given to the W&LR to raise sufficient capital for the taking over of the various companies referred to in the Act. In addition, it was empowered to raise up to £50,000 (with an additional one-third borrowing) by the creation of new shares for the general purposes of the undertaking.

Resignation of officers

Ainsworth wrote to the board in January 1872 announcing his resignation as secretary and traffic manager. He was requested to withdraw his notice for one month and, meanwhile, some consideration was given to the separation of the two posts. Ainsworth's resignation was formally accepted on 15 March, when Isaac Banks was confirmed as traffic manager at a salary to be considered. At this meeting, Martin Atock also announced his resignation to take up an appointment as locomotive superintendent on the MGWR, where he was to distinguish himself. Notices were posted in various trade journals for a

Platforms 3 and 4 at Limerick with an ex WL&WR 4-4-0 about to depart from platform 2. On platform 4 is one of the GSR Sentinel railcars. Note the magnificent signal gantry, one of two at the end of the platforms. Ian Allan Library

replacement, to include the carriage and wagon departments at a salary not exceeding £400. In due course, Mark Wardle was appointed to the post on six months' trial. Atock's departure once again brought a period of instability to the post of locomotive superintendent, Wardle resigning after only a year on the grounds of ill-health.

The company solicitor, Ambrose, agreed to act temporarily as company secretary pending an appointment to that post. J. F. Nicoll was appointed as secretary in June 1872 at a salary of £400 per annum, with M. J. Kennedy as his assistant at half that figure. Ainsworth asked for a testimonial following his period of 13½ years as secretary, during the last 4½ of which he had also been traffic manager. It was decided to present him with a testimonial of £500 in consideration of his long service and the arduous duties he had had to perform during that period. This was opposed by some of the directors, one commenting that 'since resigning he has plainly shown his intention to give the Board all the trouble he can', a reference to claims made by him for monies owing to him. The earlier resolution of giving him a testimonial was rescinded at a meeting on 27 August, but after Ainsworth attended the board, it was again reinstated. Suggestions were also made of appointing him to the board, but there was considerable opposition to this proposal also.

Problems with the GWR agreement

Under the 1872 agreement, the GWR had guaranteed the W&LR an ordinary dividend of 4% per annum by means of rebates etc. During 1873, however, it refused to pay as its interpretation of the agreement was that it was conditional on the W&LR working ratio being held at 47%, leaving 3% to go into the reserve fund and 50% for dividends. In 1873, the working ratio had in fact gone

up to 54%. This refusal was to lead to considerable acrimony both amongst the directors and the shareholders, as we shall now see.

There were clearly two factions on the board: those who were led by the chairman, Abraham Stephens, in favour of further negotiations with the GWR, and a minority, led by J. F. Lombard of Dublin, who were critical of the actions of their colleagues and would have preferred to continue negotiations for amalgamation with the GS&WR. Stephens issued a circular to the shareholders in March 1874, 'in consequence of the interruption caused by a section of the shareholders' representatives opposing the interests (of the company)'. The amount claimed from the GWR to enable the dividend to be paid was £2,420 1s 2d. The circular referred to the difference of interpretation as to clause 25 of the agreement. The GWR stated that if it were to pay the amount due, it should be entitled to control the Irish company's income and expenditure and to appoint officers. In anticipation of receiving this figure, the directors decided to pay a 3% dividend in February 1874.

A letter was received from Sir Daniel Gooch in August pointing out that the GWR was reluctant to change the existing agreement. A letter was also read from Dr George Atkinson, a board member from Dublin, expressing the great dissatisfaction in Dublin amongst shareholders at no dividend being paid for the half year to June, commenting that 'the Dublin shareholders are so tired of the disappointments they have suffered'.

Also in August, a motion was introduced by Atkinson seeking the termination of the company solicitor's engagement, but an amendment moved by Mr Denny saw Ambrose remain in his position.

At the half-yearly meeting held on 28 August, an amendment was put to the meeting calling on the chairman to continue negotiations with the GWR. The question of the legality of this amendment was raised by some shareholders since prior notice of intention to put it forward had not been given. The solicitor said it was in order, but a protest signed by eight shareholders, including William Malcomson and six directors, was handed in expressing a contrary view. As a consequence the meeting was adjourned for four weeks.

Shortly after the adjournment, Stephens reported that one of the directors, Henry Slattery of Waterford, had reduced his shareholding and no longer appeared to qualify as a member of the board. It seemed that whilst his name appeared in the shareholders' register for certain shares, some of them had not been paid for. Slattery was duly informed that he was no longer regarded as being a director. John Riall of Clonmel, who had seconded the amendment at the August meeting, and who was therefore regarded as pro-GWR, was elected in his stead, despite the fact that Slattery had, in the interim, paid the amount outstanding on his shares.

The secretary is suspended

Prior to the reconvening of the meeting, Counsel's Opinion was sought on the legality of introducing the amendment, it stating that it was 'quite a harmless one and does not commit the company to any definite action'. The next board meeting was held on 6 October 1874, and when Riall endeavoured to take his seat, a protest was handed in against the 'so-called election . . . the same being invalid, there being no vacancy.' The chairman endeavoured to adjourn the meeting to allow tempers to cool, but Lombard moved a motion that business be proceeded with. The voting was four each way, the chairman's casting vote being against Lombard's motion. Another motion put forward by the chairman was for the suspension of the secretary as it was felt that Nicoll had forfeited the confidence of the board, having supported the 'rebels'. Slattery, who was in attendance, tendered his vote, which was refused by the chairman, who, along with his supporters, left the meeting after calling an adjournment. The rebels continued the meeting, however, some of them entering personal protests in the board minute book.

The board meeting was again resumed four days later, the rebels absenting themselves. Nicoll also being absent, a motion was passed unanimously that the assistant secretary be ordered to make a transcript of the proceedings of the board of 6 October up to the declaration of the adjournment, all subsequent entries being cancelled, as had been directed by Counsel. Thus, nine pages of entries were cancelled — and are still to be seen in the relevant minute book! Nicoll was now formally suspended and he was ordered to hand over all books and documents to his assistant, M. J. Kennedy. A circular was issued to shareholders on 12 October making reference to a notice appearing in the press signed by Nicoll (who had left Waterford with the keys of both the safe and the seal box), calling a meeting to be held at the Imperial Hotel in Dublin on 22 October. The circular pointed out that the meeting had been summoned by a minority of the board, one of whom (Slattery) had legally ceased to be a director. The circular concluded by stating that Counsel had advised that the proposed meeting was illegal.

More keys!

Orders were given that the boardroom in Waterford was to be locked and no person admitted without the prior authority of either the chairman or the vice-chairman.

Likewise, Kennedy was instructed not to give the company's books or documents to anyone without similar authority. A new safe was obtained, the old one having been forced open. Some documents, including copies of Acts, minutes and correspondence relating to conferences with the GWR, the A&EJR and the A&TR, were found to be missing. Matters reached a farcical level when Nicoll's desk and chair, which were not the property of the company, were ordered to be removed from the boardroom.

All the directors attended the board meeting in Waterford on 20 October, including Slattery and also the suspended secretary. Having heard Counsel's Opinion, the chairman put a motion for the removal of Slattery, an amendment put forward by Lombard countermanding this being defeated. Nicoll was then requested to deliver up the keys of the safe and the seal box. Before handing them over, Nicoll demanded that his desk be returned and 'put into the exact position in which it formerly was', this being done after some debate. Nicoll then handed over the keys, but not before entering a protest in the minute book. He was then asked to leave the boardroom, when the solicitor read an Attorney's letter and a writ of summons in an action for slander for words alleged to have been uttered in the boardroom at the suit of Nicoll. Arising from this, the chairman moved that Nicoll's services be dispensed with, an amendment being passed to the effect that he be given £100 in lieu of three months' notice.

At the Dublin meeting two days later, Lombard, in the chair, referred to the company as being 'a leaky old machine at all points', under a board that was 'a curious conglomeration of individuals', and under a chairman who was 'mesmerised' by some of his colleagues. The meeting called on Stephens to resign and a committee of investigation was set up. Kennedy was officially appointed secretary at a board meeting on 3 November. At that meeting, the investigating committee sought access to the company's books and any relevant correspondence.

Sir Daniel Gooch of the GWR wrote a long letter to Stephens on 30 November, in which he referred to the suggestion made that the line should be worked and managed by a joint committee of three directors from each company. With a view to carrying this into effect, two officers of the GWR, Messrs Armstrong and Voss, had

The approach to Waterford from the west on 18 June 1939. On the left are the 'Limerick' and 'Kilkenny' engine sheds, separated by a turntable. In the background is the toll bridge and, across the River Suir, the city of Waterford.
W. A. Camwell/IRRS collection

inspected the W&LR line and its rolling stock. The inspection was thorough and the subsequent report outlined a number of failings. Accommodation for locomotives at Limerick and Waterford was deficient, but there was an excess at Clonmel and Ennis. The arrangements for Foynes line trains at Limerick was criticised, other stations also coming under notice. It was suggested that the station at Longpavement should be closed, while a number of others of timber construction should be renewed.

This report led the Paddington board to the conclusion that a rather larger investment (estimated to be in the region of £26,300) would be required than had been anticipated in placing the line in a satisfactory condition. To secure some harmony on the Waterford board and a cordial co-operation in the interests of both companies, the GWR now agreed to alter clause 25 of the 1872 agreement to increase the figure of 50% of gross receipts to 55%, thus allowing the outstanding shortfall to be paid. Sir Daniel concluded by stating that he hoped this concession would 'induce all parties in Ireland to work harmoniously with you, so as to promote the prosperity of the Company and develop the resources of the district'.

Despite this apparent solution to the problems besetting the board and the shareholders, matters failed to improve. Protests were registered at every meeting to the attendance of Riall. One piece of good news for the board was the announcement in December of the withdrawal of Nicoll's slander case against the chairman. Things were, however, set to worsen. At a special meeting held in Waterford on Tuesday, 12 January 1875, it was proposed that four directors be removed. Slattery, who had precipitated some of the bad feeling on the board, did not stand for re-election as he had recently moved to live in London. Stephens, however, was allowed to remain on as chairman in deference to his long connection with the company. He resigned his position on 4 February, but remained as a director. He was now 69 years of age and had been a shareholder since 1845. His two principal opponents, Lombard and Atkinson, proposed and seconded respectively a motion placing on record the thanks of the board for his long and faithful service. He remained as a director until 1889, having served in that capacity for 30 years. He was replaced as chairman by Thomas Synnott of Dublin. Nicoll was now reinstated as secretary, and was additionally offered the post of general manager, a post which he declined. The matter of keys still caused a problem as Abraham Denny, one of the directors removed, held one of the keys to the seal box and refused to hand it over, necessitating the box being again forcibly opened and the lock changed.

Investigation of the traffic manager

It was reported in January 1875 that the Bank of Ireland had withdrawn an overdraft facility for £20,000 allowed to the company; a deputation was appointed to wait on the bank seeking a renewal. Later, the company was obliged to find an alternative banker. Nicoll wrote to the board on 26 January pointing out major problems with locomotives and rolling stock regularly breaking down, quite a sizeable proportion of the locomotive stock being in the workshops for repairs. The traffic department was in 'a completely disorganised and demoralised state — it will take a year at least to weed out all the bad and inefficient elements in it'. The permanent way, by the admission of the engineer, required very considerable outlay to put it in efficient repair. This was a damning report, the upshot of which was the appointment of a committee to investigate matters. Daniel McDowell, locomotive superintendent of the W&CIR, was engaged to report on the locomotive works and stock. Further details in this regard are recorded in Chapter Fifteen.

Obviously anticipating an adverse report, Isaac Banks, the traffic manager only since March 1872, submitted his resignation at the beginning of January. Banks had been at the centre of controversy in July 1873 following the dismissal of a member of his staff, Richard T. Clarke. Clarke had forwarded an unauthorised telegram to the secretary regarding the men's pay at Limerick, and had also assisted in drawing up a subsequent memorial on their behalf. There was obviously more to this incident, as Clarke later made charges against Banks. So serious were these that comparisons were ordered between Railway Clearing House returns and the company's cash receipts back to January 1871. It was decided to appoint an outside agent to investigate further, James Grierson, the GWR accountant and later to become general manager, being appointed. Grierson's report was received in October 1873, Banks being cleared of all charges of dishonesty, although it was accepted that serious irregularities had existed for some time in the traffic department in relation to shortages of cash with certain individuals.

A year later it was decided to dispense with Clarke's services, but he refused to accept salary due to him, instead, seeking a year's pay and £150 expenses in lieu of notice. It is not clear what influence Clarke had, but a board minute of 26 January 1875 ordered his reinstatement and the payment of his salary for the period he was out of employment. Arising from these revelations, Banks had been removed from Limerick to Waterford, with Thomas O'Malley being appointed traffic superintendent at the former location. O'Malley also fell foul of the board. In December 1877, the secretary was instructed to notify him of the board's intention of dispensing with his services, but offering him an opportunity to resign. O'Malley chose the latter option, he being paid three months' salary and expenses due to him. He was not replaced at Limerick. John Roberts was appointed traffic manager in April 1875 at a salary of £600 per annum. Robert Andrews, who had been appointed as locomotive superintendent in March 1873, was replaced by Thomas Armitage, who had previously been with the Dublin & Belfast Junction Railway, and before that with the Dublin & Meath Railway. His salary was fixed at £250 per annum, with a free house, coal and light.

This was not to be the end of Richard Clarke, however, for he was apparently appointed as Agent at Listowel. In June 1886, the chairman reported on investigations carried out which led to the directors deciding to remove him from Listowel and 'to place him in some other position on probation'. In the following October, memorials were received from a number of the Limerick butter buyers seeking Clarke's reinstatement as stationmaster at Listowel. The board however decided that this would not be possible in view of the way the officer in question had conducted himself. Later in the month, no less than 46 pig buyers wrote in similar vein, but the board held to its original decision and no further mention is made of Clarke.

Tramways and a proposed extension at Waterford

In December 1873, notices were published for two tramway schemes for the city of Waterford. The Waterford Railways Junction and Tramway Bill proposed a line commencing by a junction with the W&LR seven furlongs west of the terminus, crossing the river on a new bridge and connecting up on the south side of the River Suir with the authorised Waterford Dungarvan & Lismore Railway. From the latter's terminus a further tramway, approximately a mile in length, would run eastwards along the south quays. If constructed, this line would have had the potential to divert much of the company's goods traffic from the last mile of its line, and it was therefore strenuously opposed.

The second scheme, under the title of the Waterford Free Bridge, Railways Bridge & Tramways, envisaged nine separate tramways, and was considered to benefit not only the public and the port of Waterford, but would also be of material advantage to the W&LR, and in fact, would afford equal accommodation to all the railways terminating in Waterford. This scheme involved the replacement of the old wooden toll bridge (constructed in 1793) by a new, free, combined road and rail bridge. The principal tramway was to commence at the

4-4-0 No 298 and train at Waterford North station. In this view one can clearly see how Mount Misery had an overpowering effect on the station. Photographer unknown/S. Kennedy collection

'Kilkenny Goods Yard Gate', cross over the new bridge and run along the quays as far as the GWR quay yard at Adelphi Wharf.

The directors determined on assisting the second scheme as far as they legally could and resolved that a payment of £300 be made on account of expenses already incurred in its promotion. It was also decided that the GWR be requested to make the necessary Parliamentary deposit on behalf of the W&LR. It was announced in March 1874 that both schemes had passed the examiner on Standing Orders, but they were causing considerable controversy in both railway and public circles in Waterford. The matter was finally resolved when the GWR intervened and persuaded both parties to withdraw their Bills and confer further with Paddington to produce a more general scheme which would more equitably serve the interests of the public, the port and the railway companies.

Following on the withdrawal of the tramway schemes Tighe, the engineer, was instructed to prepare plans for an extension along the north side of the river. He was requested to prepare two sets of plans, one under the cliff of Mount Misery and the other directly along the river front. Consideration was also given to a possible connection across the river, which would necessarily involve the construction of a new bridge, possibly freeing same for the use of the citizens of Waterford. The directors announced that they would be prepared to assist in such a public work by paying over a capitalised amount based on the rent they were currently paying in tolls.

It took some time to prepare the necessary plans, Parliamentary notice not being published until November 1875. This indicated a line extending from the 'Old Terminus or Goods Station and terminating in the townland of Mount Misery in the Old Timberyard at a point in the south-eastern corner of that yard at or near the southern-most end of the lane or passage leading

under No 13 Sion Row from the public road leading from Waterford to New Ross to the River Suir'. Reclamation of the riverbed would be undertaken and a quay or wharf wall would be constructed eastwards from the north end of the toll bridge. The scheme was defeated in 1876, mainly due to the strenuous opposition of the GWR, which had steamer services operating from the south side of the river.

We have spent a good deal of time discussing the affairs of the board and the shareholders during this difficult period in the company's history. It is important, however, to deal with these matters in some depth as the departure of Stephens represented a turning point in the Waterford company's affairs, which thereafter began gradually to improve.

Deep-water extension at Waterford

Reference has been made above to a proposed extension of the line at the Waterford end to deep water. One of the problems was that the company was forced to pay tolls on all goods traffic brought across the river, whether by the bridge or by lighters. In January 1873, a deputation from the Bridge Commissioners had met the board inquiring whether they would unite with the commissioners to make the bridge free of tolls, but no agreement was forthcoming, and in fact it was to be 1908 before the bridge was freed. The old wooden bridge was replaced in 1912. In September 1877, the 1875/56 plans were dusted off and it was decided to carry out the extension, to include Sion Row and a tunnel at Mount Misery rather than along the riverside. It was also decided to take powers to double the section of line from Newrath to Dunkitt. Notice was given to the W&CIR that powers would be included in the Bill to enable it to use the extension if it desired. In any event, it was hoped that it would not oppose the Bill.

It soon became clear that there would be opposition from other quarters, when

petitions were lodged with the Harbour Commissioners from ships' masters and cattle dealers to the proposed running of steamers from the dock premises. Despite opposition, the Bill became law on 22 July 1878. Difficulties were encountered in regard to valuations of property necessary for the construction of the tunnel, the engineer being requested to negotiate with the holders of property. In March 1879, James Connington was appointed to the post of piermaster and the GWR was informed that steamers were about to come to the new wharf. It agreed that as from 1 April its Milford steamer reaching Waterford on a Friday would, after discharging its cargo at the Adelphi Wharf, go over to the railway wharf and start from there on a Sunday. Also, on one day per week, a cattle steamer would sail from the railway wharf.

In June, the Crown & Treasury Solicitor wrote agreeing to accept a sum of £60 10s 0d compensation for the removal of the RIC barracks at Terminus Street. Specifications for the railway extension were submitted in April 1880 and it was arranged to advertise for tenders. That of Messrs Falkiner & Stanford was received on 29 June in a sum of £31,210 10s 0d, this being accepted and they were ordered to proceed at once with the works. Three months later, the contractors wrote suggesting the substitution of an open cutting in place of the tunnel at Mount Misery, in return for which they were prepared to allow a reduction of £1,000 from the contract price. Never happy to accept what was offered, the company sought a reduction of £1,400, a compromise of £1,250 being agreed. The BoT agreed to the substitution, as did Waterford Corporation.

Concerns were expressed in December 1881 at delays in progressing the works, the engineer being of opinion there had not been sufficient reason given for these delays. Tighe was requested to inform the contractors that no further payments would be made in respect of extra works unless ordered in writing as such. An engine and wagons were requested by the contractors in February 1882, the engineer being informed to act as he thought best in this regard. The tender of the Railway Signal Co at £900 was accepted in April for the necessary additional signalling, and that of John Lysaght at £2,998, for a new goods shed. Fears were expressed in July in reference to the rock cutting, the danger of slips being considered. There was further correspondence with the contractors towards the end of 1882 in regard to the continued slow progress of the works. The extension, passing under the Clonmel and New Ross roads by bridges, was finally opened on 26 May 1883, it having been found necessary to refer the dispute between the company and the contractors to the arbitration of the BoT. The extension was doubled in the following year.

Waterford station from the east during reconstruction works for the accommodation of the F&RR&H Co. The train, in charge of GS&WR 'D17' 4-4-0 No 11, is standing at the combined platforms 3 and 4, while to the left are the new bay platforms 1 and 2 used by D&SER trains. The station building can be seen in the background, with Mount Misery on the right of the picture. Photographer unknown/S. Kennedy collection

Permanent way and bridges

In September 1876 the engineer suggested that as rails were now moderately priced, an additional 2,000 tons should be purchased, allowing for the re-laying of about 30 miles of line during 1877/78. This suggestion was adopted and tenders were sought. Tighe also mentioned the necessity of bridge renewals, referring in particular to the remaining timber structures. He recommended their replacement with iron tops, and he was requested to prepare plans for the consideration of the board.

Correspondence had been entered into late in 1873 with landowners in the vicinity of the Robertstown viaduct, who had offered to subscribe towards the making of an embankment there. Lord Monteagle wrote to the BoT in February 1876 complaining that he believed the viaduct was dangerous, leading to an inspection by Lt-Col (later Gen) Hutchinson. He described the viaduct as being constructed entirely of timber and consisting of 15 spans of 20ft each. The piers were of usual construction, each having four piles. The piers were spanned by two timber baulks 12in by 12in, strapped together one above the other, the lower one resting on a bolster 9ft x 12in x 12in. Upon careful examination, Hutchinson saw no reason to see any immediate danger from its condition. He confirmed that it was the company's intention to 'do away with this viaduct in connection with a reclamation project'. In February 1879, with an offer of £1,000 towards the work from Mr Stratford, the company agreed to make and maintain the embankment.

Similar doubts were expressed regarding the Shannon Bridge in July 1877. Following an inspection by the engineer, the bridge was declared to be quite safe with little or no fear, provided trains crossed over it at the reduced speed of 15mph as laid down by the board. It was however agreed that a new bridge should be put in. It was again carefully examined on 17 October 1878 and Tighe described it as follows. There were twelve river and four land spans, the total length being 514ft 8in. The land piers were all of timber, the first river pier consisting of a single tier of timber piles, the next a cluster of piles comprised of timber and iron and so on alternately. Tighe confirmed that the bridge had been badly designed and

erected. On testing the south main girder, there was no more than half an inch deflection, although it did vibrate as trains passed over it, and with some lateral yield. Following the collapse of the Tay Bridge on the night of 23 December 1879, some concerns were voiced as to the stability of the Shannon Bridge. Col Rich carried out an inspection in February 1880. He had two engines of 88 tons run over it, and had some of the timber piles bored and probed. He found the condition of the bridge to be 'better than he expected and as safe for trains as when opened'.

The stolen railway

A letter was received in August 1876 from the secretary of the Parsonstown & Portumna Bridge Railway offering to negotiate for the sale of that undertaking on reasonable terms. The full story of this short railway does not concern us here as it was worked by the GS&WR, but a brief summary would not go amiss in explanation of the above heading. The 12-mile line was authorised by an Act of July 1861 and was opened for traffic on 5 November 1868, being leased to the GS&WR for 10 years. Worked by the latter company, the line never made a profit, and it was closed at the end of the lease. The PWLC, which had advanced £12,000 on mortgage, took possession of the line, making no attempt to work it, nor was it successful in finding a buyer. The line lay derelict for five years, during which time it was regularly patrolled. The P&PBR and the PWLC both approached the W&LR in November 1878, to seek a working agreement, but this was declined. Following a further approach in May 1880, it was agreed that Messrs Tighe and Roberts would inspect the line and report, but there the matter rested. The PWLC security was withdrawn in 1883, leading to pilfering of anything movable. The wooden station

buildings at Portumna Bridge are said to have disappeared overnight and attempts were even made to remove the girders of a six-span bridge over the River Brosna, hence the title, 'the stolen railway'.

Dispute over Limerick Junction

Over the years minor problems occurred between the GS&WR and the W&LR in regard to the use of Limerick Junction. For example, in April 1855 the W&LR protested against additional expenditure and suggested the erection of a more convenient station under the joint superintendence of the two companies' engineers. This suggestion fell on deaf ears. Further complaints were made in September 1856 in relation to through traffic and the poor connections between the trains on the respective lines. The GS&WR trains were frequently delayed and instructions were given that all W&LR trains delayed as the result of this should be reported. A traffic minute of 17 February 1866 interestingly makes reference to the stopping of the 06.45 train at the 'temporary platform' at Limerick Junction. The traffic manager suggested 'serious consideration before so doing as it would endanger the safety of passengers thereat if allowed by the GS&WR to walk up the rails, etc'. It is not clear from the minute whether this temporary platform was at the divergence of the two companies' lines or perhaps at Keane's Points Junction, but there is no further mention of it in the minutes. In December 1866 the GS&WR wrote directing attention to the current state of the working arrangements and giving three months' notice of their termination. Arising out of this, a new agreement was drawn up by which the W&LR agreed to pay a sum of £190 per annum for the use of the facilities at the junction.

Tipperary was an important source of traffic in butter; as an example in April 1868 a Mr McDonnell stated that he would be prepared, on certain conditions, to forward to Waterford about half his annual shipments, the latter estimated at between 5,000 and 6,000 firkins. (A firkin was an old measure of volume equal to 7½ gallons.) Much of the butter traffic went to Dublin via Limerick Junction and when early in 1864 the W&LR ceased the running of the 16.00 from Waterford, the GS&WR complained that this would have the effect of diverting from Dublin the Tipperary butter traffic so long as the Limerick Junction and Tipperary rates were equal. The alteration had been made as an economy measure but the W&LR agreed to allow the GS&WR to send an engine to Tipperary to collect such traffic left after the departure of the 14.45 train. However, following a fatal accident in February 1869 to a man named Hanley, run over by the GS&WR butter engine, the W&LR notified its intention to cease the running by the GS&WR. The latter reacted by threatening to 'adopt other steps for retaining the butter to their route'. This may in part have been the reason for a Bill promoted in 1871 for a branch from the GS&WR main line near Limerick Junction to Tipperary.

It is clear from a perusal of the GS&WR board minutes that the impetus for a separate branch came from the L&NWR. In a letter dated 14 October 1871 its general manager stated that in the absence of an independent line to Tipperary, it (the L&NWR) 'could not appoint agents or take other necessary steps to control the through traffic by our route over your line'. The branch would have deviated from the GS&WR main line north of the square crossing, paralleled the W&LR line for almost two miles and then turned northeast, approaching Tipperary parallel to Limerick Street and terminating beside the Church and Butter Market at No 141 Bohercrow Street, in line with the Church. The Bill was successfully defeated by strong opposition from the Waterford company.

The GS&WR referred, in February 1877, to the 'very small' rent hitherto paid by the W&LR for the station accommodation provided at Limerick Junction, and called for a settlement of this long-outstanding question. It advised that returns were to be made at once. The W&LR immediately responded by referring to the serious inconvenience suffered by it in shunting for the conveyance of GS&WR traffic; in its view the rent it was paying was quite ample — the shunting in question, amounting to 5,500 miles per annum, was costing it in the region of £750. Nothing further was heard from the GS&WR until April 1880 when it gave three months' notice of its intention to determine the 1867 agreement, this agreement having allowed for the payment of a sum of £190 annually for the use of the

GS&WR station and associated facilities. Tighe was immediately instructed to prepare plans for a timber station to enable the company to work its traffic to and from its land at the junction.

Copies of the plans were sent both to the GS&WR and the BoT, the latter being informed of the company's intention to erect a station and platform 'at the actual junction'. The GS&WR replied to the effect that it could not understand how the W&LR could consider the notice given 'a sudden and unexpected one'. Furthermore, it never intended that a separate station would be built, but that a new agreement might be reached; in addition it was totally against the provision of the proposed station which would entail unnecessary expense and great inconvenience to the public.

The BoT approved the plans subject to proper signalling arrangements for the crossing on the level of the two companies' main lines. In addition, it required the erection by the GS&WR of platforms to the northwest of the crossing, the provision of a footbridge and the stopping of all (GS&WR) trains north of the crossing. Lt-Col Hutchinson also complained of the short platforms in the angle at the south side and the danger of shunting over the GS&WR line. Tighe explained that the plan was submitted on the understanding that the GS&WR would come up to the junction points on the south side for and with traffic. Hutchinson condemned this idea and inquired whether the W&LR could make a car and foot road between both stations, Tighe stating in reply that the land was GS&WR property.

Tighe informed the board on 9 June that he had men employed in cutting away the bank on the south side for a siding. At the north side he was constructing a temporary platform at the company's cottages, also a platform on the south side in the angle of the two lines for the interchange of passengers. He suggested that the GS&WR be requested to reinstate a diamond crossing for a double line to Tipperary, taken up by it in 1860, as plans were now being drawn up to double the line as far as Tipperary. Tighe reported on 18 June that the platforms would be completed within a week and inquired if a shed and lamps should be put up, these being approved. It was suggested to the GS&WR that the W&LR might, at their own expense, provide a platform in the narrow strip between the two companies' lines with proper arrangements for the convenience of passengers.

The W&LR directors decided to proceed, omitting altogether the platform on the GS&WR system; they informed the latter company that revised interchange arrangements would come into effect as from 21 July. The GS&WR however persisted in its belief that the existing arrangements were

quite adequate and threatened to cease all through booking arrangements, the W&LR in reply, stating that it would apply to the Railway Commissioners for the necessary order to compel the former company to exchange traffic at the point of junction. On 23 July, Tighe advised that he was getting up a timber platform for down trains.

Lt-Col Hutchinson reported again on behalf of the BoT in August 1880. He commented that the two stations were almost 400 yards apart and thus passengers would be 'terribly inconvenienced . . . unless some provision is to be made for their transfer'. W&LR trains had ceased to use the GS&WR station as from 21 July. Regrettably, the BoT correspondence file relating to this period at Limerick Junction is no longer extant and we have to rely on a brief reference and diagram extracted from the bound volumes of each year's inspections and kindly supplied to the author by Peter Rowledge. Under the new arrangements trains for Limerick reversed into the curved (or back) portion of the new platform, those for Waterford running in to the front of it. From this it would appear that the separate down side platform may not have been finalised. Hutchinson remarked that 'the interchange passengers and their luggage (had) to pass on foot between and across lines of rails for the space of about 330 yards . . . large numbers of passengers and the area is badly lit'. He was of opinion that the Waterford company should be called upon to cease the new arrangement and revert to the old system of working pending a decision by the Railway Commissioners. He commented further that the old method of working contravened BoT regulations regarding the reversal of passenger trains, but short of 'removing the station to the crossing where it ought originally to have been built', he saw no real adequate remedy. If the W&LR were allowed to continue to use its new station a shuttle train might be run between the two stations.

Tighe submitted further plans in August 1880. These were discussed at a meeting in Holyhead between Messrs Findlay and Grierson, respectively of the L&NWR and the GWR, but were deemed unsatisfactory due to their close proximity to the crossing. Common sense eventually prevailed and in December 1880 it was agreed that the Waterford company should continue to use the GS&WR station for a period of 10 years from the following 9 May at the existing terms, viz £190 per annum. Approval was given in March 1881 for Tighe to remove the temporary shed and other items, and at the same time it was agreed to defer the doubling of the line to Tipperary. This latter was of course never carried out although further reference was made to the subject in July 1883 when it was estimated that it would cost in the region of £10,000.

Chapter Eight

A SHORTER ROUTE TO DUBLIN

Two schemes to serve the area north of Clonmel appeared in 1845. The grandiosely titled Thurles, Carrick-on-Suir, Clonmel & Nenagh Central Tipperary Railway Co was intended to connect Clonmel with Thurles and Nenagh through the collieries district. It was reported to have the support of the Mining Company of Ireland and was expected to derive a large and remunerative traffic, estimated at upwards of 200,000 tons annually, from coal alone. At a meeting of shareholders in April 1846, the decision was taken to abandon any attempts, at least for the present, of obtaining an Act. This was effectively the end of the first scheme. The second scheme, under the title of the Clonmel & Thurles Railway Co was to join the two points named in its title with a branch to the Slieveardagh Collieries. Included among the subscribers were John and William Riall, Joshua Malcomson, Samuel Perry and Thomas Samuel Grubb.

At the W&LR half-yearly shareholders' meeting in February 1846, the Earl of Glengall made reference to the new line as competing with the W&LR, most of the Clonmel traffic up to then going via Waterford; if the new line was constructed much of this traffic would flow northwards. At what was described as a highly respectable meeting of the C&TR shareholders held at Hearn's Hotel in Clonmel in April 1846, consideration was given to dissolving the company. This hurdle was overcome and the Clonmel & Thurles Railway Act received Royal Assent on 18 July 1846. Before we look at some of the details of the line as described in the Act, it is important to note that reference was once again made to the company at the W&LR half-yearly meeting in August. Mr Fennell inquired whether there was a clause in the Thurles & Clonmel Railway Bill (sic) compelling it to construct a viaduct over the River Suir at Clonmel so as to join the two lines. Mr Riall, who was in attendance, said there was no such clause in the Bill. It must be remembered that at this point in time, there were plans for the W&LR line to run to the south of the river here, as described in Chapter One.

The C&TR was to form a junction with the W&LR, then swing northwards to cross the river (despite the earlier reply to Mr Fennell),

passing Powerstown Demesne and running parallel to the Thurles branch as eventually built, but slightly to the west, as far as Lisrouagh. There it would turn northwest and follow the line of the present R688 road through Rosegreen to connect with the GS&WR Holycross to Cashel line just west of the latter town in the townland of Hore Abbey. A branch was to deviate from the GS&WR line in the townland of Thurlesbeg, following the line of the Cashel branch as later built to Ardmayle, from whence it would turn almost due east through Laffansbridge (also referred to as Laffan's Bridge by the companies) to a terminus in the townland of Lanespark and parish of Killenaule. Capital was to be £400,000 in £25 shares, with additional borrowing powers up to one-third of that amount. Section 38 of the Act empowered the company to amalgamate with, lease or sell to the GS&WR, while Section 41 enabled the new company to take, lease or purchase the section of GS&WR line between Cashel and Thurles. The latter was most likely Holycross, the point of junction with the GS&WR main line.

Birth of the Southern Railway
The powers for the line expired in due course and we have to move forward almost 20 years to a W&LR board meeting on 19 November 1864 when the directors considered Parliamentary Notices, including one for the Southern Railway Company (SR). This short but imposing title was appropriate as the scheme envisaged tramways in

The two-road engine shed and water tank at Clonmel. The track disappearing behind the shed is the Clonmel to Thurles branch. W. A. Camwell/IRRS collection

Tipperary, Cork and Waterford and railways between Thurles and Clonmel, Youghal, Fermoy, Lismore, Cappoquin and Dungarvan. It was largely promoted as a shorter route to Dublin, avoiding Limerick Junction. Working arrangements were proposed with the GS&WR, W&LR and the Cork & Youghal Railway. There was also a rival scheme under the title of the Clonmel Lismore & Dungarvan Railway Co.

At a meeting of the provisional committee held at No 1 Great College Street, Westminster, on 5 January 1865, those present included Peter Graham in the chair, Thomas White and E. N. Burgess. Also present were the secretary, R. F. Mulvany, the engineer, John S. Burke and the solicitor, B. Kernaghan. It was announced that letters had been received from the Tipperary County Surveyor, which were considered highly favourable to the undertaking. By the following May it became clear that Parliament was in favour of only the section of line from Clonmel to Thurles, the extensions to the south of the former therefore being withdrawn.

At a board meeting of the SR held on 18 July 1865 Peter Graham was elected chairman. The Graham family, which were to be closely connected with the affairs of the company for many years, were eminent and wealthy London furniture manufacturers. It is said that their large financial involvement in the affairs of the SR brought about the bankruptcy of the long-established firm of Jackson & Graham of Oxford Street in London in the late 1870s. At the same board meeting, it was reported that Thomas White had resigned as a director, but he was shortly to be appointed as the line's contractor. In October the directors decided to reduce Mulvany's salary to £250 per annum, payable quarterly. He had recently been paid an amount of £291 13s 4d, his salary up to the date of the passing of the company's Act in July 1865.

A contractor is appointed

Early in December, it was announced that a contract had been entered into with Thomas White, a railway contractor of Salt Hill, near Slough, for the construction of the entire line at an amount of £217,300. The line was to be completed and ready for opening on 1 October 1867, and the works including the erection of three ordinary roadside stations, at Killenaule, Cashel Junction (Farranaleen) and Fethard, along with the necessary junctions with the GS&WR and the W&LR. Permanent way was to consist of rails weighing 60lb per yard with transverse sleepers of Irish larch or Baltic timber from Memel or Dantzic (sic).

Reporting to the shareholders at their first meeting in December, Graham made reference to the apparently excessive expenses involved in obtaining their Act. He reminded shareholders that the Bill, as originally submitted, was based on almost 92 miles of line; Parliament, in its wisdom, had chosen to grant most of this mileage to other companies. Also in December, it was reported that the W&LR had raised objections to the site of the proposed junction at Clonmel, situated as it was proposed between the goods shed and the engine shed; at this period the latter was situated beside the station. If located here, the goods yard would 'be much cut up'. Tighe recommended that it should be located about 400ft to the east of the engine shed.

Poor finances and the surrender of a contract

The company suffered a severe financial setback in May 1866 when it was reported that its backers, the Imperial Mercantile Association, had gone into liquidation. White, who had commenced work at the Thurles end of the line, had to reduce his works to the minimum. It is to be regretted that this was to be the first of many such setbacks which dogged the company for many years to come. In deference to the wishes of the W&LR, the company obtained an Act in July 1866 allowing of the necessary deviation at Clonmel. The Act also empowered the construction of branch lines

from Graystown, roughly equidistant between Fethard and Horse & Jockey, to various collieries in the Ballingarry area. Powers were also granted for an additional £60,000 capital. There had, in addition, been moves to provide railway accommodation to the town of Cashel from Farranaleen, but despite a well-supported meeting held in the town in July, the Cashel Junction Railway Bill was withdrawn. In October, a Professor Sullivan was requested to report on the coal district of Killenaule 'at an expense not exceeding £25'.

The question of accepting the surrender of White's contract was considered in December 1866. Before making any decision, White was called upon to report on his total expenditure and liabilities to date. At the same time the company's officers were requested to render any outstanding accounts. By the early part of 1867, work was at a virtual standstill, with the line left in the care of watchmen. White owed freight charges to the W&LR and in July it seized some 3,000 sleepers which he had in store. In addition, a number of creditors, including Messrs T. & C. Martin of Dublin (sleepers) and the Ebbw Vale Company (rails), served writs against the company. The directors appear to have completely lost heart about this time and the board minutes indicate that no board meetings were held between then and September 1868. It was reported that the chairman and the secretary were the only people to turn up, and even the former failed to do so after some months. The shareholders likewise appear to have lost interest, no half-yearly meetings being held during 1868.

When the directors did finally meet again on 23 September 1868 consideration was given to the abandonment of the project. It was reported, however, that a subscription of £1,750 had been received and it was therefore decided to resume operations. It was also reported that the company's engineer, John Smith Burke, had died on 19 May; he was succeeded by Sir Charles Fox, who agreed to hand over to the representatives of the late Mr Burke one-half of the profits of the fees to be paid to him (Fox). Sir Charles immediately set about inspecting the line and reported his findings to the board in October.

Further correspondence arrived from Thomas White, addressed from the Bombay, Baroda & Central Indian Railway, in which he stated he was now preparing to leave Indian matters in charge of his son and return to Ireland. He was of the opinion that he should still be allowed to carry out the remaining works on the SR as he 'had looked for the return of a profit as a recompence (sic) for embarking on the undertaking at its earliest stage'. A sense of bitterness at not being allowed to resume the works is evident in a letter from him

dated 16 March 1869. Some three and a half years later, White was again in India carrying out Government reclamation works and 'working on doing no good for himself beyond earning scanty bread, being kept down by having to work with money borrowed from natives'. At this stage he even sought £1,000 of the £20,000 owed him, presumably to pay off his debts. In truth, of course, he might have been little better off in the SR contract. White's contract was formally surrendered by agreement in May 1869.

Negotiations were entered into with Messrs Brockett Shields & Muir of London but do not appear to have progressed very far as a provisional contract was then awarded to a Mr Maxwell Bury. A brief article in the *Clonmel Chronicle* for 21 December 1869 reported that work would resume in the following January, the Thurles to Fethard section to be completed within six months and the entire line in 18 months. Hopes were expressed that the local people would subscribe a sum of £35,000 after the railway had been opened. These projected dates were, however, to be wildly optimistic. Funds were so low early in 1870 that Peter Graham had to lend money to pay the office rent. No board meetings were held until July when the directors heard that six Court Judgments had been obtained against the company, which was not in a position to pay any of them. When all the movable goods were auctioned at Thurles on 2 August, only £2,000 was realised. It was in this context that the directors decided to go to Parliament in 1871 seeking powers for landowners to subscribe, to borrow £30,000 from the PWLC, to seek capital or dividend guarantees from the GS&WR, and, if possible, to obtain a baronial guarantee.

The directors approached the GS&WR in March 1871 seeking to negotiate a working agreement on the basis of 50% of gross receipts for a period of 10 years from the time of completion of the main line. The branch to the collieries was to be completed within two years. Ilberry replied on behalf of the GS&WR confirming it was prepared to accept the terms offered for the main line, but would only work the collieries branch at cost.

Yet another contractor

It was also announced in March that yet another contractor, Frederick Appleby of Manchester, had been appointed. Appleby offered to have the Thurles to Fethard section ready for opening by May 1872, the remainder of the main line and the branch to Slieveardagh by March of the following year. The tender for the main line was £130,000 with an additional £40,000 for the branch. He agreed to take preference shares to the extent of £55,000 in part payment. Work recommenced but was suspended

within a month as unpaid landowners refused to give up possession of their lands. There was at least one exception to this as it was agreed to give Thomas O'Mahony a free pass for himself and his wife, to be renewable annually, on completion of the line from Thurles to Clonmel, in return for facilities afforded to the company as to the possession of land. Perhaps this was given as an incentive to others to do likewise! Work recommenced yet again in August but it was not long before the directors were complaining that Appleby was not carrying out his duties satisfactorily. Yet another offer came in November 1871, when J. P. Ronayne of Cork advised that he would prosecute the works if Appleby withdrew, which the latter agreed to do.

Terms were finally agreed with Ronayne in July 1872, by which time much of the works between Thurles and Laffan's Bridge, a distance of 9½ miles, had been completed. Despite a measure of agreement arrived at with the GS&WR, this latter company appeared reluctant to subscribe any capital, so the Southern directors again turned to the W&LR for financial assistance. Application was made for a subscription of £50,000, which was approved by the latter company. As a natural follow-on, a working agreement was proposed on the basis of 60% of gross receipts up to receipts of £17 per week, reducing by 1% for each £1 increase per week until a figure of 55% was reached for gross receipts in excess of £22 per week. The subscription was to be paid on the basis of £25,000 upon completion to Fethard, a further £15,000 when opened to Laffan's Bridge, and the final £10,000 on completion of the main line. When the W&LR discussed the question of a subscription with the GWR, Sir Daniel Gooch is reported to have commented that the Killenaule branch would be 'the cream of the Irish lines'.

Ronayne applied in May 1874 for payment of £10,000 on account of monies due to him. He was informed that the board was in the course of negotiating a loan with the PWLC. The latter body required the company

to procure from the Judgment Creditors releases of its judgments and accept in lieu, ordinary fully paid-up shares at a 25% discount. A cheque for £10,000 was handed to Ronayne in June following receipt of £26,666 from the PWLC, the first instalment of a loan of £55,000. The W&LR was, however, causing great loss to the Southern board due to its alleged delay in fulfilling its subscription contract; a cheque for £5,000 was duly lodged to the credit of the company in October, Ronayne getting a further £4,600 of this figure. By the end of 1874, bottom ballast had been laid for 12 miles, with rails for 11 miles on hand. Work was virtually suspended through the spring and summer of 1875 and, at the suit of Ronayne, office furniture and some rails were seized. In addition, the company's bank account was attached by the Chancery Court.

In August 1875, the engineer, Michael Betagh, was given three months' leave to go to India, his position being once again filled by Sir Charles Fox. Further complications arose in May 1876 when Ronayne died unexpectedly and his executors pressed for payment of outstanding monies, amounting to £16,000. The W&LR paid over a further £20,000 which was used to liquidate this debt. Work, which had once again been at a standstill in January, was now concentrated on the Clonmel to Fethard section; the works were taken over by Ronayne's former assistant, W. F. Madden.

Troublesome officers

Difficulties surfaced in 1877 with certain of the company's officers. It would appear that Kernaghan, the company's solicitor, was in poor health in February. In reply to a letter from him, the board advised that it preferred not to enter into any discussions with him, 'in his present state of health of the extraordinary theories he sets up in that letter'. These 'theories' appear to have related to payment to him for his services. In response to its reply, Kernaghan offered his resignation, but sought to withdraw it in March. In the following month it was

Above left: **Fethard station looking south towards Clonmel on 23 April 1955.** H. C. Casserley

Above right: **Fethard station building as seen from the road approach.** H. C. Casserley

suggested that Peter Graham's attorney might advance a sum of £50 per month for up to four months to enable Kernaghan to go abroad and obtain the rest and change advised by his doctors.

Meanwhile, R. F. Mulvany, the secretary, reportedly applied to Walter Graham for a temporary loan of £117 18s 4d to pay salaries and office expenses. Mulvany was severely censured for taking such action without the approval of the board. His failure to competently perform the duties of secretary was discussed in June, leading to a request for his resignation, the board offering to pay him a year's salary when it was in a position to do so. The offer was refused and he was therefore dismissed in July. In course of time, both Kernaghan and Mulvany sued the company. The former passed away in December 1877 and was replaced as solicitor by Edmond Power of Clonmel, while J. F. Quinton was appointed secretary the following month.

A measure of the financial state of the company at this time was its inability to pay accounts of £4 9s 0d and £12 4s 9d for printing and £13 11s 0d for advertising in the *Irish Times*. In fact, one newspaper refused to carry advertisements for Wharncliffe meetings. Throughout 1877, work had been at a virtual standstill due to shortage of funds. It had been decided to have intermediate stations at Fethard, Farranaleen, Horse & Jockey and Laffan's Bridge. The directors considered dispensing with Farranaleen and Horse & Jockey on the grounds of cost, but were advised against this course by

Sir Charles Fox. Work was restarted in September 1878 and by the following month, 280 men were at work between Fethard and Laffan's Bridge.

Agreement over Thurles

In April 1879, the GS&WR agreed to pay the expense of converting the existing engine shed into a new goods store and the provision of a new turntable for Thurles station. The SR was to pay for the necessary signalling and the laying-in of the junction, the former being installed by Messrs Saxby & Farmer. Finally, after some 14 years, the BoT inspected the section of line between Clonmel and Fethard, on 9 June 1879. Col Rich passed it as fit for public traffic, this portion of line being opened on Monday, 23 June. Initially, the BoT had sought the provision of a turntable at Fethard, or the use of tank engines, but this requirement was withdrawn. Hardly had the line been opened when complaints were made of the excessively high charges levied by the W&LR, which was having the effect of putting some local road carriers back in business. The W&LR, for its part, threatened to cease working the SR unless works at Clonmel, including the provision of a footbridge, were completed. The footbridge was in fact ready, but Messrs. Courtney & Stephens were seeking a guarantee of payment before allowing it to be erected. The Waterford company also complained of a shortage of permanent way men on the Southern line.

11

SOUTHERN RAILWAY BRANCH

Miles frm Thurles.	DOWN Trains to Clonmel.	WEEK DAYS ONLY. 1 1, 2, 3 Class. a.m. Arr.	Dep.	2 1, 2, 3 Class. p.m. Arr.	Dep.	3 1, 2, 3 Class. p.m. Arr.	Dep.
...	THURLES ...	...	10 7	...	1 45	...	5 40
5¾	Horse and Jockey	10 19	10 21	1 58	2 5	5 52	5 57
9½	Laffan's Bridge ...	10 30	10 31	2 13	2 20	6 5	6 10
14	Farranalleen ...	10 42	10 44	2 32	2 35	6 19	6 20
17	Fethard ..	10 50	10 55	2 42	2 55	6 27	6 40
25½	CLONMEL ...	11 15	...	3 15	...	7 0	...

Miles frm Clonmel.	UP TRAINS to Thurles.	WEEK DAYS ONLY. 1 1, 2, 3 Class. a.m. Arr.	Dep.	2 1, 2, 3 Class. a.m. Arr.	Dep.	3 1, 2, 3 Class. p.m. Arr.	Dep.
...	CLONMEL ...	...	7 10	...	11 45	...	4 15
8½	Fethard ...	7 30	7 35	12 5	12 15	4 32	4 35
11½	Farranalleen ...	7 42	7 44	12 22	12 25	4 41	4 43
16	Laffan's Bridge ...	7 55	7 57	12 35	12 45	4 53	4 55
19¾	Horse and Jockey	8 7	8 13	12 55	1 0	5 3	5 8
25½	THURLES ...	8 30	...	1 15	...	5 25	...

TRALEE AND FENIT RAILWAY BRANCH.

Miles frm Tralee			WEEK DAYS. All 1, 2 & 3 Class.		SUNDAYS. All 1, 2 & 3 Class.		
			a.m.	p.m.	a.m.	p.m.	p.m.
—	Tralee	Dep.	9 15	4 0	...	...	...
4½	Spa	,,	9 27	4 15	...	...	...
6¼	Kilfinora	,,	Flag	Flag	...	...	...
8	Fenit	Arr.	9 35	4 25	..	...	...
			a.m.	p.m.	p.m.	p.m.	p.m.
—	Fenit	Dep.	10 30	6 15	...	...	...
1¾	Kilfinora	,,	Flag	Flag	...	...	...
3½	Spa	,,	10 42	6 27	...	...	...
8	Tralee	Arr.	10 55	6 40	...	...	...

A page from an 1890 timetable.
Author's collection

The contractor gave his workmen a week's notice of dismissal early in October, but agreed to continue the works if he received payment of £8,300 by 13 October. It was necessary to borrow this amount from the directors and others, who agreed to a form of Indemnity. Walter Graham wrote at the end of October to Thomas White expressing the belief that the line would be completed and opened for traffic by the end of December. Graham was somewhat optimistic with his timetable. Nevertheless, by the beginning of December it was reported that the line was ready for opening as far as Laffan's Bridge, a further seven miles. The W&LR urged the Southern to notify the BoT as soon as possible as it was anxious to commence working before 1 January. In the interim, the W&LR chairman was deputed to meet his opposite number on the GS&WR to endeavour to conclude arrangements for the use of the latter's station at Thurles. When Tighe inspected the line between Fethard and Laffan's Bridge, he discovered a number of matters requiring attention and, as the remainder of the line was nearing completion, it was decided not to open the short extension.

Opening throughout

In March 1880, Tighe carried out a thorough inspection of the entire 25-mile-long line and listed a number of shortcomings. At Clonmel, some minor works were necessary, including the provision of a stop-block, urinal and a wall at the west end of the station. In addition, the SR had not paid the cost of gas fittings or half that as agreed for strengthening the footbridge. The station and station accommodation at Fethard were 'in a very unfinished state'. The walls of the station were very damp and the chimneystacks needed rebuilding. The road to the goods shed was also incomplete and required to be carried on as far as the carriage dock siding, which was lacking a platform. Other requirements there included the proper flooring-in of the goods shed and alterations to the cattle pen siding.

The station house at Farranaleen was likewise unfinished, there was no approach road, station furniture, lamps or even lamp posts, and fencing was lacking around the platform. The goods shed and platform and the cattle pens had not yet been provided. Similar remarks pertained to Laffan's Bridge and Horse & Jockey stations. Similarly, none of the intermediate stations on the line had signals or signal cabins, while many of the cattle passes were unfinished. Tighe also reported that the permanent way in 'the Wilderness', a narrow natural defile just north of Clonmel, was causing excessive wear of wheel flanges and some of the rails would soon require removal and replacement. Finally, houses were required at four of the five level crossings on the line. Tighe also pointed out that a siding was required at Laffan's Bridge for the accommodation of traffic from the Mining Company of Ireland. He was ordered in February 1881 to proceed with the necessary siding and bank, the Mining Company of Ireland to pay an annual rent of £7 10s 0d.

The line was inspected throughout by Col Rich on 17 April 1880 but the W&LR would not agree to its opening pending completion of its engineer's requirements. A further BoT inspection was carried out on 3 June. This time, Rich called for one or two small matters to be completed, including the provision of lamps and clocks at stations. Terms were also proposed by the GS&WR for running powers into Thurles station, which were accepted. The Southern was to pay 5% on half the cost of the GS&WR's 1m 15c of line between the point of junction and Thurles station, half the maintenance of this section to be charged to the SR. The Southern was also to pay 10% interest on the cost of the old station and platform and was to pay in proportion to the work done on its behalf, for the cost of working the station.

All outstanding matters were satisfactorily resolved, the entire branch being opened for public traffic on 1 July 1880. A service of three trains each way daily was provided, two of which gave connection with main line trains to and from Dublin. Journey time was 90 minutes each way over the branch.

In August, approval was given to a scheme of arrangement filed by the directors with the Chancery Division of the High Court in England, while in December it was again found necessary to apply to the executors of the late Peter Graham for a temporary loan of £10 for petty disbursements. By the time of the approval of the above arrangement, the judgment debts amounted to some £115,000, of which £21,000 odd was owed to Thomas White. In a letter addressed to his son, Betagh stated that Thomas White 'will be paid to the penny but the Grahams claim it, so your father had better look out'.

It was not long before complaints were being made as to the working of the railway, with reports of unpunctuality, poor connections at Thurles and the diversion of traffic via Limerick Junction. The Southern directors themselves were of the opinion that little attempt was being made to develop the traffic potential of the line. In April 1881, the traders of Clonmel referred the matter to the arbitration of the Railway Commissioners. Problems also arose as to the amount which the W&LR should pay for the use of Thurles station, the view being that if it incurred any further liability in this regard, then it would cease to run trains beyond Thurles Junction.

Despite their protests and threats, and their solicitor's opinion to the contrary, the Railway Commissioners decided that the working company was in fact liable for such charges, but not rent. When the GS&WR sought the rent in October, it was informed that the revenue of the company had been attached under a Sequestration Order. In May, when the W&LR engineer reported that water supplies were required at the intermediate stations at a cost of £120, the Southern directors complained that the supply had been considered adequate when the line was opened. They also took grave exception to the notion that the W&LR should consider it had the right to deduct expenditure of this nature from the SR receipts without prior communication with the Southern board.

In an attempt to stave off the inevitable, the Southern board offered 'B' debentures in discharge of various claims, and in May 1881, Messrs Courtney Stephens & Bailey were offered £1,420 debentures at par, agreement being reached on a figure of £1,600. However, Mulvany and other judgment creditors refused to accept the debentures in discharge of their claims. In the case of the PWLC, it stated that it had no powers to accept them against loan repayments, the company for its part advising that it had no other means of discharging the debt. In fact, it had found it necessary to raise debentures even to pay their proportion of the costs of the Commissioners' inquiry. The board made an application to the Dublin Stock Exchange seeking to have its shares quoted, a request which was, understandably, refused. It also sought a reduction in the interest payable on the Government loan from 5% to 3½%, a request which was also turned down. Further writs were served on the company, including one from the Dublin *Evening Mail* for £252 odd, it also refusing to accept debentures.

Further complaints against the W&LR came to light in May 1883 when it was reported that it had altered local and through rates without consultation. This had the effect of diverting traffic to road carriers, while Dublin to Clonmel traffic was rerouted via the Kilkenny Junction Railway to Waterford. Messrs Murphy, brewers of Clonmel, stated that they would send all their traffic to Limerick via Thurles if they could obtain a rate equal to what they were paying the W&LR. The secretary was reprimanded for approaching the GS&WR seeking such a rate, which was in any event refused, as the natural route in this case was by the W&LR. The latter agreed in August to revert to the old rates.

In September 1883, the County Surveyor for Tipperary suggested that a tramway to the collieries to the east of Laffan's Bridge would be of advantage to the company, he also being of opinion that the branch to Cashel would not be worth pursuing. The secretary spoke to several members of the

Horse & Jockey station looking north towards Thurles on 23 April 1955.
R. M. Casserley

Grand Jury who thought the tramway a good idea and it was felt that the Grand Jury would support such a line if promoted by the company. Despite these encouraging signs, the directors had more pressing problems and decided not to take the matter further. An approach was made two months later on behalf of the ratepayers of certain baronies regarding a light railway to Cashel, the board being asked if it would work such a light railway or tramway. It replied that it had no capital which could be applied as a contribution but agreed to do all in its power to aid construction and would arrange to secure through rates, and, if possible, working arrangements with the W&LR. In the event, Cashel had to wait another 20 years for a railway connection, which was then provided by the GS&WR from Goold's Cross to the north.

In October 1883, a request was made for a siding about three miles from Fethard. The secretary, having called on the parties concerned and inspected the proposed site, advised that a lime kiln was situated within 20 yards of the railway boundary and in his view if a siding were laid, traffic could be considerable. Despite the positive report, there is no evidence to suggest that a siding was ever constructed there. The W&LR advised that alterations were required to the points and signalling at Horse & Jockey station, works which would cost about £90 and which would ensure safety in working there. Once again the SR objected, but when it referred the matter to its engineer, Sir Charles Fox confirmed that the works would be a great improvement and necessary to increase traffic. The W&LR refused to carry out the work unless the cost could be stopped out of SR receipts.

The company's financial situation was by now deteriorating even further. In December it was reported that there were insufficient funds available to pay salaries and office expenses until the W&LR paid the net revenue in February. It was necessary once again to apply to the Grahams' solicitors in

March for an advance of £40 to enable the company to hold the half-yearly meeting. This sum was refused, but Gen Brownrigg sent a cheque for £10 to the secretary to enable him to attend the meeting, this to be refunded when practicable. The meeting did not in fact take place due to a lack of a quorum, but the chairman's report stated that in consequence of the W&LR retaining a proportion of the receipts rightfully due to the company, the directors were 'not practically in a position to carry on the business of the company'. Another blow was struck in May when the solicitors refused to incur any further expenses on behalf of the company until their claim for past costs was dealt with.

The beginning of the end came in October 1884 when the Lords of the Treasury instructed the BoW to take possession of the undertaking. At this point, £14,633 was outstanding by way of principal, along with £11,806 interest. The directors asked for sufficient time to call a general meeting of shareholders. Early in January 1885 the BoW requested a meeting at Clonmel to enable it to take formal possession of the line and the company's books. The secretary again announced his inability to travel to London, he being instructed to forward the books and papers. The company secretary, Quinton, was officially confirmed as receiver/manager in June, formal possession being taken in October, effectively bringing to an end the affairs of the Southern Railway as an independent company. The W&LR continued to work the line on behalf of the BoW. The company had the dubious distinction of being the last to be officially amalgamated into the GSR under the terms of Statutory Rules & Order No 9 of 1925. When efforts were made that year to find anyone claiming to have an interest in the SR, none came forward, hardly surprising after a lapse of 40 years. The story of the line's remaining years up to 1900 will be dealt with later under the heading of the W&LR.

Chapter Nine

INTO THE KINGDOM

Notices of intention to apply for powers for the construction of two lines in north Kerry were published towards the end of 1863. One was for the Limerick Foynes Tralee & Killarney Junction Railway, to construct a line from a junction with the GS&WR at Tralee to Foynes via Listowel and Tarbert. This was a revival of an 1861 scheme under the title of the Tralee & Tarbert Railway. Whilst a contractor, John Watson of London, had undertaken to construct the line subject to a guarantee on the county, nothing further was done towards obtaining powers. The promoters were shown as Messrs A. F. Croom and J. Overend, with G. W. Hemans as engineer. The second scheme was the Limerick & North Kerry Junction Railway, to connect the R&NJR at Newcastle West with Listowel via Abbeyfeale. Although the gradients around Barnagh were acknowledged to be steep, the more southerly course was adopted due to the support of two prominent landowners, Lord Listowel and the Earl of Devon, the latter having promised some nine miles of land free of charge.

An Act was obtained in 1865 for the L&NKJR scheme with a capital of £130,000 including powers for making working arrangements with the R&NJR and/or the W&LR, the latter being expected to work the R&NJR when completed. Mr H. Williams Wood was appointed company secretary. No progress having been made towards construction, a further Bill was notified for the 1868 Session to allow an extension of time for construction, but nothing happened in this regard. Then, in 1870, a scheme known

as the Foynes Listowel & Tralee Tramway Co Ltd was announced with a proposed capital of £50,000. The Knight of Glyn was appointed chairman with Messrs J. Cartwright and W. Fitzgerald as engineers. As this line was being promoted under the Tramways Acts, it was intended to be worked, at least initially, by horse power. Approaches were made to the W&LR seeking traffic rebates but it was informed that a decision would only be made after the line was constructed. This was in effect to be the end of the scheme.

Yet another company was provisionally formed during 1872 under the title of the Limerick & Kerry Railway for a line from Newcastle West to Tralee via Abbeyfeale and Listowel with a branch from the latter to the coast at Ballybunion. This was in effect a re-introduction of the L&NKJR scheme of 1865. The L&KR Act received Royal Assent on 5 August 1873 for the 42½-mile line with a capital of £260,000. The W&LR had, in the interim, agreed to subscribe a sum of £25,000, £10,000 of which was to be paid upon the opening of the line to Listowel, the balance of £15,000 upon completion to Tralee, where a junction was intended with the GS&WR. This subscription was dependent on a fair working agreement in perpetuity being secured to the W&LR as well as a guarantee on the counties of Limerick and Kerry being obtained.

At a board meeting on 29 August 1873, the Earl of Devon was elected chairman of the new company, with George Sandes as deputy-chairman, John Fowler was appointed consulting engineer, William Barrington of Limerick as engineer and Thomas Naan as

secretary, to be based in Limerick, where the company's offices were to be situated. Barrington was instructed in December to proceed at once with pegging out the line and the preparation of land plans etc. It was agreed that he would be paid at the rate of £40 per mile, one-quarter of which was to be paid in shares. The question of a working agreement was raised at a W&LR board meeting in April 1874, but it was decided to defer a decision until reports were submitted from the engineer and traffic manager, when a committee would be formed to consider the matter further. By May it was clear that some important alterations had been made as regards gradients and level crossings and the matter was again deferred.

This question was allowed to drift on and it was not until October 1875 that a decision was finally taken. The line would be worked so as to secure a minimum mileage charge of 2s 10d up to receipts of £11 per mile per week, then on a percentage of receipts, which would secure to the company 3s per mile. The L&KR directors found a difficulty in acceding to the terms put forward, particularly in relation to the proposed subscription. They felt that it would be more equitable if half the subscription was made within one month after commencement of the works, and the remainder one month after the opening of the line throughout to Tralee. As regards the working agreement, it was suggested that a similar agreement be entered into as was in force with the Rathkeale company, particularly in view of the large increase in traffic expected to be brought to the W&LR system. The W&LR directors however were unmoved by this suggestion and replied to the effect that they could not see their way, in the interests of their shareholders, to make any alterations to the original proposals. This was to be the first of many disagreements between the

Ballingrane Junction photographed in 1933 looking west. The station buildings are on the down side with the Saxby & Farmer signal cabin on the up platform adjacent to the level crossing. The two lines diverged immediately beyond the level crossing, that for Newcastle and Tralee swinging to the left while the Foynes branch went straight ahead. Ian Allan Library

two companies, some of which, as we shall see shortly, were to be extremely acrimonious.

The question of the working agreement with the W&LR was not finally resolved to the satisfaction of both parties until November 1878. It was finally agreed to increase the first portion of the subscription to £15,000 when the line was opened to Listowel, the L&KR paying interest at 4% per annum on the additional £5,000 until the line be opened to Tralee when the balance was to be paid. As regards the charge for haulage, the W&LR proportion was fixed at 60% of gross receipts up to £17 per mile per week. For each £1 per mile per week increase the percentage was to drop 1%, with a figure of 55% when the receipts were between £21 and £22 per week. The mileage earnings were to be calculated on an annual average ending on 31 December each year, when the percentage was to be finally adjusted. The W&LR agreed to grant the free use of a special train to Lord Listowel for the use of himself and his family and friends, at their own risk, five times a year during his Lordship's lifetime, between Tralee and Listowel. Twenty-four hours' prior notice was to be given of special trains, which were to consist of one first class carriage. Later, Lord Listowel advised that he did not wish any such arrangement to be made and, in fact, he resigned his position as a director at the end of 1878. The line was to be worked by a joint committee, with the W&LR secretary acting as secretary to that committee.

We must now review certain other events which occurred during this lengthy period of negotiations. In December 1873, it was reported that arrangements had been made with Messrs Jackson & Wise to act as contractors. However, in January 1876 we find 12 tenders were opened for the works on the line, varying from Michael Walsh of Foynes at £171,000 to Messrs Easton Gibb of Dundee at £225,000. Henry Jackson, presumably of Jackson & Wise, appears to have been successful, but in September 1878 Messrs Falkiner & Stanford's revised tender of £197,000 was accepted.

In May 1878, certain constructional matters were agreed. A turntable was to be provided at Listowel along with a water supply and tank, the goods store platform was to be widened to 20ft and refreshment rooms were to be provided; the latter are referred to further in Chapter Nineteen. The location of the engine shed was also to be altered, if possible. At Abbeyfeale another room was to be added to the stationmaster's house, while the goods sheds at Devon Road, Lixnaw and Abbeydorney were to be increased to 30ft by 120ft. In addition, a small goods shed was to be erected at Ardfert.

At the half-yearly meeting of shareholders in December 1878, Captain Charles Bingham was confirmed as company secretary in place of Mr J. Mitson who had died at the

end of 1877; Bingham's salary was confirmed at £350 per annum while the line was under construction. The Kerry board's attention was called early in February 1879 to the defective condition of sleepers in course of delivery, this matter being again raised in the following October.

An inspection of the L&KR line was carried out in December 1879 and Tighe subsequently reported that all earthworks were in a forward state except for those at Barnagh where the contractors had not gone within 5ft of the proper depth in the cutting to the east of the tunnel. The tunnel itself was being formed from each end and was stone lined. He reported that as regards ballasting, the stones used were too large, he being in favour of at least 4in of finely broken stones being used as packing under the sleepers. As regards buildings, construction of the goods shed at Abbeyfeale was almost up to roof level, but was badly in need of dressed quoins and jambs; the stones were reported to be of a dark sandy colour. The small shed at Devon Road exhibited a similar appearance, but no other station buildings or goods sheds were in hand, except that the foundations of the station building at Listowel were nearly at ground level. Reference has already been made above to the delivery of defective sleepers, and in his report, Tighe was able to

Top: **Rathkeale station looking east. The station buildings are on the single platform on the down side. Also on the down side, behind the photographer, was a siding serving the goods store and loading bank. The signal cabin was on the up side.** Ian Allan Library

Above: **Another view of Rathkeale station, again looking east but showing the goods facilities on the right with the signal cabin on the up side.** Ian Allan Library

confirm the removal of any unsuitable larch sleepers (presumably native) and their substitution by foreign timber.

When Tighe inspected the line again at the beginning of April 1880 he was able to report some progress in relation to building works. At Tralee, the station house and building were almost up to roof level, with the goods shed also in hand. Tighe proposed the reversal of the position of the engine shed siding and also putting the turntable at the top end of the platform rails. About that time it was decided to abandon the idea of a connection with the GS&WR, although this was revived some years later. The station building at Listowel was said to be 'got up well, the outside face being all dressed punched limestone, nearly ready for roofing as is the goods shed', and some alterations to the proposed track layout were required as the BoT had insisted on Listowel being a crossing station.

The buildings at Abbeyfeale were reported to be almost complete, and it was noted that the contractors, having initially agreed to Ardfert and Abbeydorney stations being built of concrete, had subsequently expressed their intention to revert to stone. Col Rich had also made recommendations regarding Newcastle West, requiring the station to be 'looked on and worked as a terminus instead of a roadside one'. To alleviate some of the likely problems with shunting, Tighe suggested the provision of a siding at the back of the goods store and the removal of the cattle pens to the angle of ground on the same side. Tighe also commented that whilst the contractors hoped to open the line by the following September, his experience suggested that it would not be until the beginning of 1881. Nevertheless, the locomotive superintendent was promptly instructed to go over the line and prepare specifications for engines suitable for working it, a decision being subsequently taken that two engines would suffice.

BoT inspection

Despite Tighe's earlier reservations, the L&KR secretary gave the statutory one month's notice to the BoT on 13 September regarding the proposed opening of the line. Lt-Col Hutchinson inspected the line early in November, but returned a fortnight later on 25 November. He referred to the line as being 42m 68c in length, single throughout but with sidings (and stations) at Barnagh, Devon Road, Abbeyfeale, Kilmorna, Listowel, Lixnaw, Abbeydorney, Ardfert and Tralee. Listowel was the only station suitable for the crossing of passenger trains. The permanent way consisted of flat-bottomed rails 18ft to 24ft long and weighing 70lb per yard on partly rounded sleepers; ballast consisted of shingle and broken stone to a depth of 11in. The ruling gradient was 1 in 61 and the sharpest curve was of 20 chains radius. There were 12 over- and 19 under-bridges, four river bridges and 43 culverts. Although Hutchinson makes reference to the cutting at Barnagh being 93ft deep through rock, he did not comment on the tunnel.

There were 14 authorised level crossings with adequate gates and lodges, and there were turntables at Tralee, Listowel and Newcastle. As regards the latter station, it was arranged only as a terminus and to make it suitable as a passing place it would require another cross-over road and two additional signals. Finally, Hutchinson reported that strict instructions were necessary for the safe working of Barnagh station in view of the severe gradients. He instructed that the siding points should be kept open until a train departed towards Newcastle West. Trains from Tralee should

not be shunted on the main line and it was recommended that each train be provided with two brake vans and two guards, either both at the tail end or one at the centre. Permission was granted for opening the line on 15 December, subject to the completion of some minor requirements and, in fact, a service of three trains each way daily commenced running as from Monday, 20 December 1880.

In the course of his inspection, Hutchinson also suggested plans for making Abbeyfeale a crossing station, the engineer being instructed to proceed with the necessary works. However, other works were causing problems and it was resolved by the W&LR board in January 1881 that, unless outstanding works required for the completion of the line were finished within two weeks, it would have no option but to cease working the new line. At the same time it was reported that a memorial had been received from the inhabitants of Tralee for a passenger entrance at Edward Street, this request being declined. Also in January, the *Railway Times* reported that the GS&WR, whose line from Mallow via Killarney to Tralee had been opened to the latter point in July 1859, were promoting a bill to enable it, *inter alia,* to form a junction with the L&KR at Tralee.

Complaints were made at a joint committee meeting in June 1881 in relation to the inadequacy of locomotives and rolling stock in use on the line. More powerful engines were sought along with better carriages and newer wagons. Instructions were given for attention to be paid by stationmasters at either end of the line to the cleaning of carriages. Two other items raised at the June 1881 meeting were the provision of a siding near Listowel station and a flag station at Killacrim (Ennismore). A Mr Latchford operated a corn mill about ¾ mile south of Listowel station and had written requesting the installation of a siding. Following an inspection by Tighe, it was considered advisable to install a separate siding and turntable beside the running line, at which point the gradient was 1 in 82. This latter would obviate the need to use of horses for hauling wagons to the station, and it was considered that the siding should be extended to the station itself, a distance of ¾ mile.

The request for a flag station at Ennismore crossing came from George Hewson, but it was not until April 1882 that an agreement was finalised in this regard. However, as early as August 1883, it was ordered that three months' notice be given to terminate the agreement, the company stating that it did not consider itself bound to give any explanation for the decision. Despite this, the instruction was rescinded the following November, when instructions were given that trains would not be stopped

for Hewson's servants, but only for members of his family and visitors stopping at the house. Once again, in September 1884, the board decided upon discontinuing the accommodation. On this occasion it was clear that Hewson had been canvassing for proxies against the board, but again it relented. Hewson was causing some concern again in March 1889 when it was reported that he was canvassing for the proposed Newcastle and Buttevant line and yet again the decision was taken to withdraw the facility at Ennismore. This time the board refused to be persuaded to change its mind and the station was finally closed on 18 July 1889.

Reference has already been made to the intention of the GS&WR to seek powers for the connection of the two lines at Tralee. In October 1881 it submitted plans of the proposed junction arrangements, the L&KR finding itself unable to express an opinion and suggesting a meeting of the engineers and traffic managers of the companies. This was held on 29 October, and the W&LR engineer was instructed to send an amended tracing to both the GS&WR and the L&KR for approval. In December, the W&LR considered that the GS&WR should pay for the junction works, a platform extension, covered-way and conveniences. It was hardly surprising that the latter company objected. It was agreed that the L&KR should provide a ticket platform at its own expense and that it should carry out the platform and covered-way works. Plans were finally agreed in August 1882, but the matter appears to have dragged on, passenger trains not running through until 1901.

Appointment of a traffic inspector

At the half-yearly meeting of the L&KR shareholders in February 1883, the chairman reported that the development of local and through traffic continued to progress, despite 'serious difficulties with which they had to contend'. The increase was far less than might have been anticipated had the line been as efficiently worked as they had a right to expect, 'which has not been the case'. The directors went as far as stating that legal proceedings might be necessary to settle the problem. Complaints were made to the W&LR in June 1883 in reference to the want of sufficient and superior rolling stock and also to the irregularity in and the insufficiency of the train service. The question of rolling stock had been first raised at a meeting of the joint committee as far back as June 1881, but to no effect. Third class passengers had been forced to travel in first and second-class carriages 'to the great inconvenience of those who occupy them and have paid the higher fare'. The W&LR response to both complaints was that it had taken over the line in an incomplete state and that outstanding

Ex GS&WR 'J15' 0-6-0 No 151 and coach at Newcastle West, although the station nameboard simply refers to it as 'Newcastle'. Note the overall roof over part of the platform and track. On the left can be seen the goods store. The engine is facing towards Rathkeale, the line on the far side of the platform being for trains to Tralee.
Photographer unknown/S. Kennedy collection

works had not been finalised. It said it was not usual to place new carriages on branch lines and that sufficient rolling stock was provided. In fact, a banking engine was provided for assisting trains up Barnagh bank at great expense to the company!

Relations gradually deteriorated over the next couple of years and things came to a head following the appointment of a traffic inspector by the L&KR. Consideration had been given in October 1883 to such an appointment, but it had been decided to defer the matter for three months and rely on extracts from reports supplied by the W&LR traffic inspector, Mr McAdoo, being furnished monthly. It soon became clear, however, that it was virtually impossible for one inspector to adequately supervise the entire Waterford system. So we find Edmond Cooke being appointed traffic inspector to the L&KR in September 1884 at a salary of £125 per annum. He was also appointed to a similar post on the R&NJR at the same time, the latter company agreeing to find him a house and contribute half the cost of furnishing it, and for two suits of clothing per annum.

Within two months of his appointment, the W&LR had made two complaints against him: first, that he had been found smoking in a non-smoking compartment. Cooke said that he was simply holding an unlit cigar in his hand at the time, although a member of the traffic staff reported having seen him actually smoking both on the platform and in the compartment. The second complaint related to Cooke travelling in uniform in a first class compartment. The W&LR threatened to withdraw all of Cooke's facilities and he was duly instructed to travel second class while in uniform, and any class he desired when not so attired.

It soon became clear that the W&LR was being as obstructive as it could to Cooke in the performance of his duties, in not providing him with information requested. The L&KR board then decided that the solution to the problem was to appoint him a director, which it did in August 1885. In explanation, it said it had been forced into this action by the fact that all other legitimate efforts to obtain access to traffic records and station accounts had been thwarted by the actions of the W&LR. It went on to state that they would be quite willing to allow Cooke to revert to his previous position if the W&LR would co-operate and allow him the

information requested. In September 1887, the L&KR agreed to Cooke taking up an appointment as general manager of the newly formed Listowel & Ballybunion Railway, so long as it did not interfere with his duties on the L&KR.

In June 1889, it was reported that a joint committee meeting due to be held on the 16th of the month had been postponed due to the non-attendance of the W&LR representatives. Two months later, matters took a turn for the worse when George Hewson resigned as a member of the joint committee and was replaced by Cooke. Resulting from this appointment, no joint committee meetings took place for the next 21 months. Initially, the W&LR representatives attended, protested at Cooke's presence, and then walked out. Later, either one side or the other, but not both, would turn up for meetings.

In May 1889, the W&LR threatened to apply to the Irish courts for the appointment of a receiver to the L&KR in consequence of non-payment of interest on its debenture stock holdings. Before the matter proceeded further, a larger creditor, Lord Halifax, took similar action in Britain, resulting in the appointment of a Receiver. The W&LR action was heard before the Master of the Rolls in Dublin on 20 November 1890 but was in effect thrown out. At the same time, the question of Cooke's appointment was referred to the Railway Commissioners, who decided his appointment was valid, but they did not allow the L&KR its costs. By 1894, the W&LR was again dragging its feet on the matter of attendance at joint committee meetings and were threatened with steps to compel its attendance. This was despite the fact that a meeting had taken place between the chairmen of the two companies to sort out their differences.

Similar action took place with the R&NJR, no joint committee meetings taking place following Cooke's appointment. The W&LR attitude was that Cooke's appointment was illegal as he could not be a director at the same time as he was receiving a salary. The

whole affair would have been comical but for the fact that the travelling public were the ones who suffered from a poor service and inferior rolling stock.

Monorail to Ballybunion

The story of the Listowel & Ballybunion Railway (frequently referred to as the Lartigue Railway) has already been told in at least two recent publications (see Bibliography) and need not therefore be dealt with in detail at this point. Suffice, however, to state that as early as September 1883 a tramway scheme to connect the towns of Listowel and Ballybunion was being proposed by Father M. O'Connor, the parish priest of the latter place. The scheme was defeated due to strong local opposition to the fact that it would have involved a baronial rate of 1s 4d in the pound. Another scheme under the title of the Limerick & Kerry Light Railways Company also sought powers for a similar line, but to 5ft 3in gauge; this company sought running powers over the L&KR, leading to it being strenuously opposed by the W&LR. As a consequence it was withdrawn before going before the committee stage. Two years were to pass before a notice appeared in the *Dublin Gazette* of an intended line between the two points, to be worked on the Lartigue monorail principle. So it was that the Listowel & Ballybunion Railway Company became a reality with its incorporation on 16 April 1886, with the Earl of Devon as its chairman.

The Ballybunion company was, to some extent, affected by the differences between the Kerry and Waterford companies, and may even have contributed unwittingly to some of those differences. In September 1887, the L&KR suggested the laying down of a siding and the provision of a footbridge at Listowel. Estimates were received in October for a lattice iron footbridge from Messrs Westwood of Millwall in an amount of £195, which was approved by Tighe. He also approved of the other works, the company consenting to pay half the cost of the footbridge but declining to bear any expense in connection with the erection of

An Up train for Limerick at Listowel station in charge of 'J15' 0-6-0 No 156 on 12 June 1953. The station building can just be seen on the down side beyond the footbridge. The unique Listowel & Ballybunion (Lartigue) Railway had its terminus behind the railings on the right-hand side of the picture. D. G. Coakham

the siding and of a platform for the L&BR traffic. These latter works, the Waterford company believed, should more correctly be borne in full by the newcomer. A payment of £400 was sought in advance of instructions being given for the commencement of the works.

Also, in October, Captain Bingham wrote to the W&LR requesting permission for the L&BR engines to take water at Listowel. Two months later an agreement was prepared by John O'Connor, the W&LR solicitor, for water to be provided at a fixed rent of £4 10s 0d per 6,000 gallons per week, any excess over that amount to be charged at a rate of 1s per thousand gallons. The L&BR was also granted permission to erect on its own ground, a water tank capable of holding 1,000 gallons. The total amount due for water was to be paid to the W&LR. This latter requirement produced a furious response from the L&KR solicitor, who pointed out that the Waterford company was only entitled to water required for the working of the Kerry line. Any quantity over and above that was the property of the L&KR, to be disposed of as that company thought appropriate; were it not for the small amount involved and the short notice contained in the agreement, the Kerry company would not have agreed to accept it.

Another dispute arose in December 1887 when the W&LR wrote to the L&KR demanding that the balance of freight due by the L&BR for the carriage of construction materials be paid forthwith, failing which the amount due (£279 4s 0d) would be deducted from the Kerry company's traffic receipts. Needless to say, this also raised a strenuous response from the latter company. It would seem that the W&LR carried out its threat, as the traffic manager reported in the following March that he had received a sum of £245 from the L&BR against this charge, and it was agreed to

refund this amount to the L&KR. The opportunity of seeking the balance was taken to ask for other outstanding matters to be seen to, including the repair of fences broken down, without permission, at Listowel station.

The matter of the footbridge rumbled on for some time, Hutchinson having called for the provision of one when he carried out his line inspection of the L&BR in February 1888. Attempts were made in August 1892 to have the Limerick Grand Jury contribute to the cost, but it politely declined. At one stage, arrangements were made to refer the matter to the arbitration of Mr Robertson of the GNR(I), but the bridge was finally provided in August 1894.

There are some other matters which occurred during this period that merit brief mention. The L&KR complained regarding the state of Barnagh Tunnel in July 1882, this being dismissed by the Waterford company's engineer. Devon Road was made a flag station in November 1887, and a line was proposed in February 1889 from Newcastle to Buttevant, but the Order was turned down by the Grand Jury.

It was reported in July 1884 that George Hewson was quarrying stones inside the railway fences on both sides of the line at Ballintogher. Three months later Tighe reported that lime kilns were being erected and in March 1885 it was stated that the Ballintogher Quarry Company was proposing to use its own wagons. The locomotive superintendent reported that they were not to the W&LR specification as they had 3ft diameter wheels instead of 3ft 6in and the buffers were also reported to be out of line with those of the W&LR. A charge of £4 10s 0d was made in June for the haulage of two such wagons from Waterford to Lixnaw. A request for a siding to the running line was made in January 1886, this being acceded to and permanent way

materials supplied. A connection was also made to the company's siding at Lixnaw in 1888 to facilitate this traffic.

Before taking a look at the further short extension of the line to Fenit, brief reference must be made to a Bill promoted by the L&KR in the 1885 Session of Parliament. This envisaged the amalgamation of the R&NJR and the Tralee & Fenit Railway (more fully referred to in the following paragraphs) with the L&KR. This was vigorously opposed and was thrown out on Standing Orders. Immediately following this, the L&KR made allegations to the Railway Commissioners regarding the manner in which its line was being worked, the case being dismissed with costs. Then, the W&LR sought to have an arbitrator appointed to force the L&KR to carry out the provisions of an agreement of December 1880, whereby the latter company was to undertake certain works on its line. When the notice for the appointment was submitted to Lord Devon, the L&KR chairman, he refused to sign it. The W&LR then instituted proceedings for the appointment of a Receiver on foot of debenture stock held by it in the L&KR.

A short extension to the Atlantic

Tralee, the principal town of Kerry, is a trading and industrial centre. It derives its name from the Gaelic *Trá Lí*, the 'strand of the River Lee' and was founded in 1216 by John FitzThomas Fitzgerald. The town was burnt by the Earl of Desmond in 1580 as part of his 'scorched earth' policy, so the present town of Tralee owes its origins mainly to the 18th and 19th centuries. It is perhaps best known today for hosting one of Ireland's major festivals, the Rose of Tralee, held each year at the beginning of September. The town itself is situated about 1½ miles from the shore of Tralee Bay. Up until the 19th century the harbour for Tralee was at Blennerville, a village about 1½ miles distant. This latter village is today the terminus for the short length of the reopened narrow-gauge Tralee & Dingle Railway. Here, vessels of up to 250 tons could discharge at the quay, but larger ships had to anchor in the bay and discharge their cargoes into lighters at Fenit, some seven miles from Tralee.

In 1828, construction of a ship canal from Fenit to Tralee had been authorised with a loan of £24,000 provided by the Exchequer Loan Commissioners. Construction commenced in 1832, but money ran out two years later and work ceased. Labourers' wages did not apparently contribute greatly to the shortage of funds as explained by Henry Inglis, an English visitor to the area at that time. Inglis commented: 'The canal indeed employs many (about 400), but the wages are extremely low; and in this rainy climate, it often happens that the labourers, after working in the canal from five in the morning to eleven in the forenoon, are discharged for the day with the pittance of 2d.' A further loan was sought and the Treasury recommended the works being taken over by the BoW. Work recommenced in 1844 under the supervision of the BoW and the canal was finally opened for traffic in April 1846.

Even with the canal open, difficulties were encountered as it could be approached only at high water through a narrow and tortuous channel over three miles in length from Tralee Bay. Over the years, the importance of Tralee as a port grew with a new trade in Indian corn. In later years the canal gradually silted up, proposals being put forward in 1880 for the construction of a deep-water quay at Fenit with a rail connection to Tralee. It is claimed that St Brendan the Navigator was born in Fenit in AD484, although others claim he came from Annagh just across the bay. Fenit had one other claim to fame, as it was here that German guns and ammunition were to have been landed in Easter 1916 from the vessel *Aud*. Today, it is an important sea-angling centre and has extensive oyster beds.

Two pieces of legislation were passed in 1880, namely the Tralee & Fenit Pier & Harbour Order 1880 which received Royal Assent on 2 August and, 24 days later, Royal Assent was also given to an Act which incorporated the Tralee & Fenit Railway. The estimated cost of the pier and harbour works was £95,000. The pier was to be constructed from the foreshore of Tralee Bay seawards in a southeasterly direction to Great Samphire Island and then in a northeasterly direction for 330 yards from the island. The T&FR Bill as lodged included four lines of railway, two of which involved connections with the GS&WR terminus at Tralee. As the result of a petition lodged in the House of Lords by the L&KR, these two lines were dropped and the Act had lines connecting only with the L&KR.

Railway No 1 was 3f 5c in length, Railway No 2 (the actual branch) 6m 9c in length, terminating in the townland of Fenit Without on the foreshore of Tralee Bay. Capital was £45,000 in £10 shares with additional borrowing of up to one-third of this amount. The first directors included the Earl of Devon, Sir Henry Donovan, Samuel Hussey, Robert McCowen and Richard Latchford, the latter an important merchant of Tralee. Powers were given for the county

of Kerry to contribute a sum equal to a dividend on the capital expended up to £30,000 at 5% per annum for a period of 35 years after the opening of the railway for public traffic.

Section 68 of the Act made provision for the purchase of the ship canal by the company from the PWLC. In this regard, a sum of £5,400 had already been paid, the balance of the £8,000 purchase money to be paid at the rate of £200 per annum. Section 73 then made additional provision for the transfer of the ship canal to the Tralee & Fenit Pier & Harbour Commissioners, this latter body to pay the same price for the canal as the railway company had done. A schedule to the Act comprised Articles of Agreement made on 29 May 1880 between the T&FR, the L&KR and the W&LR, whereby the latter company was to work the line. Under Article 3, the L&KR was obliged to construct a single line of railway parallel to its existing line between its terminus at Tralee and the termination of Railway No 1 of the T&FR. A sliding scale was laid down for the division of the gross receipts of the line. When the average gross receipts amounted to not more than £17 per mile per week the W&LR was to retain 60%. These figures altered such that the W&LR retained 55% when the receipts amounted to £22 and upwards — the agreement was in perpetuity.

It is interesting to note from the Book of Reference accompanying the Parliamentary Plans that virtually all of the land required for the construction of the T&FR was owned by Sir Edward Denny, Bart. Under the terms of the 1880 Act, the directors duly appointed Messrs Herbert, Hewson and Hussey to be members of the T&FP&HC in April 1881. Robert FitzGerald was appointed secretary to the T&FR in September 1881, but it was not until November of the following year

A visitor to the line — 'J26' 0-6-0T No 560 (ex MGWR) at the intermediate station at Spa between Tralee and Fenit on 5 June 1961. R. M. Casserley

that his salary was fixed at £150 per annum. It would appear that FitzGerald had received no remuneration up to this time as the directors also agreed that he should be paid the sum of £100 on account.

A contract is signed
In September 1881 the tender of Messrs Falkiner & Tancred was accepted for the construction of the railway. Despite this apparently promising development, no moves were made towards construction. The problem appears to have been due to the non-production of plans and specifications for the approval of the W&LR engineer, and it was not until December 1882 that a plan of the alterations required at Tralee station was submitted. By this time the W&LR had refused permission for the contractors to commence work on the section of line between the terminus at Tralee and the proposed junction of the two lines at Mounthawke.

The matter of plans and specifications dragged on into 1883 and in March the T&FR suggested referring the question to arbitration as laid down in Article 29 of the working agreement. The W&LR in due course replied in May to the effect that it 'could not indulge in the luxury of an expensive arbitration, unless the T&FR was prepared to pay all expenses occasioned by them'. It did, however, agree to refer the plans to a BoT inspector to say what accommodation should be offered for the traffic of the T&FR. Some works were

Fenit station area photographed from the extension to Fenit Pier. In WL&WR days Fenit handled considerable volumes of fish traffic. G. Beesley

obviously being carried out by August 1883, when the W&LR complained that the contractors had taken away iron gates from Rock Street crossing in Tralee and substituted wooden gates. The former had been removed to another part of the Fenit line, and the W&LR engineer was instructed to insist that proper gates were erected at Rock Street.

In January 1884, Sir Henry Donovan reported that he had had an interview with two English gentlemen connected with the fishing off the Kerry coast, stating that they were prepared on and after 1 March to deliver about 100 tons of fish daily to the T&FR at Fenit, if facilities could be provided for landing and sending forward the fish by rail. An approach was made to the W&LR for the supply of the necessary rolling stock, the response being that the Fenit line working would be taken up only when it was completed, according to agreement. This was to be some 3½ years away.

In the interim, an application was made to the BoT in November 1883 for a certificate to authorise the deviation of about 2½ miles of the line, approval being granted in May 1884. Lt-Col Hutchinson, on behalf of the BoT, issued an award in March 1884 in relation to various works to be carried out. It was agreed that the platform roof at Tralee station should be extended northwards for a distance of 120ft; the goods store was also to be lengthened, by 25ft. It was further agreed that the W&LR should not be liable to provide such additional accommodation at Tralee as might be rendered requisite by the traffic from the T&FR line until five years after the opening of that line — this was to allow time for the traffic on that line to develop. Instructions were also given in relation to the stations on the branch. That at Spa was

to have a platform 250ft in length, the station house to resemble that on the L&KR at Ardfert. In addition to the plans submitted for Fenit station, an engine shed was to be constructed with accommodation for one engine, and a proper water crane, tank and engine turntable were also to be provided. The cost of the award amounting to £169 2s 6d was divided equally between the three companies.

Work proceeded slowly and on 31 December 1885 the L&KR wrote to the W&LR advising that the line was ready for opening and requested that Mr Tighe should carry out an inspection. Tighe inspected the line in mid-January 1886 but found 'several instances of incomplete and unfinished works'. However, the T&FR advised the BoT of its readiness for opening and Hutchinson declared the line fit for passenger traffic following his inspection only a month later. Tighe was instructed to again inspect the line, the result of which was a list of requirements. These included inadequate arrangements as to Kilfenora station, the non-completion of a gatehouse near Tralee and a lack of station furniture.

A board meeting of the T&FR held on 15 July 1886 under the heading 'Conduct of the Company's affairs' may perhaps give a clue to some of the problems. The board was reconstructed and future meetings were to be held in London, to which the company's offices were moved. FitzGerald's engagement was terminated and Charles Henry Bingham was appointed in his place at a salary of £150 per annum — Bingham already holding the post of secretary to the L&KR. Finally, a Finance & General Purposes Committee was appointed to oversee day-to-day matters.

Correspondence with the W&LR in August 1886 stated that a platform 150ft by 12ft would be erected at Kilfenora so that it could be used as a signal station. This was only one aspect of the outstanding works, yet a month later the T&FR threatened to open the line itself and seek relief from the working agreement. This could not have

been more than an idle threat as the directors must surely have realised that they would have had no prospects of working profitably a line only eight miles in length in such an isolated location! The contractor, in response to a query, advised in December that the outstanding works would cost £860. However, the W&LR engineer also advised that the removal and replacement of bad sleepers and ballast would cost a further £646. The T&FR responded by offering £600, this being rejected and the full amount was reluctantly paid over in March 1887.

Ticket and luggage label cases and dating presses were acquired from Messrs Edmondson of Dublin in May 1887 at a cost of £55 2s 0d. Also in May, the W&LR complained that its brake van No 6, apparently on loan to the contractors, was being used for the conveyance of women passengers and corn. A final inspection was carried out by Tighe on 15 June and although some works remained undone, he saw no reason why the line should not open on 1 July. In fact, the opening for public traffic took place four days later on Tuesday, 5 July with a service of three trains each way. Early indications were that virtually the whole of the line's earnings derived from passengers. No coal was carried as the local merchants considered the rate demanded by the W&LR to be prohibitive at 2s 9d per ton as opposed to 1s 6d by lighter.

Accusations of mismanagement
Reference has already been made to the difficulties encountered with the appointment of Edmond Cooke as inspecting director of the L&KR. Hardly had the T&FR been opened then he was proposed by the Earl of Devon as inspector of the new line at a remuneration of £25 per annum. Only three months after the opening of the line complaints were being made locally of mismanagement by the working company in not taking sufficient steps to develop the traffic. A specific complaint in December 1887 made reference to allegations that the W&LR had made no endeavours to secure Messrs Donovan's corn traffic. This referred to a cargo of 1,500 tons of corn which the firm had proposed to import to Fenit. Discussions also took place in relation to the working by the company of traffic to and from the pier. In this regard, Tighe had inspected the harbour extension works but had expressed his dissatisfaction with the permanent way and the viaduct giving access to the pier.

One of the three commissioners appointed by the railway company to the T&FP&HC in 1881, Samuel Hussey, resigned his position early in 1888 in protest at the working of the T&FR. The position in relation to the working of the harbour traffic continued to dominate many of the

Fenit station on 13 July 1934 showing 'J15' 0-6-0 No 102 on the 13.15 passenger train to Tralee. Note the double smokebox doors on the engine. H. C. Casserley

company's board meetings throughout 1888. Correspondence was submitted in March with the Waterford Steamship Company and Mr McCowen in regard to mackerel traffic which the steamship company proposed should be accepted by the W&LR. The traffic manager was ordered to make the necessary arrangements to secure this traffic. Two months later, McCowen was complaining of the want of carriage accommodation on Sundays; two months later again, he offered a cargo of 800 tons of timber between Fenit and Tralee at 7s per ton, this figure being declined by the W&LR. Pending the completion of an agreement for working the traffic to and from the pier, the Harbour Commissioners gave permission for the use of the pier extension by the company's engines.

The chairman of the company, the Earl of Devon, died on 17 November 1888, a sad loss. It was due to his enterprise and public spirit that the T&FR might fairly be said to owe its very existence. His just, wise and sympathetic management of his estates in Limerick and Kerry had done much to improve the prosperity of the company. Mr F. Collis Sandes was in due course elected to succeed the late Earl.

Financial matters came before the board in February 1892 when the Scottish Provident Institution, which held the entire of the debenture issue of the company, agreed to allow future receipts of the line, which were applicable to the payment of its interest to the extent of £900, to be applied to the construction of an additional siding at Tralee station. Differences between the Harbour Commissioners and the company led to the withdrawal of the W&LR engine as from 1 September 1892. From this point onwards relations between the harbour authorities and the W&LR deteriorated, so much so that when the former offered a sum

of £1,000 for engine No 42, it was turned down despite the fact that it was way above the actual value of the engine. Later, in April 1899 it was reported that the door of the engine shed at Fenit had been forced and an attempt made to house the Commissioners' own engine there. The W&LR flatly refused to allow the shed to be rented.

Financial matters

In October 1892, Mr Robert Nagle, a ratepayer, endeavoured to obtain a conditional order to quash the last Grand Jury presentment on the grounds that the line had not been completed within the five years set down in the company's Act of Incorporation. The case came before the High Court in February 1893, which decided in favour of the validity of the guarantee and the company recovered its costs. It should also be mentioned that Robert FitzGerald, who had been the T&FR's first secretary, became secretary of the Grand Jury. In April 1893 he wrote to the company stating that he had received Counsel's Opinion and as a result was unable to send the company a cheque for the presentment. Instead, he required the personal attendance of the secretary. He also refused to accept the authority sealed by the company in favour of its bankers.

Later, in May 1895, it was reported that FitzGerald, who was a judgment creditor, had seized, through the sheriff's officer, the company's books and papers and had threatened to sell them, but of what value these would have been is difficult to imagine. The company was forced to go to litigation over the matter and, in due course, the Court of Queen's Bench Division in Dublin ordered FitzGerald to return all the documents, which he did. Worse was to come as when Sir J. B. Greene, one of the arbitrators appointed under the company's 1880 Act died early in 1896, the BoT

appointed FitzGerald in his stead. The company entered a strong protest and FitzGerald resigned the position in May 1896. He obtained a judgment against the company in December 1901 for £812 11s 0d, being his outstanding salary with interest. The company had consistently claimed inability to pay due to lack of funds.

Further difficulties occurred with the Harbour Commissioners during the last years before the demise of the WL&WR. In July 1893, it was ordered that engines were not to go on to the pier as the viaduct was reported to be defective. A contract for repairs was given to a Mr H. Peet for £434. Then in October 1894, the Commissioners sought an annual rent of £200 or half the gross receipts for the privilege of working the pier traffic. This was turned down by the W&LR, and the Commissioners considered providing their own wagons. Complaints were frequently made regarding shortage of wagons, but to no effect. In February 1898, the T&FP&HC intimated its intention to charge 1d per ton on all goods carried over its line with a view to recouping the cost of track repairs and maintenance. This was also turned down by the W&LR, which now threatened to discontinue the working. Nevertheless, payments on this basis were made under protest.

The T&FR remained as an independent company following the 1901 amalgamation, but our story will be closed at this point. Brief details of subsequent happenings are related in a later chapter.

Chapter Ten

NORTHWEST FRONTIER

Mention has already been made of the GN&WR company's opposition to the supporting of the A&TR scheme by the MGWR. In an attempt to appease Lord Lucan, an agreement was signed between the three companies in June 1858 whereby the A&TR agreed not to promote any further extension northwest of Tuam, the Midland for its part agreeing not to assist any scheme for such an extension, unless the GN&WR should fail to proceed during its time with its Castlebar extension. This latter was pushed ahead 'in the hope of frustrating any attempt to construct the Swinford line and to secure themselves from competition from the A&TR line also'. The line was opened in stages, Castlebar being reached on 17 December 1862. For a more detailed description of this line, the reader is referred to the companion volume on the MGWR.

In December 1868, the A&TR wrote both to the Midland and to the W&LR advising that it was promoting an extension from Tuam to Claremorris and offering to include powers for either company to subscribe up to £20,000 and also to work the line. The MGWR refused to give any undertaking, while the GN&WR board minutes simply mention the proposed extension. The W&LR on the other hand added its seal to the Bill but went on to say that this was not to be considered in any way as binding the company 'beyond what any subsequent mature consideration as to permissive subscription or working their undertaking may be declared'. Nothing further happened at this time, but the matter was to be raised again three years later, an Act being obtained in 1872. The powers so obtained were allowed to lapse and nothing further was done for another 18 years.

During the second half of 1889 a number of schemes surfaced briefly. These included the Tuam & Westport Railway, the Tuam Claremorris & Ballinrobe Railway and the Tuam & Claremorris Direct Light Railway. In the event, an Act was obtained in 1890, promoted by the A&TR, for a 17-mile-long extension under the cumbersome title of the Athenry & Tuam Extension to Claremorris Light Railway Company, the project being passed by the Privy Council on 26 September, the Order itself following two months later.

In March 1890, the A&TR solicitors had reported that the County Mayo Grand Jury had sanctioned the undertaking and guaranteed dividends on one-third of the necessary capital, but that the Galway Grand Jury had refused the application chiefly owing to strenuous opposition from the MGWR (which favoured a line from Tuam to Ballyhaunis and which it was in fact prepared to work when completed), but ostensibly on the grounds that the Mayo Grand Jury should have guaranteed a larger proportion of the capital. However, five months later, when the latter had consented to guarantee the entire capital, it refused 'on technical grounds'.

The Mayo guarantee was, however, conditional on a satisfactory working agreement being concluded with the W&LR for a period of at least 20 years. An agreement was in fact concluded with the W&LR in September 1890 for the latter company to work the line for a period of 20 years from the date of opening on the basis of 50% of gross traffic receipts, subject to a minimum payment to the owning company of £51 per week. The A&TECLR was obliged under the agreement to construct the railway with stations, permanent way etc. 'in every respect equal to the best portion of the existing line between Athenry and Tuam', rails to be steel weighing 72lb per yard. It was also obliged to provide and pay for two engines and 30 wagons suitable for a light railway. The two engines were W&LR Nos 43 and 44, respectively named *Knockma* and *Nephin*. The W&LR wagons nominally allocated for the line are listed in the rolling stock appendix — nominally because in reality, although the extension company's rolling stock returns were shown separately from those of the working company, they were not in fact used exclusively on the extension. It is quite possible even that some of them never actually ran over the line.

At a board meeting held on 19 January 1891 it was announced that a contract had been entered into with Messrs William M. Murphy & Company for construction of the railway from Tuam to Claremorris; regrettably no amount is shown. At the same meeting, William John Kennedy, who had been the acting secretary, was formally

appointed to the post of company secretary. The company's solicitors, Messrs O'Connor & Dudley, wrote to the Midland in February 1892 inquiring whether it might assume that the latter company had no objections to the proposed junction at Claremorris. The Midland replied to the effect that it did object and it was necessary to refer the matter to the BoT to decide on it. Sir Douglas Galton inspected the layout at Claremorris on behalf of the BoT on 21 June and in due course made his recommendations.

When plans for a temporary passenger station, engine shed and goods shed for Claremorris were submitted to the W&LR in December 1892, the board called for a report which was submitted to it for consideration in the following February. The engineer reported that the deposited plans were for the junction with the MGWR to be made at the south end of the latter's station, whereas the latest plans envisaged a connection into the proposed branch of the Ballinrobe & Claremorris Light Railway. If this latter were adopted the feeling was that the A&TECLR should construct the junction and all associated works free of expense to the W&LR. In response to this suggestion the Extension company stated that it had 'gone to great lengths and incurred considerable expense, solely in the interests of the W&LR, to obtain a junction different from the deposited plans as the Waterford company considered the original junction disadvantageous. The mode of effecting the junction is a matter of indifference to our (A&TECLR) shareholders.' The extension company would construct and pay for the junction if the BoT would arbitrate and agree to the revised arrangements. It should be mentioned here that the proposed new layout resulted from the plans submitted by the Claremorris and Collooney extension, which are considered in more detail later.

Frederick Lewin, the County Mayo Grand Jury representative on the Board, intimated that the Grand Jury would strongly object to any departure from the deposited plans. Thus ended any idea of forming a junction with the Ballinrobe branch, and the proposed location of the temporary station was approved by both companies. Following a conference with the MGWR in April 1893 it was reported that it had also agreed

An AEC diesel railcar set stops briefly at Swinford on a Sligo to Limerick service on 23 April 1953. H. C. Casserley

to a double-line junction being formed 'about 100 feet east of their footbridge'. There were however three provisos, viz (i) the MGWR passenger station should be used by the W&LR, no other such station to be constructed either by the latter company or by the extension company, (ii) the junction to be made at the entire cost of either the W&LR or the A&TECLR, and (iii) the cost of the necessary alterations and additional accommodation required at Claremorris and also by the W&LR running into and through it to be borne by that company. Any differences or disputes were to be referred to arbitration.

The new line was inspected by Lt-Col Hutchinson early in November 1893 on behalf of the BoT and although he was happy enough with it, the W&LR detailed a number of additional requirements at Claremorris, including extra sidings and four cattle pens. A goods shed was sought at the temporary station 'without rails going through but with a projecting roof for wagons and carts'. The locomotive superintendent asked for a turntable and a water supply and, in lieu of an engine shed at Claremorris, he requested that the one at Tuam be extended by two-thirds. Finally, the line was opened to traffic to the temporary station on 30 April 1894 with intermediate stations at Castlegrove, Milltown and Ballindine. Prior to the opening some other matters came to light. Back in February 1893 it was reported that the contractors had refused to do any work in the existing Tuam yard as they claimed their contract

was restricted to the provision of the junction. They did however agree to erect a brick signal cabin and a signal to the north of the station. Following the obtaining of legal opinion Messrs Murphy were informed that the A&TECLR was obliged to provide additional station accommodation to cater for their traffic and of course it would be expected to pay half of the cost of maintenance and working there.

Frederick Lewin advised in November 1893 that an application had been made at the Road Sessions for a grant of £150 to make a road to Castlegrove station and inquired regarding arrangements for goods traffic. He was informed that the company would undertake to deliver goods 'which the facilities at the station enable them to work' in other words the provision of facilities was not a matter for the W&LR. Lewin returned to the question of goods facilities on a number of occasions up to May 1895 from which it would appear that they had been at least inadequate up to that time. A Claremorris extension board minute of 17 May 1895 refers to an inquiry carried out by Maj Marindin of the BoT into alleged insufficiency of accommodation at that time. Marindin laid down additional works, which he considered necessary, and it was reported that Murphy had put these works in hand.

The water supply at Claremorris proved inadequate and the contractor was instructed to make inquiries as to the possibility of piping water from the nearby Mayfield Lough or by other means. It was not possible to come to an agreement in relation to the use of the Midland station at Claremorris and it was found necessary to refer the question to the BoT to decide. Lt-Col Hutchinson arbitrated on the question of the costs of the provision of the junction and the other alterations necessary and in July 1895 he awarded an amount of £4,650 2s 9d to the Midland. Then, at the beginning of August,

the MGWR wrote advising that the W&LR would not be allowed to use the station or run through to the Collooney line until the conditions and payment for this service were agreed on. The short section connecting the two companies' stations was opened for traffic on 1 October 1895, the same day as the Collooney extension was opened. The matter of payment for use of the Midland station was in due course referred to the arbitration of Henry Plews, general manager of the GNR(I), his award being issued in August 1896.

We must now return some years and turn our attention to the proposals for a line northwards from Claremorris.

Final push northwards

As early as 1882, proposals were being put forward to effect a communication northwards from Claremorris in the direction of Collooney and Sligo. Henry Tottenham persuaded the Sligo Leitrim & Northern Counties Railway (SL&NCR) to take an interest in the promotion of such a line, which resulted in a draft agreement for the proposed line to be worked by it. Two schemes emerged in 1884: the Collooney & Charlestown Light Railway and the Charlestown, Claremorris, Ballinrobe & District Light Railway. Neither of these schemes went beyond the proposal stage and it was to be October 1890 before the notion of such a line was raised again. The W&LR now took an interest and stated that it would work such a line if the Government would advance money for its construction. The Swinford Board of Guardians reported in favour of the project and of it being worked by the W&LR.

We have already seen how various Acts had been passed to enable the Government to subsidise lines of communication. In 1889, yet another piece of legislation was enacted. The Light Railways Act of that year, applicable only to Ireland, was passed to provide for a situation where it was desirable that a light railway should be constructed between certain places for the development of fisheries and other industries, but owing to the circumstances of the district special assistance from the State would be required for its construction.

The Act was to apply only under the following conditions: (a) where the promoters of the light railway were an Irish railway company having a railway open for traffic, or (b) where the promoters had made an agreement, approved of by the Treasury, for the maintenance, management and working of the light railway by such a railway company, or (c) where the promoters in making application to the Grand Jury of any county under the Tramways (Ireland) Acts proposed that a barony or baronies in the county would guarantee the payment of dividends upon a portion of the paid-up capital of the light railway. In return the Treasury would make funds available and, in addition, application might be made to the relevant Grand Juries for a baronial guarantee on the paid-up capital of the light railway. A number of lines were constructed under the provisions of the 1889 Act, including the Claremorris to Collooney extension and the three western branches of the MGWR.

In February 1891, Messrs O'Connor & Dudley approached the W&LR Board and suggested that it might send a deputation to attend the Sligo Grand Jury to explain how it would be prepared to work the Claremorris to Collooney line being promoted by the A&TR. It was stated that another, practically identical, line was being promoted by the SL&NCR under the title of the Claremorris & Collooney Junction Light Railway & Tramway Company. In addition, a line was proposed from Swinford to Foxford, which would hopefully benefit Ballina. After protracted discussions the Sligo Grand Jury granted a presentment to the SL&NCR in an amount of £80,000 towards the construction of a line between Collooney and Swinford (then known as Swineford), leaving the question of working the line open for further consideration. The Mayo Grand Jury came down in favour of the W&LR proposals for the line from Claremorris to Swinford. It might here be mentioned that this particular line was known amongst railwaymen as the Burma Road.

Despite the division of the proposed line at Swinford, the W&LR stated that it was willing to work the entire line on the terms of the two presentments, agreeing either to construct the line if capital was advanced in line with the BoW estimates for constructing and equipping the line with rolling stock, or would take over the line when completed. Having agreed on the former, a committee was formed to negotiate with Henry

Tottenham for the transfer of the Sligo Grand Jury presentment, agreement on this issue being reached on 29 October 1891. Two Orders were passed in August 1892, viz the W&LR (Claremorris to Swineford [sic]) Railway Order and the W&LR (Collooney to Swineford) Railway Order.

Many matters were common to both Orders but there were also some interesting differences. Both laid down that rails were to be of steel and to weigh not less than 72lb per yard, the gauge was to be 5ft 3in, no gradients greater than 1 in 70, and both could be constructed and worked other than as light railways. Motive power was to be animal, steam or by any mechanical means. The railway was to be transferred to the Grand Jury if the guaranteeing areas were called upon to pay during a period of three years any money for the maintenance or working of the undertakings. No passengers or goods were to be carried on the roof of any wagon or carriage, other

than with the prior approval of the BoT! Under both Orders running powers were to be granted to the SL&NCR if required by the Treasury. Finally, both lines were to be completed by 31 December 1894.

Although a number of Acts were passed referring to light railways, none of them defined what a light railway was. Joseph Tatlow suggested that 'the most recognisable feature of a light railway is its light traffic', J. C. Conroy being of opinion that gauge was 'not necessarily the differentiating element, nor does the length or location establish it'. He felt that financial assistance, either local by way of baronial guarantees or from the State might be 'regarded as a necessary concomitant of a light railway'. Either way, the two lines in question could not be defined as light in terms of their gauge or the weight of rails. They certainly did receive financial assistance as suggested by Conroy and they were cheaply constructed as regards lack of steep gradients etc.

Regarding the Claremorris to Swinford section, the County Mayo presentment allowed for the payment of dividends at 4% per annum on a sum of £40,000, while the Treasury grant was not to exceed £59,000. There were to be stations of a substantial and permanent character at Swinford,

Above: **Above: Carrowmore station on 7 June 1961.** H. C. Casserley

Left: **Collooney station looking towards Collooney Junction on 25 August 1956. The signals in the left background control the approach to Collooney Junction. The MGWR line crosses over the spur to the right, which provided access from the WL&WR line to the SL&NCR.** D. G. Coakham

Kiltimagh and two other intermediate points if required by the BoW. At Claremorris, junctions were to be made with the MGWR and the B&CLR. It was laid down that the W&LR was to provide a service 'for ever thereafter' of at least three trains each way daily, Sundays excepted, two of which were to be passenger trains and to run in connection with those on other undertakings including the Collooney extension. In the case of this latter, the capital guaranteed by the presentment amounted to £80,000, the Treasury grant not to exceed £91,000. The company was required to erect stations at Collooney, Coolaney, Knockadoo or Carrowmore, Tubbercurry, Curry, Charlestown and Swinford and at one other intermediate point if required by the BoW. Five railways were listed in the Order, three of which represented junctions at Collooney. Rolling stock to the value of not less than £23,000 was to be provided in addition to that to be supplied for the Claremorris to Swinford section. It is interesting to note that no reference is made to rolling stock in the latter Order.

It is clear from a reading of the two Orders that the BoW had entered into preliminary contracts to carry out essential earthworks and fencing. These contracts were awarded to relieve distress and to provide employment. The *Western People* reported on sod-turning ceremonies at Tubbercurry by Canon Staunton, PP, at Kiltimagh by Father Denis O'Hara, PP, and at Swinford by Mr. A.J. Staunton, chairman of the local Board of Guardians. Contracts were awarded to Robert Worthington on 8 January 1891 and to William M. Murphy & Co on 26 January 1891 for earthworks on the following sections:

Claremorris to Swinford. Worthington between Claremorris and Lislackagh, and Murphy between Lislackagh and Swinford.

Swinford to Collooney. Worthington between Collooney and Tubbercurry, and Murphy between Tubbercurry and Swinford.

The *Connaught Telegraph* for 3 January reported that some 2,000 men were in want of work. Murphy initially engaged about 100 at Swinford; fearing a riot, 40 additional policemen were drafted in from Ballinrobe. It was a similar story at Tubbercurry where Canon Staunton was out at 7am endeavouring to prevent riots there. By the end of January, about 1,400 men were employed and the works were continued until August when many of the men left to look after the new harvest. By the following January, distress was again widespread but it was not until 1 April that the BoW awarded a further contract to Murphy for the fencing of the entire line.

A general election was held in 1892, Gladstone being returned to power. One

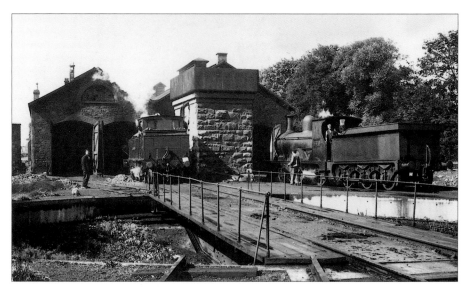

Sligo shed on 20 August 1938 with Class G3 2-4-0 No 293, ex W&LR No 48 *Granston*. On the left is SL&NCR tank *Lough Gill*.
H. C. Casserley/SLS collection

casualty of the election was William Martin Murphy who lost his Parliamentary seat. Murphy, who was also a major shareholder in the Dublin United Tramways Co, had been Nationalist MP for St Patrick's, Dublin, since 1885. The fencing contract was again only by way of remedial works and in December 1892 a resolution of the Tubbercurry Union was received urging the W&LR to progress the works and so provide employment. Two months earlier, on 21 October, William Murphy's tenders (one for each section) for the construction of the entire line had been accepted. On 16 December, however, with no works in progress, he was ordered to appoint caretakers to protect the works so far completed. Murphy wrote to the W&LR on 19 January 1893 pointing out certain difficulties which had arisen with the contract and seeking to formally withdraw his tenders. The main problem as far as Murphy was concerned was that the BoW appeared to have greatly undervalued the land required and as he had tied himself in to these estimates he was bound to lose heavily.

The board now instructed its solicitor and engineer to open negotiations with Robert Worthington and with Messrs Fraser & Falkiner, and Worthington's tender was accepted in April 1893. In August, it was reported that BoW expenditure to date totalled £65,539 17s 3d, of which £41,052 14s 0d related to the northern portion of the line. Hints of difficulties with Worthington surfaced in August 1893 when he requested a remittance of £696 to pay the current week's wages to his men. A cheque for this amount was passed to the solicitor with instructions that it only be handed over in return for Worthington's agreement to alter the notice clause in his contract from 14 days to 24 hours. It is therefore hardly surprising, when we read that Worthington's contract was determined as from 2 November, the machinery, plant, horses, etc were taken

over. Obviously unaware of the reasons behind the determination of the contract, resolutions were received from the Boards of Guardians of the Claremorris and Swinford Unions and from the inhabitants of various towns, urging continuation of the contract.

Fresh tenders were received in December, including one from Messrs Worthington and John C. Smith, who was at this time engineer to the DW&WR. Later, it had to withdraw its tender as the DW&WR would not allow Smith to act as Worthington's partner or even to become security for his son. The new contract with Messrs Fisher & LeFanu was finally approved in January 1894 and work could again resume. In June 1894 the new contractors sought and were granted permission to obtain materials at Westport and Claremorris rather than at Collooney and Sligo as they intended working northwards from Claremorris. June also saw a protest from the SL&NCR 'in the strongest manner' against the scheme for the proposed junction with its line at Collooney. Differences also soon arose with the MGWR regarding additional accommodation required at Sligo, which was to be reached by running powers over the line from Collooney. While these matters were under discussion the W&LR traffic manager suggested that Coolaney and Charlestown should be made passing stations for all trains and not just for goods and cattle as proposed. He also suggested that the name of the former be altered due to its similarity with Collooney — this was referred to the engineer who suggested the name Leyny. Lt-Col Hutchinson proposed continuing the line to a junction with the Midland at Carricknagat, but this idea was quickly abandoned.

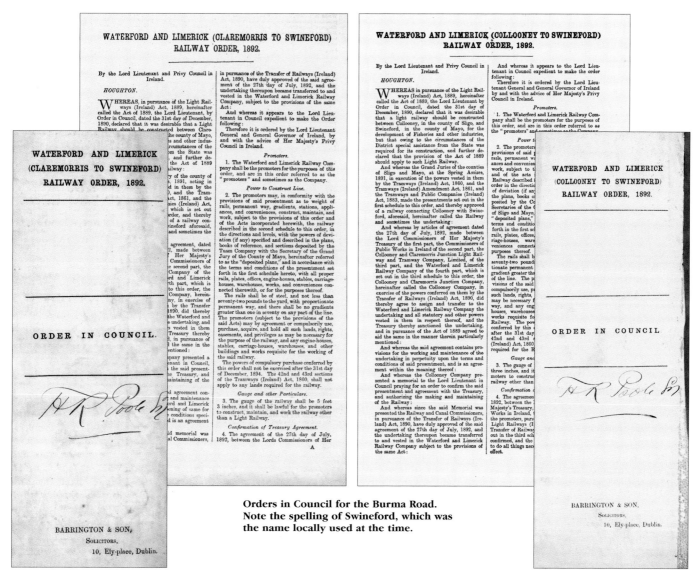

Orders in Council for the Burma Road.
Note the spelling of Swineford, which was
the name locally used at the time.

Hutchinson also made recommendations regarding junctions and stations at Claremorris and Collooney. At the former it was agreed to abandon the short line to, and the junction with, the Ballinrobe branch. The companies failed to agree on Hutchinson's recommendations for Collooney, leading to the engineer being requested to prepare fresh plans in April 1895. The BoW wrote in June with a resolution from the SL&NCR suggesting that the W&LR should make a payment of £1,750 for alterations at Collooney, £125 per annum for a shunting horse until such time as the traffic justified an engine, and a further annual payment of £125 to cover the cost of working the junction. These payments were considered to be 'preposterous demands', and the company resolved to refer the matter to the BoT. As regards the accommodation at Sligo this matter was referred to the arbitration of Edward J. Cotton of the Belfast & Northern Counties Railway. When Cotton announced his award in July the W&LR board stated that it could not accept its terms and was

taking steps to have it set aside, changing its mind a month later. The company, in due course, accepted Messrs Fisher & LeFanu's tender at £1,835 3s 0d for the necessary works at Sligo. This did not include an extension to the engine shed for which the MGWR quoted a figure of £3,150, £1,700 being accepted by the latter company in January 1896; this was to accommodate three W&LR engines.

The W&LR wrote on 15 August to the Midland to the effect that pending settlement of terms for the use of Claremorris station it intended opening its line throughout from Tuam to Collooney as from 1 October. This was to be a close call as the BoT inspected the line in mid-August and postponed the opening for a month. The contractors agreed to provide a luncheon for the opening on condition they be given assistance with invitations.

The line was in fact opened for traffic on 1 October 1895 following a further BoT inspection by Maj Marindin. The junction with the SL&NCR at Collooney was also

reported to be complete, but it was not until the end of July 1896 that Col Addison finally sanctioned its use, subject to certain requirements, a contribution of £1,250 being made in due course towards it by the Waterford Limerick & Western Railway as it became. As regards Claremorris, agreement was reached for a payment of £500 per annum to the MGWR for 10 years. Shortly after the opening it was agreed in November, that Leyney should be made a crossing place at a cost of about £550. This figure was later revised to £900 after the traffic manager recommended that the passenger accommodation should be nearly opposite the existing platform rather than staggered. In April 1896, plans were submitted for the station at Tubbercurry, a tender from John Houlahan being accepted the following month.

With the opening of this last remaining piece of the system, the W&LR jigsaw was now complete. The next chapter looks at the remaining five years of the company's independent existence.

Chapter Eleven

FINAL YEARS OF INDEPENDENCE

At the board meeting on 23 June 1887, the secretary handed in a requisition signed by 33 signatories calling for an extraordinary general meeting for the purpose of appointing a shareholders' committee to examine the company's books and accounts with a view to investigating its financial position. The board agreed, if the chairman should so decide, that notices be issued to include powers for the removal of Abraham Stephens as a director. The EGM was called to follow immediately after the conclusion of business at the shareholders' half-yearly meeting on 23 August. In his address to the shareholders in August, the chairman, James Spaight, made reference to the 'incessant agitation kept up by the Dublin Shareholders' Committee for some years past'. The requisition for an extraordinary general meeting had come at a time when the directors were fully occupied in measures to oppose repeated attempts by the MGWR to gain control of the A&EJR system. It was no coincidence that more than half the persons signing the requisition were Midland shareholders; 'the motives influencing their action in the matter will be sufficiently apparent'.

A committee of eight shareholders was appointed. These included Thomas Cairnes, deputy-chairman of the Bank of Ireland, and a director of the GNR(I), George Russell, Thomas Grubb representing the Waterford shareholders' interests and Anthony O'Connor, the only W&LR director on the committee. It was agreed that the committee would have power to appoint a skilled public accountant and such other assistance as might be deemed necessary. Eleven meetings in all were held and the report was completed on 17 February 1888. Three experts assisted the committee in its deliberations under three broad headings: Messrs R. Mackay & Co, chartered accountants of London (financial), J. S. Macintyre MICE, (permanent way, works and rolling stock) and E. J. Cotton, general manager of the B&NCR (traffic arrangements and agreements with other companies).

Investigations had shown that the permanent way and works were substantial and in a satisfactory, well-maintained, condition. The same could not be said, however, of the rolling stock and plant. Renewals had fallen seriously in arrears, the average age of the stock being excessive. In addition, the shops at Limerick were 'very deficient in facilities for getting the work in or out', although improvements were currently being made in this regard. Furthermore, the tools etc in the existing shops were old and in bad condition, overworked and insufficient. Further details regarding the locomotives and rolling stock can be found in Chapters Fifteen and Sixteen.

The company's accounts and finances were generally in fair order, except for the accounts of the revenue receipts, for which the system of keeping and checking left room for improvement. Macintyre suggested that greater efficiency and economy could be secured by the concentration of the Traffic Audit Department in Waterford. The inability of the company to pay a dividend on the ordinary shares was due to such a large portion of the capital stock consisting of debenture and preference stocks. Any further expenditure on capital was to be avoided as far as possible, strict economy being observed in revenue spending consistent with the safe and efficient working of traffic and maintenance of rolling stock, way and works.

E. J. Cotton had a number of comments to make in relation to matters of traffic and competition. Rates and fares generally corresponded to the average charged by other Irish lines. However, some aspects could be improved. The issue of single-journey passes to traders, pig buyers, cattle dealers and the like was 'most objectionable' and should be looked at closely. Free passes should be issued only by the locomotive superintendent and the engineer to their own staff. Market tickets also required to be closely monitored and possibly curtailed or even ultimately discontinued. Whilst the agreement with the GWR provided considerable benefits to the W&LR, there were drawbacks, particularly in relation to the arrangements for ensuring a dividend, which Cotton stated 'is clogged with such conditions that you have not derived the benefit which might otherwise have been contemplated'.

The loss of the Clyde Shipping Company's trade to the company represented a setback. This arose from that company's refusal to bring its steamers to the new North Wharf at Waterford, the W&LR, in turn, withdrawing through booking arrangements. As a consequence, this traffic had been diverted via the WD&LR and the GS&WR to places as far afield as Limerick and Tralee, representing a loss of almost £4,500 per annum. This was an unfortunate move and could perhaps have been avoided through further negotiations. Cotton advised the appointment of an inspector to visit stations on a three-monthly basis to balance cash and accounts and report back to the Audit Department. He also suggested that applications for stores at stations should be certified by the inspector.

Cotton was of the opinion that shunting at stations could be improved. At Limerick, for example, he felt it might be possible to dispense with one of two engines engaged in shunting, if train engines were to perform a portion of the work. Finally, Cotton concluded his report by looking into the competition for traffic between the company and the GS&WR, which he stated, 'must be detrimental to the interests of both'. He recommended the entering of negotiations with a view to establishing a system of equal rates on all competitive routes and, if possible, common purse agreements. Similar remarks were applied to the MGWR, and Cotton offered to use his good offices to bring about agreements.

Early attention was directed to a number of the issues raised in the report. Arrangements were made in April 1888 for the erection of a new building at Waterford to provide office accommodation for the Audit Department at an estimated cost of £250 to £300. As regards periodical and market tickets, free passes, etc, various changes were introduced. It was agreed that the scale for issuing tickets to traders and cattle dealers be revised in order to make them more remunerative, the entire question of market tickets being considered with a view to their eventual discontinuance. The issue of free passes was in future to be restricted to the secretary's and traffic departments as regards non-company persons. This 'objectionable' issue of passes to other persons was defeated by the traffic manager who stated that he had been reluctantly compelled to give them, 'consequent on the great competition with which he has to 'contend', referring in particular to their wholesale issue by the GS&WR.

As regards competition traffic, the committee agreed fully with Cotton's suggestions, but it was to be March 1889 before any moves were made in this direction. At that time, reference was made to correspondence with the GS&WR regarding such traffic between Thurles and Limerick and between Clonmel and Charleville, with the idea of terminating competition. However, the GS&WR stated that it was not prepared to make any changes at that time.

Signalling and interlocking

Although chronologically out of place at this juncture, it is nevertheless, a good place to review what we know of early signalling on the W&LR, before looking at the introduction of interlocking mandated by the Regulation of Railways Act 1889, referred to below. The earliest reference to signalling was in April 1854 when it was ordered that the danger signal be lowered at each station on the departure of each train. We do not know what types of signals were in use on the W&LR at this time. The earliest reference to the employment of a signalling contractor appears in a board minute of 27 September 1862 when Messrs Courtney & Stephens of Dublin estimated the cost of fittings for the working of signals and points at Ennis Junction at £56.

During the course of a directors' inspection of the line in January 1871, consideration was given to the building of a signalbox at Abbey sidings near Cahir; it was, however, decided to hold this in abeyance until the new siding was made. Other signalling matters were approved, including auxiliary signals at various locations, a signalbox at Waterford and accommodation for signalmen at Limerick Junction, Carrick and Cahir. Two years later, probably following a similar inspection, it was ordered that signalling and locking apparatus be provided at Sixmilebridge, where a new siding had been installed.

In December 1877, Tighe, the company's engineer, informed the board that nearly all the company's stations were worked 'on the old principle'; if they were to be changed to comply with BoT requirements the expense would be 'very great'. He advised that most of the signalling work in Ireland was carried out by Courtney, Stephens & Bailey of Dublin and inquired whether other firms should be asked to tender. He stressed, however, that signalling at Killonan Junction was a priority, it being agreed in February of the following year to invite tenders for this work. Various quotations were submitted in May 1878, that of the Gloucester Wagon Co being accepted, £454 for Killonan and £28 15s 0d for Caher (sic). This firm was relatively new to signalling work, having diversified into it only in 1876 following a

The starting signal for the Limerick bay platform at Limerick Junction. The line to Limerick can be seen diverging to the left. Limerick Junction North Cabin is in the background just to the right of the signal.
Ian Allan Library

downturn in wagon sales. No mention is made in the minutes of the provision of a signal cabin at Killonan, although the sum mentioned would seem rather high for signalling alone. We do know that a cabin was provided in November 1878 and that a similar sized cabin (16ft 10in x 12ft 8in) cost in the region of £148, while a 16-lever locking frame might have cost in the region of £160. Gloucester appears to have carried out some minor work in February 1881 and there is some evidence to suggest that signal cabins at Abbeyfeale and Listowel also came from this source. In addition, it had submitted plans and estimates for signalling work at Limerick Junction in 1880, presumably in connection with the proposed new station; action was deferred and there is no further reference to any works being carried out by this firm.

Early in 1882, attention turned to signalling arrangements in connection with the extension works at Waterford, a tender for £900 being submitted by the Railway Signal Company Ltd of Fazakerley (RSC). Once again, this was a firm that had been only recently set up — just nine months previously. Its founder, George Edwards, had previously been the signalling superintendent of the L&NWR before he had become head of the signalling division of the Gloucester Wagon Co. The contract with the RSC was signed in April 1882 with work scheduled to be completed within three

months. In connection with the doubling of the line between Fiddown and Waterford, tenders were submitted for Tyer's block signalling at Fiddown, Grange and the old and new stations at Waterford. The new works were inspected in November, Hutchinson confirming that the necessary signal cabins had been erected, the points and signals being properly interlocked.

A note dated 7 May 1885 instructed the removal of Cahir Abbey siding, no longer in use, thus saving signalmen's wages of 13s 6d per week. At the same time extensive alterations, including signalling and a cabin, were carried out to the station arrangements at Cahir, these also including the conversion of this station into a passing place for passenger trains with the provision of a second platform. Some difficulties were reported in the early months of 1889 with the GS&WR in respect of the interlocking of the south end of the yard at Birdhill Junction, the GS&WR company declining to become involved. This matter was resolved only after the matter was referred to the BoT, which insisted that interlocking the yard was the only satisfactory solution.

To summarise the situation which pertained at this time in relation to interlocking, company returns to the BoT provide some information. The first such return still extant appears to be that for December 1873. As regards the main line there was a total of 59 connections, only five of which were interlocked; on the branches, only three out of 52 connections had interlocking. Matters began to improve from 1877 onwards and two years later, 22 out of 82 connections had been attended to on the main line. A special return to the BoT in 1880 confirms interlocking at the following locations: Waterford, Fiddown, Clonmel (station and junction), Ennis Junction, the C&LDR junction at Limerick, Patrickswell, Ballingrane Junction and Nenagh Road. The list was increased by the addition of Abbeyfeale and Newcastle West in 1881.

The Regulation of Railways Act of 1889 brought into force mandatory changes as a result of the horrific accident near Armagh on the GNR(I). The company received a letter from the BoT in October 1890 with a draft proposed order requiring the adoption of the block system and continuous brakes within 18 months, and interlocking in two years. Robinson and Tighe were instructed to prepare a careful estimate of the cost of these requirements. In due course, figures were produced and in June of the following year, the BoT submitted a certificate totalling £29,531, made up of £13,678 for interlocking, £2,673 for the block system, £9,000 for continuous brakes and a separate figure of £4,180 in respect of Limerick Junction. In April 1891 the tender of the RSC was accepted with an amount of £3,744 18s 7d for the first phase of the interlocking,

Cahir station showing the shelter on the
down side platform. The station nameboard
announces that this is the station for
Rockwell College. The down platform
has been disused for some years and the
track lifted since this photograph was
taken. Ian Allan Library

it having been decided to start with the main line. As regards block working, the Post Office quoted a figure of £522 for one wire between Limerick and Fiddown, with an annual maintenance charge of £67 5s 0d, the engineer also reporting the cost of 14 Webb & Thompson ETS instruments at £41 each as quoted by the RSC. (In Ireland, the telegraph and telephone maintenance was carried out by the Post Office, unlike in Great Britain, where the railway companies carried out this work themselves.) Previously, in May 1890, surplus electrical appliances (unspecified) from the Lancashire & Yorkshire Railway had been offered, but no further action had been taken.

During 1892 interlocking for the remainder of the main line between Limerick and Waterford was completed with signal cabins being provided at 13 locations; confirmation of this number is indicated by a board minute of 30 August which ordered that 13 clocks be ordered for the new cabins. Plans for these cabins were drawn up by the RSC. Cabins at Tipperary, Cahir and Dromkeen were clearly of RSC design as was that at Gort. The end-of-year returns show 76 connections as being interlocked; from this time all new lines and connections were provided with interlocking when built.

By the end of May 1893, Tighe was able to report that installation of block working on the main line was complete, although the Traffic Department had not commenced using it. As regards the Ennis, Foynes and Killaloe branches, he hoped to have these completed within a matter of days. Block working between Patrickswell and Limerick eventually came into operation on 29 October 1894. In July 1893 it was reported that the MGWR was pressing for work to be completed at Athenry, but the two companies were unable to agree on the necessary works, and the matter had to be referred to the BoT in August 1894 for a

decision. Early in 1894, the BoT approved a new down platform at Ennis, along with new north and south signal cabins. Difficulties also arose with the GS&WR regarding arrangements at Limerick Junction, that company refusing to bear the costs of additional signals. Also at Limerick Junction, the WL&WR, as it had by then become, disagreed in May 1897 with the concept of providing a runaway siding for its up trains at the point of junction, even though the GS&WR agreed to bear the cost. This trap siding was later installed.

A new Thurles station agreement

An agreement had been concluded between the SR and the GS&WR in April 1881 for the use by the former of the latter's line between the point of junction and the station at Thurles, a distance of about 1½ miles. A figure of 5% was agreed on half the cost of the GS&WR line from the point of junction to the station and 10% on the cost of the old station and platform, plus 10% on the cost of new works. In addition, the SR was obliged to pay half of the maintenance cost of the 1½-mile stretch of line and a proportion of the station expenses. One amusing item raised about this time was a request from the SR to the W&LR for the removal of the block wires from the signal cabin at Thurles Junction, as it was reported that the signalman could not hear the approach of trains due to the noise from them.

In April 1882, the W&LR raised the question of liability for the maintenance of signals and the signal cabin at the junction. The SR advised that in its opinion, it was 'fairly part of the SR', and should therefore be maintained by the working company. The latter disagreed and its solicitor suggested that it continue declining to pay for it, unless it could be proved the signal cabin was on the Southern line. Another matter of concern was the withholding by the GS&WR

of SR receipts at Thurles station in lieu of rent due, the W&LR claiming it was entitled to 60% of the receipts under the working agreement, and holding the SR liable. This matter dragged on until November 1885 when the BoW agreed to pay the rent. It was also pointed out that the GS&WR was doing its utmost to divert legitimate traffic for the Southern line to its own system, and in October 1889 consideration was given to providing a new station and a separate line for SR traffic. This suggestion was put to the BoW, which agreed to the extent that there should, as a minimum, be separate cattle sidings.

Meanwhile, the agreement with the SR was due to expire in July 1890. Following a conference between representatives from the BoW and the GS&WR, a new agreement was reached in January 1893, the W&LR disapproving of some of the clauses. The Thurles Railway Station Act, 1894 received Royal Assent on 3 July 1894. Although the Act itself consisted of only two brief sections, the new agreement was included by way of a schedule to the Act. Provision was made for the GS&WR to provide 'with all due speed immediately upon the execution of these presents', a cattle siding or bank at Thurles station, the BoW paying the cost of the same. The schedule also included a list of payments to be made, either by the Commissioners or the working company for the privilege of using the line and station of the GS&WR. The agreement itself was to be in perpetuity, subject to six months' notice of determination by the GS&WR in the event of rent etc being in arrears for more than three months.

Final acquisitions

The final pieces of the jigsaw which went to make up the complete W&LR system were the acquisitions of the A&TR and the A&EJR. In regard to the former, approaches were made in August 1892 as to whether the Tuam company would transfer its undertaking to the W&LR or would accept a reversionary working agreement. The A&TR board replied in the following November, having given the matter careful consideration, that it was prepared to recommend to its shareholders a sale of the line. A committee was appointed by the W&LR board to consider the matter further and it submitted a report in late January 1893, recommending the purchase for a sum of £79,000. It was also recommended that the W&LR should execute the various works required under the Regulation of Railways

Act of 1889, at its expense. Steps were taken to realise the sum required and the purchase price was paid over on 30 September 1893.

The situation with regard to the A&EJR was somewhat more complicated, due to the fact that the Ennis shareholders were, in the main, in favour of a sale to the MGWR. As early as December 1889, an offer of £170,000 in 3½% debenture stock from the W&LR was turned down and a decision taken to accept an offer from the Midland of £175,000 in 4% debentures. Responding to this rebuff, the W&LR board instructed its solicitor to take whatever steps were deemed necessary for compulsory powers to purchase the line. At the same time, approaches were made by interested parties on the Ennis board to inquire whether the Waterford company would offer 'an advanced price'. Limerick Harbour Commissioners passed a resolution in April 1890 deploring the actions of the MGWR in opposing the line's purchase by their rivals, 'thereby interfering with and breaking up traffic arrangements existing for the past twenty years'.

Reporting in March 1892, the *Galway Vindicator* stated that at a meeting of A&EJR shareholders, an overwhelming majority had voted in favour of an agreement with the Midland company. However, the MGWR Bill seeking powers for the purchase of the A&EJR was rejected by a House of Lords Committee two months later. By mid-June, an agreement had been reached on an offer from the W&LR of £180,000 in its 4% debentures, the W&LR agreeing to pay three-quarters of the costs of the Bill in Parliament. The Ennis board duly accepted this on 17 June. When the Bill was being prepared, provision was made for the raising of an additional sum of £20,000 to provide additional station accommodation. The W&LR secretary reported in June 1893 that the GWR agreement of 13 December 1872 in relation to subsidies for the two lines had been extended for six months pending the completion of the purchase arrangements. Thus came to a conclusion the policy of acquisitions, which had been a central strand of W&LR policy throughout the years.

Miscellaneous matters

Before we take a look at the events leading up to the demise of the company, there are several matters which can be conveniently grouped together at this point. In August 1881 plans were sent to the GS&WR in respect of the provision of an end-on junction between the two companies' stations at Tralee. Amended plans were prepared three months later, copies being sent to the L&KR for its approval. The GS&WR objected to being asked to pay towards a platform extension and a covered way, which the Waterford company considered to be conveniences,

'incident to the junction'. By April 1882, the GS&WR announced it was about to erect the platform extension, at the expense of the L&KR, but questioned the necessity for a covering over it. Some 12 months later, the GS&WR applied for through rates, consideration of this matter being deferred. Almost four years on, in May 1887, the Kerry Grand Jury passed a resolution urging the completion of the connection, the W&LR responding to the effect that the directors were of the opinion that to afford the facilities sought by the GS&WR would afford them the opportunity to divert Kerry traffic to its line. The Tralee Harbour Commissioners and Lord Kenmare also became involved in this matter. Finally, the W&LR traffic manager reported the formal opening of the junction on 13 April 1888, through rates having been agreed between the two companies.

In May 1896, the GS&WR submitted plans for a waiting shed and footbridge at Patrickswell. Approval was given provided the alterations were carried out at the joint expense of the two companies, the GS&WR declining to pay any portion of the outlay. When the latter company sought the extension of a siding there in January 1898 to allow the shunting of full goods trains, orders were given that no money was to be spent on Patrickswell station. Instructions were given in February 1898 to make Long-pavement a passing station. A similar suggestion from the traffic manager in October 1899 for Craughwell was deferred; in this instance the estimated cost was £1,000 as it would have necessitated the provision of a second platform. In June 1891, orders were given not to expend any further money on the station building at Killaloe, which was referred to as being unsuitable. The decision was taken to provide a new station near to the bridge on the deep-water extension. This was finally opened in June 1894, following an inspection by Gen Hutchinson on behalf of the BoT.

The Rev J. Dunphy, parish priest of Mooncoin, approached the board in October 1887 applying for freedom from, or a reduction of, the tolls on Fiddown Bridge for the children of poor people crossing from the Waterford side to Clonmore National School. It was agreed to charge 1d for families and ½d for single children. A figure of £450 was estimated for repairs to the timber work of the bridge in August 1888, Tighe being instructed to procure some 70 tons of timber on the best terms. Ten years later, rather heavier repairs and painting became necessary at an estimated cost of £650. Meanwhile, in December 1891 the toll collector reported that cars were coming from the Waterford side as far as the toll bar and dropping off passengers, thus evading tolls for the car itself. The solicitor advised that the only remedy would be to

place toll bars at each end of the bridge. There is no evidence to indicate that this was ever carried out.

Another bridge that caused some concerns for the company was that over the River Suir at Waterford. It will be recalled that the Bridge Commissioners had levied a charge on the company in respect of goods transported across the river by lighter. When the Commissioners issued notice in July 1891 of the discontinuance of the existing arrangements, the company took Counsel's Opinion on the legality of such a charge when the goods were not landed on the south side, but placed directly into vessels. Opinion was that the Bridge Commissioners did not have the legal powers to enforce such a toll, but in the event the company agreed to pay a sum of £320 per annum. The bridge was finally freed of toll after the W&LR company had ceased to exist as a separate entity.

Various schemes were promoted in W&LR territory in connection with the various Tramways and Light Railways Acts. Amongst those promoted, but never built, were the Tuam & Dunmore Light Railway (1886), the Newcastle West & Charleville Railway, the Newcastle & Buttevant Junction Light Railway, the Tuam & Westport Railway, the Limerick Bruff & Kilmallock Steam Tramway, and a proposed branch from Goold's Cross to Cashel (all 1889). All were opposed by the W&LR, and the only one to be constructed was the Cashel branch of the GS&WR, again after the demise of the W&LR.

Difficulties with the GWR agreement

Reference was made in Chapter Seven to differences of opinion as to the interpretation of the 1872 agreement with the GWR. Further problems arose in trying to obtain payment from the latter company, and in frustration the W&LR endeavoured to have the matter adjudicated upon by the Railway Commissioners. The GWR, however, appealed against this, and in due course the matters in dispute were referred in May 1881 to C. H. Parkes, general manager of the Great Eastern Railway. Parkes submitted his award, for the two years ending June 1880, amounting to £5,200, somewhat less than the amount claimed. Apart from making a monetary award, Parkes suggested, in the interests of maintaining amicable relations between the two companies so essential to the development of traffic, that the GWR should give its assent to capital expenditure on the extension of the line at Waterford and the provision of rolling stock. One of the points in dispute had been a complaint by the GWR that the Waterford company had not sought prior approval, as required under the 1872 agreement, for capital expenditure.

Parkes was again called on to arbitrate in 1886 in respect of the accounts for the year ended June 1884, an award being made in favour of the W&LR. Suggestions were made

Extension to the east of Waterford station. This view taken from across the River Suir shows a number of wagons and what appears to be an unidentified signal cabin.
Photographer unknown

by certain shareholders in February 1892 for the sale or amalgamation of the company with the GS&WR. The 1872 agreement ran to the end of June 1893, and as early as September of the previous year the question of its renewal was being considered. Reporting to the board early in February, Bernard, who had succeeded as chairman following Spaight's death, was able to advise that a recommendation was being put to the GWR board that it should grant a rebate of 32½% on all through traffic. In addition, interest on £10,000 of W&LR preference stock held in the name of GWR directors should be payable to it. Initially, a rebate of 30% had been put forward but, in an endeavour to close the negotiations amicably, the Paddington representatives agreed to recommend the higher figure. They were also of the opinion that they should not continue to contribute the sum of £1,250 annually towards the SR, but agreed, without prejudice, to continue it during the term of the new agreement. The new agreement was to run for five years from 1 July 1893 and was to be subject to 12 months' notice on either side. It was also agreed that there would be no contribution to the Athenry lines. The draft agreement, as amended by the W&LR solicitor and traffic manager, was finally approved by both parties in June 1894. It is perhaps of interest to note that ordinary dividends to shareholders peaked at 3½% in 1872 and 3% in 1877, but between 1883 and 1900, apart from three or four occasions when ½% was achieved, no dividends were paid. The GWR investment in the company was, therefore, in no way remunerative so it is all the more surprising to see that company accepting a further, albeit short-term, agreement being entered into in 1893.

With the extension of the line northwards towards Collooney approaching completion, consideration was given to altering the title of the company to better reflect its extended status. One such was the Irish North Western Railway, a title vigorously opposed by the MGWR. As commented by

E. L. Ahrons, 'the old Waterford & Limerick Company had so outgrown its original clothes that it did not quite know where it was, and to square up with the map, changed its title on 1 January 1896 to the Waterford Limerick & Western Railway'. As such it was to be known for the remaining five years of its independent existence.

In August 1896, the WL&WR solicitor reported that the GWR board had deferred the question of extending the agreement beyond June 1898. The Paddington directors, in so restricting the period of the agreement, were obviously of a mind to look further into their Irish operations. In truth, of course, the W&LR, and the W&CIR with which it also had rebate arrangements, was far from an economic proposition. Its only saving grace was that it kept the GS&WR, and by extension the L&NWR, from taking all the cross-channel traffic. By this time the GWR was close to becoming involved in the affairs of the Fishguard & Rosslare Railways & Harbours Co and this is an opportune time to briefly consider the Welsh connection.

The Welsh connection
It will be recalled that the first ideas for a western extension of the GWR towards Fishguard had been put forward in 1844. We will briefly recap on this early history and bring matters up to date, so that we can better grasp some of the reasons for the apparent change of heart towards the W&LR in the closing years of the 19th century. A prospectus had been issued by the South Wales Railway in the summer of 1844 for a line from the Cheltenham branch of the GWR at Standish to cross the Severn at Hock Cliff, between Fretherne and Awre, thence via Chepstow to Newport, Cardiff, Bridgend, Neath, Swansea and Carmarthen to Fishguard;

there was also to be a branch from Whitland to Pembroke. The company was incorporated by an Act of 1845, an Act in the following year empowering a branch from near Clarbeston Road station to Haverfordwest. Work commenced at various places along the proposed route in the summer of 1846 and by August 1847 had reached to within some seven miles of Fishguard. However, soon after this the general financial difficulties which affected all railways obliged the directors to suspend operations and the decision was taken to concentrate on the line east of Swansea.

In addition, the famine in Ireland had brought a halt to the proposed connecting railway works in Ireland — the WWW&DR and the Cork & Waterford lines. In March 1851 a fresh agreement was concluded, with the GWR providing for the eventual completion of the SWR to Milford Haven rather than Fishguard, the line being leased to the GWR for 999 years. In 1852, an Act was obtained for the abandonment of 14 miles of the original line between Fishguard and the junction with the Haverfordwest branch and for an extension from the latter to Neyland Point on Milford Haven. The line to Neyland was opened on 15 April 1856, the port at this point owing its creation to Brunel. A steamer service was begun almost immediately to Waterford and by August of that year a second steamer had been put on. Waterford now had a three times per week service each way. The port was called Milford Haven until 1859, then Neyland, but by the end of 1859 became known as New Milford, a name it retained for more than 40 years. The shipping services to Waterford and Cork, as we shall see in Chapter Twenty, were taken over from Captain Jackson of Milford on 1 February 1872. The Cork service was handed over to the City of Cork Steamship Co in 1876.

In 1872, Edward Cropper of Penshurst in Kent obtained powers to construct an 8½-mile railway from the GWR near Clynderwen (then known as Narberth Road) to slate quarries at Rosebush, north of Maenclochog; it was opened on 19 September 1876 for passenger traffic. The Rosebush & Fishguard Railway was formed in 1878 to make a line from Cropper's railway to Fishguard. Only half a mile was constructed when the name was changed in 1884 to the North Pembrokeshire & Fishguard Railway Company (NP&FR). The Maenclochog line had, meanwhile, closed at the end of 1882.

Birmingham businessmen Joseph Rowlands, a solicitor, and James Cartland, a brass founder, acquired a controlling interest in the NP&FR in 1892 and also agreed to purchase the harbour works at Rosslare (then known as Greenore). An Act was passed in 1893 for the Fishguard Bay Railway & Pier Company with powers to make a pier and a short line to connect it with the NP&FR. Then, in 1894, a further Act vested in the company the pier at Rosslare Harbour and the Waterford & Wexford Railway, the company's title being altered to the more familiar Fishguard & Rosslare Railways & Harbours Company. Rowlands tried to persuade the GWR to purchase the Welsh portion of his undertaking, but only got an agreement for traffic facilities. He then promoted a Bill for the extension of the NP&FR to join the L&NWR at Abergwili, just north of Carmarthen. The Bill passed through Parliament in 1895 despite strenuous opposition from the GWR.

The Maenclochog line was reopened with a nine-mile extension to Letterston on 14 March 1895 for goods and on 11 April for passengers. Rowlands went back to Parliament in 1897 for a further extension eastwards to give access to Swansea and both the L&NWR and the Midland Railway. The Bill was defeated, but the GWR now stepped in, fearing the L&NWR might avail of the opportunity of a short sea route to Ireland, and entered into negotiations with Rowlands to acquire the F&RR&H, which it did in February 1898. An agreement was reached in the following May between the GWR, the GS&WR and the F&RR&H whereby the latter undertook to complete the harbours at Fishguard and Rosslare and to provide steamers, the GWR, for its part, to construct a railway from Clarbeston Road to Fishguard. This was confirmed by an Act of 1899.

More importantly, as far as the WL&WR was concerned, the F&RR&H obtained powers to construct various railways in Ireland — one to connect the Waterford Dungarvan & Lismore Railway across the River Suir at Waterford to a junction with the WL&WR in the townland of Newrath, and another from a junction with the goods extension of the WL&WR in the townland of Mount Misery to join with the W&WR at Rosslare Strand, thereby gaining access to Rosslare Harbour. Powers were also obtained to acquire the undertakings of the WD&LR and the Fermoy & Lismore Railway. These powers were similar to those originally taken under the Cork & Fermoy & Waterford &

Wexford Railway Act of 1890, nothing further being done at the time to progress that particular venture and, in fact, the powers for the Waterford to Rosslare section were repealed by a further Act of 1893. The second schedule to the F&RR&H Act of 1898 made reference to the proposed amalgamation of the W&CIR and the W&LR (sic) with the GS&WR.

DW&WR expansion towards Waterford

The Dublin Wicklow & Wexford Railway reached Wexford in August 1872 and a connection from Macmine Junction, some 9½ miles north of Wexford, to New Ross was opened on 19 September 1887. The section between Macmine and Palace East had previously been constructed by the Waterford New Ross & Wexford Junction Railway. Further details of the history of this line can be found in the companion volume on the Dublin & South Eastern Railway. The Act for the New Ross extension had been obtained as far back as August 1877, but even before the ink was dry on the legislation, plans were being formulated for a further extension to Waterford. An Act for the latter was obtained in July 1878 and authorised the construction of four lines. The principal one was from New Ross to a point close to Newrath House in Waterford, with a branch crossing the River Suir over an opening bridge to connect with the WD&LR. Connections were also to be made with the W&LR and the W&CIR companies' lines. Despite occasional reminders from the Dungarvan company, the powers eventually lapsed and it was not until September 1896 that further approaches were made by the DW&WR to the WL&WR seeking its approval of the scheme. Once again, a bridge was to be constructed across the river and a connection made with the WD&LR. The principal line was to terminate by a junction with the WL&WR at Ferrybank. Railway No 2 was to be a short branch running from the goods extension of the latter company and terminating by a junction with that system close to the road bridge to the west of Waterford station.

The WL&WR directors expressed themselves in favour of the extension but not the projected bridge. Parliamentary notice duly appeared in the local press, powers being sought for a guarantee of £2,000 from the WL&WR. The DW&WR was prepared to guarantee a similar amount and expected that the GWR would guarantee £3,000 a year. Capital for what was to be a separate undertaking was to be £200,000, which was believed to be sufficient to complete all the works, including the Suir bridge. It was suggested that work should be completed as soon as possible to forestall the F&RR&H project. The WL&WR board agreed to the guarantee if an undertaking was given that the works would be completed within two

and a half years, the existing Waterford station and premises and no other to be used by the projected line, and the chairman of the company was to have a seat on the board of the new undertaking.

The DW&WR (New Ross & Waterford Extension) Act received Royal Assent in August 1897 and included provision for the bridge across the river to connect with the WD&LR. This part of the work was to be left in due course to the F&RR&H company to complete. Considerable delays ensued in completing the line and it was not opened for goods traffic until February 1904. Full details of the fascinating story of this extension can be found in the companion volume on the Dublin & South Eastern Railway, already referred to above.

Narrow-gauge connections

Two narrow-gauge companies made connection with the W&LR system: the West Clare Railway at Ennis and the Tralee & Dingle Light Railway at Tralee. Although their histories have been related in other publications, some brief mention must be made in relation to their impact on the W&LR system. The forerunner to the WCR was the Kilrush & Kilkee Railway promoted in 1860 to connect the two towns by means of a 5ft 3in gauge line. The scheme also included the reclamation of waste land at the Poulnasherry estuary by means of an embankment on which the railway was to be constructed. A portion of the embankment was completed but the railway scheme went no further than the planning stage. The West Clare Railway Co was formed in 1883 under the auspices of the Tramways (Ireland) Act of that year and was authorised by an Order in Council in May 1884. This first section was for a line connecting Ennis with Miltown Malbay, a distance of 27 miles, built to a gauge of 3ft. A separate company, the South Clare Railways Co., was formed in June 1884 to extend the WCR to Kilrush and Kilkee. The WCR was opened on 2 July 1887, the SCR on 3 August 1892 for freight and for passenger traffic on 23 December of the same year.

Some alterations were necessary to the A&EJR yard at Ennis station to accommodate the newcomer, the narrow-gauge company having its headquarters there. The WCR commenced from the rear of the down main line platform and ran parallel to the A&EJR line towards Athenry, before diverging to the left after somewhat more than a mile. Complaints were made from time to time regarding the inadequacy of the goods and cattle accommodation at Ennis. Partly due to this, the WCR was somewhat slow in making payments in respect of rent and its proportion of the cost of working the station. At one stage, the A&EJR endeavoured to collect the rent, the WCR being advised not to pay it to it as it was more correctly due to the working company. When the W&LR

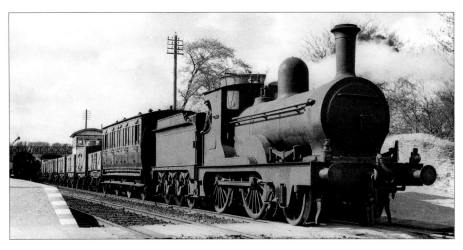

2-4-0 No 290 in CIE days, far removed from its home territory at Macmine Junction on the D&SE section. This engine came from the Glasgow factory of Messrs Dübs & Co in 1893 and was originally numbered 43 and named *Knockma*. One of four of the eight members of the class to be rebuilt, No 290 received its new boiler in June 1926. Photographer unknown / S. Kennedy collection

engineer submitted proposals to his board in December 1894 for alterations at Ennis station, the narrow-gauge company was approached seeking a contribution. However, due to its inability to pay the amount involved, the alterations were subsequently abandoned.

The T&DLR was another of those lines arising from the passing of the Tramways (Ireland) Act of 1883. Initially sanctioned in 1884, the powers were allowed to lapse due to the lack of a contractor. These powers were renewed in September 1888, construction work commencing before the year's end, with Robert Worthington as the contractor. The 37¾-mile line was opened for traffic on 1 April 1891. Approaches were made to the W&LR in March 1894 inquiring if it would work the 3ft gauge line. The Waterford company agreed to consider terms when the T&DLR was put in efficient order and condition, but the matter was never pursued. There was no direct connection between the W&LR and T&DLR lines, there being only an interchange siding for goods transfer with the GS&WR; passengers from both broad gauge lines had to walk between the relevant stations.

Amalgamation proposals

Having looked at the various connections, we now return to the WL&WR. By March 1898 the possibility of an amalgamation with the GS&WR was being seriously considered and certain guidelines were set down following a meeting in Paddington. Some measure of agreement was arrived at in relation to the exchange of GS&WR stock

for that of the Waterford company. In general, the staff of the WL&WR were to be taken over by the GS&WR. The GWR was of the opinion that, in the interests of the public, a running powers agreement should be entered into between the two companies. Other provisions related to the New Ross & Waterford extension of the DW&WR. The GWR was to be at liberty to negotiate, with the concurrence of the WL&WR, for the abandonment by the DW&WR of the NR&WER line, and the GS&WR representatives made it clear that that company would come under no obligation as to construction of that line.

The GS&WR announced its early agreement to the proposed terms and it was decided to issue a circular to the WL&WR shareholders setting forth the terms for them. The BoW wrote expressing concern in relation to the Collooney extension and sought a guarantee regarding its interest in that line, and were informed that the conditions for its working had not yet been discussed. In response, the BoW requested that any agreement for sale be submitted to it in advance for approval. Consequent on a meeting of shareholders and directors in the following June a requisition was received from shareholders representing about £50,000 of shares calling for an extraordinary general meeting to consider the actions of certain directors who had dissented from the proposed amalgamation and, if considered necessary, their removal from the board.

When the GS&WR and WL&WR Companies Amalgamation Bill came before the House of Commons Committee in June 1899, Counsel for the GS&WR stated that the company proposed to give to the Waterford company 'the benefit of an administration strong and powerful, able to carry out improvements, able to spend money in providing a sufficiency of accommodation, in the enlargement of stations, in the general service of the line, in the provision of rolling stock . . . that system (the WL&WR) is at present . . . a weak system (and) would

certainly not be able to stand efficiently by itself . . . The fact is that the W&L (sic) Company has never been able to live alone; it has always been dependent on GW assistance and subsidy.'

A long list of petitions against the proposed Bill was submitted. These included the North Kerry line companies, the L&KR, R&NJR and the T&FR. Such an amalgamation would be detrimental to the public interest and would cause serious loss and injury to the petitioners, as the GS&WR would divert much of the traffic over its own line from Tralee via Killarney. Needless to say, there was also strong opposition from the MGWR, which was currently competing with a weak company for traffic in Connaught. If the GS&WR took over the entire WL&W system, it would be a stronger competitor; on the other hand, that was exactly what the traders and inhabitants of the district wanted. Early in the proceedings, Counsel for the MGWR suggested that the Waterford system north of Ennis should be taken over by it with the balance passing to the GS&WR.

The first witness was Percy Bernard, chairman of the WL&WR since 1893. He confirmed the company had received a total of £213,302 since 1872 in rebates and subsidies from the GWR, of which more than £50,000 had been received in the last five years. The figure for 1898 amounted to almost £11,500, but this was not the whole picture; in addition, the likely diversion of traffic would be a very serious matter and the total figure might well be in the region of £15,000. Bernard confirmed that the passing of the Fishguard Act in 1898 had considerably altered the equation as, instead of working cordially with the WL&WR, the GWR had now teamed up with the GS&WR to develop the Cork to Waterford line via Dungarvan and to extend it eastwards to Rosslare. Section 72 of the 1898 Act in fact referred to the provisional agreement already reached between the GS&WR and the WL&WR/W&CIR companies for amalgamation. If there was no amalgamation and the GWR subsidies were lost, the Waterford company would be forced to reduce the train service and also staffing levels, particularly in the workshops at Limerick. As it was, the company required a large capital expenditure to improve stations and rolling stock. Amalgamation with the GS&WR now seemed to be the only option open to it.

Thomas Cleeve JP, a member of the Limerick Harbour Commissioners and of the Chamber of Commerce, a director of Messrs Matterson, bacon curers, and chairman and managing director of the Condensed Milk Co of Ireland, gave evidence regarding the latter company. He stated that its business amounted to some 4,000 tons per month, about half of which was given to the GS&WR. He believed that the WL&WR was not sufficient for business requirements and found the GS&WR much more satisfactory. In the course of cross-examination, however, he conceded that the trades people of Limerick had passed a resolution emphatically protesting against the sale of the local company, which would create a monopoly and deal a serious blow to the trade and commerce of the city. Sir David Roche, a deputy lieutenant of the county, said he was unhappy with the service provided by the WL&WR to the north of Limerick, with poor or no connections with the Midland at Claremorris. He felt that the granting of running powers into Limerick for the latter company would assist in solving this problem.

Various other parties confirmed these views, in particular William McCowen, a partner in the Tralee firm of Robert McCowen & Sons, grain merchants and the town's largest employers. Imports into Tralee in 1897 amounted to 75,435 tons, of which 29,137 related to this firm; comparable figures for 1898 were 69,302 and 22,406 tons respectively. The drop was attributed to the WL&WR ceasing to work the Fenit Pier traffic from 1 June of that year. This was brought about when the Harbour Commissioners introduced a levy of 1d per ton on all goods going via the railway. McCowen also referred to the very large fish traffic handled at Fenit and, not for the first time, mention was made of a shortage of wagons. Figures for 1893 indicate that the Waterford company held third position amongst Irish railways for fish traffic, behind the MGWR and the CB&SCR.

R. G. Colhoun, the manager of the GS&WR, gave evidence and stated his company's view that the traffic was insufficient to support two competing railways. He referred to the considerable improvement brought about by the formation of the GNR(I) in 1876 — at that time the Irish North Western Railway was impecunious, which he opined was analogous to the current situation with the WL&WR. Reference was made to the latter company's trains only

waiting 25 minutes at Limerick Junction to make a connection with GS&WR trains. Fish traffic from Fenit could more conveniently be worked by handing it over to the GS&WR at Tralee, rather than sending it via Limerick Junction. Colhoun was totally opposed to a division of the Limerick to Sligo line between itself and the Midland.

Frederick Vaughan, traffic manager of the WL&WR, stated that he had concentrated on trying to improve tourist traffic. However, he found it very difficult to increase traffic as it was surrounded by the GS&WR and the MGWR, both of which were antagonistic towards the company. Finally, Joseph Tatlow, the MGWR general manager, was examined. Asked had his company been offered the construction of the Collooney extension, he confirmed it had been approached, but had declined any involvement as it was heavily involved in the construction of the three western extensions at the time. In addition, it favoured an alternative line from Claremorris to Ballaghaderreen, which would have been a shorter route to Sligo. He confirmed that the amalgamation would cause serious injury to the Midland. However, if it was to take over the Waterford company in its entirety, it would seek running powers from Waterford to Rosslare and offer reciprocal powers to the GS&WR between Limerick Junction and Ennis.

The upshot of the House of Commons Committee's deliberations was that the case for amalgamation had not been sufficiently proved and the Bill was duly thrown out, but was reintroduced in the 1900 Session, at which time the Midland introduced an alternative. After much deliberation, the latter was thrown out and the GS&WR Amalgamation Bill received Royal Assent on 6 August 1900. Adequate provision was made for the compensation of the various classes of shareholders in the WL&WR. Section 23 of the Act provided for four additional directors on the GS&WR board, two from the existing WL&WR board and one each, either resident in or near or

conversant with the trade of Limerick and Waterford. Section 25 was important as it safeguarded the locomotive, carriage and wagon works at Limerick for a minimum period of 20 years from 1 January 1901. The new owners were obliged to pay out annually in wages a sum equivalent to that expended in the works by the WL&WR; there was a proviso, however, that wages in Limerick were not to exceed those paid to equivalent grades at Inchicore Works, Dublin. Running powers were granted to the MGWR between Athenry and Limerick, and to the DW&WR between Waterford and Limerick. In the event, the latter company's trains did not run beyond Limerick Junction. The MGWR exercised these powers for passenger trains until 1905 and for goods until 1910, although cattle specials continued up to 1912. The DW&WR ran goods trains to Limerick Junction between May 1904 and June 1908.

Other sections of the Act provided protection for the extensions north of Tuam — the GS&WR was obliged not to sell or lease the A&TECLR, and as regards the line north of Claremorris, a service of at least three trains each way daily was to be provided, in direct connection with services on the SL&NCR and, as far as possible, with those on the MGWR at Collooney. The SL&NCR were to be given all reasonable facilities, including running powers to Claremorris as granted under the Order, through rates and fares. Sections 46-48 of the 1900 Act dealt separately with the SR. Should gross receipts on that line be less than £10,451 5s 2d in any year, the GS&WR was to guarantee and account for the gross receipts at a minimum rate of that figure. Section 48 laid down that the company should, within three months of the passing of the Act, make proposals to the BoW for the purchase of the SR undertaking for a sum of £54,000. In the event of the purchase proceeding, the GS&WR was obligated to relieve the guaranteeing area to the extent of two-fifths of its annual liability under the existing guarantee but, as we shall see in the next chapter, the SR remained independent until 1925.

And so the independent existence of the WL&WR effectively came to an end after a period of 55 years. The following chapter takes a brief look at some of the post-1900 events to bring the history of the line up to the present time.

View of Ennis station looking towards Limerick on 12 June 1957. Note the goods store on the left behind the platform. The narrow-gauge track on the right has one of the CIE West Clare section Walker diesel railcars on view. Outside the station on either side of the road are two P-class Leyland Tiger provincial buses.
D. G. Coakham

Chapter Twelve

NEW CENTURY, NEW MANAGEMENT

One of the first acts carried out by the new owners of the railway was the closure to traffic of the WL&WR station at Rock Street in Tralee and the transfer of its activities to the GS&WR station, which was effected in 1901. The provision of a new crossover at Tralee in 1914 enabled direct access by Fenit trains to and from the GS&WR station, as prior to this they had to reverse. In Chapter Eleven we saw how the DW&WR proposed an extension of its line to Waterford in 1877 and how the powers gained under the Act of 1878 were allowed to lapse. The new line, as authorised under the DW&WR (New Ross & Waterford Extension) Act of 1897, was duly opened for goods and cattle traffic on 15 February 1904, passenger services commencing on 27 April. Initially, DW&WR trains ran through the back of the station at Waterford over the goods lines and reversed into a west facing bay at the Limerick end of the station. Within months, complaints were being made by the DW&WR in regard to the inadequate accommodation provided by the GS&WR at Waterford. With the further imminent arrival on the scene of the F&RR&H company, it was decided that the time had come for improvements in the facilities there.

Before taking a brief look at the reconstruction works at Waterford we must, for a moment, return to the F&RR&H following the passing of that company's Act of 1898. The contract for the construction of the railway from Rosslare Strand to Waterford was awarded to Messrs Robert McAlpine & Sons of Glasgow, while the contract for the bridges across the Suir and Barrow rivers went to Sir William Arrol & Co. also of Glasgow. The works at Rosslare Harbour were undertaken by Charles Brand & Co, yet another Glasgow firm. Construction work on the railway got under way in June 1900 at Wellington Bridge, extension works at Rosslare pier commencing in May 1902. Three ships were ordered for the new service from Fishguard, the first of these, the TSS *St George*, being launched at Cammell Laird's yard in Birkenhead on 13 January 1906. The steamer service was officially inaugurated on Saturday, 21 July of that year. The first commercial sailing took place on 30 August to coincide with the opening of the railway.

Whilst the F&RR&H company was obliged to provide steamers for the new route, an agreement dated 27 May 1898 engaged the GWR 'to work manage and maintain the portion of the Fishguard Company's undertaking on the English side including the steamboat service between Fishguard and Rosslare'. This agreement was incorporated in the Fishguard company's Act of 1899.

Waterford reconstruction and Limerick improvements

The main drawback to any reconstruction at Waterford was the close proximity of Mount Misery, towering as it did over the station. Before any improvements could be carried out it became necessary to cut back the rock face by some 50ft. How much cutting back was effected can be judged when one realises that the present through platform (Nos 3 and 4) is situated where there was once rock. At the western end, the main road from Limerick and Clonmel, which up until then ran behind the station building, was diverted to pass on the river side of it. The new road was supported on concrete piles over the river, the first extensive use of ferro-concrete in Ireland. A group of buildings behind the station and adjacent to the toll bridge, occupied as houses, shops and public houses, were removed to allow room for the new passenger station. Three through roads were provided, with one being the through platform road, the platform itself becoming the country's longest at 1,210ft. It was in effect two platforms with central access provided by a scissors crossover in the middle, a feature frequently used in Ireland. The usual accommodation, including waiting rooms, offices and a refreshment room was provided on this platform. There were four bay platforms facing west (Nos 5 to 8) and two facing east (Nos 1 and 2). The F&RR&H line approached Waterford from the east, joint track with the DW&WR running from Abbey Junction to North (or New) Wharf Junction.

Prior to the amalgamation of 1900, the GS&WR had carried out a detailed survey of the Limerick station area. This was a prelude to the extensive alterations carried out in 1909/10. These alterations brought about a number of important improvements in the working of the station. A connection was made between the C&LDR and WL&WR lines

at the station, enabling trains of the former company to arrive at and depart from one of three platforms rather than being restricted solely to No 4. This alteration also led to the abolition of the C&LDR signal cabin. The cabin at the locomotive shed was also closed following a re-arrangement of crossovers there. Similarly, Ennis Junction signal cabin was abolished. A new signal cabin, known as Limerick Check, was opened in 1910 and soon became the most important box in the station area. New crossovers enabled through running from the Foynes loop to the down main and Ennis lines. A new locomotive shed was built in 1911 to replace the original one located in the Works area.

Other improvements carried out by the GS&WR included the installation of a new siding in December 1904 on the up side at Dromkeen, and the provision of a new, 20-lever signal cabin on the Limerick side of Newrath crossing. Improvements to track-work at Clonmel, including the moving nearer to the station of facing points at the up end of the loop, and the working of two sidings by ground frame, enabled the station to be worked by one signal cabin instead of two; this work was sanctioned by the BoT on 6 March 1907. At Fiddown, a new crossover was installed at the Waterford end of the station in October 1914, enabling longer up trains to use the down platform. A 204ft-long platform was sanctioned at Powerstown Park, just north of Clonmel on the Thurles branch on 17 June 1916; this was in connection with the adjacent racecourse and remained in use until about 1941.

The world at war

Great Britain declared war on Germany on 4 August 1914 and within 24 hours the entire railway system of England, Scotland and Wales had been brought under Government control. This was effected under the provisions of the Regulation of Forces Act of 1871 and saw the setting-up of the Railways Executive Committee. There was no immediate impact on Irish railways, but in December 1916 the locomotive men on the GS&WR demanded a permanent wage increase of 6s per week or a war bonus of 10s per week. With no agreement in sight, a strike was threatened from midnight on 16 December. Notice was withdrawn after the Government announced its intention to take possession of the Irish railways under the Regulation of Forces Act. The official announcement, made on 22 December, stated that the Irish Railways Executive Committee would take control of the railway system with effect from midnight on 31 December. Compensation would be payable by the Government to bring net receipts during the period of control up to the corresponding figures for 1913.

Full control of the railways passed to the newly formed Ministry of Transport on 15 August 1919, although it was to be 26 September 1919 before the Irish Branch was formed, powers being transferred to it on 1 January 1920. This latter was placed under the control of H. G. Burgess, earlier Irish traffic manager of the L&NWR, under the title of Director-General of Transport (Ireland). Traffic matters, including the operating railways section, came under Percy Wharton, formerly of the GS&WR. Control of the railways finally came to an end on 15 August 1921. In the intervening period, the cost of working had increased dramatically, the eight-hour working day playing a major contribution in this. As an example, the wages bill for the Irish railways was then £5.8 million as compared with £1.55 million in 1913. Compensation for the period of Government control was set out in the Irish Railways (Settlement of Claims) Act of 1921, a sum of £3 million being awarded; of this figure the GS&WR received £878,458.

The Easter Rising broke out on Monday, 24 April 1916, services on the GS&WR being totally suspended until 1 May, gradually returning to normal after 8 May. Loss of revenue was estimated at £21,000, compensation of £5,500 being paid later. The entire period from 1916 right through to mid-1923 was one of unrest in Ireland, particularly from 1919 onwards. In an attempt to quell some of the unrest, a volunteer force known as the Black & Tans was recruited. As part of the opposition to this force and other measures, what was known as the Munitions Strike occurred in May 1920. On Tuesday, 25 May 1920 a group of L&NWR workers in Dublin refused to handle munitions of war. They were quickly supported by fellow workers in other companies, including the GS&WR, who refused to work trains when munitions were offered for conveyance or British armed troops boarded trains with the intention of travelling. This quickly led to major disruption of rail services as crews were suspended countrywide. It was not until the following December that a conference of railway workers was held, resulting in a decision to return to work. A number of such incidents occurred at various locations on the WL&W section, including Limerick Junction, Tipperary, Fethard and Waterford. A raid on Tubbercurry station in July led to the seizing of 22

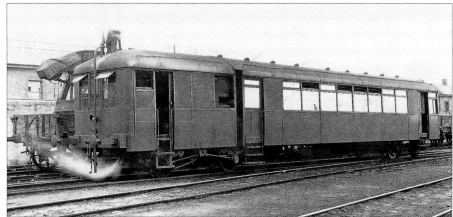

barrels of treacle. Earlier, the pay carriage, hauled by *Fairy*, was robbed near Limerick and an amount of £1,666 1s 2½d was subsequently written off by the company.

Civil war
It is not intended to go into details of the period of unrest which prevailed in the country during the 1922/3 period. Suffice to say that the first shots of the Civil War were fired with the occupation of the Four Courts in Dublin on 28 May 1922. The Anti-Treaty (or Irregular) Forces quickly saw the benefits in cutting communications in attempts to make it extremely difficult, if not impossible, for the Government to retain effective control of the country. Raids on the WL&W section during the Civil War period are too numerous to be dealt with in full. What follows, therefore, is no more than a brief description of some of these events.

During the nine months or so between July 1922 and March 1923, a total of 22 signalboxes were either destroyed or badly damaged. This compares with a total of 110 for the entire GS&WR system, 92 of which were totally destroyed. The station buildings at Foynes were destroyed by fire on 14 July 1922, damage being estimated at £15,000. Bridges were seen as legitimate targets — the river bridge at Cappagh level crossing, between Cahir and Bansha, was severely damaged by explosion on 17 July, services

Top: **General view looking towards Limerick station showing Roxborough Road bridge.** Ian Allan Library

Above: **The new order – a Sentinel railcar at Limerick in 1933.** Ian Allan Library

being suspended beyond Cahir. In August, two cases were reported of the company's permanent way staff being threatened. One of these involved a gang working in the Castlegrove-Milltown section who were fired on by Irregular Forces, their permanent way trolley and tools being thrown into a nearby river. Ganger Lynch was taken at night from his cottage on the Claremorris-Collooney section and warned not to carry out repairs.

Reporting to the board on 1 September, John F. Sides, the engineer, advised that two under-bridges had been seriously damaged in the Thurles-Clonmel section, repairs not being possible due to the operation of Irregular Forces. A similar but worse situation existed on the Cahir to Waterford section of the main line. There, Sides reported destruction or severe damage to 11 under- and two over-bridges, permanent way having been torn up in 16 places. The North Kerry and Collooney lines were effectively closed due to the presence of the Irregulars.

By September, action also involved the ambushing of trains and the removal of

Three 0-4-0 tank locomotives owned by Siemens Bauunion for use on the Shannon electrification scheme. In total, more than 100 engines were used, including a small number of electric locomotives. They operated on two gauges, 600mm and 900mm, all being built in and shipped from Germany. At the conclusion of the contract all the materials and rolling stock were shipped back to Germany. The two engines nearest the camera are identifiable as Type Ra1 Nos 1031 and 1030.
Photographer unknown, G. Beesley collection

goods, such as tobacco, bacon, sugar, flour and footwear. However, what appears to have been the first attempt to send a train to destruction, at Aherlow Bridge, was foiled when the driver refused to co-operate. Instead, the train was set on fire, two carriages being totally destroyed and two others seriously damaged. Sides, reporting again in October, advised that the company's staff had repairs well in hand on the Carrick-Fiddown section when the work was taken over by the military authorities. They reported on 20 October that the section was fit for traffic; Sides disagreed and pointed out that the Military had in fact undone some of the company's work and he refused to certify the line fit for traffic. Within days, the Carrick-Clonmel section was closed following the malicious derailing of a passenger train at Nicholastown. The 15.00 ex-Limerick was held up there by armed men on 31 October, passengers, parcels and mails being taken from the train. The engine was detached and brought back to collide with the carriages. A special train from Waterford was severely damaged on 14 November after it was run into a gap in the permanent way created by the blowing-up of Carriganeen Bridge (No 109) near milepost 44.

Towards the end of October, with damage to the system becoming a major problem, the authorities decided to set up the Railway Protection, Repair & Maintenance Corps. Some unemployed railwaymen were numbered within its ranks. A number of engines were armour-plated and the Corps set about carrying out repairs. In addition, Lancia

armoured cars were fitted with flanged wheels. The Corps was successful in restoring services to the Thurles-Clonmel branch, although one incident outlines the difficulties which it encountered and the vulnerability of the Lancias. On 15 October, one of these cars was out on patrol between Farranaleen and Laffansbridge when it was stopped by a wall of stones across the line at the 11¾ milepost. Upon stopping, the occupants were immediately fired on from all sides, causing them to make a retreat, following which coping stones removed from an over-bridge were thrown down on the car, disabling it. There then ensued a four-hour battle, the crew of the Lancia eventually being forced to surrender when their ammunition ran out. The car was relatively undamaged and was recovered later the same evening.

An incident occurred on the Castle-connell line on 13 November when the 18.15 passenger train was set on fire between Lisnagry and Castleconnell. It was reported that the stationmaster at the latter place succeeded in bringing the engine and burnt carriages to his station, the driver, fireman and guard of the train having gone missing. Later in the same month the military authorities advised the company that they were about to commence repairs to the Tuam-Sligo section. Their optimism was short-lived, however, as their repair train was captured and derailed, further damage being done to the permanent way. Two incidents at Limerick Junction are worthy of mention. On the morning of 9 January 1923, the engine of the 08.50 passenger train from Limerick ran into the station, through the back road and collided with a van; the train had been ambushed between Oola and the junction and the engine set off. The second, similar, incident involved a stock special from Limerick. The engine was detached at the 19¼ milepost and sent off without a crew. Arriving at the junction, it broke through No 16 points and ran on to the main line, before coming to a stand some four miles to the south near Emly, at milepost 111¼.

The end of the Civil War effectively came

in March 1923, a unilateral ceasefire being declared on 30 April. Before this came about there were, however, two incidents of note during March involving the WL&W section. On the 5th, the 16.50 passenger train from Tralee was held up at Barna and the crew and passengers removed. The train was set on fire and then sent off down the steep gradients of 1 in 61 and 1 in 81, eventually crashing into the buffer stops at Newcastle West, six miles away; damage was estimated at £4,272 18s 11d. On the 21st, another spectacular incident occurred when the 18.50 passenger train from Ballingrane was held up and set on fire. On this occasion, the train ran through Foynes station and on to the harbour siding. The engine ended up in the harbour and the carriages destroyed by fire; damage this time was given as £4,705.

Towards Amalgamation

Following the signing of the Anglo-Irish Treaty on 6 December 1921, a commission was set up in 1922 to consider the future of the railways. Two opposing views were put forward, the majority one being in favour of government purchase of the railways. It was suggested that the Government should set up a national railways board which would have absolute powers of management, rather than putting them under the direct control of a Minister of the State. The minority view was that the new Government would have more than enough commitments without incurring the heavy financial burden involved in the purchase of the railways. Instead, it was envisaged that they should be put under government control for a period of, say, three years. Having considered the commission's reports, the Government formed the view that the various railway companies should voluntarily agree to amalgamate; failing such an agreement, the Government would force an amalgamation.

Talks had in fact taken place in April 1922 between the boards of the GS&WR and the CB&SCR and they had agreed to amalgamate. It was decided, however, to postpone proceeding with this pending the outcome of the commission's deliberations. The D&SER was averse to any amalgamation with the GS&WR, preferring instead to join a grouping with the MGWR and the GNR(I). In the event, the latter company was excluded from the amalgamation talks due to its cross-border operations. The D&SER had two difficulties in relation to the proposed amalgamation. The London & North Western Railway had granted it a loan of £100,000 in 1902 towards the completion of the New Ross to Waterford extension. This loan entitled the L&NWR to a seat on the D&SER board, and its successors, the London, Midland & Scottish Railway, now sought a seat on the board of the amalgamated company or else the repayment of the loan.

It was, in time, granted a seat, this right being taken away from it when the capital of the GSR was later drastically reduced. The second obstacle related to the division of cross-channel receipts which effectively provided the D&SER with an annual subsidy of £20,000. It wished to hold on to this subsidy, the other companies objecting to this arrangement.

The Railways Act, which was passed into law on 24 July 1924, provided for the amalgamation of the Great Southern & Western Railway (GS&WR), Midland Great Western Railway (MGWR), Dublin & South Eastern Railway (D&SER) and Cork, Bandon & South Coast Railway (CB&SCR) and the absorption by the amalgamated company of all other railway companies operating wholly within the Irish Free State. The GS&WR, MGWR and CB&SCR proposed a preliminary amalgamation scheme in accordance with Section 10 of the Act, the D&SER declining to agree to it. This preliminary scheme, once it had been approved by the Railway Tribunal established under the Act, enabled the Great Southern Railway Company to be formed and incorporated on 12 November 1924. In pursuance of the provisions of the Act, the Railway Tribunal proposed and settled a scheme for the amalgamation of the Great Southern Railway and the D&SER, these companies being dissolved and their assets vested in the Great Southern Railways Company with effect from 1 January 1925, the new company absorbing the other minor and narrow gauge operating companies at the same time. Most of the smaller non-operating companies wholly within the 26 counties were absorbed under a number of Statutory Orders & Rules during 1925, these including the T&FR and the A&TECLR. The last one of all was the Southern Railway, the Order for it being issued on 18 November 1925.

Electricity and sugar

Between Ennis Junction and Longpavement station, on the up side just beyond the Shannon bridge, a 1¼-mile-long branch was constructed in 1928/29 to serve the newly completed hydro-electric power station at Ardnacrusha. The siding itself was handed over to the Electricity Supply Board in 1931. Constructed by the German firm of Siemens Schuckert, with civil engineering work carried out by its subsidiary, Siemens Bauunion, the Shannon electrification scheme was at the time the largest undertaking of its kind in Ireland. To move all the equipment in to the construction site Siemens decided to lay narrow-gauge tracks from the Ennis to Limerick line near Longpavement station. Two gauges were employed, 900mm and 600mm, consisting of light prefabricated track and at its maximum there were about 62 miles of permanent way, 93 900mm gauge locomotives, 13 of 600mm gauge,

An AEC diesel railcar set on a Limerick to Tralee train at Ballingrane in September 1959. David Murray / IRRS collection

and a total of more than 1,000 wagons. In addition, there was a short length of electric railway, employing four locomotives. The hydro-electric power station was officially opened on 22 July 1929.

The (Irish) standard-gauge branch initially shared one line of rails with the 900mm gauge line, thus forming a mixed-gauge section. With the completion of the power station all the narrow-gauge track and rolling stock were removed back to Germany, and by 1931 there were no signs left of the system. Even the broad-gauge line was little used in later years, the facing points from the main line being disconnected in 1965. Trackwork on the branch was subsequently lifted apart from a short section at Longpavement. The connection was reinstated early in 1975 when a ground frame was installed in a hut, the siding being used in connection with wagons running to a refuse dump. The siding points and associated ground frame were finally removed in October 1980.

A private concern, the Irish Sugar Manufacturing Co, was established in 1926 in Carlow to produce sugar from Irish-grown sugar beet. Within seven years, however, the company was in financial difficulties, arising from a strike of growers complaining of low beet prices. The government, conscious of the importance of promoting native industry where possible, set up Cómhlucht Siúicre Éireann Teoranta (CSE, The Irish Sugar Co) and took over the Carlow factory. Additional factories were built at Mallow, Thurles and Tuam. The Mallow factory was completed in November 1934, and the other two in the following month. Tuam and Thurles were, of course, within the territory of the lines covered in this volume. Within a year, the four factories were producing 70,000 tons of sugar and by the 1980s this figure had risen to about 200,000 tons, produced from approximately 1.6 million tons of sugar beet. The railways benefited greatly from this new traffic.

Today, now privately owned by Greencore, only two factories remain in production, at Carlow and Mallow, with only the latter served by rail, but it has been announced recently that the Carlow factory is to close. The Tuam factory closed in 1985, that at Thurles four years later.

To give some idea of the volume of traffic carried by the railways, we will take a brief look at the 1959/60 beet season. In total, Tuam received 10,650 wagons (87,100 tons) in a campaign lasting 55 days, while Thurles received 15,600 wagons (140,000 tons) in 75 days. This brought a considerable volume of additional traffic to the W&L section. In addition, some beet from North Kerry line stations and the Fenit branch went to the Mallow factory. In an effort to improve the railway's position in regard to competition generally, CIE (formed in 1944, the result of the Transport Act, as described later) formulated a Rail Development Plan during the 1970s. As far as beet traffic was concerned, a joint working party comprising individuals from CIE and CSE met and it was decided to build a central depot alongside the South Wexford line at Wellington Bridge station. The first trainload of beet was despatched from there on 25 September 1979 and a fleet of 165 dedicated wagons was provided for this traffic in 1984. Rebuilt from vacuum-braked container flat wagons at Limerick Works, these consisted of two old 'corrugated' open wagon bodies mounted one above the other, each wagon having a capacity of 20 tonnes. For the 1989/90 season, a service of three trains daily was provided from Waterford to Mallow via Limerick Junction. With the closure of Cahir Viaduct in October 2003, referred to later, these trains were rerouted via Kildare.

A fire, a tribunal and another world war

A serious fire broke out in the main smithy and machine shop at Limerick works at about 19.15 on the evening of 17 May 1936. The roofs of both buildings fell in at about 20.30. The fire may have been caused by sparks from a shunting engine or from the engine of the 18.50 passenger train, the weather having been extremely dry. Three or four wagons caught fire, but this was quickly extinguished. Two engines and a tender undergoing repair in the erecting shop were hauled clear as were two Sentinel coaches, none being damaged.

As part of an economy drive introduced by the GSR, the lines between Killonan and Limerick Junction, and between Fiddown and Waterford were singled in 1929. The junction at Killonan was removed in 1931, two separate lines from Limerick serving Limerick Junction and Ballybrophy. Double-line working was restored between Limerick and Killonan in 1947, at which date a new signal cabin was provided at the latter place to replace that removed in 1931. In addition to singling, a large number of stations were reduced to the status of halts during the 1930s. A few further stations were similarly treated by CIE during the 1950s and 1960s.

There were two new pieces of railway legislation in the 1930s, the Railways (Miscellaneous) Act of 1932 and the Railways Act of 1933. The former made provision for the discontinuance or reduction of train services on lines constructed or operated partly out of public monies, in other words the baronial lines. Recognising that the GSR had from the outset been grossly over-capitalised, the 1933 Act provided for the restating of its capital and the remission of certain debts due to the State. The company was authorised, with the consent of the Minister for Industry & Commerce, to reduce or terminate services on any railway line, provided an adequate replacement service was put on. Resulting from these powers, all train services were discontinued on 114 miles of line and passenger services on a further 82 miles. As far as the ex-WL&WR system was concerned, the Tralee-Fenit branch lost its passenger service as from 1 January 1935.

During the period from 1925 to 1938, GSR passenger train revenue fell from £1,497,105 to £844,485, passenger numbers declining from 15.75 million to just under 11.6 million. Freight fared rather better, receipts falling from £1.54 million in 1925 to £1.28 million in 1938. However, some classes of merchandise suffered badly, with timber traffic down 49%, manures by 40%, potatoes down 57% and pigs by 59%; in contrast, grain fell by only 7.8% and cattle by just 4%. Following the passing of a resolution in the Dáil and Seanad (respectively the lower and upper houses of the Irish parliament) in December 1938 a tribunal was established to inquire into the prevailing position of public transport in Ireland (aviation excepted), and in particular the circumstances which had led to the unfavourable financial position of the GSR, and if possible, to suggest changes to effect improvements.

In its submission to the tribunal the company proposed the closure of 861¾ out of 2,340 track miles. These proposals would have seen the termination of all services between Thurles and Clonmel, Birdhill and Killaloe, Tralee and Fenit, Ballingrane and Foynes and between Claremorris and Collooney. Two reports were in fact put to Government. The majority one envisaged the closures and the compulsory acquisition of licensed hauliers being spread over a number of years, during which time the circumstances of the company were expected to alter and, hopefully, improve. The minority report was put forward by Dr Henry Kennedy, who was of opinion that services should not be discontinued until a more detailed inquiry was carried out into the affairs of the GSR. He also believed that the GSR should be looking to its northern neighbour, the GNR(I), and considering the introduction of diesel trains and railcars.

The reports were only completed early in August 1939, less than a month before the outbreak of the Second World War, which brought about more serious problems for the railways. One thing it did do was to effect a considerable reduction in road transport generally, although this did not assist the GSR as it struggled to provide some semblance of a service in the face of serious fuel shortages due to its dependence on imported coal. A new timetable had just been introduced on 11 September 1939. On the WL&W main line there were three down passenger trains from Limerick, at 08.40, 16.40 and 18.50, journey time being about three hours. There were also two mixed trains, at 11.15 and 21.45, and two goods, at 06.25 and 23.45. In the up direction there were four passenger, one mixed and two goods services. The only Sunday service was the 12.45 from Limerick to Limerick Junction, there being no return working. The Limerick to Sligo line had two through daily workings with an additional passenger train to and from Tuam only. In the down direction there was a train from Claremorris to Limerick at 09.05 with no balancing working, while there was also a Tuam to Sligo working each way.

On the North Kerry line there were two passenger trains each way on weekdays, with an additional working to and from Abbeyfeale. There was also a through mixed train, at 06.00 from Limerick and 17.20 from Tralee. The Thurles to Clonmel branch had one passenger and one mixed train each way on weekdays, plus an additional passenger train each way on Wednesdays and Saturdays only. There was one goods train each way on the Killaloe and Fenit branches. Apart from the one working referred to above, none of the other lines had a Sunday service, nor had these been provided in the previous summer timetable.

As the war progressed, severe strains were placed on the Irish railway system as fuel supplies dwindled. The GNR(I) operated cross-border services, and with a judicious re-arrangement of engine working diagrams, it was possible to stock up on additional coal in Northern Ireland. The GSR, on the other hand, had to cope with inferior quality coal. What was known as 'duff' was employed, various experiments being carried out with briquettes made from coal dust, cement and various other products. Locally produced anthracite proved to be unsuitable for locomotive use, and even turf was resorted to as an emergency measure. These inferior products resulted in copious quantities of clinker being produced, the end result of which was fires going out. When this happened, lorries were despatched with slightly better quality coal to get trains moving again. Journeys which should have taken a few hours were frequently delayed for up to 12 and more hours en route.

It had been proposed to withdraw passenger services on the Foynes branch as from 1 January 1940, this being postponed. A general, 25% cut in GSR train services was announced as from 1 July 1941, main line Sunday passenger services being withdrawn a fortnight later. Further severe cut-backs were announced in the following October. By April 1944 passenger services were being reduced to two days a week and goods to three days. Services on the Killaloe and Fenit branches were withdrawn under the Emergency Powers (Reduction of Railway Services) Order of 1944 at the same time. Services were gradually restored, resuming operation on six days a week in August 1945.

Another new owner and a further inquiry

Faced with the prospect of the GSR being unable to continue in operation after the war, at least in its then current form, the government of the day decided in 1944 to bring about an amalgamation between the GSR and the Dublin United Transport Company, which operated the bus and tram services in Dublin. When the Bill giving effect to this came before the Dáil for its second reading it was defeated and the Government went to the country, surely a unique event for transport legislation to bring about the downfall of a government. The Government was returned with an increased majority and the legislation was passed on 21 June 1944 as the Transport Act of 1944. A new company, Córas Iompair Éireann (roughly translated as the Transport Company of Ireland) was formed with

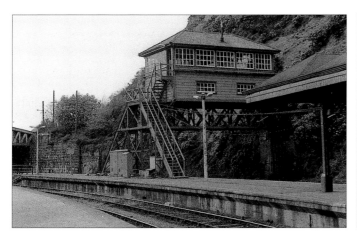

Above left: **Waterford North station showing the unusual Central Signal Cabin constructed over the through lines. In the background is the bridge carrying the main Clonmel road over the line, while to the right is Mount Misery.** W. E. Shepherd

Above right: **Rosbrien Junction, Limerick, with the Castlemungret branch diverging on the right.** David Murray/IRRS collection

Augustus Percival Reynolds as chairman. Reynolds, who was managing director of the Dublin United Transport Company, had been appointed chairman of the GSR in 1942, by the Minister for Industry & Commerce under the Emergency Powers Order No 152.

Any hopes of a full post-war recovery were to be short lived as the winter of 1946/7 was to be the worst in living memory, leading to further serious fuel shortages as coal could not be moved from the mines in Britain, which was aggravated by the nationalisation of the mines. On the W&L section, there was a passenger train ex-Limerick at 12.30 on four days a week, with a similar service from Waterford; journey time was 6h 35m in the down direction and 5h 10m in the up direction. On the Sligo line, a train left Limerick on Mondays, Tuesdays and Thursdays only at 08.00, arriving in Athenry at 11.07. After a wait of 4½ hours, a prospective passenger could resume his journey for Sligo, arriving there at 20.20. Tralee also had one train each way, but on four days a week. Even this service was to be drastically reduced. Within a month, passenger trains were reduced to three days a week. The arrival of American coal supplies coupled with a thaw in the arctic conditions eased the situation somewhat, although passenger services only returned to a four-day week in May.

With little or no improvement in the financial state of the new company, Daniel Morrisey, the Minister for Industry & Commerce, appointed Sir James Milne, the last general manager of the GWR, 'to examine and review the position of rail, road and canal transport' and to report on how matters might be improved for the future. CIE put forward proposals for the closure of 43 branch lines, including Ballingrane to Foynes, Claremorris to Collooney, Tuam to Claremorris and Tralee to Fenit.

The inquiry considered that branch lines formed part of the national system of highways and should not be closed if their retention was necessary or desirable in the public interest. The feeling was that any

such proposals, based solely on the grounds that they were currently unprofitable, should be rejected. It was recommended that before the closure of any branch line was sanctioned, there should be a public inquiry. There was even a suggestion of reviving the principle of a local authority guarantee. Scheduled long-distance bus services running parallel to the railway should be withdrawn when railway services were improved and road freight services should be ancillary to rail.

It was felt that the railway should be re-equipped so as to make it more amenable to passengers. Rolling stock should be improved so that more rapid and frequent services could be provided, for both passengers and goods. Consideration should be given to the introduction of diesel railcars; stations on routes to be served by them, and which were not required for goods services, should be converted to halts. Goods traffic should be concentrated in one station within certain areas, with road transport to connect to outlying districts. Finally, it was suggested that there should be co-ordination of road and canal services of the Grand Canal Company with those of CIE under a common ownership.

In specific relation to the W&L section, CIE had submitted plans for the reconstruction of Limerick Junction station. The inquiry team were of opinion that whilst there was a strong justification for improving the layout there, it was recommended that the plans be reviewed and a modified, less costly scheme be prepared. At Waterford, CIE had proposed to reconstruct the North Wharf and to provide a new goods store at a

cost of £89,000. The inquiry's view was that the scheme as proposed did not provide proper facilities for the existing traffic, although it was accepted that the existing facilities were inadequate and antiquated. At Limerick, Sir James Milne and his advisers were of the view that the locomotive repair shops were adequate but the equipment in use there was worn and old. As an example, lifting was carried out by hand-operated gantry cranes. Extensive repairs, including the changing of boilers and cylinders, were carried out there, spares coming from Inchicore. With regard to wagon repair shops, these were adjudged to be adequate although modern repair methods should be introduced. The upshot of the Milne Report was that Percy Reynolds was replaced as chairman of CIE, his successor being Thaddeus C. Courtney who had started his railway career with the CB&SCR. CIE and the Grand Canal Co were amalgamated under state ownership as from 1 June 1950. Although chronologically out of place here, it might be mentioned that CIE's operating activities were placed under the management of three new companies as from January 1987, the railway operations being taken over by Iarnród Éireann (IE or Irish Rail), CIE retaining the functions of a holding company.

A new branch

CIE announced on 11 February 1955 that it had applied for powers under the Transport Act 1950 to construct a railway from Limerick to Castlemungret to serve a cement factory at the latter location. This was to be the first standard-gauge branch line to be constructed since 1942 when the GNR(I) had built the Gortnagallon branch as a wartime measure. Prior to this, Cement Ltd transported cement by road from the factory to Carey's Road Yard where it was loaded into wagons; this was an expensive and labour-intensive operation, hence the first suggestions for a rail connection being made in 1953. As originally planned, the line was to have been constructed further to the south with five public-road crossings and two farm track crossings. There was strong opposition to these plans from local landowners, which resulted in the first 1¾ miles of the branch being realigned. Limerick County Council also insisted on an over-bridge where the main Limerick to Cork and Tralee road crossed over the proposed line. In due course, a compromise was reached whereby a level crossing was substituted, provision being made for a bridge if the county council insisted on this in the event of the road being realigned.

The Order authorising the branch was made early in November 1955 and the contract for construction of the three-mile-long line was awarded to Messrs Murphy Bros of Cork, with construction being commenced on 3 September 1956. The branch diverged from the North Kerry line about 200 yards beyond Rossbrien crossing, just short of milepost 2. Work was straight-forward, permanent way being laid by CIE. This consisted of flat-bottomed rail, most of which was second-hand, some of this dating back to W&LR days (1894), with other rails coming from the GS&WR and MGWR. The official opening of the branch took place on 1 October 1957, the ceremony being attended by directors of both CIE and Cement Ltd, and by the Mayor of Limerick.

From its opening the branch was worked by manual staff on the 'one-engine-in-steam' principle. In August 1964, however, this was altered with the line in effect becoming a siding, control being by telephone. The telephones were located in Limerick Check cabin and in a subsidiary hut at Carey's Road and at the marshalling yard at the factory. Under the new arrangements, no train could leave either Carey's Road or the factory without permission from the Limerick Check signalman. About this time, trains of new bulk cement wagons began running between Castlemungret and a new bulk storage facility at Cabra in Dublin. Traffic inward to the branch included oil imported through the port of Foynes.

It soon became clear that the section of line between the turnout to the factory and Limerick was becoming very congested. Apart from the oil and cement trains, the latter consisting of both bulk traffic and also bagged cement, there were the regular Limerick to Cork and Tralee goods trains and barytes traffic from Silvermines to Foynes. It was decided, therefore, to eliminate Cement Factory Junction and to extend the Castlemungret branch into Carey's Road alongside the North Kerry line. Work was commenced in late May 1966 and the new line was brought into use in mid-December.

Dieselisation and closures
It was decided in 1954 to experiment with a diesel railbus on the Thurles to Clonmel branch. An AEC Regal road bus was converted to rail use by fitting Howden-Meredith patent wheels. This enabled the

running of a two-train passenger service on the branch. However, No. 2508 as introduced had an entrance on one side only, making it unsuitable for the branch, and it had to be returned to Inchicore for modification. Although it remained on the branch until 1956, it was not sufficiently large to cater for the traffic on offer and would perhaps have proved more suitable for a shorter branch line.

AEC diesel railcars began operating some services on the Tuam to Claremorris line during the summer of 1955. Later, as the 'A' class diesel-electric locomotives began operating on the main lines, railcars were displaced and began to work the Limerick to Waterford and Tralee lines. A set was based in Tralee and worked a morning service to Limerick, then continuing to Waterford. A second set based in Waterford worked in the opposite direction. By September 1956 the 'A' class locomotives appeared on the Limerick to Waterford and Sligo goods services. By 1958 there was only one steam working from Limerick, the 11.15 to Foynes and its return working at 16.15; this service was finally handed over to diesel operation in the winter timetable of 1959. With the closure of the Harcourt Street line in Dublin, one of the displaced diesel railcar sets was sent to work the Thurles to Clonmel branch as from 1 January 1959. Finally, on 15 February 1960 'A' class locomotives replaced steam on the North Kerry line.

Yet another inquiry was set up in July 1956 under the chairmanship of James P. Beddy, who had been involved in the 1939 tribunal. Under the terms of the Transport Act 1950, CIE were 'obliged to provide or secure or promote the provision of an efficient, economical, convenient and properly integrated system of public transport for passengers and merchandise by rail, road and water'. Under that Act, CIE could not withdraw services on unremunerative branch lines other than by authority of exemption orders made by the Transport Tribunal established under the Act. The committee, however, had a different approach, believing that services could be provided almost as well, or better, by other means. Railways it considered to be necessarily an expensive form of transport suited only to conditions of dense traffic.

Large-scale closures of lines occurred in 1963 as CIE made an attempt to balance the books. The Clonmel to Thurles branch closed to passenger traffic on 9 September of that year, being closed entirely as from 27 March 1967. It might be mentioned here that Laffansbridge had developed a traffic in coal from the nearby Ballingarry Collieries near Killenaule. A new siding and crossover had been installed there in 1963 to cater for this traffic, which consisted of nine wagons daily, sent via Clonmel to Waterford for shipment to Newport in South Wales.

Coincidental with the 1963 closure, a large number of stations closed to passenger traffic. Details of the stations involved can be found in Appendix A.

The line between Claremorris and Collooney lost its passenger services on 17 June 1963, a limited goods service remaining until 3 November 1975. Trackwork was left *in situ* and still remains over most of the line, albeit severed at both ends and unused for 30 years. The North Kerry line passenger services ceased on 4 February 1963; on the same date the Ballingrane Junction to Foynes line also lost its passenger service despite the local authorities offering to reduce charges on railway property in their districts. Goods services between Ballingrane Junction and Listowel were officially withdrawn as from 29 November 1975. The section between Listowel and Tralee remained open for freight with a service operating on three days per week each way. Listowel was closed on 10 January 1977, only Ardfert and Abbeydorney remaining open for beet traffic. Finally, on 2 June 1978, these remaining stations closed for all traffic. Trackwork, however, remained *in situ* between Ballingrane Junction and Tralee, and it was the summer of 1988 before lifting finally commenced.

Although the Foynes branch closed to passenger services in February 1963, it was not until 1998 that the running of passenger trains was officially prohibited due to the unsatisfactory condition of the track. Even before the 1963 closure, traffic had been sparse, the service being provided by the attaching of an ex-MGWR six-wheeled carriage to the daily goods train. From a freight point of view, however, Foynes has a rather chequered career. Oil traffic was killed off by the opening of the Whitegate refinery near Bantry, only to be revived when the branch to Castlemungret was opened in 1957. Extensive works were carried out at Foynes during the 1960s to cater for barytes, lead and zinc concentrates from the newly opened Silvermines area on the Ballybrophy branch. Work included the provision of a new jetty for the export of this material. During 1993, grain, molasses and smokeless fuel were added to the materials handled at Foynes, the former running three days a week to and from Portlaoise, while the latter ran to Belfast.

Limerick Junction alterations
The late E. L. Ahrons once referred to Limerick Junction as being 'one of the most extraordinary junction stations that ever existed, which may also be described as typically Irish'. Lt-Col Hutchinson, reporting on a collision which occurred there on 7 December 1882, commented that the arrangements were 'of a very peculiar, and so far as I know, of a perfectly unique character'. He went on to state that so long as the station arrangements remained

unaltered, 'it is to be feared that the present most objectionable mode of working the traffic must continue, and I can only hope the occurrence of the present collision may rouse the directors of both companies to again seriously contemplate the remodelling of the station'. Col Rich had similar comments to make when he investigated another collision there in July 1890. He recommended the alteration and improvement of arrangements, urging that trains should not be reversed into and out of platforms. Rich referred specifically to the W&LR platforms, which he describes as being in 'a very dangerous and improper state'.

These various comments largely fell on deaf ears, even following the absorption of the WL&WR system by the GS&WR in January 1901, and it was not until 1966 that plans were announced for several alterations designed to improve the working of main line trains. Estimated to cost in the region of £100,000, the scheme would, in future, allow trains on the Cork main line to have direct access to the platform rather than running past and then reversing in to the station. In addition, a new curve would be provided to enable trains from Dublin to Limerick and vice versa to avoid Limerick Junction station altogether.

Work got under way in July 1966 with the clearance of the area behind the North cabin. All platforms were raised to standard height, the main line one being extended northwards; the famous scissors crossing was moved to the new halfway point of the up and down portions of the platform. New facing crossovers were necessary at either end of the main line platform to allow direct run-in and a further crossover was provided to the north of the station near Kyle crossing so as to gain access from the down main line to the Limerick Direct curve. In addition, minor alterations were carried out to sidings, the signalling also being upgraded.

One of the reasons put forward for the alterations was the impending closure of the Cork to Rosslare route via Dungarvan and the resulting rerouting of Rosslare boat trains via Limerick Junction. As far as the operation of Limerick to Waterford trains was concerned, there was little or no change, with reversals remaining the order of the day. The ultimate solution to the problems of the layout here would have been the construction of an entirely new station at the point of intersection of the two companies' lines.

Improvements at Waterford
It was decided to improve facilities at Waterford early in the 1960s. Both the 'Kilkenny' and 'Limerick' locomotive sheds were demolished in 1963, while in the following year the CIE wharf was disposed of to the Waterford Harbour Commissioners. The wharf had in fact been rebuilt in reinforced concrete in 1951 to accommodate three ships instead of two as previously, with a depth of 22ft 8in available at low water. The new wharf had been opened by the Minister for Industry & Commerce on 17 November 1951.

A £120,000 scheme commenced on 6 February 1967, the object of which was the replacement of the old W&LR building which had served the city for 103 years; demolition of the old building was completed by May 1967. The locomotive maintenance depot closed in March, only fuel and watering facilities for railcars remaining. Work on the new station building was completed at the end of 1968 and it was brought into use in January of the following year. A three-storey building occupied almost the same site as the old building and housed offices. A new staff dormitory was built at Sion Row near the East cabin. The old bay platforms, Nos 1 and 2, were filled in and converted into a passenger car park.

Further alterations were carried out in 1974 when the main running roads between West and Central cabins were diverted closer to the river. This was to allow for the provision of a new container terminal on the site of the goods yard. This diversion led to the removal of virtually all sidings and the turntable at the river side. Platform No 4 was lengthened by about 75 yards at the same time that the goods yard was connected to the main line at both ends in October 1975. This enabled locomotives to run round their trains without having to shunt them. The removal of the Bus Éireann (Irish Bus) services to a new purpose-built bus station on the city side of the river in 2000 led to the closure of the restaurant at the station. For some years prior to this, buses had been using the area previously occupied by the west-facing bay platforms.

Two accidents at Cahir Viaduct
In the early morning of 21 December 1955 a serious accident occurred at Cahir Viaduct when a loose-coupled beet special ran through Cahir station and fell through the floor of the viaduct into the River Suir below. At the time of the accident, the late running down night mail was standing at the up platform in Cahir station. The beet train, consisting of 'Woolwich' 2-6-0 No 375, 32 laden wagons of beet and a 20-ton brake van, had originated in Bridgetown and was en route to the Thurles factory. As the driver and fireman were both killed, it has never been possible to ascertain precisely what happened; the weather on the night was clear and dry. What we do know is that the train ran past the home signal, into the station at a speed variously estimated at 30 to 45mph and entered the down loop, ran through the buffer stops at the end and out on to the viaduct. No 375 and 22 of the wagons broke through the floor of the viaduct. The latter, although built for double track, has always been single.

Staying with Cahir Viaduct, at approximately 06.00 on the morning of 7 October 2003, the 03.35 Limerick to Waterford bulk cement train, consisting of two diesel-electric locomotives (Nos 134 and 186) and 22 laden four-wheeled cement wagons, derailed while crossing the viaduct. The locomotives and the first wagon remained on the rails, the next nine wagons derailing but staying upright. The remaining 12 wagons fell through the bridge and into the river. No defects were found in the bridge and the train was not exceeding the speed limit of 40mph. The official report into the occurrence concluded that the variable stiffness of the bridge beams, combined with the rigidity of the type of wagon, caused one of them to jump the track.

Fears were widely expressed that the damage to the bridge might sound the death knell for the Waterford to Limerick line, which has been losing money for many years. However, a contract for the reconstruction of the bridge was awarded to a consortium led by Irish Enco at an estimated cost of 2.8 million euros. Work was completed on 18 August 2004 and IE announced that the passenger service on the route would be improved, with three trains each way daily operated by diesel railcars. In fact, the Cahir bridge was officially reopened by the then Minister for Transport, Séamus Brennan, on Thursday, 23 September 2004. An enhanced passenger service recommenced the next day. Since then, all passenger services between Limerick Junction and Rosslare Europort are now operated by two-car railcar sets, normally of the '2700' class.

A panoramic view of Cahir Viaduct, the scene of two spectacular accidents.
W. E. Shepherd

Chapter Thirteen

TRAIN SERVICES

A timetable published in May 1848 for the opening of the line to Tipperary shows departures from Limerick at 06.00, 11.30 and 15.30 on weekdays, journey time being 1½ hours for the 25 miles. There were two trains on Sundays, at 07.30 and 16.00. Trains left Tipperary at 08.00, 15.30 and 19.30 on weekdays and at 09.30 and 18.00 on Sundays. Intermediate stops were made at Killonan, Pallas and Oola. All trains carried first, second and third class passengers, the respective through single fares for passengers being 4s 0d, 3s 0d and 1s 8d, while dogs were charged 3d each, irrespective of distance. First and second class return tickets were available between any two stations, for return on the same day at one and a half times the single fare. Those issued on Saturdays were available for return on Saturday, Sunday or Monday.

A GS&WR timetable for 1 October 1848 shows W&LR trains departing Limerick for Tipperary at 08.05 (mail), 11.00, 14.05 and 21.50 (night mail). The mails ran on seven days per week, the remaining two trains on weekdays only. Journey times varied from 43 to 70 minutes. In the down direction, trains left Tipperary at 13.20, 15.50 (mail), 19.10 and 01.25 (night mail), the latter providing a connection out of the 19.30 night mail from Dublin. The only intermediate stations shown were Junction and Pallas. It was reported in December 1848 that arrangements had been concluded with the GS&WR whereby one train each way daily would be discontinued early in January. In addition, two of the down trains from Dublin were to be so arranged that they would be brought from the Junction into Limerick as one so that there would only be one night and two day trains leaving Limerick for Dublin and one day and one night train from the latter into Limerick. Furthermore, with the expected opening of the GS&WR to Buttevant, Limerick connections would also be made in that direction, thus adding additional revenue to the W&LR.

About this time, *Berry's Irish Railway & General Advertiser* indicated down trains at 06.50, 11.30, 14.00 (mail), 18.45 and 00.45 (night mail), and from Limerick at 07.00, 10.45 (mail), 13.10, 16.30 and 21.50 (night mail). Once again, only the mails ran on Sundays. Intermediate stations were now shown as Killonan, Boher, Dromkeen, Pallas, Oola and Junction. Only the 06.50 and 18.45 down and the 07.00 and 16.30 up carried all three classes of passengers. Journey times varied between 1¼ and 2 hours for the 25-mile journey.

In December 1849, Saunders suggested making the 07.00 from Limerick a slow goods train with a single composite carriage attached, this suggestion being approved by the board. In February 1850 it was agreed that third-class passengers be accommodated with return tickets at single fare and a half, returnable on day of issue. Fourth class travel had been introduced in the previous October by the MGWR board when it agreed to include wagons with seats on certain trains to and from Mullingar. Also in February 1850 it was resolved that open cars (bogie wagons) be attached to local trains on market and fair days to take fourth-class passengers at reduced rates. Return fares from Tipperary to Limerick were agreed at 2s. At this time the single fares for other classes were 4s, 3s and 1s 10d for first, second and third classes respectively. The question of through working of GS&WR wagons was raised in May 1850, with the secretary being requested to write to the latter company proposing a conference. The GS&WR responded by suggesting that the W&LR should make a fixed rate for all goods in wagons. Rates of 2s 6d per ton from Limerick to the Junction were suggested, agreement finally being reached two months later.

The ever-present financial difficulties of the company led, in August 1850, to consideration of a reduction in the service provided, a committee being appointed to report on the expediency and practicability of this measure. There is no indication that any service reductions were made at this time, but in December of the same year the secretary was requested to take all necessary steps to prevent the 16.30 from Limerick from stopping at the Junction. The extension of the line to Clonmel in May 1852 saw a service of five through trains each way on weekdays and one on Sundays, the best journey time being 2h 40m for the 49¼-mile journey. The GS&WR received a complaint in August 1852 on the subject of the late arrival of its Dublin trains at the Junction. This matter was to be a regular cause of complaint in the years ahead.

A timetable for November 1858 has through services from Limerick to Waterford departing at 07.30, 11.30 and 16.00. In addition, there was an 08.00 from Clonmel to Waterford and a 17.45 Limerick to Tipperary. On Sundays a train left Limerick at 12.20. Through journey times varied from 3h 45m to 4h 10m. By now the direction of travel had been reversed, departures from Limerick being shown as down trains.

1869 working timetable

The working timetable effective from 1 July 1869 provides us with some additional information. There were seven trains in the down direction, at 05.15, 09.20 (mixed to Junction and goods from there to Waterford), 11.40 (mail), 16.00, 19.00 (a goods train running only to Oola), 22.45 (pick-up on Tuesdays and Thursdays from Junction to Waterford) and 22.45 (mail). There were two trains on Sundays, at 06.30 (mixed) and the 22.45 night mail. The 05.15 took goods and cattle offering from Limerick Junction. The down day mail would, if required, stop at Oola and Kilsheelan for first-class passengers only; a note also indicated that it ran into the siding at Fiddown for ticket checking. As this train provided a connection to the Milford steamer due to depart Adelphi Wharf at 16.00, every exertion was to be made to ensure an on-time arrival in Waterford at 15.10. There were corresponding up workings, including a 16.00 Waterford to Junction pick-up on Tuesdays and Thursdays. The latter train also ran on Saturdays, when it was extended through to Limerick so as to work out a Sunday excursion. Journey times had not improved greatly since 1858, the fastest train being the 10.20 up mail which took 3¼ hours from Waterford to Limerick, the slowest being the 22.45 down mail which occupied five hours for the 77¼-mile journey, an average of just over 15mph. One must, however, remember that all trains had to reverse into and out of Limerick Junction, while from there to Waterford it was a single-tracked line.

The Ennis line had three trains each way on weekdays, down at 10.20, 14.25 and 18.30, up at 07.40, 12.30 and 16.30; there was no Sunday service on the branch. There were trains from Limerick to Killaloe at

10.45 and 16.30, with up workings at 08.40 and 12.50. It was not possible to travel from Limerick to Killaloe and back on weekdays unless one was happy to spend only an hour there, but one could comfortably do the return journey in the opposite direction. There was one train each way on Sundays. Finally, the 1869 working timetable shows Foynes branch trains leaving Limerick at 10.20 (to Newcastle West only), 14.10 and 17.30, and up trains at 07.00, 14.20 (from Newcastle West) and 15.50. All three classes were catered for on each of the branch line trains. The Foynes and Newcastle West sections were economically worked with just two engines. A Limerick engine made one return trip to Foynes at 14.10 to connect with the Kilrush to Tarbert and Foynes steamer service. The second engine, shedded at Foynes, worked the 07.00 up to Ballingrane; there it left the train for 80 minutes while it ran light to Newcastle to bring up the 08.05. The two trains were combined at Ballingrane and arrived in Limerick at 09.50. This engine then worked a round trip to Newcastle West before repeating the morning's movements.

We shall now consider the public timetable for January 1883. By this time the North Kerry line to Tralee, the Southern Railway to Thurles and the extensions to Athenry and Tuam had been opened and were being worked by the W&LR. There were five weekday workings each way on the main line, with only the mail trains running on Sundays. The 13.35 down and the 09.45 up were shown as express trains between Limerick and Limerick Junction. Making no intermediate stops, they completed the 22-mile run in 40 minutes, an average of 33mph.

Two trains ran through from Limerick to Tuam, at 10.20 and 15.30, with arrivals respectively at 14.35 and 19.40. A combined mail and goods train (mail only on Sundays) left Limerick at 02.30 and ran only as far as Ennis, arrival being at 04.00. A 'connection' left Ennis for Athenry at 10.00 and, with a further two-hour delay there, it was possible to travel on to Tuam by the 10.20 from Limerick, which had by then caught up with any overnight travellers from Limerick! In the opposite direction, trains left Tuam at 06.00, 08.45 (to Athenry only), 11.15 and 15.45 (goods and mail to Ennis and mail only on to Limerick), with an additional midday train from Ennis to Limerick.

The North Kerry line had four departures from Limerick, the earliest at 05.00. The 10.10 ran to Newcastle West only, the 13.35 was an express (arriving Tralee 17.00); there was also a 10.00 (Mondays excepted) from Newcastle West to Listowel, returning from the latter station at 16.05. There was one train each way on Sundays, at 07.30 from Limerick and 17.50 from Tralee. On the Killaloe branch, a mixed train left Limerick at 10.40, passenger trains at 15.35 and 19.25;

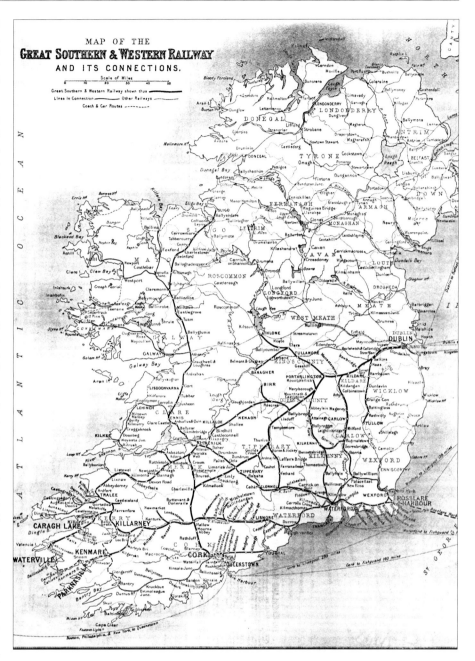

Map of the GS&WR including the WL&WR network, which it took over in 1900.

the latter train provided a GS&WR connection to Nenagh, the other two providing connections to Roscrea. Trains departed Killaloe at 08.35, 13.15 (mixed) and 17.55. Finally, on the Southern Railway trains left Clonmel for Thurles at 07.10, 11.00 and 16.20 with return workings at 08.40, 13.50 and 17.45. No Sunday services were provided on either the Killaloe or Thurles branches.

Generally, connections between main line and branch line trains were not good. If, for example, one came up on the 09.45 from Waterford, due in Limerick at 12.52, a Tralee train left at 13.35, but a prospective passenger had to wait until 15.30 for a train to Ennis or Tuam and 15.35 for the Killaloe branch. In the reverse direction, a passenger wishing to catch the 16.00 to Waterford would have

had to leave Tuam at 06.00 and would have had 6¼ hours to kill in Limerick; the 10.00 from Tralee left one just short of 2¾ hours to amuse oneself in Limerick. Our prospective passenger could leave Killaloe at 13.15 and arrive in Limerick an hour later, which missed the 13.35 to Tralee but did provide a comfortable connection for Ennis and Tuam.

As regards the cross-channel steamer services, the boat left Waterford at 17.00. The 13.35 train from Limerick did not arrive in Waterford until 16.40, leaving only 20 minutes to get to Adelphi Wharf. Prospective passengers would most likely have travelled on the 11.00 from Limerick, allowing themselves 2¼ hours to make the connection. The scheduled arrival in Paddington was 10.45 the following morning.

Waterford and Limerick Railway.

WORKING TIMETABLE JULY 1868

WATERFORD AND LIMERICK RAILWAY.

Distance from Limerick	DOWN LIMERICK TO WATERFORD		Week Days 1 Pass. 1 2 3 a.m.	2 Pass. and Goods 1 2 a.m.		3 Mail 1 2 a.m.	4 Pass. 1 2 3 p.m.	5 G. S. & W. Butter Engine p.m.	6 Goods p.m.	7 Pick up Tuesdays and Thursdays p.m.	p.m.	8 Mail 1 2 p.m.	Sundays 1 Mixed. Pass. 1 2 3 a.m.	2 Mail 1 2 class p.m.
Mls.										Arr.	Dep.			*
—	Limerick	D.	5 15	9 20		11 40	4 0	—	7 0	—	—	10 45	6 30	10 45
8	Boher ..	..	5 35	9 45		11 55	4 20	—	—	—	—	—	—	—
11¼	Dromkeen	..	—	Flag		—	4 30	—	Flag	—	—	—	—	—
13¾	Pallas ..	..	5 50	10 10		12 10	4 40	--	Flag	—	—	11 30	7 10	11 30
18¾	Oola ..	..	Flag	—		Flag	4 55	—	8 30	—	—	—	—	—
21¾	Junction	A.	6 17	10 35		12 32	5 5	—		—	—	12 0	7 40	13 0
				Goods Arr.	Dep.									
		D.	6 45	—	11 15	12 45	5 25	6 30		—	10 45	12 15	7 50	12 15
24¾	Tipperary	..	7 10	11 40	1 5	1 0	5 40	6 45		11 10	11 35	12 45	8 15	12 45
29½	Bansha ..	..	7 30	Flag		1 15	5 55			Flag		—	Flag	—
38¾	Caher ..	..	8 0	1 50	2 30	1 35	6 15			12 20	12 30	1 30	8 55	1 30
49¾	Clonmel ..	..	8 35	3 10	3 55	2 0	6 40			1 15	1 30	2 15	9 40	2 15
55½	Kilsheelan	..	8 55	—	—	Flag	6 55			—	—	—	Flag	—
63	Carrick ..	..	9 15	4 40	5 0	2 35	7 20			2 15	2 25	2 55	10 20	2 55
67¾	Fiddown ..	..	9 30	5 15	5 25	2†52	7 30			2 40	2 45	3 10	10 35	3 10
70	Grange ..	..	9 40	—	—	—	7 35			—	—	—	Flag	—
77¾	Waterford	A.	10 0	6 0	—	3 10	8 0			3 20	—	3 45	11 20	3 45
			A.M.	P.M.	P.M.	P.M.	P.M.			A.M.		A.M.	A.M.	A.M.

No. 1.—The 5 15 a.m. will bring on from Limerick Junction Goods and Cattle offering, to within two waggons of engine load.

No. 3.—The 11 40 a.m. stops at Oola and Kilsheelan for 1st class passengers only; & at Fiddown, runs in on siding to be checked.

Mem.—This Train being in direct connexion with Milford Boat Express Service, leaving Waterford at 4 0 p m., every exertion is to be made to keep and bring in the Train to Time.

Distance from Waterford	UP WATERFORD TO LIMERICK		Week Days 1 Goods a.m.		2 Passenger 1 2 3 a.m.	3 Mail 1 2 a.m.	4 Pasngr. 1 2 p.m.	5 G. S. & W. Butter Engine p.m.	6 Pick-up, Tuesdays, Thursdays, and Saturdays, p.m.		7 Passngrs. and Goods 1 2 p.m.	8 Mail 1 2 p.m.	Sunday 1 Mail 1 2 3 class p.m.
Mls.			arr.	dep.					arr.	dep.			*
—	Waterford	D.	—	5 10	6 0	10 20	2 30	—	—	4 0		8 30	8 30
7¼	Grange ..	..	—	—	6 15	—	Flag	—	—	—		—	—
10	Fiddown	..	5 50	6 0	6 25	10 40	2 52	—	4 35	4 45		9 0	9 0
14½	Carrick ..	..	6 15	6 45	6 40	10 50	3 10	—	5 0	5 30		9 15	9 15
22	Kilsheelan	..	—	—	7 0	—	Flag	—	—	—		—	—
28	Clonmel ..	..	7 30	8 35	7 20	11 20	3 50	—	6 15	6 45		10 0	10 0
39	Caher ..	..	9 15	9 55	8 0	11 45	4 20	—	7 30	8 0		10 45	10 45
47¾	Bansha ..	..	10 25	10. 35	8 20	12 5	4 40	—	—	—		—	—
52¾	Tipperary	..	10 50	1 0	8 35	12 15	4 50	7 15	8 50	9 35		11 30	11 30
55½	Junction	A.	1 20	—	8 45	12 30	5 5	7 30	10 0	—		12 0	12 0
		D.	—	1 50	8 50	12 40	5 25				9 0	12 15	12 15
59	Oola ..	..	—	—	9 5	Flag	5 35				—	—	—
63¾	Pallas ..	..	2 15	2 25	9 15	1 0	5 45				9 25	12 40	12 40
66	Dromkeen	..	—	—	9 25	Flag	5 50				—	—	—
69½	Boher ..	..	—	—	9 35	1 15	6 0				—	—	—
77¾	Limerick	..	3 0	—	10 0	1 35	6 30				10 5	1 20	*1 20
			P.M.	P.M.	A.M.	P.M.	P.M.				P.M.	A.M.	A.M.

* *Will stop at all Stations, if necessary, to set down or take up Passengers—but Stations where Train not timed to stop must signal when they have Passengers.*

No. 6, as a rule, to do Carrick Siding work on days Pick-up runs, and on Saturdays this Train to run on to Limerick, to bring out Sunday Excursion Train.

GENERAL NOTES AND ORDERS.

It is required that Goods or Cattle Trains shall be on the sidings *at least* 10 minutes before Passenger Trains are due to pass them.

Speed of all Trains, when passing over Viaducts at Dunkitt (near Waterford), not to exceed 10 miles an hour.

The large figures denote where Trains (whether following or in opposite directions) are fixed to pass or meet each other at Stations, on the Single Line.

W&LR Working Timetable, July 1868. Author's collection

For many years the Limerick to Waterford services were operated by small engines; ie these services were the preserve of 2-2-2s, 0-4-2s and 2-4-0s right up to the 1890s. Included among the singles were three Bury engines dating back to 1847. Goods traffic was worked by the 0-4-2s, some of which dated from the 1850s. Improvements began during Appleby's tenure as locomotive superintendent with the two 4-4-0s, Nos 9 and 12, working the night mails. The appointment of J. G. Robinson brought about a reversion to the 2-4-0 type, but of a more powerful design than previously used. Whilst average speeds appeared low, one must take account of the gradients on the main line, reversals into and out of Limerick Junction and the fact that most of the line was single-tracked.

November 1890 and June 1900 working timetables

In November 1890, the early morning train for Waterford left Limerick at 06.00 and was followed by the limited mail at 09.35. This latter was due in Waterford at 12.25, having run non-stop as far as Limerick Junction, still referred to simply as Junction in the timetable. The boat train left Limerick at 11.40 and was followed by a second limited mail at 14.45. On arrival at Limerick Junction, the 14.45 became a goods train; on no account was this train to be delayed as the engine was scheduled to work back the 21.00 up mail. A passenger train left Limerick at 16.00 and the night mail at 23.00. In addition to the above-mentioned goods, there was a 21.00 down arriving in Waterford at 05.35 the following morning. On Saturday evenings, however, the 21.00 was described as an express goods, due in Waterford at 00.46. As it ran in connection with the Sunday morning sailing from North Wharf it took no wagons for intermediate stations and did not go into Limerick Junction. On other days of the week the engine of this train was to be available, when required, to assist the 23.30 up goods between Clonmel and Cahir.

There were corresponding up workings from Waterford. A note stated that if the GS&WR Dublin goods train was not on time at Limerick Junction to connect with the 23.30 goods, wagons from the GS&WR line were to be forwarded to Limerick by the 07.47 passenger train from the junction. As regards Sundays, there was one through train each way, along with a 12.00 to Limerick Junction only, this train returning to Limerick at 13.50.

Services on the North Kerry line now comprised the 04.50 mail for Tralee, 07.00 passenger to Listowel (extended to Tralee on Saturdays), 11.00 express mail for Tralee, 16.55 (Saturdays excepted) to Tralee and 17.45 (Saturdays only). The 19.00 up mail was required to stop at Devon Road on Listowel fair and market days if passengers so wished. There was one train each way on Sundays. The Foynes branch had three trains each way on weekdays only. By 1890 the Fenit branch was open for traffic with two trains each way on weekdays. Between Limerick and Tuam there were again three trains each way, with two additional workings as far as Ennis only. There was the usual mail service each way on Sundays. Both the Killaloe and Thurles lines had three trains each way, there being no Sunday service on these branches.

Four pages of notes followed the tables and provide useful information in relation to various train workings. The boat trains, at 11.40 down and 10.15 up, particularly the former, were the heaviest trains on the system. The timetable indicated that the 11.40 was to take only perishable traffic for shipment on the same day. This, however, often necessitated a tail of cattle wagons, fish vans and covered wagons of butter, eggs and other perishables. The up train was restricted to passenger-carrying vehicles between Waterford and Limerick Junction, although it was allowed to take on horse boxes and carriage trucks from the latter point.

To complete our review of train services we will take a brief look at the company's final timetable, published in May 1900, and by now of course under the brand of the WL&WR. The system had by this time reached its maximum extent with the completion of the link to the MGWR and SL&NCR systems at Collooney. On the main line there were three mail trains each way

Limerick and Kerry, Rathkeale and Newcastle Junction, and Foynes Branch Lines.

Miles frm Limerick	UP TRAINS TO FOYNES AND TRALEE.	WEEK DAYS.										Satdy. only.		SUNDAYS.	
		1 (Mail) 1, 2, 3 Class. a.m.		2 1, 2, 3 Class. a.m.		3 Exp. Mail 1, 2, 3 Class. a.m.		4 Goods. p.m.		5 1, 2, 3 Cl. Except Sat'day. p.m.		6 1, 2, 3 Class. p.m.		Mail. 1, 2, 3 Class. a.m.	
		Arr.	*Dep.*	*Arr.*	*Dep.*	*Arr.*	*Dep.*	*Arr.*	*Dep.*	*Arr.*	*Dep.*	*Arr.*	*Dep.*	*Arr.*	*Dep.*
...	LIMERICK ...	...	4 50	...	7 0	...	11 10	...	...	...	4 55	..	5 45	...	**7 30**
7¼	Patrick's Well ...	5 10	5 11	7 35	7 45	11 30	11 32	...	...	5 15	5 16	6 10	6 15	7 48	7 50
11	Adare ...	5 20	5 21	...	...	11 39	11 40	...	...	5 24	5 25	6 25	6 28	7 58	8 0
17¼	Ballingrane Junc.	5 38	5 40	8 20	8 30	11 53	11 55	...	...	**5 40**	**5 43**	6 45	6 48	8 15	8 18
Foynes Branch. 17¼	Ballingrane Junc.	...	...	...	...	...	12 0	...	1 45	...	5 50	...	6 55	...	...
20¾	Askeaton ...	...	...	...	...	12 8	12 10	1 55	2 0	5 58	6 0	7 3	7 5	...	...
26¾	FOYNES ...	...	...	...	...	**12 25**	...	2 15	...	6 15	...	7 20	...	...	...
19¼	Rathkeale ...	5 45	5 50	**8 38**	**8 50**	12 0	12 5	...	...	5 48	5 53	**6 54**	**7 3**	8 23	8 28
24½	Ardagh ...	6 5	6 8	9 8	9 13	12 18	12 23	...	...	6 6	6 10	7 19	7 23	8 41	8 43
27¼	NEWCASTLE ...	6 15	6 30	9 23	10 0	**12 30**	**12 45**	...	...	**6 20**	**6 35**	7 33	7 48	8 50	9 5
33½	Barnagh ...	6 49	6 50	10 25	10 27	1 0	1 3	...	...	6 54	6 55	8 7	8 8	9 22	9 25
38	Devon Road ...	7 2	7 5	10 40	10 43	1 12	1 13	...	...	7 4	7 5	8 17	8 18	9 34	9 35
41¼	Abbeyfeale ...	**7 15**	**7 20**	10 53	11 3	1 22	1 23	..	...	7 14	7 15	**8 26**	**8 27**	9 43	9 45
45¼	Kilmorna ...	7 29	7 30	11 17	11 20	1 33	1 35	...	...	7 25	7 30	8 37	8 42	9 54	9 55
50¾	Listowel ...	7 45	8 0	**11 35**	...	1 50	1 55	...	...	**7 50**	**8 5**	9 2	9 15	10 6	10 10
57¼	Lixnaw ...	8 13	8 15	On Saturdays this train will leave Listowel 11.45 a.m., arriving at Tralee 12.45 p.m.		2 9	2 10	...	...	8 19	8 20	9 29	9 30	10 27	10 30
62	Abbeydorney ...	8 28	8 30			2 19	2 20	...	...	8 30	8 32	9 40	9 42	10 39	10 40
65½	Ardfert ...	8 39	8 45			2 28	2 30	...	..	8 40	8 45	9 50	9 55	10 50	10 56
70¼	TRALEE ...	9 0	...			2 40	...	...	...	9 0	...	10 10	...	11 15	...

☞ No. 3.—On Fridays the Engine and Carriages working 3 p.m. train from Tralee will return from Listowel at **4.30 p.m.**, calling at intermediate Stations, and arriving in Tralee at 5.20 p.m.

9

Working Timetable, 1890. Author's collection

plus one through passenger service; the best times were now 3h 10m. As regards goods services, the 13.30 from Limerick was shown as the 'Milford Boat Express' and was due into Waterford at 16.40. In addition to the through services, there was an 05.40 down on Wednesdays and Saturdays which ran only to Tipperary, with a return working at 07.45 (as a passenger train). On the same days a goods train left Waterford at 05.00 for Clonmel, returning as a mixed train at 08.30.

The North Kerry line had the usual three trains each way, the fastest of which was the 10.15 down mail which was scheduled to arrive in Tralee at 13.30; two trains each way provided a Fenit connection. There was one train each way on Sundays, including a connection to Fenit. The Foynes branch had two weekday trains, one of which was mixed. The Killaloe and Thurles branches had two passenger, one goods and one mixed each way. There was no Sunday service to Thurles, but one train operated each way during the summer months to and from Killaloe.

As mentioned above, the line to Collooney was now open throughout, with running powers over the Midland into Sligo, the distance from Limerick to Collooney being 140 miles. The only through passenger train was the 10.12 from Limerick which was shown as a mail service to Ennis, passenger to Tuam and mixed on to Sligo, where it arrived at 17.00. This was a marathon journey by any standards and even more so when one considers that there were no on-train catering facilities. The longest intermediate stop, 15 minutes, was at Claremorris Midland, barely long enough to grab a cup of tea. It would have been possible to arrive on the early morning boat at Waterford and reach Sligo on the same day, but few people would have contemplated such a journey, dare one say, even hardened railway enthusiasts! Likewise, the 08.50 from Sligo would enable an intrepid traveller to reach Waterford at 20.10 or Tralee at 21.40, but in the latter case he would have a 2¼-hour stopover at Limerick.

The main line passenger trains were by now being worked by the three 4-4-0s, Nos 53, 54 and 55, and goods services by the Dübs and Kitson 0-6-0 engines. The Tralee line had been worked in the early 1890s by a pair of 2-4-2T engines, Nos 13 and 14, these being based for many years at Tralee shed. Four larger 4-4-2Ts entered service in 1896/7, primarily intended for working the Sligo line, but they also appear to have worked the North Kerry road. These were Nos 16, 17, 18 and 21. Prior to the introduction of the 4-4-2Ts on the Sligo extension, a pair of 0-4-4Ts, Nos 51 and 52, were to be found on the line to Tuam.

Sunday trains

Reference has already been made to the question of running Sunday trains on the W&LR system, and to services actually provided through the years. It was agreed as early as August 1850 that Sunday excursion trains would be continued so long as they did not interfere with the hours of Divine Worship. Up until 1862, every railway in Ireland ran Sunday trains, but in that year the W&LR suddenly resolved, at Malcomson's instigation, no doubt influenced by his Quaker tradition, to discontinue them. The subject was raised again in September of that year when the *Railway Times* reported that the Limerick people could not travel to Tramore, whereas in England, those living in London could avail themselves of seaside excursions to Dover, Brighton and even the Isle of Wight. The people of Dublin and Cork could likewise enjoy of such outings to places like Howth and Kinsale. The chairman, in reply to questioning by a Mr Delahunty, said that the board was of the belief that Sunday train traffic was not 'a description of traffic which compensated for the enormous risks incurred'.

The traffic manager submitted a return of earnings from Sunday trains in October 1863 showing that for the six months to 30 April of that year, receipts by the two trains concerned (10.20 up and 12.10 down) amounted to £436 17s 10d, the average number of passengers 179½. Jacob suggested the withdrawal of these trains on the main line, which was agreed to, despite a memorial from Limerick Corporation for their continuance. However, it was agreed to run Sunday trains on alternate weeks during the summer months of 1864. By now, the Sunday Trains Compulsory Running Bill was before Parliament, endeavouring to force companies, who provided passenger services on six days per week, to run Sunday trains. The *Railway Times* reporting in September 1864 on the half-yearly meeting of shareholders, referred to 'a good deal of dissatisfaction in the neighbourhood by the withdrawal of Sunday trains, which fell upon the lower classes'. A Mr Hackett said he understood the savings in a half-year amounted to no more than £200, whereas the receipts ran to almost £1,100. We do not have company figures for 1864, but returns are available for 1865. Receipts for the months of May, June and July totalled £200 0s 3d, later figures indicating a total of £360 for all Sunday trains in that year. As regards numbers travelling, these were broken down into 2,225 on up trains and 1,024 on down trains, respective receipts being £226 and £134, making totals of 3,249 passengers and receipts of £360.

The Sunday Trains Bill was defeated but was brought back to Parliament in the 1865 session under the hand of Sir Colman O'Loghlen, chairman of the A&EJR; returns were sought regarding numbers travelling and receipts for each of the three years to October 1862. The Bill was again defeated in the 1865 session. Among the opponents was Mr J. A. Blake, MP for Waterford City, in recognition of which Malcomson was instrumental in having a free pass issued to him for three years. Reference was made to the policy of the W&LR directors 'which was open to serious animadversion and a charge of pharisaism was justly brought against them'. Adverse comments were made in the *Railway Times* to the effect that only four Irish members of Parliament had opposed the Bill, its defeat being occasioned by no fewer than 53 Scottish members. Sir Colman O'Loghlen commented that he felt he had a right to complain of them forcing their peculiar views on the observance of the Sabbath into a question which solely affected Ireland, and where those views were not generally sympathised with. The proposed legislation reappeared in 1866 as the Sunday Travelling (Ireland) Bill, being defeated yet again by a majority of 200 to 83. Later, with Malcomson's departure, the directors were less troubled about running Sunday trains.

Goods services

Apart from the albeit brief references to goods services as enumerated in the various extant working timetables, some other contemporary references appear relative to specific traffics. Reference was made in August 1860 to iron ore traffic going via Waterford from the Shallow Mine or Nenagh to Llanelly in Wales, a traffic estimated at 1,000 tons per annum. A request was made in July 1864 for a covered shed at Waterford to accommodate the ore pending shipment to Wales. A Captain King wrote in November of that year seeking a special rate of 4s 6d per ton for ore from Birdhill to Waterford and a covered store or shed at the latter place to hold, say, two cargoes. The board declared itself 'hardly disposed to go to such expense' although it did ask its engineer to prepare estimates.

A ballast pit had been located at Cappagh, 3½ miles east of Bansha from an early date but had apparently been closed by January 1861. Another siding was provided at Toureen almost a mile further east in January 1859 to cater for timber traffic. A letter was received in January 1861 from the Rev G. Baker stating that he had a large quantity of timber on his estate and requesting the reopening of Cappa (sic) siding. The board decided that this traffic could be accommodated at Toureen siding. A further request was made in February 1863 when Baker mentioned a figure of 5,000 tons of timber. The board explained its objections to increased siding accommodation, although Baker tried again in January of the following year when the traffic manager said: 'It was worthy of consideration whether there should be a second line of rails between Bansha and Cahir.' Finally, in February 1864, the board relented and instructed Tighe to lay in a siding at Cappagh at a cost of £147. This was to be subject to Baker's guarantee to pay the cost if he did not send 2,000 tons of timber during the next two years at a rate of 4s 10d per ton. It was completed and ready for use in the following May. In July 1866 the traffic manager recommended the removal of the siding, but a decision was deferred. Instructions were finally given in June 1867 for the points to the siding to be removed and it was reported as closed in the following month.

Despite the board's apparent objections to additional sidings, one was installed at Cratloe in April 1863 to cater for timber traffic brought to the line by a Mr Cunningham. He sought a reduction in the rate for timber from 5s 6d a ton to 5s, a rate of 5s 3d being quoted and accepted.

Butter from Tipperary was another traffic that got a mention, the GS&WR complaining in February 1864 when the company stopped running the 16.00 from Waterford, a decision taken on the grounds of economy. The suggestion was made that the GS&WR might send a goods engine from Limerick Junction to Tipperary to take any butter remaining for transit to Dublin after the departure of the 16.45 train. This was in fact done, and this engine working became a feature of the timetable for some years. For example, it appears in the working timetable for July 1869, leaving Junction at 18.30 and returning from Tipperary at 19.15. Notice was given to cease the running of this engine in April of that year, the GS&WR asking a reconsideration of the decision as it bore the entire cost of its running. If the W&LR insisted with the notice 'they (the GS&WR) will adopt other steps for retaining butter traffic to their route'. One wonders if this may have been the reason for the GS&WR putting forward proposals in 1871 for its own branch to Tipperary.

Post Office mails

Down through the years the company was in constant dispute with the postal authorities regarding the level of payment made, the General Post Office in turn complaining of delays in the working of the service. Reference has been made to the early provision of mail services. However, in January 1851 it was noted in newspaper reports that the Post Office intended to run the mails from the Junction to Limerick by car. Two directors were requested to take the necessary measures to retain the service for the railway. Three months later, the Postmaster General sought proposals for the carrying of the night mails. A figure of 3s per mile was requested if 20 minutes were allowed for the journey. The postal authorities considered the figure to be too high and the matter was referred to arbitration. The company was in due course awarded a figure of 2s 10d for the night mails and 1s per mile for the day mails.

With the proposed opening to Waterford, a figure of 1s per mile was quoted for the day mails, which was accepted. In January 1859 the chairman stated that the Post Office had offered £1,000 for permission to run the mails in charge of the company's guards by any train, the company being merely bound to run a train daily to meet the GS&WR day mail at the Junction. It was agreed that a figure of £1,200 be sought, the former figure being accepted in the following November after some tough bargaining. Two years later the Inspector of Mails inquired if the service could be accelerated by 20 minutes. The traffic manager confirmed that this could be achieved if there were no intermediate stops and additional payment was made, and he was instructed to inquire what compensation the GS&WR had received for passing intermediate stations.

When the subject of payment for the night mails was raised in June 1862 the chairman reported that the postal authorities in London had hinted at a figure of £1,000, he being instructed to get as near as possible to £2,000 per annum. Later in the month, it was reported that £3,000 would be offered for the day and night mails, a five-year contract at this figure coming into operation from the following 1 November. It was agreed that a number of gatemen between Tipperary and Limerick should be allowed an additional 1s 6d per week for additional duties in connection with the night mails.

September 1864 saw the Inspector of Mails complaining of delays to trains, resulting in comments that the line was the worst in Ireland for delays 'which has a very prejudicial effect'. Hints were made that payment for the service might be stopped. It was agreed that delays in general had become too frequent and the matter was referred to the appropriate officers. The traffic manager and the locomotive superintendent agreed that they would fine those in charge of trains more than 10 minutes late in the absence of a satisfactory explanation. Further complaints were made in October when the Postmaster General stated that the time had arrived for taking action to protect the postal services. It was ordered that the load of the mail trains was to be limited for the future and the Post Office was to be requested to allow an additional 15 minutes between Limerick Junction and Waterford. By December the Postmaster General was obviously becoming quite frustrated at what he saw as a lack of action on the part of the company and he could only conclude that the company wished a hostile step to be taken by him. He presumed that the company did not expect the December account to be certified for payment. In reply the company again sought additional running time, on this occasion 15 minutes extra in departure and arrival.

Proposals put forward in February 1865 to alter the mail services on the Cork and Kilkenny lines as from 1 April were considered and it was agreed that considerable delays would be experienced at Limerick Junction or else additional trains would be required, the latter estimated to cost an extra £1,000 per annum. Alterations were made which disrupted the connection into the up main line day mail. This led to a memorial from the Mayor of Limerick requesting the running of a short train, perhaps an engine and a single carriage, between Limerick and Limerick Junction to meet the up day mail. Inquiries were made as to the charge for such a service, he being advised that 1s per mile would not adequately compensate the company although it would accept that figure. There is no evidence that such a train was laid on and in fact a letter was sent to the GPO in June 1868 suggesting a modification in the service to do away with the delay of one and a half hours at the Junction. The GS&WR eventually persuaded the Post Office to agree to the up mail being retimed, the W&LR altering its service to make a more reasonable connection.

Details were given to the board in December 1869 of remuneration received for the mail service provided by it. This indicated that on the main line, 48,202 miles were run during the year in connection with the day mail, for which £2,000 was paid, equating to 9¾d per mile, while 56,210 miles were run for the night mail. In the latter instance, £1,000 was received, equal to only 4¼d per mile. The branches fared even less well, only ¼d a mile being received for the Castleconnell line, while in the case of the L&FR, 41,000 miles were run with a payment of only £20 for the year. The company sought a total figure of £5,000 for the main line services, this being declined by the Post Office, which also declined a suggestion of arbitration. A figure of £4,000 was then sought, but by September 1871 the chairman was informed that he should seek an additional £1,500 but could, if necessary, accept £1,000, viz a total of £4,000 — this is in fact what was accepted.

The question of the subsidy was again raised in October 1882 when the board considered the small sum being received by the company, the traffic manager being requested to ascertain what other companies received. The Postmaster General refused to increase the payments, although the company was 'so strongly impressed with the justice of their claim and the insufficiency of the sum paid to cover the expenses incurred, (they) beg to suggest the matter be at once referred to arbitration'. The response from the Post Office was that the company, if not satisfied, should terminate the agreements, due notice being served.

With the matter still unresolved, although the service was being temporarily continued at the existing terms, a rate of 3s per mile was considered equitable, or else a figure of £10,000 per annum was sought along with an agreement for 10 years. The Post Office eventually agreed an additional £1,659 per annum, being 3s per mile for an additional service between Limerick and Limerick Junction. In June 1886 a subsidy of £2,000 per annum additional was offered for an accelerated service between Limerick Junction and Waterford, this being accepted. In May 1889 it was reported that the Tralee mails for Cahir, Clonmel and Waterford had been diverted over the GS&WR route, where the latter company's train departed Tralee earlier. This was accepted without demur.

More complaints of late running and lost connections were made in February 1891, followed by three more in the following month, all involving the night mail. In its defence, the company pointed out that there was only a four-minute margin at Limerick Junction which was insufficient. In October of the following year the company agreed to the Post Office putting post boxes on the up and down night mails on the main line, at no extra charge. In 1893, a sorting carriage, without exchange apparatus, was introduced between Waterford and Limerick Junction, the one carriage doing the return journey the same night. The GS&WR altered this arrangement in 1902, the sorting vehicle then working right through between Limerick and Waterford.

By 1897 attention had again turned to the inadequate remuneration received for the postal service, the traffic manager being of the opinion that a figure of about £28,000 was required. It was agreed that £16,000 would be accepted — the wide divergence between the figure required and that sought makes one wonder as to their veracity. It was agreed in March 1898 that the entire matter be referred to the Railway Commissioners for a decision, the company now seeking a sum of £20,000. Meanwhile, the locomotive superintendent suggested the conversion of three old third class carriages to provide sorting accommodation on the night mails. When the Commissioners had deliberated on the WL&WR application, they stated that the sum of £20,000 was unreasonable and awarded a figure of £8,000 per annum. This was in November 1900 and the company response was that it 'had no interest in obtaining further Counsel's Opinion'. It was something its new masters would have to consider in due course.

Road services

With the opening of the line to Dunkitt, Charles Bianconi was authorised to provide a road service thence to Waterford, charging 8d for each inside passenger and 6d for each outside the horse-drawn car, the service to commence from 12 December 1853. By July 1858, Bianconi's cars had given way to a local operator, a Mr Dobbyn. This latter gentleman was offered 10s per week to operate a service, this figure being declined and in the following month it was decided to discontinue the service. He appears to have reluctantly agreed to the payment but in November he was informed that the company no longer required his omnibuses or vehicles 'for any purpose whatsoever, nor will the Company be responsible for any expenses or tolls connected with the running of such conveyances from Waterford city to our terminus'. In the following

Working Timetable, June 1900.
Author's collection

month, two offers were received for the service, viz from Messrs Power at 16s per week and from Messrs Cummins for 10s 6d per week. Despite all of this, it was agreed to go on paying Dobbyn. Arrangements were later made for the provision of a car service between Fiddown station and Portlaw, in connection with the Malcomson enterprise at the latter village. It was reported in July 1868, however, that through bookings had rather abruptly ceased, the operator being dissatisfied with receiving no payment for the trouble in booking through passengers. It was agreed to pay 5% of the rail receipts as an incentive, which was accepted.

In March 1864, it was reported that a car had commenced operating between Carrick-on-Suir and Waterford, it being decided to take no action at that time. It was still running in the following month and the traffic manager was requested to arrange with the locomotive superintendent for the running of a train each way daily from Waterford to Carrick-on-Suir. This service was to be well placarded, with return fares at 3s, 2s and 1s, but complaints were made as to the first class fare being too high, this being soon reduced to 2s 9d. The train obviously had the desired effect as the car service ceased operating on 22 April.

Various other road services operated over the years, including those from Dromkeen to Doon and Cappamore, Boher to Hospital and Castleconnell to Newport. In the latter case, an annual sum of £50 was settled upon for a two-horse car, the proprietor, Christopher Cullen, agreeing to run in connection with the Sunday trains.

Chapter Fourteen

ACCIDENTS

An accident at Limerick Junction on the morning of 13 September 1848 led to a report being submitted to the board by Mr Rogers, superintendent of police. The report stated that the driver of the engine *Glengall* was conducting the train at a speed 'not authorised by the arrangements of the Directors'. On reviewing the matter it was decided to refer the case to the Magistrates, it having been established that the driver was seen 'in a state of intoxication or apparent intoxication' by several individuals in the company's employment. Resulting from this accident a printed circular was issued to all officers and servants informing them that not only could they expect instant dismissal for such an offence but the might of the law would also be used against them.

A derailment of the 06.00 down train occurred on 2 December 1852 about 2½ miles on the Cahir side of Bansha. The engine overturned and unfortunately Thomas Enright, the stoker (fireman), was killed. The inquest found that the driver and guard of the train had acted properly and no blame could be attached to the company. Luckily, no passengers were injured as the carriages remained upright. However, Captain Wynne RE commented on the state of the permanent way, orders being issued in January 1853 for the line to be put in perfect order. This led to a considerable increase in the number of men employed on the permanent way.

A very serious accident befell the 16.15 down train from Limerick on New Year's Day 1854 at Anner Bridge near Kilsheelan resulting in another fatality. On this occasion both the engine and carriages were derailed and fell down a 14ft high embankment. The engine, having completely rolled over, ended up on its wheels at the bottom of the embankment. Regrettably, Driver John Smith died at the scene, his fireman suffering severe injuries including a fractured collarbone and arm. None of the passengers received serious injuries, but a sum of £35 was later paid to three of them. Smith's widow was given a lump sum of £60; subsequently Mrs Smith requested the board to reconsider its decision and grant her an annuity, but the board considered 'a sum of money best for Mrs Smith'.

Thomas Lunt, the locomotive superintendent, submitted a report to the board which gives us some additional information on this particular accident. The train consisted of the Stothert & Slaughter 2-2-2 *Waterford*, a covered wagon (the BoT report refers to it as a guard's van) and first, second and third class carriages, all of which went down the embankment. Lunt was unable to establish the cause of the accident with certainty, but believed it had been caused either by a broken rail which had become brittle owing to severe frost, or a broken spring link over the driving wheels. The breakage of the rail could have resulted from a breakage of the latter. Lunt recommended that the Stothert engines be withdrawn from service pending the alteration or strengthening of the spring links on the remaining engines of the class. He commented that they were 'rather an unsteady class of engine for a curved line'.

Captain Tyler investigated the accident on behalf of the BoT. It appeared that the engine had given a sudden jump about 100 yards before it derailed, dragging its train after it. By the time of Tyler's inspection of the scene on 14 January, the wreckage was still in situ although the permanent way had been replaced to enable services to resume. The line in question consisted of 71lb/yd rail in 21ft lengths laid in cast-iron chairs fastened by wooden trenails to larch sleepers spaced about three yards apart. Chairs had been broken for a distance of about 60 yards before the point of derailment. Anner Bridge consisted of wrought-iron lattice girders with a span of 62ft; the bridge was skewed at an angle of 55°, Tyler commenting that a cross-jumping motion given to an engine passing at speed over all skew girder bridges would be imparted to a more than ordinary extent by this bridge.

The Stothert engines were unique for their time in that they were outside-cylindered and this, Captain Tyler considered, might have contributed to the accident. He suggested that the company should in future work its passenger traffic with inside-cylindered engines, and that a speed limit of 15mph be placed on Anner Bridge. Tyler also commented that another member of the same class, *Limerick*, had suffered a derailment on a straight piece of track in December 1852, the accident near Bansha already mentioned above. Following consideration of the BoT report, Lunt was instructed to carry out Captain Tyler's suggestions as far as possible. Despite this, it was reported that No 5, another of the Stothert engines, came off the line near Limerick on 2 August 1860 and fell down a 4ft embankment. Pim, by then the locomotive superintendent, claimed that the outside-cylinder construction caused oscillation at high speed, estimated on this occasion at 20 to 25mph. The engine was running light at the time and only recently out-of-shops and in thorough working order.

A near accident on 6 February 1871, when the driving wheel came off the engine of an up train, drew the comment from the board that Mr Lunt would have received the severe censure of the board 'were he not now leaving the line'. A fatal accident near Pallas station on 27 May 1858 was investigated by Captain Tyler, who commented that William Nichill's death resulted from his own recklessness in endeavouring to exit a moving train on the wrong side. He went on to recommend that the permanent way should be shifted to the centre of the bridge, instead of being only 2ft from the middle girder; similar remarks could be applied to about two dozen other bridges of similar construction on the W&LR.

A scathing letter from the Board of Trade
Reference was made in earlier chapters to financial cut-backs introduced by the board in the early years. This parsimonious attitude was to lead to a scathing letter being issued to the directors following a head-on collision between two trains near Bansha on 6 April 1859. Tipperary lay on one side of Bansha, Cahir on the other, both being telegraph stations at this time, although Bansha was not. The timetable arrangements were that the 07.20 up goods train from Waterford was due to meet and cross the 11.30 down passenger train at Tipperary. There was, however, a general order in place allowing stationmasters to alter passing places to cater for late running trains or for special trains. This was catered for by sending telegraph messages. To ensure that such messages were fully understood, it was not sufficient for stationmasters receiving these messages to simply reply 'noted' or 'all right'; they were obliged to repeat them in full and carefully file a copy for future

reference. To further ensure safety, the stationmaster so altering passing places was obliged to consult with the driver and guard of the train, following this with a written authority allowing them to proceed beyond the original passing station.

On the day in question, the 07.20 up goods train was already late by the time it arrived at Cahir and was further detained there by shunting work. After consulting with the crew of the goods, the stationmaster at Cahir decided that the crossing with the 11.30 down passenger train should be made at Bansha and, in this context, telegraph messages were exchanged between Tipperary and Cahir at about 12.35. It would seem that, contrary to regulations, the Tipperary stationmaster sent the written order to the driver of the passenger train by the hands of a porter rather than delivering it in person. The driver later stated that he had never received the order, while the guard claimed that he was not informed where the trains were to meet.

The passenger train then went on its way to Bansha. There, the stationmaster stated that he always asked the engineman on the train's arrival for his written order, but coincidentally omitted to do so on this occasion. While he was standing on the platform the guard gave the signal for the train to start, without the stationmaster's permission. The guard contradicted this evidence and claimed he had requested and received permission. In addition, there was a regulation requiring the stationmaster to ring a hand-bell as a signal to the guard to start his train, but it had not been the practice at Bansha to do this for some considerable time.

While all this was going on at Bansha, the goods train had left Cahir. For those early days it was a heavy train, 204 tons worked by two tender engines and with two brake vans. The two opposing trains met on a curve less than a mile from Bansha. The crews of both trains, except for one of the guards on the goods train, had time to jump off before the collision occurred. It would seem that in his haste to leave his charge, the driver of the passenger engine may have left his regulator open or else it had been opened by the collision. He had managed to put it into reverse and, following the collision, it ran back to Bansha where it was stopped by the signalman diverting it into a siding. It was extremely lucky that injuries to passengers were of a minor nature.

Captain Ross in his report into the accident was scathing in his comments regarding the non-observance of rules and regulations, particularly in relation to such important matters as the altering of passing places. Had proper attention been paid to these regulations, the accident would most likely not have happened. In sending the report to the company, the BoT stated that

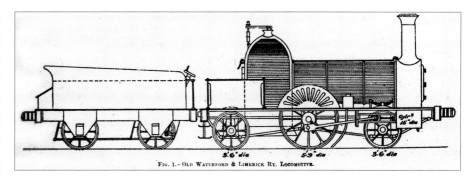

Fig. 1.– Old Waterford & Limerick Ry. Locomotive.

Drawing of one of the Stothert, Slaughter engines of 1846. It is incorrectly drawn as the trailing wheels should have outside bearings. Locomotive Magazine

the directors 'apparently with the object of effecting the petty economy of not having a separate wire and proper instruments, servants and regulations for the telegraphic train service, have adopted a mode of working the single line, which appears to place responsibility on no-one, and to be so fraught with danger that it is providential that some serious accident has not happened long ago upon the line'. The letter concluded by commenting that their Lordships trusted that this warning would induce the directors to at once alter such a reckless system of working as responsibility would fall on them for any future accident.

Arising from this accident, the stationmaster and head porter at Tipperary were dismissed, as were the driver and guard of the passenger train. A board minute of 2 June comments that the suggestions contained in the report were already in force, while orders had been given to have additional telegraph stations at Fiddown and Bansha. There was a sequel to the Bansha accident six years later, when Payne, by that time with the DW&WR, reported that Driver Hall, just before emigrating to Australia, had admitted to him that he had in fact received, and destroyed, the train order. It was decided, in view of the lapse of time, to do nothing towards reinstating the Tipperary stationmaster, Daniel Hickie.

Two accidents at or near Clonmel in November and December 1860 are worthy of brief comment. The November derailment resulted from a stone being placed in points and a £25 reward was offered for information leading to a conviction. The second derailment occurred a month later after a large stone, estimated to weigh about 2cwt, was placed on the rails. Following this incident, it was reported that a porter who had recently been discharged had been arrested on suspicion of the offence.

Regulations are again ignored

A number of minor accidents and incidents occurred over the next eight years, none of any great consequence or interest. We return to Clonmel, however, to consider a serious collision which took place there on 29 March 1869. Like the Bansha accident 10 years previously, that at Clonmel resulted from the crossing of two trains being

altered. On the day of the accident the 09.20 down goods train was due to cross the up passenger train at Clonmel at 15.50. Due to being delayed en route the goods train was already 40 minutes late by the time it arrived at Cahir, 11 miles west of Clonmel. The stationmaster at Cahir therefore decided to hold it there and allow the passenger train up from Clonmel to pass. While he was in course of informing the guard that his train would be held to await the arrival of the passenger train, the driver was performing shunting operations. The stationmaster then directed his assistant to telegraph accordingly to Clonmel and enter the transaction in the telegraph book, both of which were done.

With the shunting completed, the goods train was re-formed and appears to have left Cahir while the stationmaster was in his office. Although the guard later denied that he had been instructed to remain at Cahir, he appears to have harboured some doubts as some discussion took place on the subject with his driver. It should be mentioned that on this occasion, no written order was handed to the crew of the train. In his defence, the stationmaster claimed, quite incorrectly, that such orders were only to be given to trains authorised to go forward and not to those being detained.

In any event, the passenger train left Clonmel at 15.54. At about 1½ miles west of the station and running at about 20mph, the driver saw the goods train bearing down on him about 200 yards distant on a falling gradient of 1 in 132. Both drivers shut off steam and reversed their engines, all four footplate staff then jumping off. The collision was estimated to have occurred at about 12mph, both engines being much damaged. All the passenger carriages were more or less damaged, four goods wagons being completely destroyed and two others considerably damaged. Fourteen passengers were reported to have sustained injuries as well as both guards and the driver of the goods train.

In evidence it transpired that the goods train guard had left Cahir some nine months previously under similar circumstances. Lt-Col Rich, who investigated the accident on behalf of the BoT, felt that the stationmaster had not maintained his authority, 'so necessary to the proper and safe working of the station and railway'. Arising from this accident the company decided to alter the method of working the line to the train staff system. Rich also recommended that trains should run to and from up and down platforms. In future, the staff, or ticket, should always be given personally by the stationmaster to the driver in the presence of, or through the guard. It was to be almost 12 months before the last of the personal injury claims was finally settled.

In the 20 years following the accident at Clonmel, a series of collisions occurred across the system and, as we shall shortly see, the BoT inspecting officers repeatedly referred to lack of interlocking and the inadequacy of braking systems. Before dealing with these accidents, however, we will briefly look at two derailments. The first of these occurred at Tuam on 2 November 1873 when an empty passenger special was partly derailed on a set of facing points at the south end of the station. The points in question were worked by an adjacent hand lever and when not in use were locked by a bolt passing through them; this latter was covered by a ferrule cut to such a length so as to act as a wedge. It appeared that a split had developed in the ferrule which prevented it from acting as such. Lt-Col Rich commented on the company's lack of a weighing machine, as he was of opinion that there appeared to be very little weight resting on the trailing wheels of the engine involved. He also recommended interlocking.

The second derailment occurred on 21 August 1875 at Longpavement on the ex L&ER line. In this instance the tyre on the right-hand leading wheel of the engine fractured as the train approached the Shannon Bridge. The engine and tender ran down a 20ft high embankment, the former ending up on its wheels at the bottom of the slope. Driver Cowie and Fireman McGrath were both injured, the fireman succumbing to his injuries the next evening. Although the entire train derailed, only the engine and tender went down the embankment. The cause of this accident was found to be an incorrectly sized tyre, it having been held in position with a packing strip. Lt-Col Rich passed comment on the poor state of the rails, the condition of which rendered their speedy renewal a matter of necessity.

A series of collisions

Two collisions occurred in the space of just over a month on 20 October and 29 November 1873. The October collision occurred at Ballyglunin, only six miles from the scene of the Tuam derailment, when a special train of empty cattle wagons and passenger carriages ran into the 18.55 passenger train from Athenry which was standing in the station. On that day a cattle fair was held in Tuam, causing some disruption to services. As a result, the passenger train did not leave Athenry until 19.58, arriving in Ballyglunin at 20.22, having taken 24 minutes for the journey of nine miles. As it was, it had overrun the station and had to set back about two carriage lengths. This operation had only just been completed when the special ran into the rear at a speed estimated by Lt-Col Rich as about 7 or 8mph. The train consisted of 16 empty wagons, three empty carriages and a brake van, hauled by two locomotives.

Both drivers on the special claimed that the station signal was clear when they first saw it, but that it was changed to red after they had passed the distant signal. The driver of the leading engine was clearly negligent in allowing the train to approach the station at too high a speed when he knew that the passenger train was ahead of him; he was also aware that the Ballyglunin down distant signal was never lit. Rich recommended that the distant signals on either side of the station be moved out and that all signals and points be interlocked. White, the driver of the leading engine, was dismissed by order of the board, the driver of the train engine receiving a reprimand and a fine of a week's pay.

The November collision took place at Limerick Junction station. The accident occurred when a mixed train leaving the W&LR platform on the back road collided with a train arriving from Limerick. The former train left the platform against signals after the driver had received the right-away from the guard. However, he omitted to check the position of the starting signal and collided with the arriving train. It also came to light that his fireman was forward on the running plate oiling his engine as the train departed. Lt-Col Rich described the accident as being one of a class 'that will sometimes occur with the best men'. Yet again, interlocking was recommended.

On 4 November 1875, the 05.30 goods train from Limerick collided with the 04.00 mixed train from Waterford, which was performing a shunting operation at Carrick-on-Suir station. Luckily there were no injuries to staff or passengers. Once again, it was a case of approaching a station at too great a speed, the 05.30 having run through both the distant and home signals. The fireman was described as being 'a young and inexperienced lad'. Both he and his driver were instantly dismissed and it was ordered that the company's solicitor take the strongest steps to have the driver prosecuted. However, it soon became clear that Driver Franklin had been employed continuously for almost 21 hours. Immedi-ately after the accident he was found in a deep sleep on a station bench and it was assumed, quite incorrectly, that he had been drinking. Following receipt of the BoT report it was decided to defer prosecuting Franklin and his fireman was re-employed. As in previous accidents, it was recommended that points and signals be interlocked.

Neglect at Patrickswell

Following the Carrick-on-Suir accident another six years went by with nothing serious to record. The 1880s, however, produced a spate of collisions, the first of which occurred on the evening of 13 September 1881 near Patrickswell station. Before dealing with the accident itself, it is opportune to make some reference to the arrangements for trains leaving Limerick station for the North Kerry road. Outgoing W&LR trains bound for either Foynes or the North Kerry line were pushed out of the terminus as far as Limerick Check cabin by the train engine before proceeding on their way. Departing C&LDR trains made a very sharp turn right off the end of their own platform, passing Carey's Road yard to join the North Kerry line at Foynes Junction. The effect of this was that C&LDR trains reached the latter point in about two minutes whereas W&LR trains took seven or eight minutes to do so. Despite this time difference, the latter trains were only allowed the same overall running time to Patrickswell.

Tuesday, 13 September 1881 was the first day of the Limerick races. On that evening a special train for Foynes left Limerick at 18.05 carrying a ticket. The special should, in the normal course of events, have been followed out by the 18.15 passenger train to Tralee, after which there was to be a GS&WR special departing for Cork. However, as the Cork special was ready to go, he was let away at 18.27, also carrying a ticket. The Tralee train, carrying the staff, moved off only one minute later. In his evidence, Stephen Glynn, the chief clerk to the superintendent at Limerick and who was in charge of operations that day, stated that he warned the driver of the Tralee train to run cautiously as far as Patrickswell as the GS&WR train was just ahead of him.

Fate now intervened as the Foynes special stopped at Patrickswell with a suspected hot box, the Cork train being pulled up behind him. It appears that the driver of the Tralee train either forgot or ignored what had been said to him as he approached the station at excessive speed and collided with the rear of the train ahead of him. In all, some 55 passengers on both trains complained of injuries. Lt-Col (later Maj-Gen) Hutchinson criticised the driver of the Cork train for having stopped at least 120 yards in rear of the disabled train; had he moved forward another 70 yards he would have brought the rear of his train well within the protection of the distant signal. Whilst this might not have prevented the collision, its effects would have been lessened. The guard of the GS&WR train also came in for criticism for being tardy in going back to protect his train; at the moment of impact he had only gone back about 100 yards although his train had been stopped for perhaps five minutes — there were considerable discrepancies in the timings given for various events. Hutchinson was of the opinion that the collision would probably have been prevented if the line had been worked on the absolute block system, or if the Tralee train had had more brake power available, or indeed if the down distant signal had been situated some 500 yards further out. Finally, Hutchinson commented on the objectionable practice of backing Foynes and Tralee trains out of Limerick station.

Just over a year later, on 7 December 1882, a more straightforward collision took place at Limerick Junction when a Waterford bound passenger train was being pushed out along the back road. The train ran through a set of facing points and came into collision with three empty carriages standing in a siding. Criticism was levelled at the GS&WR, who operated the station, for not having the points held over while movements were taking place at them. It was also clear that the driver was setting back at an excessive speed. Lt-Col Hutchinson referred to the arrangements at Limerick Junction as being 'of a very peculiar, and so far as I know, of a perfectly unique character'. He went on to state that the practice of propelling passenger trains was 'objectionable'. Yet again, mention was made of interlocking.

For the next collision we move to the Southern Railway's Thurles branch. On 2 April 1883 the 13.50 mixed train from Thurles to Clonmel, due to depart from Fethard station at 14.53, was run into by a cattle special running ahead of its time. There were a number of factors involved in this accident: the cattle train was a heavy one with inadequate brakes and overran the signals at Fethard at a higher speed than was advisable; the driver had worked over the branch on only three occasions previously

and was clearly unfamiliar with the steep gradients; likewise his fireman had been on the branch only five times. The driver should have requested a pilotman to accompany him or should have arranged for the fireman off the mixed train to travel with him. It was also reported that there had been a failure of the block instruments at Farranaleen, but this was denied by the linesman.

Hutchinson was back in December of that year to investigate another collision, this time at Carrick-on-Suir station. During shunting operations there on the morning of 5 December, the 05.00 Waterford to Limerick Junction goods train was run into by the 06.00 passenger train which was due to stop there. The collision occurred about 530 yards inside the up distant signal on a falling gradient of 1 in 833. The point of collision was about 125 yards short of a water tank at which the passenger train was supposed to stop. It need hardly be said that the points and signals were not interlocked. The company's rules stated that the goods train should have been moved on to the down loop rather than leaving it on the main line when a passenger train was due. There was also a delay in putting the distant signal to danger following the arrival of the goods train; again, there was some conflict as regards times, but it appeared that it remained at clear for at least two to three minutes. Hutchinson concluded his report with the comment that 'it is almost needless to say that had the block system been in force and properly worked between Fiddown and Carrick, this collision would not have taken place'.

Tuam Junction at Athenry was the location for a collision on 2 January 1884 between an MGWR up mixed train and a similar train from Tuam bound for Limerick. The W&LR train ran through signals and collided with the first two carriages of the Midland train which was just leaving for Dublin. Such was the violence of the collision that these carriages ran back for almost a quarter of a mile before being stopped just short of the level crossing at the Galway end of Athenry station. Three pig drovers complained of their injuries as did the driver and fireman of the W&LR engine.

The Tuam driver claimed that he passed the distant signal at clear and that the home signal was thrown to danger when he was only about 150 yards from it. This was strongly denied by the signalman, his evidence being corroborated by an MGWR ganger who witnessed the accident. One point of criticism was the fact that the weight available for braking on the Tuam train was only 27 out of 175½ tons. Hutchinson stated that it was most desirable that engines working mixed trains should have a steam brake fitted and that heavier brake vans be employed. He concluded his report with a similar remark to that in his report on the Carrick collision, viz 'It is hardly necessary to remark that with a proper system of junction block working this collision would have been prevented.' This was all set to change following the Armagh accident of 1889.

One final collision is worthy of mention, that at Limerick Junction on 19 July 1890. This involved a passenger train from Limerick running into a light engine going to shunt a carriage from the GS&WR platform. The collision, which might have been very serious, brought to light a very lax system of working at the junction station, as well as 'very imperfect station arrangements'. The stationmaster appeared to be responsible for having allowed, for some time past, engines to move about the west side of the station and yard without signals of any kind from the signalmen, and without proper communication between the shunter and the signalmen. The shunter was described as being a very young man with insufficient experience to be entrusted with such responsible duties. He, and the driver of the light engine, passed a signal at danger.

Once again, it came to light that the train from Limerick was fitted only with a screw brake on the tender and a similar device in the guard's van. Lt-Col Rich recommended that the arrangements and signalling at Limerick Junction be altered and improved. Yet again it was stressed that trains should not be backed into and out of the platforms, and it was also pointed out that no engine should be allowed to move about the yard without proper signals. Rich commented that the W&LR bay platforms were in a very dangerous and improper state and appeared to have been altered without reference to the BoT. The various alterations in the track layout required to reduce the need for backing trains at Limerick Junction station were to take almost another 80 years to be carried out.

Although outside the timescale of the WL&WR, it might be mentioned that a serious accident occurred at Kiltimagh on 19 December 1916 when a ballast train from Tuam ran through the station and collided head-on with a special of goods from Sligo. The collision resulted in the deaths of six ballastmen and a further six were injured.

Limerick Junction station looking east. Trains for Limerick used the platform on the right in the middle distance while Waterford-bound trains used a platform behind the photographer. Use of the latter required reversals in both directions. The up and down main line platforms are on the far side of the main station building.
Ian Allan Library

Chapter Fifteen

LOCOMOTIVES

Consideration was given in February 1846 to obtaining tenders for the supply of engines, three such being opened at a board meeting on 16 April. That of Messrs Stothert, Slaughter & Company of Bristol (later to become the Avonside Engine Co) was considered the most favourable, although Vignoles was requested to obtain further particulars from them before a final decision was made. In due course an order was placed with Stotherts for six engines and tenders to be delivered at Limerick on or before 1 April 1847 at £2,400 each. The six locomotives (Type I) were delivered in March 1847 and were unnumbered, carrying names only as follows: *Glengall*, *Bessborough*, *Waterford*, *Limerick*, *Suir* and *Shannon*. They were subsequently numbered 1 to 6 after William Dargan relinquished his haulage contract in 1853 (as described later), but today, we cannot be absolutely certain as to which number was allocated to each of the names.

The new locomotives were unusual for the time, at least in Ireland, in that they were outside-cylindered. It seems likely, as was usual at that period, that the engines were designed by the manufacturers, with little input from the company other than a broad outline of their requirements. A newspaper report on the first engine, *Glengall*, gives her total weight as 32 tons, 7 tons of which related to the (empty) tender. Allowing for 3 tons of water and about 2 tons of coke, the laden tender probably weighed 12 tons. The same report stated that *Glengall* was tested at 70mph — a high speed for those days.

The first locomotive superintendent, William Martley, was requested in February 1848 to report to the secretary on whether two of the Stothert engines might be adapted for goods traffic and the probable cost of same. There is no further reference to the report, but we do know that no such work was carried out. Following Martley's dismissal, it was Khlos who was asked to explain the apparent disparity in locomotive expenses in January 1849. These varied from 7.264d per mile for *Waterford* to 12.825d for *Glengall*. Another newspaper report in October 1849 stated that the company's engines in use between Limerick and Tipperary 'consume turf in preference to coal'. Reference was made to a poor woman's cabin being set on fire at Pallisgreen due to 'flakes of fire falling from the engine as it passed by'. Again, in September 1850, it was reported that locomotive expenses for the previous half-year had amounted to £779 for 549 tons of coal and 175 kishes of turf. Another interesting board minute in August 1855 gave instructions to experiment with the use of 'quarter coal on the engines'.

One of the class, *Waterford*, was involved in the derailment at Anner Bridge in December 1853. Captain Tyler, the BoT inspector sent to inquire into the accident, was of opinion that the company should, in future, run its passenger trains with inside-cylindered engines. He also commented that another engine of the class, *Limerick*, had been derailed in December 1852. Further details of these accidents can be found in Chapter Fourteen. The locomotive superintendent, Thomas Lunt, stated that these engines 'are all rather an unsteady class of engine for a curved line', although it should be said that both of these accidents occurred on straight track. No 6 burst a tube in December 1855, reportedly the first time this had happened, although two tubes had previously been plugged in the workshops. One locomotive was converted to a tank engine, possibly in the second half of 1857 as company returns show a tank engine from that time, believed to be No 6, but this is not certain. By April 1857 an offer had been received to purchase two of the Slaughter engines but this offer was declined. However, in October 1860 the company advertised two engines and three tenders for sale.

Dargan's haulage contract
By December 1850, the W&LR had decided to adopt a measure popular with many companies at this time, namely that of arranging a haulage agreement and passing over the train working to a third party. Thus, such an agreement was concluded in April 1851 with William Dargan, the contract initially being for a period of 18 months or until the opening of the extension beyond Tipperary, including maintenance of way and policing. Initially, the charge was 1s 8d per train mile for three months, Dargan promising to reduce this if possible after the experience of that period. The contract was in fact extended and remained in force until the line reached Dunkitt in August 1853.

In the period during which Dargan undertook the haulage, four of his engines were added to the W&LR list, a report of 1 September 1852 stating that three locomotives had been added to stock, which were Dargan's property. The fourth was a mystery engine, which we shall return to shortly, but first of all we will deal with the three of Type III, which were originally supplied new to the Newry, Warrenpoint & Rostrevor Railway as its Nos 1 to 3, the first two in 1848, the third in 1849. They were almost identical to a batch of Bury engines on the GS&WR, a slightly larger example of which, GS&WR No 36, is preserved at Cork. They were, however, found to be too heavy for the Newry company's track and were most likely transferred away shortly after Dargan took over the working of that line in May 1850.

The Burys had bar frames and D-shaped fireboxes with a low crown. They probably also had standard Bury four-wheeled tenders, but at some point these appear to have been swapped with those on the Stothert engines. They were numbered 8 to 10 after the W&LR took back the working of its lines in 1853. All three survived until the 1880s, having been rebuilt between 1865 and 1871. By April 1875 it was reported that they were fit only for light passenger trains. When tubes failed in No 10 in March 1885, it was ordered that only a 'cheap set be put in', although she also received new cylinders at the same time. Following No 10's withdrawal in 1888 she was put to work driving sawmill machinery at Limerick Works, where her cylinders and motion were still to be seen 50 years later.

The so-called mystery engine which, after August 1853, became No 7 in the W&LR list, was almost certainly a Dargan engine. A board minute of 19 January 1853 refers to the possible purchase of two second-hand engines offered by Dargan, and about this time the GS&WR loaned him two, possibly because the two for sale were not immediately available. It seems that the W&LR took only one of these two engines from Dargan, probably because it already had six new locomotives on order, which were beginning to arrive. This one appears to have arrived towards the end of the haulage

Upper right: **0-4-4T No 15 *Roxborough*,** one of two engines built at Limerick, including parts of 0-4-2 engines bearing the same numbers. The original No 15 was supplied new in 1853 by Sharp Stewart & Co. A new boiler supplied by Kitson in 1893 for old No 4 was most probably used in No 15. The bogie used in No 15 came from 4-4-0 No 12 which was rebuilt as a 2-4-0 in 1894, the year No 15 was built. It had a short working life, being withdrawn in November 1912. Ian Allan Library

Lower right: **2-2-2 No 28 outside Limerick Shed.** Behind the locomotive is the Locomotive Superintendent's office. Although devoid of nameplates in this view, No 28 was in fact named *South of Ireland*. Note copper-capped chimney and polished brass safety valve cover. The tender to which it is coupled does not appear to be the original as a drawing in Andrews' report of 1874 shows a four-wheeled tender of Kitson design. No 28 was withdrawn in 1901, shortly after this photograph was taken. Ian Allan Library

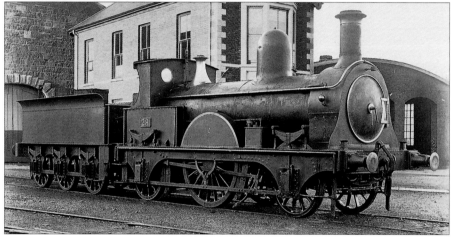

contract, as a return to the House of Lords in March 1853 shows only nine engines on the roster. The fact that the W&LR gave it a number between those of the Stotherts and the three Burys already described, possibly indicates that the engine was built sometime after March 1847, but before No 8 was completed in 1848.

Various suggestions have been put forward as to the origins of No 7. Some references have been made to this engine having come from the Waterford & Tramore Railway, but this is not possible as the first of its engines arrived only in May 1853. The only possible second-hand company engine available at this date was the Dublin & Drogheda Railway 2-2-2 No 12 *Firefly*, purchased second-hand by that company in 1843 from the contractors, Messrs Jeffs. This was sold 'practically as scrap' for £350 and could not therefore have been No 7. Exhaustive investigations lead us to conclude that this was a Grendon engine, as the A&EJR requested in 1872 that the W&LR let it have a crank axle from its Grendon engine to replace that in one of its. It seems clear that this most likely came to the W&LR via William Dargan. The only known dimensions are as shown for Type II in Appendix C. It appears in the 1861 listing with a load of seven carriages, but was apparently gone by 1867. It is a pity that it did not last long enough to be included in the diagrams prepared in 1874 by Messrs Dean and Andrews!

Fairbairns and Sharps

Hemans was instructed in October 1851 to apply to Messrs Sharp & Co and Messrs Fairbairn as to what terms they would require to supply two coupled engines. In the following month the latter's tender at £2,160 each, payment by bills at six months

and renewable if required, was accepted for two engines. We will revert to these shortly as additional engines of the same type were added to stock in 1854/5. In June 1852, four coupled engines were ordered at £2,300 each from Sharp & Co. These were Nos 13 to 16 of Type V, delivered between August 1853 and March 1854. In the interim, Sharp had written asking permission to be allowed to transfer one of the engines to the Dublin & Belfast Junction Railway; this was agreed to on the understanding that a replacement be delivered by November 1853. The company appears to have been slow in settling the account with Sharp as it was reported in January 1854 that the fourth engine would not be delivered until paid for.

These engines came with six-wheeled tenders and it was ordered that they be numbered on the bufferbeam of the engine and on the back of the tender. By March 1865 it was found necessary to renew the boilers and cylinders and, as Sharp quoted £618, it was decided to carry out the work gradually. In fact, the first (No 16) was not done until 1867 and the last (No 14) was completed in 1871. In the 1861 listing, these engines are shown as being capable of taking 12 carriages or 30 wagons. An incident involving the burning of the firebox and tubes of No 15 occurred on 31 May 1887, it being reported a week later that Driver T. Malone had not put in an appearance since

the incident and he was duly dismissed. No 13 received serious damage in February 1884 when it fell into the turntable pit at Clonmel. Arising from that incident, steamraiser John Reddin was dismissed. Parts of No 15 were reportedly used in the construction of the similarly numbered 0-4-4T built in 1894.

The two Fairbairn engines, Nos 11 and 12, were delivered in January and June 1853 respectively and were of the 2-4-0 design (Type IV). In February 1853, Fairbairn wrote offering additional engines at £2,490 each, the board deciding to take another four. Two came in January 1854 and two in the following April, numbered 17 to 20. Complaints were made in May 1854 that the cylinders of the last engine delivered were defective, similar remarks being made in May 1858 regarding the boilers. This might suggest that the workmanship was not all that good, but nevertheless with one exception, they had long lives on the W&LR. The 1861 list shows them capable of taking 12 carriages, and although considered as passenger engines, four of the class were rated at 28 wagons, the remainder at 25, while in 1890, they were rated at 11 wagons or three carriages on the main line. Andrews' report in 1874 states that No 19 had been condemned while two more, although both at work, were regarded as being in a dangerous condition. No 19 was in fact withdrawn in 1875, while another member

A period photograph of the Limerick shunter, 0-4-0ST No 29, supplied in 1865 by Sharp, Stewart & Co, maker's No 1653. No 29 spent most of its working life at Limerick, being unofficially named 'Darkie'. It was withdrawn in 1924 as GS&WR No 228. H. Fayle/IRRS collection

of the class survived until 1901. When McDowell inspected the locomotives in 1875, he described them as being 'pretty fairly adapted for ordinary passenger trains'. It was also reported that Nos 11 and 17 received six-wheeled Stothert tenders (the Fairbairn tenders were also six-wheeled and had a water capacity of 1,500 gallons).

Next comes a period of some uncertainty. A seventh Fairbairn engine, No 21, arrived in December 1855, but there is no reference in the company's records to an order being placed. However, there is a reference in November 1855 to a Fairbairn engine being taken only if approved of on inspection. This probably refers to No 21, which may therefore have been an engine held in stock by the manufacturer. It has been stated that one of the engines had 16in by 21in cylinders, whereas the remainder had 15in cylinders. It is unlikely that No 21 was any different in this regard to her sisters unless of course she was, as surmised, a stock engine.

Another locomotive is stated to have come from Fairbairn via William Dargan in 1855. Type VI 2-2-2T No 19 had apparently been built for the Ballymena, Ballymoney, Coleraine & Portrush Junction Railway, which had refused to take delivery and it thus passed into Dargan's hands. We know little further about this engine, although a six-wheeled engine with 5ft wheels was advertised for sale at Waterford in 1879. Andrews, the then locomotive superintendent of the W&LR, referred to No 19 in September 1874 as being a passenger engine which had been condemned. (Another No 19 has also been mentioned, but this must

be dismissed entirely as there is no evidence to suggest that such an engine ever existed.)

Following a great number of failures and breakages in the locomotives, Lunt was requested, in November 1856, to furnish a detailed statement of the deficiencies of every engine. He was also censured for having, without reference to the board, returned a faulty cylinder from locomotive No 13 to Sharp, Stewart & Co. In January 1857, he was once again called on to report on the state of the locomotives. As a result of a memorial from the drivers in October 1859, Pim, who had been appointed in place of Lunt, was instructed to provide weather-boards on the engines at a cost of £4 each.

Kilkenny and Ennis acquisitions

Next came the engines handed over when the working of the W&KR was undertaken in 1861. These were six in number, in three batches, becoming Nos 22-27 on the W&LR. Although some doubt exists as to the exact numbering of the engines concerned, three 4-2-2Ts were purchased in 1846 from Messrs Tayleur (builder's Nos 241-243). One was apparently sold to contractors Carlisle & Hutchings of Cork for £750 in 1859, the other two being transferred to the W&LR and possibly becoming Nos 22 and 23 (Type VIII). They had the distinction of being the first side-tank engines in the world, these tanks being very deep and long. No reference is made to them in W&LR service and they were returned to the W&KR at the end of the lease in 1867. It was reported that they were scrapped immediately without being numbered back into the Kilkenny stock. The late Bob Clements even went as far as to state that he had reservations as to whether they ever came to the W&LR, or if they had already been scrapped by 1861.

Type IX represented two 2-4-0 tender engines and were supplied by Stothert, Slaughter in September 1852. There is some

confusion regarding their numbers, Bob Clements referring to them in one source as W&KR Nos 6 and 7 (W&LR Nos 26 and 27), and in another as W&KR Nos 4 and 5 (W&LR Nos 23 and 24). What we do know is that one was returned to the W&KR in 1867, the other, probably No 24 or 27, being retained until 1872. Two 2-2-2 engines, W&KR Nos 4 and 5, became W&LR Nos 24 and 25 (or 6 and 7/W&LR 26 and 27). Classified as Type X, they were supplied by Messrs Kitson in 1853. Both returned to the W&KR in 1867 where they became Nos 4 and 5.

It has to be said that the W&KR stock was in poor condition when it was taken over in 1861. The rolling stock committee expressed its anxiety to know more of their present state and what was required to make them more effective, along with the cost of same. The locomotive superintendent, Pim, submitted a report on their condition in March which showed only one of the locomotives as working, two either awaiting or wanting repairs, two under repair and one 'in pieces at Kilkenny and Limerick'. The cost of putting them into efficient working order was shown as £2,540 2s 11d. It was also found necessary to employ two boilermakers, two helpers and three fitters to put them in order. Five of the engines were returned to the W&KR in July 1867.

Three engines came from the L&ER when that railway began to be worked by the W&LR in 1861. L&ER No 1 (Type XI) was an 0-4-2 purchased from Fairbairn in 1859 at a cost of £2,550. Following on the placing of the order in March 1859, the manufacturers came back with an improved specification, including a stronger firebox and an additional pair of wheels under the tender. This became W&LR No 1. Whereas the original dimensions show the cylinders as being 15in by 22in, a GWR diagram of 1874 has them at 16in diameter. No 1 was reported as worn out in May 1883 when the locomotive superintendent requested the provision of a new engine, this latter being ordered in September; its final fate is unknown. Type XII was an 0-4-2 tender engine, ex-L&ER No 2, taking the same number on the W&LR. Built by Fairbairn in 1856, the original owners are unknown, it being sold to the L&ER in 1859 by William Dargan. No 2 had a six-wheeled tender holding 1,550 gallons of water, although just before being scrapped in 1900 a four-wheeled one was inherited from an unknown source. There is very little reference to the locomotive in W&LR days.

L&ER No 3 (Type XIII) is another engine the origins of which are shrouded in some mystery. Messrs Sharp Bros of Manchester show a design, No E143, as relating to a six-wheeled engine for William Dargan in connection with the Dublin to Cashel contract. Importantly, it was stated that the engine comprised parts made by Sharp Roberts, and this must date these items back to at least 1843 when the company name was changed. The builder's number was 279 and it was delivered in April 1845. Reference is made in *Freemans Journal* for 5 May 1845 to the trial trip of Dargan's engine *Lady McNeill* built by Sharp Bros. Nearly four years later the engine was involved in a collision with another Dargan engine between Limerick Junction and Charleville, while in July 1850 she was sent to Limerick for onward transmission by canal to Athlone in connection with the MGWR Galway contract. Then, in June 1854, Dargan's manager requested the GS&WR to carry out repairs to the engine *Pioneer*, the cost to be paid by the Killarney Junction Railway Co. Apart from two Sharp Roberts 0-4-2s on the Ulster Railway, *Lady McNeill* was the only other such to have operated in Ireland, so it seems that she was renamed in the intervening four years.

The W&LR records refer to an engine for sale at Inchicore in 1859, Dargan having applied to have a locomotive repaired about this time. It seems likely therefore that L&ER No 3 was in fact *Pioneer*, the former *Lady McNeill* of 1845. The price asked was £1,550 and this would seem to indicate a major overhaul having been carried out at Inchicore before the locomotive was offered for sale. *Pioneer* was offered back to the GS&WR in April 1861, but it declined to negotiate for her. No 3 had a comparatively short working life on the W&LR, being scrapped about 1873. Bagnell had written in July 1863 asking to purchase it, but the price asked, £1,100, was apparently regarded as being too high.

A period of stability
Reverting again to the W&LR, Pim had previously reported to the board in December 1860 regarding the requirement for a more powerful class of engine to work goods and mineral traffic effectively. He was ordered to prepare drawings and specifications for two locomotives. In the following March, Stothert offered to supply one 2-4-0 tender engine for £2,700 free on board at Bristol, or two for £50 each less. Dimensions included cylinders 16in by 24in, four coupled wheels 5ft diameter and a heating surface of 1,090sq ft. The firm also agreed to take two of its old engines back for £250. This offer was not accepted, further tenders being received in May 1861. It was not until after Atock's arrival in November 1861 that an order was placed with Messrs Sharp, Stewart & Co for two 0-4-2 goods engines at a cost of £2,134 each, free on board at Liverpool. In the interim, Atock produced a report for the board showing that only nine engines were in good working order with a further four requiring slight repairs. Eleven engines were not in good working order, the remaining six (the Stotherts) not being worth repairing.

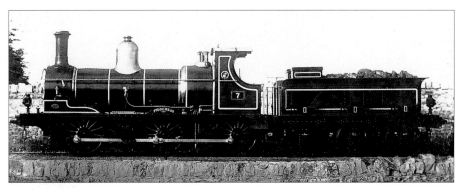

The two new Sharp 0-4-2s, Nos 4 and 5, (Type XIV) were delivered in June 1862 and, far from being of a more powerful nature, were almost exact copies of the four purchased from the same firm in 1853. The 1862 engines had two No 8 injectors instead of pumps, 1in inside frames, a round dome on the middle ring of the boiler and a safety valve trumpet on the flush firebox casing. A third engine, No 6, was ordered in December 1863, being delivered in August 1864. The dirty and dangerous state of No 4 resulted in the sacking in May 1878 of Joseph Miles, locomotive foreman at Waterford. Two members of the class, Nos 5 & 6, were later rebuilt at Limerick as 0-6-0s, in 1893 and 1890 respectively. This followed a recommendation by Henry Appleby in October 1882 for such a conversion. No 6 received new steel frames and a steam brake at the time of her rebuilding at a combined cost of £92. These two engines were subsequently named *Bee* and *Ant*. Bob Clements stated that No 6 was a right-hand drive engine, the other two presumably being left-hand. In 1890, Nos 4 and 5 were rated at 15 wagons (the rebuilt No 6 at 17 wagons), or three carriages each. They became Nos 223 and 225 on the GS&WR, lasting until 1901 and 1907 respectively.

In December 1863, it was decided to order a 2-2-2 engine from Kitsons of Leeds, similar to the two W&KR engines taken over in 1861. This has been incorrectly reported to have been exhibited at the Ballsbridge Exhibition in 1865, the DW&WR engine *Banshee* being the only engine to appear there. Ahrons described No 28, later named *South of Ireland*, as being an enlarged 'Jenny Lind' type with inside bearings for

Top: **An ex-works photograph of 0-6-0 No 7** *Progress* **as reconstructed at Limerick in 1893.** Ian Allan Library

Above: **2-4-0 No 10** *Sir James*, **named after the company chairman, Sir James Spaight. This engine was the first of eight built by Messrs Dübs between 1889 and 1894. Renumbered 263 by the GS&WR, it remained in service until 1906. An engraving of the locomotive was shown in** *The Engineer* **for 14 February 1890, drawings appearing in the issue for 12 September 1890.** Ian Allan Library

the driving wheels and outside for the carrying wheels. It had a heating surface of 882sq ft and a grate area of 14.58sq ft. No 28 (Type XV) arrived in 1865 and was for many years based at Waterford shed, working daily to and from Limerick. In later years it was reported on the Foynes branch. At the time of the 1874 report, No 28 had completed 224,130 miles and had patches on the bottom of the boiler and the inside firebox. Following a collision in Waterford yard in October 1882 a new crank axle was fitted.

The year 1865 also saw another arrival from Sharp, Stewart, 0-4-0ST No 29, ordered for shunting duties at Waterford. Messrs Neilson had offered a contractor's engine for £850, but Atock confirmed that whilst adequate for shunting duties, it would not be suitable for running. He recommended a heavier engine which would suffice for operating the proposed Clonmel to Carrick short train due to commence on 1 April 1865, although in fact the saddle tank did not arrive until

Vulcan Foundry 4-4-0 No 12 *Earl of Bessborough* was built in 1886 to replace an old Fairbairn 2-4-0 of 1853. It was prone to derailments and was rebuilt in 1894 as a 2-4-0. It is seen here rebuilt, prior to 1900. Views of the locomotive in this guise are rare. Séan Kennedy collection

21 December of that year. No 29 (Type XVI) was a diminutive locomotive with her saddle tank running the full length of the boiler and smokebox. As built she had a trumpet safety valve cover with an extension piece and there were no side-sheets to the cab. In 1874, Andrews confirmed that it was in use for shunting duties at Waterford, but was however better known for a period of service at Limerick, where reported in use by March 1880.

A board minute refers to the custom of allowing persons to travel on engines, and excessive speed in Limerick yard. It was ordered that the speed of engines shunting, *Darkey* (sic) excluded, was not to exceed four miles per hour. No 29 was unofficially named *Darkie* following transfer to Limerick, but as noted, the 0-4-0ST was referred to as such in the board minutes. *Darkie* was in the news twice in July 1881. First, it was reported that it had been sent without orders to Pallas and a fortnight later it assisted a train on the Foynes branch without staff or ticket. Although only a shunting engine, it was apparently painted in 1899/1900 in passenger livery of red-brown with black bands and yellow stripes. A report of a derailment of *Darkie* on the Killaloe branch in January 1914 incorrectly refers to it as being an '0-2-0'. (It is hardly surprising therefore that it was derailed!)

A statement was prepared in August 1868 showing a comparison of mileages and coal consumption for drivers in connection with a bonus scheme. This indicated that Driver Thomas Wixted returned a mileage of 16,377 for the half-year ended 30 June and a consumption of 15.20lb per mile. The highest consumption was by Driver James McHanehan who returned 26.06lb per mile. Four drivers each received a gratuity of £3 and four firemen £1 each. In the following April it was announced that Atock had made a 10% reduction in wages, partly by dismissal and partly by reducing pay. In November 1869, Atock confirmed that he had given notice to nine carpenters, two smiths and two strikers, thus reducing expenditure further, although he commen-

ted that the remaining staff were barely enough for ordinary repairs. It was about this time that the company began sending wagon wheels and ironwork to England in order to reduce costs.

Atock wrote to the board in December 1870 recommending the purchase of two goods locomotives to meet the increased traffic requirements. Various tenders were received in March 1871, the order being given to Kitson for delivery of two engines and one tender in six months at £4,000. There was a delay in the delivery of these engines due to 'disaffection of employees' in Leeds. Type XVII represented a pair of 0-4-2 engines, Nos 3 and 7. One of the engines was mated to a Fairbairn tender in stock. In 1888 plans were drawn up for the proposed renewal of No 3, but in the event, all she got was a new boiler from the Vulcan Foundry. No 7 was, however, rebuilt at Limerick as an 0-6-0 in July 1888, the first of six extensive rebuilds to be carried out in the works. Following this rebuild, and in recognition of this new experiment at Limerick, the engine was named *Progress*, a name which was carried until 1893, when renamed *Wasp*. No 3 was officially withdrawn in 1892 and parts were used in the construction of a new 0-4-2T bearing the same number. These locomotives were to be the last to be introduced during the tenure of Martin Atock, who had brought 10½ years of stability to the locomotive affairs of the W&LR.

Six more outsiders added to stock

The last of the acquisitions to come from worked companies were the six A&EJR and A&TR engines added to stock in 1872. The Ennis tender engines were 0-4-2s (Type XVIII) built in 1862 by Messrs Fossick & Hackworth for the Dublin & Meath Railway, probably its Nos 3, 4 and 6. They were purchased by the A&EJR in 1869 when the Meath company signed a working agreement with the MGWR. Under this, the D&MR was free to dispose of locomotives as it saw fit. As related in Chapter Six, these engines had a rather chequered career on the A&EJR. In a valuation prepared in November 1872,

Wardle referred to them as having been badly used and in bad repair. He would not advise valuing them at more than £350 each as all required general repairs and they were too small for the W&LR. They became W&LR Nos 22, 23 and 24, the latter having been named *Gort* by the Ennis company. It was decided in 1888 that No 22 was not worth any expenditure, while No 23 was reportedly unfit for renewal in December 1890. The surprise is how long they actually lasted in W&LR service.

Wardle referred to the Tuam engines as follows. Nos 1 and 2, named *Drumconora* and *Lough Cutra*, were two small Grendon 2-2-2 passenger engines, 25 years old and which were not worth more than their weight for old material, say 40 tons for the two. 'No 3 of Bury make . . . frames badly broken, say £220.' It is therefore not surprising to record that they never entered service with the Limerick company, although Nos 30, 31 and 32 may have been allocated to the company.

Correspondence was entered into with various manufacturers early in 1873 with a view to obtaining further passenger engines. In April a letter was read from the Vulcan Foundry regarding some alterations required from the original specification. These included larger wheels (details not specified), steam dome on the boiler, a screw jack and Low Moor plates for the boiler shell and firebox, all of which would increase the cost per engine by £90 to £2,625 each for two engines. It was decided to accept this tender, but it was then deferred and in June the GWR was approached to see how much it would charge for building them. In addition, Andrews was asked to examine new W&CIR engines and to report back. In due course, the tender of the Vulcan Foundry was accepted for four 2-4-0s, the builder being persuaded to defer payment until the engines had completed 1,000 miles in service.

Nos 25, 30, 31 and 32 of Type XIX were all delivered in May 1874 and shortly after their arrival it was proposed to name them *Waterford, Limerick, Ennis* and *Tuam*. This was the first occasion on which any reference is made to naming engines at all, apart from the original Stotherts, but it was not until about 1886 that the W&LR actually adopted the procedure, these four being named, respectively *Verbena, Lily, Myrtle* and *Dahlia*. Nos 31 and 32 received new cylinders in 1885 and 1883 and new boilers in 1892 and 1902 respectively. On 1 October 1880, Vulcan's tender for a further four engines of this type was accepted at £2,025 each. These

4-4-2T No 21 *Blarney Castle*, one of four engines from Kitson of Leeds. No 21, as GS&WR No 274, was rebuilt in December 1924 with an 'S' boiler. It was withdrawn in 1949 and broken up in the following year.
L&GRP/G. Beesley collection

engines, Nos 8 and 35 to 37, were delivered in April and May 1881 and differed from their predecessors in having, amongst other detailed changes, straight framing, Rams-bottom safety valves and ashpan injectors. They were later named, respectively *Primrose*, *Duncannon*, *Violet* and *Camelia*. Two more engines, identical to the second batch, were ordered from the same builders in May 1882, Nos 38 and 39 being delivered in November and December of the same year and later named *Hyacinth* and *Shamrock*. The whole class was withdrawn and scrapped between 1902 and 1911.

One report leads to another

As detailed earlier, a traffic agreement was signed with the GWR in April 1872. Arising out of a dispute over payments to be made under this agreement, the suggestion was put forward by the GWR that it might, in future, appoint officers to manage the company's affairs. To this end it made arrangements for various of its officers to come over and inspect the facilities in Ireland. Its locomotive superintendent, William Dean, visited the railway between 7 and 11 November 1874. Prior to this, however, Robert Andrews prepared a report in September on the condition of the locomotive stock of the company, which was

updated as necessary by Dean.

This report is interesting in that it throws some light on the general condition in which the company maintained its locomotives. It would be unfair to criticise too severely the various locomotive superintendents, who did their best in difficult circumstances and were starved of cash. Of 32 engines reported on, four were new, three of which were replacements for the A&TR stock taken over two years previously and fit only for scrap. There is a minor error in the report in that the three Fossick & Hackworth engines attributed to the A&TR, in fact, represented the engines taken over from its southern neighbour, the A&EJR. At the other end of the scale, however, Andrews condemned five engines and reported a further three as being dangerous, but still at work. This meant that 25% of the stock was either condemned or dangerous, while a further

six were not at work or were under repairs. Other engines, whilst not falling into any of these categories, were also obviously in poor condition. Three engines had in excess of 300,000 miles on their boilers, another 11 having run more than 200,000 miles.

Resulting from Andrews' report, tenders were submitted to the board early in 1875 for new engines from various builders. The to procure the services of two competent engineers to examine the state of the engines and of the locomotive department. It was announced in February that Daniel McDowell of the W&CIR and John Wakefield of the DW&WR had agreed to inspect and report. It is interesting to note that a superintendent from the smaller neighbour was chosen, for neither did the W&CIR have a good record with its locomotive stock, so McDowell was obviously highly regarded. In the event, Wakefield took no part in the exercise, McDowell's report being submitted to the directors at the beginning of April. In it, he dealt with the state of the current stock, the character of the repairs currently being carried out, and the appliances available for the repair and maintenance of locomotives. Finally, McDowell looked at the various tenders submitted for new locomotives.

McDowell found 23 engines in running order, five in shops for general repairs and two being rebuilt, making a total of 30, two fewer than Andrews' report — two engines having recently been broken up, being 21 years old. Of the 23, only five were in good

Above left: 0-6-0 No 56, one of three engines supplied by Kitson in 1897. Note that both the engine and tender sport the company's crest. Interestingly, the number and crest on the cab side have been transposed from their usual position. Four basically similar engines came from Dübs in 1893 and 1895. As GSR No 237, this engine was rebuilt in December 1926 with a new boiler. In this form it survived until October 1951.
Ian Allan Library

Left: 2-4-0 No 273, ex No 20 *Galtee More*, at Waterford Shed. It was withdrawn in 1909.
Photographer unknown/S. Kennedy collection

A superb view of 4-4-0 No 53 in full livery. The engine number has been placed high up on the cab side, but below the handrail. In contrast, the 0-6-0s from the same maker had their numbers above the handrail. Note the copper-capped chimney and the jack on the running plate, a feature of quite a number of WL&WR engines. No 53 was named *Jubilee* in celebration of the company being in existence for 50 years.
Ian Allan Library

order, four more were in fair running order, the remaining 14 requiring to be taken in for general repairs — four of these being described as in very bad order. With regard to the recently arrived Vulcan engines, McDowell stated that while they were pretty fairly adapted for ordinary passenger trains, they were not so well suited for mixed trains as engines of the same weight ought to be. He also felt that the injectors were too small. Despite this, they were obviously quite successful on the W&LR, for as we have seen above, a further six were later added to stock. In McDowell's opinion, the shop accommodation at Limerick was very good, the only piece of equipment required being a radial drilling machine, estimated to cost between £150 and £200. All current repairs were requisite and necessary, but taking into consideration the state of the stock, McDowell was of the view that more men might be employed with advantage. He also thought that the engines were not sufficient in number, even supposing them to be in fair order; four more would be required as soon as possible.

Finally, McDowell turned his attention to the specifications and tenders received for new engines. Whilst he had received every assistance from Andrews in relation to the inspection of engines and repair facilities, Andrews 'declined going into the matter of

new engines and said he had already stated to this (the W&LR) Board what was his opinion on the subject'. McDowell put aside tenders for engines from Sharp, Stewart, Beyer Peacock and Vulcan Foundry as being unsuitable for W&LR traffic. He regarded the engines offered by Kitsons, duplicates of Nos 3 and 7 delivered to the company in 1872 as being very good for goods trains 'but much too slow of speed for mixed traffic'. Next, he considered the engines offered by Dübs to be well designed for mixed traffic. His only reservation was that he would not recommend 17in cylinders as they had too long a wheelbase; 16in cylinders would better suit the company's requirements. Finally, McDowell turned to two designs offered by Messrs Avonside, one of which would be ideal for traffic requirements. The 16in Dübs engines would cost £145 more than the one offered by Avonside.

Some new and some old
Not surprisingly, the next five engines were supplied by Avonside, the only such, apart from the original Stothert, Slaughter engines, to come from the Bristol manufacturer. In February 1873 the secretary was requested to write to Avonside seeking tenders for two locomotives similar to two recently supplied to the W&CIR (Nos 10 and 11). The manufacturers quoted £3,000 each in the following June, but on 27 April 1875 a revised tender of £2,695 each was accepted for four engines for delivery in November. In the event, they were not delivered until February or March of the following year; these were Nos 19, 26, 27 and 33 (Type XX). They were not in fact exact copies of their W&CIR counterparts, having slightly larger wheels, making them useful for working passenger trains. Ahrons also related that they were very useful on passenger trains and this is borne out by the fact that the

GS&WR allocated numbers within the passenger grouping to them.

At least two of the class had unpainted brass domes and another difference to the W&CIR engines was that they had Ramsbottom safety valves fitted. No 27 was one of two W&LR engines to be fitted in 1886/7 with the Appleby-Robinson patent adjustable vortex blastpipe. The drawing illustrating the article in *The Engineer* for July 1887 shows a 4-4-0 engine and it may be that it was intended to fit it to further engines. Following comparative tests it was reported that an annual saving of £80 could be made in coal consumption, based on a mileage of 30,000 per annum.

No 27 was rebuilt in 1899 as an 0-4-4T and named *Thomond*, and as No 279 was rebuilt again in December 1927 receiving a GSR 'S'-type boiler with which it survived into CIE days until withdrawn in 1953. Robinson had also apparently intended to rebuild No 26 as a tank engine, but his departure to the Great Central Railway at Gorton in England and the transfer of the engine to the GS&WR put an end to this. However, a new boiler was fitted in 1901 and it lasted as GS&WR No. 278 until 1910. The other two engines of this type were scrapped in 1901/2. No 278 was derailed at Felthouse Junction on 19 January 1910 while working tender-first on the 20.15 Waterford to Wexford goods. Regrettably, the fireman was fatally injured, the accident being attributed to a tight coupling between the engine and the tender. This locomotive was scrapped immediately after this accident, being the last remaining 0-4-2 in service on the GS&WR.

The fifth Avonside engine was the 0-6-0T No 34 (Type XXI). This engine appears to have been offered to the Newry, Warrenpoint & Rostrevor Railway in September 1877, when she was described as 'a second class six-wheeled tank . . . and priced at £1,160'. A shunting engine had in fact been offered to the W&LR in February 1877, an offer of £1,000 being accepted by Avonside in October. It was inspected in November and again in March 1878, instructions being given that it was not to be shipped from Bristol until the locomotive superintendent's requirements were completed; arrival on the W&LR was in mid-1878.

It has been stated that this was originally a 7ft-gauge engine which had come from a South Wales colliery line. Stephenson Locomotive Society records show the builder's number as 1243, while the *Industrial Railway Record* for June 1966 makes reference to a six-coupled tank engine used by Messrs Furness & Buxton on the construction of the broad gauge Minehead & Watchet Railway which was advertised for sale in August 1874. It is possible that Avonside reconditioned the engine before offering it for sale. No 34 was not fitted with the vacuum brake and spent its entire working life shunting the yard at Waterford, probably replacing *Darkie* on that duty. Allocated the number 229 by the GS&WR, it was condemned immediately on being taken over by that company.

Two new engines came from the Vulcan Foundry in 1883. Instructions were issued in August 1882 for the preparation of drawings for four new goods engines, but in the event, two were ordered in October at £2,500 each, for delivery by the end of January 1883. It is possible that Nos 40 and 41 (Type XXII) started life with 18in cylinders as Robinson later stated that he had reduced the cylinder diameter. They were the first six-coupled engines on the W&LR, and although they were not named when new, the names *Vulcan* and *Titan* were later painted on them. They had three-ring butt-jointed boilers with ½in plates, the firebox crown being slightly domed. As GS&WR Nos 230 and 231 they lasted until 1909 and 1910 respectively.

We now come to yet another mystery engine. In November 1883 the board accepted Messrs Stephensons' tender of £2,350 for an engine to replace the old Fairbairn 0-4-2 No 1. The new 0-6-0 No 1 (Type XXIII) was delivered in March 1884. However, it has been claimed that the engine in question had been built about five years earlier, possibly for service in Russia, but had remained on the maker's hands. Problems were encountered early on and Stephensons agreed to make good cylinder joints and to supply new axle brasses at their own expense. In November 1886, they also agreed to supply a new firebox, a sum of £20 being allowed for the old one.

No 1 was always regarded as being a poor steamer, this probably resulting in the fitting of an Appleby-Robinson blastpipe, and similar fuel savings to No 27 were recorded. No.1 was rebuilt as a saddle tank in 1899, the tank extending only over the boiler and not over the smokebox. The open cab was apparently retained, the frames being lengthened to accommodate a small coal bunker. The tender was retained by the GS&WR, and was attached to '101' class 0-6-0 No 193, as such surviving at least until 1924, but No 221, as No 1 had become, was withdrawn in 1909.

For the next engine, the company once again purchased a second-hand locomotive recommended to it by Appleby. No 42 (Type XXIV) had originally been built in June 1862 and used on the construction of the Anglesey Central Railway. This was named *Miers* after Richard Hanbury Miers, a director of that company and first chairman of the Neath & Brecon Railway. The engine was transferred to the latter company in June 1867, becoming its No 3. It has been suggested it was sold to a South Wales firm in 1882 and was possibly used on the construction of the Rhondda & Swansea Bay Railway, but evidence is lacking

0-6-0 No 58 *Goliath*, built by Kitson in 1897. It later became GS&WR No 239 and was classified 'J25' by the GSR; she was withdrawn from service in 1949.
H. Fayle/IRRS collection

in this regard. Appleby would have known of this locomotive and wrote to the board in December 1882 advising that there was a shunting engine for sale at Neath, the asking price being £90. He also informed it that repairs and gauge conversion would cost a further £98.

The board agreed to the purchase and the 0-6-0WT arrived in Limerick in the second half of 1883. No 42 was a well tank with outside cylinders, steam distribution being by Gooch valve gear actuated through a rocking arm from a lever on the left-hand side of the footplate. There was no cab when it worked in Wales, one most likely being fitted when it was regauged. The firebox was flush with the boiler barrel and was surmounted by a large dome and spring balance safety valve. It was fitted only with a handbrake operating through wooden brake blocks on the trailing wheels. Water capacity was 800 gallons, the boiler being fed by one injector and one pump.

Reference was made in Chapter Nine to the proposed purchase of this engine for £1,000 by the Fenit Harbour Commissioners in January 1899, this extraordinary offer being declined by the WL&WR. Following the dispute with the Harbour Commissioners, No 42 was brought to Limerick to shunt the yard, with the rear section of the coupling rods removed, thus operating as an 0-4-2. It was allocated the number 232 by the GS&WR which decided to return her to Fenit. While en route on 1 February 1901, however, she collided with 4-4-0 No 6 at Abbeyfeale and was immediately condemned. This appears to confirm that new numbers were allocated to WL&WR engines in 1900 and quickly applied.

Three engines were ordered in 1886, two passenger engines, one each from Vulcan Foundry and Dübs, along with a goods engine from the latter manufacturer, all three being replacements for similarly numbered engines. The Dübs 4-4-0 No 9 (Type XXV) was a less

impressive engine than her Vulcan Foundry sister, No 12 (Type XXVI). No 9 sported a copper-capped chimney, polished brass dome cover and smokebox wing plates, with lubricators on each side of the smokebox. There was also a boiler feed on each side of the barrel just ahead of the leading coupled wheels. The tender springs were below platform level whereas they were above it on No 12. A feature of the Dübs tender was the awkward location of the handbrake which was placed too close to the shovelling plate, and in the fireman's way. No 9, which spent its later days on goods workings, was later named *Garryowen* and lasted as GS&WR No 262 until 1912.

No 12 *Earl of Bessborough* (Type XIX) was basically a bogie version of the Vulcan 2-4-0s of 1874 to 1882 and was the most powerful engine on the W&LR system. Possibly the first engine named on delivery, apart from the original Stotherts, it had cast nameplates on the leading splashers and below these was the company crest. This may also have been the first W&LR engine to have rectangular numberplates. Both engines worked on the night mails; No 12, however, was prone to derailment and was converted to a 2-4-0 in 1894, the replaced bogie being used in the construction of 0-4-4T No 15 in that year at Limerick. No 12 became No 265 under the GS&WR renumbering, but she was soon withdrawn from service and scrapped in 1907.

The Dübs 0-6-0 No 24 (Type XXVII) was basically a goods version of No 9, the design being based on the Vulcan goods engines of 1883. It had an identical boiler and tender to No 9. Cylinders were originally 17in diameter, probably being reduced to 16½in, while boiler pressure was reduced from

Top: **2-4-2T No 14 *Lough Derg* as built by the Vulcan Foundry in 1891. As GS&WR No 267, it was armour-plated at Limerick in August 1922. Rebuilt in 1925 with an 'S' boiler, it was withdrawn in 1935 and finally scrapped in July 1938. Sister No 13 *Derry Castle* was sold to the Cork & Macroom Direct Railway in 1914 as its No 6, being later renumbered 491 by the GSR.** Ian Allan Library

Above: **4-4-0 No 54 *Killemnee* at Waterford, one of a pair delivered in 1896 from Kitson of Leeds. As GSR Class D15 No 297, this engine lasted until 1928.**
Courtesy Green Studios, Dublin

160psi through 150 to 140psi. The leading sandboxes were combined with the lower sides of the smokebox. Later named *Sarsfield*, we know nothing of its working life and, as GS&WR No 227, it was withdrawn in November 1910.

The Robinson era

In January 1884 Appleby put proposals to the board suggesting alterations and improvements at Limerick. This led four months later to the appointment of an assistant locomotive superintendent, John George Robinson, at a salary of £3 per week. Due to Appleby's failing health, he was already in full control of matters for some time before he was appointed locomotive superintendent in March 1889. Robinson was to bring new thinking to locomotive matters at Limerick, and over the next 11 years the locomotive stock was transformed. Ahrons described the W&LR engines of the Robinson era as being 'the prettiest engines in Ireland' with

their polished brass work and attractive red livery, and were a precursor to Robinson's Great Central Railway designs. A change in livery from green to crimson lake akin to the Midland Railway in England, along with polished copper-capped chimneys, certainly made a huge difference.

Appleby had been instructed in April 1888 to issue advertisements for four-coupled engines identical to No 12, apart from the substitution of 6ft for 5ft 6in coupled wheels. In the following September, Robinson was requested to ask various manufacturers for their lowest prices for engines to their own design, that of Dübs at £2,340 being accepted in November, this figure being later increased to £2,450 to allow for alterations in the design. Exactly when the decision was taken to revert to a 2-4-0 layout is not clear, but the frequent derailment of No 12 must have been instrumental in the change. No 10 *Sir James*, the first engine of Type XXVIII, was delivered in May 1889, a duplicate (No 22 *Era*) being ordered in August at the same price. Two more engines of the same type were ordered from Dübs in April 1891 at £2,400 each, these being delivered in March 1892 as Nos 22 and 23 and named *Galtee More* and *Slieve-na-mon* respectively. In all, there were eight engines of this type, a further four engines being ordered from the same builder, with two delivered in June 1893 (No 43 *Knockma* and No 44 *Nephin*) and two more, No 47 *Carrick Castle* and No 48 *Granston*, in June 1894.

The boiler was of the three-ring type with

the dome on the middle ring. The first four engines were the only members of the class fitted with smokebox wing plates. Another difference in the first four was the use of curved coupling rod splashers over each coupled wheel centre, the remaining four having continuous splashers. Tenders were similar to that on No 9.

They were very free-running engines, working for a time on the main line before being transferred to the Sligo road. Four of the class, Nos 276, 290, 291 and 293, were rebuilt in 1925/6 by the GSR, receiving new boilers. It was reported that they had shallower fireboxes on account of the frequent flooding of the Sligo line at Ballycar. Rebuilding also saw the round cab spectacle plates replaced by square ones and extension of the cab-side sheets. No 291 (ex-No 44) had the distinction of being the last surviving W&LR engine to be withdrawn, in August 1959. The four rebuilds were in fact long-lived, remaining in service into the 1950s.

The first passenger tank engines to be acquired by the company were ordered in July 1890. Nos 13 and 14 (Type XXIX) were in effect a tank version of the Vulcan 2-4-0s of 1874 and came from the same source. After they had been ordered, Tighe expressed reservations about their weight, intimating that they would be refused if they weighed more than 44t 5cwt in full working order. In the event, No 13, *Derry Castle*, steamed for the first time on 19 June 1891, and tipped the scales at 45 tons. The leading axle box had lateral play, the trailing ones being of the Webb radial type. No 13 (as GS&WR No 266) was sold in 1914 to the Cork & Macroom Direct Railway, becoming that company's No 6, and later GSR No 491 after the 1925 amalgamation. No 14, *Lough Derg*, was armour-plated at Limerick in August 1922, this protection being removed 12 months later and it was rebuilt in 1925 with a GSR 'S' boiler. At the time of rebuilding, the plain coupling rods were replaced by a fluted type, bunker capacity being increased by the fitting of coal rails, the latter subsequently replaced by plates. It was also reported that it carried a GS&WR double smokebox door and built-up GSR chimney for a time. Although withdrawn in 1935, No 14 was used on the Broadstone wash-out until 1938.

Type XXX was represented by two engines, Nos 3 and 15, nominally rebuilds of earlier 0-4-2s, but most likely they only incorporated some parts into what were basically new engines constructed at Limerick. A new boiler had been ordered for old No 3 in October 1890 and for No 15 in March 1893, the former from Vulcan and the latter from Kitson. The Kitson boiler had in fact been ordered for No 4, but most likely went direct to the new engine. Although grouped together, they were not identical as rebuilt, No 3 being an 0-4-2T and named *Zetland*, while No 15 became 0-4-4T *Roxborough* utilising No 12's bogie. The two engines had a rather pleasing appearance and owed much to Robinson's design skills so admired later in his Great Central Railway engines. No 3 worked the Killaloe branch for a number of years. As GS&WR Nos 260 and 268 respectively, they both survived until 1912.

Between 1893 and 1897 a total of seven 0-6-0 goods engines (Type XXXI) were acquired in various batches from two manufacturers. Two engines, Nos 45 and 46, *Colleen Bawn* and *Erin-go-Bragh*, were initially ordered from Dübs in 1893, followed by Nos 49 and 50, *Dreadnaught* and *Hercules*, from the same builder in August of the following year. A board minute of 21 October 1892 refers to Dübs offering two engines at £2,250 each on condition that additional engines for the Claremorris and Collooney line were purchased from it also. It was ordered that the two 1894 engines be charged to the Collooney contract account, Nos 49 and 50 therefore being, nominally at least, allocated to the C&CR.

When, in May 1896, it was decided to purchase a total of six engines from Kitson, the order included three goods engines of Type XXXI. These were Nos 56 to 58, *Thunderer*, *Cyclops* and *Goliath*, which were slightly different from their predecessors. The Kitsons had larger boilers and plain cast-iron chimneys, whereas the Dübs engines sported copper-capped chimneys. On the Kitsons, the numberplates were placed above rather than below the hand rails, while the Dübs engines had their front sandboxes incorporated into the leading splashers. No 56, at least, had a coat of arms on the cab side as well as on the tender. It would appear that Nos 49 and 50 had 17½in cylinders, all others being 17in.

Nos 49 and 50 and the three Kitson engines, which had become GS&WR Nos 235-239, were rebuilt by the GSR with Inchicore '276'-type boilers, also receiving standard GS&WR vacuum brake equipment. GS&WR-type cabs were fitted in later years to all but No 49, which was withdrawn in 1927. The two 1893 engines became Nos 233 and 234 in the GS&WR list but had shorter lives, being withdrawn in 1919 and 1911 respectively.

Prior to the above order the company had already changed its allegiance for locomotive supply to Kitsons in August 1894 with an order for two tank engines. No 51 *Castle Hacket* and No 52 *Brian Boru* (Type XXXII) were of the 0-4-4T type and were basically a development of the design that had originated in Robinson's reconstruction of No 15 as the 0-4-4T *Roxborough*, which as GS&WR No 268 survived until 1912. No 51, which became GS&WR No 294, was an early victim, being scrapped in 1910, but No 295 (ex-No 52) was rebuilt in November 1926 with a

GSR 'S' boiler, at the same time acquiring enlarged tanks and square windows in replacement for the round cab spectacle plates. Both were based at Limerick shed and worked Sligo line services, No 295 being employed for short spells at Birr to work the Roscrea branch and surviving until 1954.

The next group of four Kitson engines, 4-4-2Ts Nos 16 *Rocklands*, 17 *Faugh-a-Ballagh*, 18 *Geraldine* and 21 *Blarney Castle* (Type XXXIII), were ordered in two batches, two each in August 1895 and May 1896, the latter pair being charged to revenue; all four were ordered for working over the extended Sligo line. As they were nominally ordered for the C&CR, they were subject to inspection by the BoW engineer. They were not confined to this section and also worked the North Kerry line. Renumbered 269-271 and 274 by the GS&WR, all were rebuilt between December 1924 and June 1926 with 'S' boilers, their weight being increased from 46t 19cwt to 50t 12cwt. Their original neat appearance was somewhat spoiled by the rebuild which also saw tank capacity increased from 1,040 to 1,200 gallons. One of them worked on the D&SE suburban section services for a short spell in 1927, with all four eventually ending their lives on the CB&SC section. No 274 had the distinction of working the last passenger train on the Cork & Macroom section on 12 July 1935. Three were scrapped in 1949, but No 269 survived until 1957.

The other engine making the total order for six placed with Kitson, in May 1896, was an additional member of a class of 4-4-0s to a design based on an enlarged bogie version of the Dübs 2-4-0s, two of which were ordered from Kitson in August 1895 at £2,325 each. Nos 53 to 55, *Jubilee*, *Killemnee* and *Bernard*, (Type XXXIV) were principally employed on the Waterford mail and boat trains. Many parts were interchangeable with the 1893 goods engines, particularly the boilers and motion. The bogies were of the swing-link type. The late Bob Clements queried whether Nos 53 & 54 had copper-capped chimneys. He also believed that

0-6-0 No.2 as supplied by Kitson of Leeds.
Ian Allan Library

No 55 may have carried the name *Duke of York* for a short period in September 1897, which would have coincided with the Duke and Duchess of York's trip from Adare to Killaloe on 1 September in that year. Photographic evidence in the form of a view of No 55 with the Royal train, however, clearly shows the name as *Bernard*. This engine retained this name until 1919, long after all other nameplates on WL&WR engines had been removed by the GS&WR.

Nos 296 and 298, as they had become, received new boilers respectively in 1924 and 1927, both remaining in service until July 1950. Both were fitted with new chimneys, smokebox doors and square cab windows when they received new boilers, No 296 additionally having 16½in cylinders provided in 1939 when given a GS&WR pattern cab. No 297 was scrapped in 1928.

Finally, in December 1898 the decision was taken to order another new goods engine from Kitson for £2,980, only this time with a Belpaire firebox. This was the first engine to appear on a principal Irish railway with a Belpaire firebox. An order for two more of the same type at £3,380 each followed in October 1899. No 2 (Type XXXV) was reported to have arrived and to have completed 1,000 miles by April 1900. It became GS&WR No 222 and was rebuilt in October 1924 with a new '235' class round-topped boiler, lasting until 1949. Possibly anticipating difficulties in obtaining payment if the proposed merger went through, Kitson wrote to the WL&WR in August 1900 inquiring as to the method of payment to be adopted for the two additional engines. In September the company approached Kitson about possible disposal, in response to which the manufacturers advised that they would do their best to relieve the company of the two remaining engines on payment of £480 each, subject to their being able to dispose of them to some other company. The GS&WR inquired in November as to whether these engines were being charged to the revenue or capital account and, in advising them of its efforts to dispose of the two engines, the WL&WR indicated that the lowest price that could be accepted was £2,500 each, ie the cost of No 2 less the payment of £480 to Kitson.

The company was obviously still pursuing the matter of their disposal at the end of November when it was noted that 'the DW&WR will not take the Kitson engines but will give storage accommodation at a moderate charge'. With the merger having come into effect, the GS&WR decided in January 1901, it would have to take them, but the company was able to advise that the MGWR had agreed to purchase the two engines. The latter company made payment to the WL&WR in February, the cheque received from the MGWR being forwarded to Kitson & Co. It is of interest to note that Nos 4 and 11 appear in the table of engine loads in the final WL&WR timetable for June 1900, and that No 4 was illustrated in WL&WR livery in the June 1900 edition of the *Railway Engineer*.

The two additional engines were to have been named respectively *Samson* and *Dragon*, although Harold Fayle quotes *Shamrock* for No 4 and *Samson* for No 11. The former names are confirmed by the WL&WR stock register dating from 1898, as referred to in the Acknowledgements. An official Kitson photograph of No 4, mentioned in the previous paragraph, clearly shows the name as *Shamrock*, adding further to the confusion over the years. In any event, they became MGWR Nos 141 and 142, being named *Limerick* and *Athenry* by that company. In November 1924 they were allocated Nos 612 and 613, but in April 1925 they became Nos 233 and 234 in the overall GSR renumbering scheme, taking two vacant numbers in the ex-WLWR goods engine list thus reflecting their ancestry. No 233 was scrapped in 1929, but No 234 survived into CIE days, not being withdrawn until 1950.

The Fenit engine

Although not part of the WL&WR locomotive stock, brief mention needs to be made of the 0-6-0ST *Shamrock*. The company worked Fenit Pier on behalf of the Harbour Commissioners between 1887 and 1899; the engine used was generally No 42. It will be recalled that a very generous offer was made for this engine and declined by the company in 1899. Faced with working the pier themselves, the Commissioners purchased an 0-6-0ST from the contractor, T. H. Falkiner. *Shamrock* had been built in 1892

Above: **An interesting photograph of No 141** ***Limerick*** **of the MGWR. It was one of two ordered from Kitson shortly before the company's amalgamation with the GS&WR. Both were purchased by the MGWR. Originally to have been WL&WR No 4 and named** ***Samson*,** **No 141 has its new nameplate and numberplate attached over the original name and number. A photograph exists of it in WL&WR livery. As Class J17, No 141 eventually became GSR/CIE No 233 and was withdrawn from service in 1929.** H. Fayle/IRRS collection

Below: **'The Intruder' – built in 1892 by Hunslet for the contractor T. H. Falkiner in connection with the construction of the Kenmare branch of the GS&WR,** ***Shamrock*** **was purchased by the Fenit Harbour Commissioners following the company's refusal to continue working the line in 1899.** ***Shamrock*** **was taken over by the GS&WR in 1900. Numbered 299, it remained in use on Fenit Pier until its closure in 1941, when it was removed to Limerick. It was finally withdrawn from service in 1957.** A. W. Croughton

by Messrs Hunslet as a typical contractor's engine, with a saddle tank resting only on the boiler. Two similar engines were in fact supplied to Falkiner for use in the construction of the Kenmare branch in Co Kerry. Peter Rowledge comments that it had frames set for standard (4ft 8½in) gauge. After the GS&WR took over the working of the North Kerry and Fenit lines in 1901, it purchased *Shamrock*. The name was retained by the Harbour Commissioners, being removed by the GS&WR when becoming its No 299, at the end of the renumbered list of WL&WR engines. A new boiler was fitted in 1937, the locomotive remaining in use on Fenit Pier until it closed in 1941. It subsequently spent some time based in Cork and was finally withdrawn in 1957.

Liveries and renumbering

Up until about 1876 the locomotives were painted a medium green. This was replaced by brown, lined out in light blue and with yellow edging. Later again this was changed to Indian red with the same lining. Robinson introduced a new livery for the passenger engines akin to the crimson lake of the English Midland Railway, his goods engines being painted black with red and white lining. Many of the engines sported highly polished brass dome covers and copper-capped chimneys like those on the GWR. In a few instances, the boiler lagging bands were also of polished brass. It is interesting to note that when Robinson suggested a new crest to coincide with the change of company name in 1896, he replaced one of the original Stothert engines depicted on the crest with his No 53. Rather than being in his new livery, No 53 appeared on the crest in green. It is possible of course that this particular engine was painted green to celebrate the company's jubilee year, otherwise it is difficult to explain how Robinson could have made such a fundamental error. A new livery was applied to GS&WR engines about 1900, viz black with red and white lines, and this was applied to WL&WR engines as they went

through shops. During the 1914/18 war, GS&WR engines were spray-painted a battleship grey, a drab livery which was perpetuated by the GSR.

Following the take-over of the WL&WR system, the GS&WR renumbered the goods engines in the series 221 to 239 and the passenger engines from 260 to 298 inclusive. These numbers were in due course retained by both the GSR and CIE. Some of the engines were quickly withdrawn by the GS&WR, the vacant numbers being applied to newly built GS&WR engines.

Chapter Sixteen

ROLLING STOCK

The report prepared by Robert Andrews in 1874 provides us with a useful basis for details of the earlier rolling stock, although contemporary evidence from the board minutes proves that there are, in fact, a number of inaccuracies in relation to builders and dates of construction quoted in that report. A recently discovered rolling stock register drawn up by the WL&WR in May 1898, based on a survey undertaken in 1890 with information suitably updated, has kindly been made available to the author. This register, which had been kept up-to-date by the WL&WR until the end of 1900, has proved invaluable in enabling the full story of the company's passenger and goods stock to be told. These two documents, supported by board minutes and rolling stock statistics, presented in the half-yearly reports to shareholders from December 1860 onwards, have helped to eliminate most of the gaps that previously existed in our knowledge.

American-style bogies
Until the appearance of an article by the late George Mahon in the May 1964 issue of *The Railway Magazine*, it was generally accepted that the first bogie carriages to operate in regular service in Britain and Ireland were those introduced on the narrow gauge Festiniog Railway in 1873, main line bogie carriages following a year later when the Midland Railway rolled out of its Derby workshops the first Pullman cars to operate in Europe. Mahon, however, provided conclusive evidence that the Waterford & Limerick had in fact set this precedent some 25 years earlier with the introduction of American-style bogie carriages in 1848 for the opening of its line. It was Richard Osborne's experience with the Philadelphia & Reading Railroad that was to make itself felt on the W&LR and produce this unique 'first' in the railway history of these islands.

Consideration had been given by the W&LR as early as February 1846 to the purchase of carriages, but it was not until the end of July that instructions were given to order two first class carriages from Rogerson, Dawson & Russell of Dublin (hereinafter referred to as Dawson). These were to be 'agreeably to specification' and as the contract price for the bodies alone

First and Second Composite No 79, one of three such vehicles obtained from the Gloucester Railway Carriage & Wagon Co, nominally for the Claremorris & Collooney extension. Delivered in 1893, this carriage was 31ft in length and had accommodation for 14 first and 20 second class passengers. It became GS&WR No 928 and survived until 1958. Courtesy Gloucestershire Record Office

was £630 each, it is evident that they must have been considerably longer vehicles than the standard length carriages being built for other railways at that time. In December 1846, Osborne advised of materials required, which included 50 tons of best American white oak, 500 tons of best red pine, 100 tons of best pitch pine and 100 tons of second quality memel (timber from a Baltic fir), an advertisement for the same appearing in the *Railway Times* for 16 January 1847. At the same time, glass for four second class and six third class carriages was ordered; the quantity required for the second class carriages indicating that the design had about 12 windows on each side.

Reporting to the shareholders in February 1847 the chairman announced that 'in consequence of the very high prices demanded for carriages and wagons of all descriptions your directors have decided on building their own'. At the same meeting, Osborne was able to advise that two long second class carriages had been completed and that the materials for the rest of the second class and third class carriages was ready for putting together. However, the framing had been delayed awaiting the completion of a proper shed and machine shop. Referring to the design of carriage he was introducing he stated that they were spacious and better lit 'and being strongly built afford protection and safety in case of accidents. The end platforms are made very strong and heavy and so arranged that they receive the first concussion and must be broken and crushed before the end of the car itself can be injured.' In his opinion they offered by

far the safest means of conveyance that could be used on railways.

From the foregoing evidence it is apparent that all 12 passenger carriages constructed for the opening of the line were American-style vehicles carried on two short-wheelbase four-wheeled bogies. There were also three bogie luggage vans built in the same style. When the line from Limerick to Tipperary was inspected in April 1848 by Captain John Simmons, on behalf of the BoT, he made reference to the bogie carriages as follows: 'The carriages adopted are peculiar, being also introduced from the United States, consisting of a body about 40ft in length supported on two bogie frames, one at each end, which are free to turn round spindles, fitting into sockets in the under framing of the body. This framing extends at each end about 3ft beyond the body of the carriage, which is entirely in one compartment, the entrance to it being by a door from this platform. These carriages are well adopted for going around curves, the bogie frames being short and wheels close together, but I think it yet remains to be proved whether they are adapted to very high speeds.'

Ex WL&WR Third No 941 at Kingsbridge station, Dublin, in GS&WR livery. This coach started life as an Ashbury four-compartment second class four-wheeler, No 3, of 1872, length 21ft 6in. It was converted to a Third in 1888/9. S. Kennedy collection

The Railway Times for 8 July 1848, referring to the opening of the GS&WR to Limerick Junction, stated that the train in which the W&LR directors arrived at the Junction excited considerable attention 'from the peculiar construction of the carriages, being of the style used in America; they are entered from either end, and are very capacious and convenient'. Despite these complimentary remarks problems were encountered, the traffic manager of the GS&WR, George Ilberry, pointing out that the W&LR stock was incompatible with that of the GS&WR, and requiring the latter company to use its own vehicles for some time. Osborne's departure from the W&LR in August 1848 spelt the end for the bogie carriages and his successor Abraham Khlos soon recommended that they be cut in two. As early as January 1849 the board ordered that this work be carried out on one of the long carriages, and another was similarly treated two months later, while in May one of the composites was ordered to be cut 'so as to form two thirds'. The reference to composite carriages would indicate that the seating in at least two of the bogie vehicles had been altered since entering traffic. Two firsts, two seconds and two thirds were produced by cutting the bodies of three bogie carriages in half, each of them having to be equipped with an additional drag box to accommodate drawgear at the newly created end.

Another of the bogie carriages was withdrawn in 1849 and it was probably the body from this that became the temporary booking office at Boher. The eight remaining bogie carriages all appear to have been taken out of service about 1851/53, one of them becoming another temporary booking office, this time at Bansha. Following Khlos's departure from

the company in May 1849, G. W. Hemans took control of rolling stock matters and reported in August 1852 that, 'a great deal of the American type of carriages and wagons on the line, which have been a long time lying out of use, have now been altered and made serviceable stock'. Although this probably refers to the shortened vehicles, which would still have had an American look about them with a platform at one end and multiple side windows, it is possible that one or two of the bogie carriages might have been kept in use to deal with peak traffic loads pending the arrival of additional stock.

Three Dublin builders

At the beginning of 1851, Hemans sought tenders for carriages and in early April he was authorised to conclude a contract for two composites and two thirds, but this never happened. The proposal was overtaken by the commencement of the haulage contract in the same month and by July an agreement had been reached with Dargan for the supply of seven carriages: two firsts at £400 each, two seconds at £375 each and three thirds at £300 each. They were all built by Fagan of Dublin and in view of the prices, and the fact that they were available for inspection at his factory, it is fair to assume that they were new vehicles. However, Dargan appears to have had ownership until the end of the haulage contract, the W&LR paying £2,500 to him for the seven carriages in August 1853.

In February 1852 Hemans was asked to ascertain on what terms he could obtain two additional composites in Dublin as a result of which he was able to secure two carriages from Hutton for £750. One of these, a first, was actually built by Hutton in 1849, but the composite had been built by Fagan. At the end of March the GS&WR accepted an offer of £700 from the W&LR for the purchase of two composites, and in April a coupé composite was purchased from it for £350. In addition, it was agreed on 23 September to purchase four thirds from the GS&WR at £250 each, Hemans being instructed 'to be

particular in selecting good carriages'. All the carriages obtained from the GS&WR were built by Fagan in 1848 and, excepting one third that had its body rebuilt as a first in 1859, the 15 Fagan vehicles on the W&LR had long lives; seven of them lasted for over 40 years. The coupé composite was one of two composites altered in late 1862 into third brakes with accommodation for mail bags for the night mail train. It was subsequently rebuilt as a composite in 1874, which survived until about 1895. The Hutton carriage was altered into a first class saloon at Limerick in 1867 and in this guise it survived long enough to become No 903 in GS&WR ownership.

On the same day that it was agreed to purchase the four thirds from the GS&WR, the tender of Richard W. Johnson and Thomas W. Kinder, trading as the Railway Carriage Company, Bromsgrove (which moved to Oldbury in 1854), was accepted for three composite carriages at £450 each. It was stipulated by the W&LR that these carriages should be 'in every respect equal to those at present in use on the Galway line, with the exception of stained glass and cushions in the second class'. Delivery took a year, and when the carriages arrived in September 1853 the finance committee wrote to Hemans expressing its concern that they were 'totally different and much inferior' to the pattern shown to officers of the company in Dublin. On 21 October the board recorded that the carriages supplied by Johnson and Kinder were not equal to their contract, which it called upon it to fulfil. In reply, Johnson and Kinder submitted an account for altering the carriages which resulted in the original contract price being greatly exceeded but, following an interview, it agreed to put glass in the second class compartments, make the windows secure and give an allowance for split panels. Its account for the carriages was settled in January 1854 at the contract price less a deduction of £56 for alterations, but its claim for repairs was submitted to arbitration by George Miller, the GS&WR engineer.

In February 1856, the locomotive superintendent, Thomas Lunt, reported on the need for new carriages. On the same day, Mr Dawson was in attendance at the board to solicit an order, but he was directed to send in an estimate and it was ordered that estimates be also requested from Wrights of Birmingham, Ashbury of Manchester and Worsdell & Evans of Birmingham. Resulting from this exercise it was agreed on 22 March to offer Dawson £420 each for two composites which he had tendered at £450, the offer being accepted a week later. However, it was not until 13 August that an order for two first class and two second class carriages was placed with Joseph Wright of Birmingham, whose firm was to become the Metropolitan Railway Carriage & Wagon Co

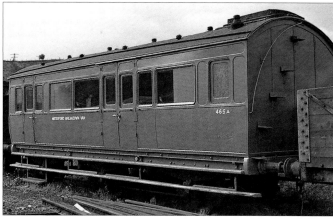

in 1863. The two first class carriages from Wright had very long lives, lasting for 52 and 60 years, but the two thirds were replaced in 1894/5.

Following this interlude with the two Birmingham manufacturers, the W&LR continued its dealings with the third Dublin coachbuilder for the supply of carriages. On 27 March 1857 it ordered two thirds, which Dawson proposed to convert from composites, and two third brakes with luggage compartments. Jonathan Pim, who had succeeded Lunt, soon reported that the converted composites were not suitable and it was agreed to order two new thirds in their place. Upon delivery of these four carriages the passenger stock reached a total of 33 vehicles, which Pim reported in February 1859 as comprising five firsts, five seconds, twelve thirds and eleven composites. The total was to increase by six when four thirds and two third brakes, ordered from Dawson on 4 May 1859, were delivered. The majority of the 14 Dawson carriages were replaced between 1888 and 1893, but one of the 1856 composites did last until 1896; a third brake of 1859, which had been converted into an accident van for Tuam survived as GS&WR No 38A, and one of the 1859 thirds worked until 1901, the GS&WR allocating it No 958.

Kilkenny line stock

When the W&LR commenced working the W&KR on 28 January 1861, it took over sixteen passenger carriages, two passenger brake vans, four horse boxes and two carriage trucks. In March 1861, the rolling stock committee was anxious to know of their condition and what would be required to make them effective and keep them in working order. Pim estimated that it would cost £124 for the carriages and £44 for the brake vans, horse boxes and trucks. The GS&WR objected to the Kilkenny stock running over its line, Pim having to satisfy Miller when the stock had been lifted to the correct height for through running. The precise renumbering of the W&KR carriages in the W&LR stock list is not known but, as

Above left: **Waterford Breakdown Van No 83a, ex WL&WR, although its original number is unknown.** D. G. Coakham

Above right: **Waterford Breakdown Van No 465A. Originally Saloon No 77 built at Limerick in 1891, it was renumbered 900 by the GS&WR. In 1954 it was converted to an Ambulance Coach for use on pilgrimage specials to Claremorris for the shrine at Knock. Withdrawn in 1963, it became 465A, and was presented to the Railway Preservation Society of Ireland in 1976.** D. G. Coakham

there is a reference to a 'want of trimming and painting' of two firsts, Nos 45 and 52 (previously seconds) in September 1866, it is apparent that they were renumbered together with the L&ER carriages in a sequence following on from the last of the Dawson carriages delivered in 1859.

It was reported by June 1862 that the carriages on the Kilkenny line were deteriorating due to the lack of attention, Martin Atock being advised of the necessity to preserve them 'by having them immediately varnished'. With the working agreement nearing its end, Atock, in his report of 25 September 1865, noted that the W&KR carriages were all so very old that they required rebuilding, and so recommended that they should all be given back. When the working agreement concluded on 31 May 1867, the W&LR returned the same 24 items of carriage stock to the W&KR that it had taken over in 1861 at an agreed valuation of £1,179.

Limerick and Ennis stock

The L&ER procured all of its passenger stock from Dawson, the first order placed on 12 March 1859 being for one first class, one second class and three third class carriages and one first/second composite carriage, and including two horse boxes and a carriage truck. Two brake vans were ordered on the same day but only one was delivered as a passenger van, the company having agreed to Dawson's suggestion that one of them should be completed as a goods

brake. They were all delivered by 1 October, but in the meantime an additional first/second composite was ordered on 11 June. One further passenger vehicle was obtained from Dawson, a third class carriage that was delivered by mid-March 1860. All of this passenger stock passed into W&LR control on 22 April 1861 when it took over the working of the L&ER, but it did not become its property immediately, as arbitration was required before the terms of sale were settled in the latter half of 1863. As noted above, the carriages were renumbered in the W&LR stock list in a sequence together with the Kilkenny stock. All but one of the L&ER carriages were replaced between 1886 and 1894, but the first class carriage, which had become No 43 on the W&LR eventually being downgraded to a composite and finally, in 1896, to a third class, survived as GS&WR No 962 until 1906.

In connection with a requirement for two composites for Killaloe passengers on the Castleconnell line, which was raised in June 1864, Atock offered to convert two third class carriages that were unfit for running at £150 each. He stated that he also had two composites laid up for general overhaul which could be adapted for £20 each. The latter course was ordered by the board, but Atock must have subsequently received approval for the thirds as Nos 7 and 8 were completely rebuilt at Limerick in 1865 and 1866 respectively in which condition they ran for over 20 years. Atock's only other contribution to the passenger-carrying stock was made just before he left to join the MGWR. On 15 August 1871 he suggested procuring three new second class carriages to replace one that was worn out and two others that were fit only to be made into third class. Three tenders were received, from Ashbury, Metropolitan and Midland Railway Carriage & Wagon Co, Birmingham, and on Atock's recommendation the board agreed to order the three new carriages from Ashbury at £276 10s each. They were numbered from 1 to 3 in the carriage list and lasted until 1907/08, running as GS&WR Nos 939 to 941 from 1901 onwards.

Tuam and Gort stock

The carriage stock was increased by 11 passenger carriages, three passenger brake vans, two horse boxes and a carriage truck from 1 November 1872 when the W&LR commenced working the A&TR and A&EJR. The entire rolling stock for both companies had been built by the Bristol Wagon Works. When the MGWR gave notice of its intention not to renew the working agreement for the A&TR after its expiry on 27 September 1870, the A&TR set about obtaining its own rolling stock. It placed an order with Bristol for two carriages, a first/second composite and a third class, and also a passenger brake van, which were delivered in early 1871. Either later in the same year or in 1872 it took delivery of a first/second composite smoking carriage and a horse box.

Finding that the W&LR would not operate its line, the A&EJR also ordered its own rolling stock from Bristol on a seven-year deferred payment system, the first order being placed in 1869 for three carriages and a passenger brake van. The carriages were a first/second composite, a second class and a third class which, together with the brake van, were ready for delivery by December. By mid-1870 it was necessary to obtain more vehicles and a further three passenger carriages, identical to those in the first batch, were ordered together with a horse box, these being delivered in December of the same year. On 19 April 1871 a carriage truck was ordered and it would have been about the same time in the following year that an order was placed for a first/second composite and a third class, as on 12 August 1872 both of these carriages were recorded as having been delivered.

The 11 Bristol-built passenger carriages from the two Athenry companies, although only three years old at the time of their transfer to the W&LR, were described as being 'sadly neglected and require very considerable repairs. A bad bargain to us altogether.' They took up vacant numbers formerly carried by the Kilkenny stock in the W&LR carriage list, passenger brake vans, horse boxes and the carriage truck being renumbered in the respective lists according to type. One of the thirds was replaced in 1886, but the other carriages ran until replaced by new vehicles built at Limerick between 1891 and 1899.

Carriages from Birmingham

In November 1876, the secretary inquired as to how carriages that had been sanctioned were to be obtained and in reply he was directed to obtain specifications, drawings and tenders from various manufacturers. Six tenders were received, and that of Metropolitan for three composites and six third class carriages was accepted in March 1877 at £368 and £281 each respectively. A month later, Metropolitan wrote declining proposals

made by the W&LR, indicating that to build the carriages to the company's design could not be done at the price tendered. It had priced for oak solebars and headstocks, oak framing and mahogany panels and mouldings, whereas the W&LR wanted top quarters rounded and solebars, headstocks, framing and panels of teak. The Metropolitan tender was for roofs covered with well-painted canvas, but the W&LR wanted the roofs to be covered with oil cloth. Furthermore, the company specified expensive rugs for the first class instead of ordinary carpets and the lamps in the large compartments were not to the Metropolitan specification. When it was pointed out that it would cost an additional £58 per carriage for the composites and £51 per carriage for the third class to satisfy these demands the company decided to accept the Metropolitan tender on the terms and specifications offered without any extras, except that the top corners of the windows were to be made rounded. The Metropolitan vehicles were soundly constructed and gave 30 or more years of service. Two of them were converted for mail traffic, No 66 becoming brake and mail van No 50 in 1899 and No 61 having its body rebuilt as a Post Office van in 1900.

Obviously conscious of its previous problems in attempting to specify carriage design, the company decided, in mid-1880, to request Alexander McDonnell, locomotive superintendent of the GS&WR, to produce drawings and specifications suitable for inviting tenders, for which he was paid a fee of 20 guineas. Having considered the seven tenders submitted, it was decided, on 23 October, to accept that of the Bristol Wagon Company for eight composites and to select patterns of cloth and hair from the samples submitted. However, just one week later the matter was reconsidered and it was decreed that the tender of either the Birmingham RCW Co or Messrs Ashbury be accepted in accordance with the chairman's

wishes, which were in favour of the Birmingham company. Construction of the carriages had not commenced by the following February when the locomotive superintendent, Edward Barry, visited the Birmingham RCW Works, although the materials were in the process of being prepared. Four of the carriages were delivered before the end of June and the remainder of the order was completed in the following month. Nos 69 to 76, which became 919 to 926 when taken over by the GS&WR, were solidly built vehicles, four of them having a life of over 65 years and lasting into CIE days.

Appleby takes over

Apart from the two third class carriages rebuilt in 1865/66 and composite No 10, which received a rebuilt body in 1874, the company had not constructed any new passenger carriages since Osborne's time. Not long after Henry Appleby's arrival on the W&LR in August 1882 complaints were received about the standard of third class carriages in use. Correspondence with the BoT ensued, and in August 1883 the company undertook not to use any carriage on Parliamentary trains that did not comply with the Regulation of Railways Act, 1844. Appleby was asked to furnish drawings and a report on the steps to be taken to improve the third class carriages. He advised the board, in a letter dated 2 October, that the alterations required by the BoT would affect 25 third class carriages and that he had heard that the North London Railway had several carriages for sale. The board, on the other hand, ordered Appleby to prepare drawings for six new third class carriages for the purpose of inviting tenders. Although these were received in March 1884, it was decided that only three thirds should be ordered from Birmingham RCW, but on 10 April the decision to proceed was deferred and the matter was not taken up again for some time.

Far left: **Radio Train Coach No 935.**
This coach began life as WL&WR No 92,
a 48ft First and Second Lavatory Bogie
Composite built by Metropolitan in 1896.
It became an Invalid Coach in 1919 and
was converted to a Radio Studio coach in
1953 and renumbered RS21 in 1964.
It was presented to the Railway
Preservation Society of Ireland.
The photograph was taken at Kingsbridge,
Dublin (now Heuston) on 20 April 1957.
D. G. Coakham

Left: **Bogie Third Brake No 937 at Glanmire**
Road, Cork on 16 April 1952. Originally
WL&WR Second and Third Brake Composite
No 102, it was constructed at Limerick in
1898 with seating for 20 second and 24
third class passengers. It was converted
to a Brake Third in 1929 and withdrawn
in 1955. D. G. Coakham

In May 1885, Appleby reported that he had not purchased any of the stock sold by the L&LSR owing to the high prices — this was actually purchased by the DW&WR. Meanwhile, J. G. Robinson had taken up duties as Appleby's assistant in August 1884, so the locomotive department was in a strong position when the matter of renewing the five condemned third class carriages was raised again in December 1885. One replacement, a 26ft third class carriage, had already been built at Limerick earlier in the year and permission was sought and given for the employment of two additional men for the renewal of stock. This event marked the beginning of passenger stock construction at Limerick on a regular basis, which commenced at a rate of two per year. Still short of carriages, Appleby suggested in March 1887 that broad-gauge vehicles then being disposed of very cheaply by the GWR might be purchased. The GWR, however, cautioned against such measures and thereafter the company stepped up its output of carriages from the Limerick works to an average of six per year. Five carriages were built on 24ft underframes, but 30ft was generally adopted as the standard until 1895, five vehicles being completed to this latter length during Appleby's time.

The Robinson era

When Robinson took over the reins from Appleby he carried on replacing the worn-out stock with new carriages built in the Limerick shops and by 1893 the total number of passenger-carrying vehicles that had been constructed there in just nine years had reached 37. Of these, thirty-five were replacements, the other two being additions to stock. This consisted of twenty-three third class, three third brake and ten composite carriages plus a directors' saloon. Saloon No 77 and composite No 78 were the two additions to stock; the former, which was completed in 1891, was the first

W&LR carriage to be constructed to an increased length of 30ft 5in. It became GS&WR No 900 in 1901 and in 1954 it was converted into an ambulance coach for Knock pilgrimage traffic. It was later transferred to service stock as No 465A, and was subsequently presented to the Railway Preservation Society of Ireland (RPSI) in 1976 — one of only two W&LR passenger vehicles to survive into preservation.

Despite the increased output from its own works, there was a need to obtain additional stock for the upcoming opening of the Collooney extension, and in February 1893 tenders were sought from nine manufacturers for the supply of five new composites. Consideration was first given to ordering these coaches from the Lancaster Railway Carriage & Wagon Co, but it was decided on 25 May to procure three composites at £620 each from the Gloucester Carriage & Wagon Co and three thirds from Bristol at £410 each. All but one survived into CIE days, one of the third class having been maliciously destroyed during the troubles in 1923. Another of the Bristol third class carriages was converted into a turf wagon in 1942 and was not broken up until 1955. Although these vehicles were nominally designated for the Collooney line, this seems to have happened some time after delivery, as on 20 December 1894 the traffic manager reported that he required nine thirds, three composites and three tri-composites for that line. In January 1895 Robinson recommended consideration of the question of substituting long bogie tri-composites to enable a reduction in the number of third class carriages, but the board decided to order the nine third class carriages from Metropolitan. At the same time, however, it did give Robinson authority to build a 48ft frame at the works 'as opportunity offers'. A month later the tender of Metropolitan for the supply of the tri-composite carriages with lavatories at £520 each was accepted, the three vehicles

in question being built to the length of 30ft 5in as introduced on the directors' saloon some four years earlier.

Meanwhile, the Limerick workshops continued to construct new carriages, turning out two third class, four third brakes and a tri-composite in 1894/95. They were built to the standard 30ft length, and all but third brake No 94 were replacements for worn-out stock. Three 30ft 5in coupé composites, Nos 12, 26 and 99, followed in 1896, but in seeking suppliers for 48ft bogie carriages, the W&LR turned to outside manufacturers once again. On 25 January 1896 it was agreed to order two bogie third class carriages from Ashbury at £755 each and two bogie first/ second composites with lavatories from Metropolitan at £1,200 each. On the same day two 30ft 5in third class carriages at £476 each were also ordered from Ashbury. One of the Metropolitan composites, No 98 (later GS&WR No 935) had an interesting career, becoming an invalid coach in 1919, with accommodation for 19 first class passengers on bunks. It was converted into a Radio Studio coach in 1953, CIE later giving it the number RS21 and, finally, it was presented to the RPSI in 1976.

Eight carriages were built at Limerick in the years 1897-99 including two bogie composite brakes, the only bogie vehicles to be built there since Osborne built his American style bogies some 50 years earlier. These were Nos 102 and 103, which were completed in late 1898 and became Nos 937 and 938 under GS&WR ownership. They both survived well into CIE days, it being 1955 before they were withdrawn from service. They were preceded by four composites and two thirds, which were turned out in 1897. One of the composites, No 56, was a coupé vehicle with lavatory and, as No 916, it survived until 1952. Finally, two third brakes were built in 1899, one of which was maliciously destroyed in 1923, the other lasting as No 997 until 1958. With the exception of these last two vehicles, all of the passenger carriages constructed or purchased by the company since 1894 were built on steel underframes, which were referred to as 'iron underframes' in the stock register.

Lighting, brakes and comfort

Before leaving the story of the passenger carriages, it is opportune to detail some general points of interest. Complaints were made in December 1860 regarding the lamps in carriages, which were reported to give a 'very bad light'. In response to an inquiry, George Ilberry of the GS&WR advised in November 1877 that that company used mineral oil in its carriage lamps at a cost of 1s per gallon. It was asked for the loan of several lamps to enable the company to carry out trials, but it appears that the GS&WR was slow in producing them. Possibly as a result of such a trial, the GS&WR was asked in July 1879 if it would sell two dozen of its lamps to the company and, about this time also, a sample of a colza lamp as used on the L&NWR was inspected.

In September 1895 Messrs J. Stone & Co, Deptford, approached the W&LR offering to fit up a carriage with electric lighting for trials at no expense to the company. The matter was deferred, but in December the traffic manager stated that he thought a considerable saving could be effected and better lighting achieved by using electricity, permission being granted to try the experiment on one carriage. And so it was that coupé composite No 12 was turned out of the works on 24 February 1896 complete with electric lighting. In April 1896 Robinson submitted correspondence with Stones in which it quoted £75 per carriage for the complete installation of electric light in two bogie composites and £55 per carriage for two bogie thirds. It was agreed that this be adopted for the carriages of that type which were under construction by Metropolitan and Ashbury. The order was extended to include four other vehicles then under construction, which resulted in two complete trains being so equipped in August 1896.

In October 1897, it was agreed to fit eight more carriages with Stones equipment at £65 each to produce two further train sets with electric lighting. In this case a double-battery system was installed. The single-battery system, as originally supplied for the first two train sets, was brought into line with the double-battery system between January and April 1898, the coupé composite being dealt with in September of the same year. Meanwhile, it had been decided to equip the directors' saloon with electric lighting and this work was completed in January 1898. Although Robinson reported the success of the 18 vehicles equipped with electric light to a board meeting in July 1898, it was decided to defer the fitting of any further vehicles. However, composite

No 32 was so equipped in September of the same year, possibly using a spare set of parts, and the two bogie composite brakes completed at the end of 1898 had electric lighting installed before they entered service in January 1899. The GS&WR had not adopted electric lighting for its own stock and, as the company had gas production facilities at Inchicore, the electrically lit WL&WR carriages were converted to gas lighting after their absorption by the former company.

In March 1861, it was reported that an offer had been made to supply Shaw's Patent brake for carriages, this offer being declined. Twenty-three years elapsed before we again find a reference to brakes, when in March 1884 the locomotive superintendent submitted tenders for applying steam and vacuum brakes to engines and carriages, the decision being taken to equip just one engine with the vacuum brake. Six months before the disastrous accident at Armagh, which led directly to a requirement for all companies to install continuous automatic brakes on their passenger trains, the W&LR received an estimate in January 1889 from the Vacuum Brake Co for the fitting of this type of brake. Robinson recommended that vacuum brake equipment to the value of £241 should be procured to permit the fitting of six carriages and two vans at Limerick works. The board, however, decided not to proceed, 'although there is no probability of any change being made in the selection of the brake'. By the time he reported to the board again on the subject of brakes in the following November, the continuous automatic brake had become mandatory, and Robinson sought instructions as to procuring brake fittings from the GWR at Swindon. The chairman was requested to ask the consent of that company to provide the castings, excluding rigging, and valves for guard's vans from its works at Swindon.

As early as October 1852, instructions were issued for the ordering of rugs for the first class carriages. When it was suggested in February 1861 that the second-class carriages be fitted with cushions, as was the practice on both the Dublin & Drogheda Railway and the MGWR, W. L. Payne, the traffic manager, complained that it would reduce the number of passengers travelling first class. The question of upholstery in the second class carriages was raised again in January 1880, when it was decided that rep should be employed in place of American cloth, no doubt on grounds of cost. When additional rugs were required in October 1882, an offer was made by Messrs Cannock & Co of Limerick to supply 60 such items at a cost of 19s each, this figure being considered excessive. The subject of providing smoking compartments was raised by the BoT in September 1868, but it was to be three years before instructions were given

for one such compartment to be provided in first and second class carriages.

Non-passenger vehicles

Under this heading we shall take a look at the company's luggage, parcel and brake vans, horse boxes and carriage trucks. The first luggage van was an eight-wheeled bogie vehicle with compartments built at Limerick in 1846 to Osborne's American-style design. Two more vehicles of this type followed in 1847, but after Osborne's departure it appears that some of them were cut in two to make short vans. Two 'old carriages' were also converted to brake vans by Lunt in late 1855, and these probably also had their genesis in the bodies of bogie vehicles. According to Pim there were seven passenger vans on 31 January 1859 and we know that one more was added in 1859 or 1860. In March 1870, it was decided to have six of these vehicles rebuilt by the Midland Railway Carriage & Wagon Co, Washwood Heath, Birmingham. Two former W&KR passenger vans were in use from 1861 until they were returned in 1867.

Until the middle of 1887, the passenger vans and goods brake vans were numbered in a combined list, and this accounts for the fact that the two brake vans from the L&ER became Nos 15 and 16 on the W&LR. The Tuam and Gort lines contributed Nos 17 to 20, three of which were passenger vans and one a goods brake. Four new passenger brake vans were added to stock in 1880 in fulfilment of an order placed with Birmingham RCW on 30 October, and these became Nos 38 to 41 when passenger vans and goods brakes were numbered in separate lists. Between 1889 and 1895, six additions to stock were built at Limerick, the last two (Nos 51 and 52) being nominally allocated to Collooney stock. Three of the earlier passenger vans were replaced in 1891/92 and a further three in 1896/97. Finally, in 1899, a brake and mail van, converted from Metropolitan composite No 66 of 1877, replaced the old No 50 of 1899, and No 31 the last of the A&EJR vehicles was replaced by a Post Office van built at Limerick in 1900. The latter was one of two Post Office vans on the WL&WR, the other being the rebuild of Metropolitan third No 61 of 1877. These became Nos 999 and 1050 respectively on the GS&WR and lasted into CIE days, albeit both running as luggage vans prior to their withdrawal in 1959.

The first horse boxes for the line were supplied by Messrs Brown Marshall to an order placed by the W&LR in November 1851. Delivered in 1852 (not 1848 as shown in Andrews' report of 1874), these seven vehicles were all rebuilt by the Midland RCW in 1870. No 7 survived as GS&WR No 1027 until 1926 when it was sold to the SL&NCR as a replacement for its horse box destroyed at Sligo during the Civil War. No 4 was replaced by a new vehicle built at Limerick in 1889 and the other five were similarly replaced between 1896 and 1898. As we have previously noted, four horse boxes came from the W&KR, but it is not known what numbers they carried while they were under W&LR operational control from 1861 to 1867. The two L&ER horse boxes, Nos 8 and 9 built by Dawson in 1859, lasted until replaced by new vehicles built by the W&LR in 1891 and 1893. Similarly, the two Bristol-built horse boxes inherited from the A&EJR and A&TR were replaced in 1891 and 1895 although No 10 had actually been withdrawn in 1888. An attempt was made to procure nine additional horseboxes in 1867 but, despite receiving tenders from Ashbury, Brown Marshall and Metropolitan, the matter was indefinitely deferred on 13 August. Fifteen years later, on 14 September 1882, four new horse boxes (Nos 12 to 15) were ordered from Metropolitan 'according to Mr Appleby's design at £125 10s each'. A solitary addition to the stock was made in 1892 when No 16 was turned out of the Limerick workshops and on 27 August 1896 orders were given for eight horse boxes to be built, Nos 17 to 22 being additions to stock completed at Limerick in 1897/8.

Brown Marshall also supplied the W&LR with its first carriage trucks, four of which were ordered on 26 July 1852, the supplier's account for the same being presented in January of the following year. No 2 was rebuilt in 1874 and replaced in 1890 and No. 1 was replaced in 1883, the other two having been withdrawn in 1875. Two more carriage trucks came from Dawson at sometime during 1856-59, and these were replaced in 1886-88. There were two W&KR trucks in operation on the line from 1861-67, and Nos 8 and 9 respectively were the carriage trucks built by Dawson (1859) and Bristol (1869) for the L&ER and the A&EJR, both of which lasted until 1887. A new No 5 was built in 1888 to replace one carriage truck 'found missing' in a census of stock, and in 1889 another vacant number was filled when No 7 was completed at Limerick. The last two carriage trucks to be built by the WL&WR were Nos 1 and 6, which were both completed during the first half of 1899.

Early goods stock

As we have already noted, for economic reasons, the W&LR decided to build its own rolling stock and this policy applied as much to goods wagons as it did to passenger carriages. In reporting on progress made during 1846, Osborne advised the shareholders in February 1847 that he had made twelve four-wheeled covered wagons for produce traffic (later referred to as vans) and seven four-wheeled open wagons for other goods, all to carry 4 tons each. In addition, he had completed three eight-wheeled long covered cars each capable of

carrying 9 tons of grain, thereby putting his American experience to work once again. During 1847 a further fourteen covered wagons and five open wagons were added and the bogie stock was increased by one more grain car and four long flat cars, bringing the total stock to 46 vehicles. A further 22 vehicles were added in 1848, possibly after Osborne's departure as none of them was of the bogie type, which included fifteen open coal wagons and three coke wagons.

Brown Marshall and Dawson

With a stock of just 68 wagons it must have been difficult enough for Dargan to operate adequate freight services after he took up the working of the line in April 1851, and he would probably have had to use a considerable number of his own wagons to supplement the fleet. The situation had apparently become quite difficult by late October when Hemans was requested to report to the board on the state of the whole working stock in the possession of the contractor. As a result, Brown Marshall's tender for the supply of 25 cattle wagons and 25 covered goods wagons was accepted on 1 November 1851. In the following year, Hemans was empowered and authorised on 9 June to order a further 25 wagons of each type from Brown Marshall, but these do not appear to have arrived until the first half of 1853. It is known that the cattle wagons were Nos 69-118 and that they were followed in the list by 44 of the covered wagons up to No 162. It must therefore be assumed that six of the covered wagons were replacements for earlier vehicles.

The opening to Waterford on 11 September 1854 placed demands on the company for an increase in the wagon stock and on the 22nd of the same month Lunt was authorised to proceed with the building of 25 new wagons. However, before they started to appear it was resolved on 2 February 1855 to hire 40 covered goods wagons from

Parcels Van No 1050, ex WL&WR Postal Van No 61, was constructed at Limerick Works in 1900. It is photographed at Waterford on 20 April 1954. D. G. Coakham

Dawson at £12 per wagon for the first year and £15 for the second year, with an option to purchase at £120 each at the end of the first or second year. After 18 months on hire, Nos 163-202 were purchased for £114 each in August 1856. Lunt actually built 30 covered wagons at Limerick during 1856 which were numbered in sequence following the 40 Dawson vehicles. On 19 January 1859 an order was placed with Dawson for the supply of 70 covered wagons at £98 17s 6d each, but on 16 June it was decided to substitute 35 of the wagons on that order with 20 open coal wagons at £82 each, four third brakes and two third class carriages. Delivery continued into 1860, and Dawson appears to have forgotten the adjustment to the order, the W&LR noting in April that 65 covered wagons had been received and asked Dawson for 'an allowance off the price for being in excess of the order'. Dawson agreed to a deduction of £6 17s 6d per wagon, the oversight also leading to the suspension of Mr Rogerson from the wagon building company. Two of the Dawson covered wagons, Nos 47 and 50, replaced old worn-out vehicles, Nos 233 to 320 being additions to stock.

Kilkenny goods stock

On 28 January 1861, when the W&LR commenced working the W&KR, it took over 46 covered wagons built in 1856 by Ashbury; 30 open wagons built by Walshe of Waterford; two cattle wagons by Dawson; four covered wagons converted from hopper wagons; ten ballast wagons; six timber trucks; and three goods brake vans. Apart from the timber trucks and goods brake vans, which were numbered separately, the rest of the W&KR goods vehicles were

**Six-wheeled 29ft 9in Carriage Truck
No 1045 on 20 April 1957. No 1045 was
built at Limerick in 1887.** D. G. Coakham

renumbered from 321 to 412 in the W&LR
goods stock list. In March 1861 the Rolling
Stock Committee was anxious to know of
their condition and what would be required
to make them effective and keep them in
working order. Pim was therefore requested
to prepare a statement of repairs necessary
to 'enable this plant to be safely and
efficiently worked'. His estimate, presented
at the committee meeting held on 19 April,
showed that it would cost £390 for the 98
wagons which, apart from the Ashbury
wagons, had to be lifted to the correct
height in order to work over GS&WR lines.

The Walshe wagons would appear to have
been the least robust as 20 of them,
Nos 354-373, were replaced by new open
wagons ordered from Dawson as early as
8 October 1861. The remaining ten,
Nos 374-383, were replaced by new open
wagons built by the company at Limerick in
1865. However, they do not appear to have
been broken up immediately as a board
minute of 16 June 1866 mentions a request
from a Mr Mannix 'for ten wagons lying near
the Limerick terminus (about being broken
up) to be used on the Newcastle line for
horse traction'. Atock advised that the 'old
W&KR plant is not fit to run or charge for'
and the board decided that it was better not
to interfere, as being old W&KR plant, it was
likely to be surrendered at short notice.

The Ashbury covered wagons, Nos 321-
353 and 384-396, appear to have been the
best of the lot, 19 of them being rebuilt in
1864/65 as part of an order given to Atock
on 5 January 1864 to reconstruct and convert
30 wagons of the W&KR stock into cattle
wagons at an estimated cost of about £40
each. As the cattle wagon stock increased by
only 27 vehicles at that time it must be
assumed that one of the 30 vehicles
reconstructed was not rebuilt as a cattle
wagon and that the total included the
rebuilding of the two original cattle wagons
built by Dawson as well as four of the ballast

wagons. The 10 vehicles making up the
balance of cattle wagon rebuilds appear to
have been Nos 397-406 in the W&LR list.
The six surviving ballast wagons were
originally Nos 407-412 but, following their
renumbering together with the other ballast
wagons in the fleet as Nos 26-31, their place
was taken by six new covered goods wagons
built at Limerick in 1865. It is not known if
these six ballast wagons were rebuilt or not
during their time under W&LR control.

When the working agreement concluded
on 31 May 1867, the W&LR returned 85
wagons to the W&KR, noting in a board
minute of 29 June that 17 Ashbury wagons,
one engine and tender, one drilling machine
and one lathe had been retained against the
additional value of £4,174 16s 7d put into
the rolling stock during the working of the
Kilkenny line. In fact, the W&LR kept all 27
of the Ashburys that had not been converted
into cattle wagons. It also retained the 30
open wagons built as replacements in 1862
by Dawson and at Limerick. Included in the
total of wagons returned were the six timber
trucks and the three goods brake vans. Apart
from these, the only original W&KR items of
stock returned were the 29 rebuilt cattle
wagons (19 of which were Ashburys) and
five ballast wagons, Nos 27-31. The difference
was made up by the transfer to the W&KR
of 46 wagons originally built for the W&LR,
viz the last 11 of the covered wagons built
by Dawson in 1859, and the six covered
wagons and 29 open wagons built at
Limerick in 1865/6.

Additions and rebuilds
On 25 November 1862 a scarcity of coal
wagons was reported and Atock, having
indicated that he could turn out about three
wagons per week at about £40 each, was
given authority to commence building 10
additional open coal wagons. In March 1866
Atock was ordered to increase his manufacture of new open coal wagons by two
each month until 24 were added to stock,
and a couple of weeks later, having
estimated that it would only cost an
additional £10 per month in wages to
produce an extra wagon, he was instructed

to increase his output to three wagons per
month. It would appear this latter batch of
wagons were Nos 534-557.

In December 1862, Smith & Knight,
contractors to the MGWR and the Great
Northern & Western Railway, offered the
W&LR 40 ballast wagons and, following a
visit to Roscommon, Atock was able to
report that he had seen 12 of them and
found them to be good and strong and able
to carry 5½ tons of coal. Smith & Knight
accepted the W&LR offer of £45 per wagon
and the wagons arrived on the company's
lines in January 1863. They were initially
numbered O1 to O40 but in July, after it was
ordered that they were to be W&LR-branded
and charged to capital, they were allocated
Nos 450-489.

On 15 December 1866, it was reported
that 97 of the W&LR wagons were in need
of reconstruction and Atock was given
authority to proceed. Progress was steady
and he was able to advise the board on
30 May 1868 that 50 had been rebuilt up to
March of that year at which time his staff had
been reduced. Having made the point that
the staff was too small to do anything but
patch-up the remaining wagons, and that he
would need seven carpenters, one smith,
one striker, one painter, one labourer and
one fitter in addition to his remaining staff,
Atock was 'given liberty to engage the men
asked for at once'.

The gunpowder wagon
The question of the carriage of gunpowder
was raised in June 1868 and it was
considered advisable that arrangements be
made to confine the carriage of such to
goods trains, and only then in special vans,
similar to those used by the GS&WR. In
response to an inquiry, Atock informed the
board that as he had no van which could be
reconstructed for the purpose, a special van
was required, strongly built of iron, lined
inside with wood and sheet lead, and fitted
with a strong and well-secured door. Having
been requested to consider the matter
further, Atock suggested making the
necessary alterations to one of the existing
goods wagons then in course of rebuilding,
at a total cost of £115. An entirely new
gunpowder van on the other hand would
cost about £160. Instructions were given for
the alteration of an existing van, No 135
being reconstructed in its new guise, in 1869.

Limerick & Ennis stock
When the L&ER placed its first order for
rolling stock with Dawson on 12 March 1859
40 covered goods wagons were included,
the first of which were delivered in July with
the order completed in October. Also
included was a goods brake van, originally
ordered as one of a pair of passenger vans,
the company having assented to a suggestion
made by Dawson in April that one should be

completed as a goods brake. A subsequent order resulted in Dawson delivering four open wagons in March 1860. This goods stock, together with four ballast wagons, came into W&LR hands when it took over the working of the L&ER on 22 April 1861. However, the matter of the sale of the L&ER rolling stock to the W&LR was subject to arbitration and was not finalised until the latter half of 1863, and it was following this that the goods wagons became Nos 490-533 in the W&LR list; the solitary goods brake van became W&LR No 16 in the separate brake van list. The four ballast wagons were immediately taken in hand and rebuilt as open wagons before the end of 1863.

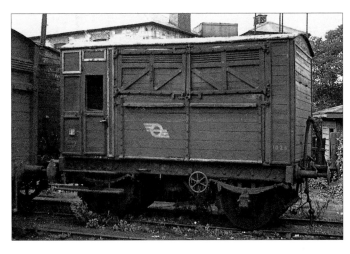

Horsebox No 1026, ex WL&WR No 6, built at Limerick in 1898. This photograph was taken on 21 August 1954. No 1026 was withdrawn in 1961.
D. G. Coakham

The Metropolitan wagons

It was not long before the 76 numbers left vacant in the W&LR list were filled, the five ballast wagons being replaced by open wagons inherited from the A&EJR and A&TR in 1872. Interestingly, the 71 other vehicles were all replaced by wagons procured from Metropolitan as follows: 20 cattle wagons and 20 open wagons ordered on 19 October 1869; one of the 12 covered wagons ordered on 23 August 1870; and 30 of the 40 covered wagons ordered on 27 September 1871, seven of the latter order being additions to stock. The balance of 11 covered wagons ordered in August 1870, together with 14 more of the same type ordered on 11 April 1871, were in fact reconstructions of worn-out Dawson wagons and cost only £65 each, the ironwork from the old wagons being sent to Metropolitan for re-use. A further 25 covered wagons at £108 15s each were ordered from Metropolitan on 22 March 1877, all of which were replacements for old stock, but we have jumped ahead a few years and must now return to 1872.

Tuam and Gort stock

The W&LR commenced working the A&TR and A&EJR on 1 November 1872 and, as a result, the wagon stock gained a further 54 vehicles: 46 covered wagons (31 from the A&EJR and 15 from the A&TR) and four open wagons from each company. Both companies also contributed two goods brake vans. All these vehicles had been built by the Bristol Wagon Works in 1870-1, the Andrews Report incorrectly showing the covered wagons as having been built by Metropolitan. The covered wagons became Nos 564-609 and six of the open wagons took up vacant numbers previously occupied by the W&KR ballast wagons. Of the other two open wagons, we know that one became No 17. The four goods brake vans were Nos 17-20 in the W&LR brake van list.

A change of suppliers

In 1875, the company moved away from its previous suppliers for new wagons when it placed an order with the Railway Carriage Co, Oldbury, for 100 covered wagons at £116 each on 24 November. Nos 613-712 were additions to stock and 30 of these vehicles survived into GS&WR ownership. Two were replaced early in their lives, probably due to accident damage, and the others were replaced by vehicles built at Limerick between 1889 and 1897. We have previously noted the 25 covered goods wagons purchased from Metropolitan in 1877, of which all but six were replaced before 1901. On 9 August 1877 a quantity of 50 open coal wagons were ordered from the Swansea Wagon Company, 32 as replacements and 18 as additions to stock. The GS&WR inherited 23 of these, the remainder having been replaced by wagons built by the company.

Timber trucks

The timber trucks were numbered in a separate list until about 1879 when the 18 vehicles of this type were given the numbers 731 to 748. Eight of these vehicles, Nos 741-748, had been built in 1867 as a result of the GS&WR stopping six pairs of timber trucks at Thurles in December 1866 as 'unsafe to travel'. They were replaced between 1880 and 1889 by new vehicles built at Limerick. The earlier timber trucks included six built for the opening of the line and rebuilt by Dawson in 1860 and four new ones acquired in 1859 or 1860, all of which were replaced between 1884 and 1889 by new vehicles also built in the company's shops. This requirement for extra timber trucks had been driven by an urgent need in May 1859 to transport 300 tons of timber awaiting movement at Cahir and a similar requirement in November 1860 to move 800 tons of timber, also awaiting loading at Cahir.

Mr P. O'Brien of Clarecastle, who in 1888 was to supply the W&LR with Irish oak for wagon underframes, made complaints in December 1885 as to the unsuitability of the company's timber trucks for long timber. He suggested the use of long flat trucks as employed by the GS&WR. In response, the board said it would have no objections if O'Brien built his own trucks. At a later date, it was reported that damage had been sustained to two coal trucks due to their use for the carriage of heavy timber, instructions being given that only timber trucks should be used for this traffic, 'on pain of fine or dismissal'. The W&LR did, however, build an additional timber truck (No 730) in 1885. In 1889, the timber truck fleet was increased by 11 vehicles with the addition of Nos 720-729, and No 749 and in the following year Nos 718 and 719 were added. All were built at Limerick and probably replaced wagons built by Metropolitan or Swansea in 1877. Finally, in 1896, two old timber trucks, Nos 734 and 735, were rebuilt at Limerick as flat wagons. They were dedicated to the transport of furniture vans and became Nos 6122 and 6123 on the GS&WR.

More new wagons

Another change of supplier came in 1880 with the placement of two orders for open-centre covered wagons with the South of Ireland Wagon Company, Cappoquin. The first order for 50 was placed on 10 June and the second order for a similar quantity on 30 October, the vehicles being additions to stock as Nos 750-849. All of the vehicles supplied under this order, and all subsequent wagons built for the company, survived into GS&WR ownership. The W&LR went back to Swansea when it ordered 100 open-centre covered wagons on 14 September 1882, these being delivered in 1883. The next contract, which was for replacement stock, was placed with Stableford of Coalville on 8 September 1887 and was for 25 open wagons and 75 covered wagons. In the following year, Stableford supplied 12 wagons to Messrs W. J. Shaw & Sons of Limerick, and these are described below in the section on private owner wagons.

A total of 150 new wagons were ordered from Swansea in two separate contracts. On 29 August 1890 the W&LR ordered 50 open wagons as stock replacements and then, on 15 January 1891, it followed up with an order for 55 open-centre covered wagons, 25 fully covered wagons and 20 covered cattle wagons, all of which were additions to stock and numbered in sequence from 951 to 1050. Forty-three of those displaced by the Swansea open wagons were reclassified as locomotive coal wagons, Nos 1051 to 1093, many being rebuilt from 1892 onwards. Between 1892 and 1894 the company turned out 20 covered cattle wagons from the Limerick shops, the first time that it had built additions to stock in any quantity since 1867. In 1895 the company reverted to outside suppliers again, ordering 40 covered cattle wagons and 14 open wagons from the Gloucester RCW, on 31 August.

Fisher & LeFanu

In December 1893, it was reported that R. W. Worthington, contractor for the Collooney extension, had ordered 12 low-sided wagons from the Bristol Wagon Co. Worthington went bankrupt about this time and Robinson submitted correspondence that he had exchanged with Bristol and recommended offering £60 each for them. After some consideration it was decided that the W&LR 'could not entertain the idea of taking the wagons'. The Collooney contract was taken over by Messrs Fisher & LeFanu, and it was agreed to take the wagons over at a valuation when the Collooney line was completed, the price to be left to the arbitration of the locomotive superintendent of either the GS&WR or the MGWR. Further correspondence followed in June 1894 in regard to 20 more wagons which Fisher & LeFanu proposed to procure, and it was agreed to take the additional wagons on the same terms.

Robinson reported in October 1895 that he was being asked to take over 32 wagons and also four additional wagons with iron frames. He suggested building up the sides of the 36 wagons to carry coal and was ordered to inspect the wagons and report further. By 24 October they were all at Limerick for inspection and two weeks later Robinson was able to report his estimate of their present value as £1,051 18s. LeFanu wrote in December offering the 24 wagons

built to W&LR specification at £55 each, at the same time proposing to retain the 12 original Bristol wagons, and in response the W&LR offered £1,130 12s, which was accepted. Fisher & LeFanu decided to offer the 12 unsold wagons at £32 10s each in January 1896, and this was agreed to by the company. The Bristol wagons built in 1893 were Fisher & LeFanu Nos 16-27 and the other 24 comprised Nos 7-15 built by Swansea, Nos 28-37 built by Metropolitan, and Nos 38-42 built by Bristol, all of which were delivered in 1894. The 10 Metropolitan vehicles were taken as additions to stock and the other 26 were replacements.

Tubular frames

During the late 1880s, two Americans, Messrs Goodfellow and Cushman, designed a lightweight tubular-framed bogie wagon, built almost entirely of steel and iron, which resulted in a low tare weight allied to a large carrying capacity. Another advantage of these wagons was that they were capable of being assembled without expensive workshop equipment. In due course the Tubular Frame Wagon Co was set up to manufacture wagons to this novel design in a workshop adjacent to the Furness Railway's works at Barrow-in-Furness. Trials of the wagons were carried out on several English lines, including the Great Northern and Lancashire & Yorkshire railways. Robinson reported to the W&LR board in May 1890 on the result of a visit to London where he had inspected some sample wagons and recommended that they be tried out on the company's line.

It was initially agreed to hire six wagons built to this design, with an option to purchase. Considerable delays occurred in signing an agreement with Col W. M. Jefferds, who was the Tubular Frame Wagon Co representative in England, but eventually two wagons arrived at Limerick in July 1891. These were of two types, low and high-sided, but, due to the delay in their delivery, the company refused to take the other four wagons. It would appear that they were not entirely to the satisfaction of

Robinson, as they were reported to be 'still lying on the company's line' in September 1892, the manufacturers offering to make such alterations as would satisfy Robinson. They were eventually returned to traffic on 4 August 1893, following modifications, including conversion into covered vans, and the lease was renewed. They were used mainly for the carriage of hops and bran between Clonmel and Waterford. However, by August 1895 the Tubular Frame Wagon Co was in liquidation and the wagons were offered at £175 each, a counter-offer of £75 each by the W&LR being accepted by the liquidator in February 1896. No 1178 measured 33ft 10in in length, No 1179 being 8in shorter. They became Nos 2988 and 2989 on the GS&WR, and both were withdrawn in 1922.

Following the purchase of the two tubular frame wagons, the company built 20 open coal wagons as additions to stock in 1896. Robinson had sought authority in November 1895 to procure 75 coal wagons and 25 covered cattle wagons, but it was considered that none of the tenders could be accepted. Instead it was decided to erect a shed for building and repairing wagons, and Robinson was directed to draw up plans and prepare an estimate. When the question of procuring new wagons was again considered in May 1896 it was ordered that frames and wheels be procured and the wagons put together in the new shops. Originally, 70 of these wagons were to be open coal wagons provided with tarpaulin supports and 30 were to be open-centre covered goods wagons. On receipt of the tenders for the frames and wheels it was decided to build 100 coal wagons with tarpaulin supports and omit the covered wagons, the frames to be purchased from Ashbury and the wheels from the Patent Shaft & Axletree Co.

Bacon and butter

Bacon traffic was an important business for the company, with several firms in Limerick involved in this business. Amongst these was Messrs William J. Shaw & Sons (established 1831) who had their factory beside the Markets Tramway in Limerick. An approach was made to the W&LR in March

Open Goods Wagon No 1157, one of a batch of 14 ordered from Gloucester Railway Carriage & Wagon Co in 1895. These and 40 cattle wagons from the same supplier were to be the last goods vehicles to be obtained from an outside supplier. Later vehicles were constructed at Limerick, although some of these were on underframes supplied from outside. Note the symbol to the left of the weight markings. Known as the 'Illiterate Symbol' it was first introduced in Britain to enable shunters and others who could not read to quickly identify a particular company's vehicle. Courtesy Gloucestershire Record Office

1888 with a proposal that Shaws build their own wagons for bacon traffic between Limerick and Waterford. The proposal was agreed to in principle, an estimated 15 wagons being required. Shaws suggested a rebate of 1s per ton on all goods carried in their own wagons, which was accepted. It appears that the W&LR may have made arrangements with Stableford for 12 covered wagons for W. J. Shaw & Sons to be added on to the W&LR order in progress as the traffic manager reported that the first bacon wagon entered service on 9 July 1888, the other 11 being delivered in October and November. It was agreed to charge £10 per annum for greasing and inspecting the 12 wagons. One additional wagon was purchased from Stableford in December 1889, but in August 1895 Shaws wrote to the W&LR suggesting the taking over of the 13 wagons. The transaction was completed in January 1896 and they became Nos 1200-1212 and later Nos 2990-2912 on the GS&WR, No 2990 being the last to be withdrawn in 1922.

In recognition of the importance of bacon traffic to the company, six covered goods wagons, Nos 192, 296, 393, 397, 505 and 562 were altered in August 1891 for the conveyance of bacon traffic on passenger trains between Limerick and Waterford. They were marked accordingly, and strict instructions were issued that they were to be used only for bacon or butter traffic from Limerick to Waterford and for soft goods from Waterford to Limerick.

The final years

The WL&WR constructed five covered wagons in 1897 and on 4 November 1897 it ordered 25 iron underframes from Metropolitan and wheels from R. Y. Pickering & Co to enable them to build 25 open coal wagons at Limerick. When these vehicles were introduced in 1898 a similar number of existing open wagons, Nos 360, 361, 363 to 377 and 380 to 387, were reclassified as locomotive coal wagons. Finally, five additional covered cattle wagons were turned out in early 1898. During 1899 and 1900 15 covered cattle wagons, Nos 126-140, were built at Limerick and the wagons they displaced were renumbered in place of worn-out vehicles. One of those renumbered was the gunpowder wagon, No 135, which became No 235 in early 1900.

Ballast wagons

Osborne referred in his report to shareholders in February 1848 to having sufficient sets of wheels to build, inter alia, 20 ballast wagons. We know that 15 ballast wagons were actually built in early W&LR days, and in October 1854 the locomotive superintendent was instructed to convert ballast wagons 'into proper receptacles for carrying coal', presumably by raising the sides. In

January 1859, Pim reported that there were 15 ballast wagons and 10 more came from the W&KR in 1861. Four more were inherited from the L&ER and six were obtained from Dargan and were possibly those rebuilt by Dawson in 1861. These latter vehicles were converted into open goods wagons, Nos 443-449, the L&ER ballast wagons having been similarly treated in 1863. The 15 original ballast wagons had already been rebuilt by the W&LR in 1862. One of these was replaced in 1882 and four in 1883. Ten new ballast wagons and five replacements were built at Limerick in 1888, one of them being rebuilt again in 1894. Four others were replaced in 1891 and one in 1892.

Private owner wagons

We have already referred to the bacon wagons owned by W. J. Shaw & Sons, but there was at least one other private owner of wagons which ran on W&LR lines. In March 1885, the locomotive superintendent reported that two wagons destined for the Ballintogher Quarry Co were not to the company's standards as the wheels were of only 3ft diameter instead of 3ft 6in. In addition, there was a problem with the height of the buffers. This led to a request from the quarry company asking the company to alter the wheels and to withdraw the haulage charge between Waterford and Lixnaw. As regards the latter, it was agreed to charge the normal empty wagon rate, while it was suggested that it would be preferable to return the wheels and axles to the manufacturers. The two wagons were lying at Limerick awaiting repairs in February 1888, this being the last reference to them. There is no indication that the W&LR ever took them into its stock.

The Fenit Harbour Commissioners approached the W&LR in October 1894

Covered Cattle Wagon No 1144, one of an order for 40 delivered from Gloucester Railway Carriage & Wagon Co in 1895. Courtesy Gloucestershire Record Office

inquiring the rate at which the company would undertake the haulage of the Commissioners' own wagons from Fenit to Tralee. The traffic manager expressed the company's willingness to quote through rates, subject to the wagons being built in accordance with the specification of the locomotive superintendent. Twelve open wagons and six open-centre covered wagons were leased from the Bristol Wagon Co in 1899, and having been examined and found correct to Clearing House specification and drawings, they were permitted to run with mixed trains or on fast fish specials. At first they carried their own numbers, 1-12 in the case of the open wagons and 13-18 for the covered wagons, but at some stage they became GS&WR Nos 4667-4684. Of even more interest is the fact that the Commissioners leased two tubular 33ft 10in bogie open wagons, built by the Lancaster RCW in 1900, which later became Nos 4050 and 4051 on the GS&WR. No 4050 was altered to a covered fish van in 1903.

Over the years, various other companies approached the board regarding the possible use of private owner wagons. These included Messrs Bannatyne of Tralee and Messrs Murphy Bros of Clonmel, the latter apparently getting as far as having three built by Swansea. They were offered to the W&LR in February 1893 by the builders, the company declining to accept them. Interestingly, Murphy Bros approached the board again in November 1894, but there is no evidence to suggest that these wagons ever entered service either with Murphy or the W&LR.

Chapter Seventeen

DESCRIPTION OF THE LINE

The present terminal station at Limerick retains the handsome two-storey stone building of 1858, which today contains offices and a refreshment room. A low wall with railings fronts on to the street and gives an impression of spaciousness. It has four platforms facing more or less directly to the east and flanked by a carriage siding on each side, these being covered by an overall roof for most of their length. The longest platform is No 1 on the north side at 552ft, next is No 3, 537ft long; platform No 2 is 397ft long, while No 4 on the south side is 343ft in length. This latter was the C&LDR platform and was shortened by some 30ft in 1961 to make room for a bus office. In the scheme of things, platforms Nos 1 and 2 are normally used for departures to Limerick Junction and the Ennis direction, No 3 for arrivals. No 4 platform, apart from being the C&LDR platform, was also used for Tralee line arrivals and departures. Initially such trains could depart only from this platform, but later alterations enabled them to also use Nos 2 and 3 platforms.

The principal goods yard is on the north side of the station, known locally as the Top Yard, beyond which is a large goods shed and loading bank, while in between used to be a small wagon turntable giving access to the Markets Tramway. To the west of the Top Yard is the Upper Yard consisting of five roads. On the south side of the running lines is a second goods store — Tobin's Store — reached by a roadway, which now also acts as a terminus for provincial bus services. Just beyond the two goods stores was the Roxboro' Road bridge of bow-string girder construction. Immediately to the east of the bridge is a series of crossovers from north to south. The Locomotive Shed signal cabin was situated at this point on the up side until 1910 when the Check cabin took over its functions.

The present Check cabin is the main box in the station area with 50 levers, of which six are spare. It controlled Ennis Junction, the main line out to Killonan and the Foynes Loop junction as well as entrance and exit to the goods yard, the Works and the eight-road engine shed, with its 55ft diameter turntable. Beside the Check cabin was a 130ft-long wooden platform used up to 15 June 1963 for the checking of tickets of

certain trains, notably the 09.00 Galway to Limerick passenger train. Limerick Works, with its red-brick offices was situated in the triangle formed by the main line, the Foynes Loop and the Roxboro' Road. The works were an important part of the life of Limerick and as recorded elsewhere survived the amalgamation of 1901 and in fact remained in use as a locomotive repair shop until 1936 and as a wagon building shop well into CIE days. It is still the principal location for overhaul of Iarnród Éireann freight wagons.

The ¾-mile-long Markets Tramway branch started at the wagon turntable behind the Top Yard Store and ran at right angles to the 'store bank'. The line crossed two public roads on the level before the Market was reached — Roxboro' Road and Mulgrave Street. The former was the scene of an accident on 5 July 1933 between a train and a motor hearse, no injuries being sustained other than to the hearse! In the Market Yard a wagon turntable gave access to an extension of the tramway, which crossed Cathedral Place to the bacon factory of Messrs Denny, this section ceasing to be worked after 1931. The line between Roxboro' Road and Mulgrave Street also served Messrs Shaw's factory and traffic continued to be handled there and in the market itself up to about 1940 when the line was cut back to the first level crossing, where a siding was used by oil tank wagons for the adjoining bus garage. This traffic ceased during the 1950s and the remaining section was finally taken out in August 1961.

To clarify the position regarding signal cabins, there were at one time no fewer than six within a mile of the terminus, viz Limerick Station cabin at the end of platforms 1 and 2, installed by the W&LR; the Locomotive Shed cabin, which was on the up side at the entrance to the locomotive yard; the original Check cabin also on the up side; Ennis Junction cabin, on the up side, which worked not only the junction but also the Munster Fair siding opposite; the Cork Direct cabin, controlling the entrance to and exit from No 4 platform and finally, Foynes Junction cabin. Between 1901 and 1915 considerable rationalisation was carried out which saw this number reduced to three. The facilities at Limerick station were much improved between 1960 and 1962 with the provision

of modern waiting rooms, booking and parcels offices. The original station of 1848 was 540 yards to the east of the present buffer stops and consisted of a large shed constructed over six lines. It was just on the city side of Roxboro' Road bridge, the latter originally known as Meagher's Viaduct. This was in use until the present building was opened in 1858.

As constructed, the main line to Limerick Junction was single but was soon doubled. On leaving Limerick it is level for rather more than a mile as well as being straight for the first 1½ miles. In 1929, the GSR, as an economy measure, singled the section from Killonan to Limerick Junction, the section from the former point into Limerick station remaining double tracked.

Ennis Junction (00.70) was, as stated above, a former block post. Here the Ennis line diverged on the down side. Until 1910 there was a double line junction here, even though the Ennis line became single almost immediately beyond it. As a result of the removal of the junction in 1910, today there are three running roads, viz a single line on the north side for up and down Ennis line trains, and separate up and down main lines for Limerick Junction. Killonan (04.20) has platforms on both sides of the line with a level crossing at the Waterford end. The main buildings were on the down platform. The signal cabin is on the same side of the line. On 25 November 1931 the signal cabin at Killonan was closed and the junction removed. The section thence to Limerick was then worked as two single parallel lines, the old up line serving main line trains, the former down road trains for Ballybrophy. Double line working was reintroduced on 17 October 1947 by CIE when Killonan Junction was reinstated.

Boher (07.50) was a former block post, closed to traffic in 1963. There were two platforms with a passing loop. A siding and loading bank were provided on the up side at the Waterford end as was the signal cabin. The station buildings were on the down platform. Dromkeen (11.46) was another block post and a passing place. There were two platforms with the station buildings on the up side. The signal cabin was at the Waterford end of this platform, beyond which was a level crossing followed by a short goods loop and loading bank.

Right: **J15' 0-6-0 No 170 and 'D19' 4-4-0 No 6 arrive at Limerick with the 09.10 from Sligo on 30 June 1938.** H. C. Casserley

Centre right: **Oola station looking west towards Limerick on 23 April 1955. Two horse-drawn conveyances can be seen on the public road.** R. M. Casserley'

Pallas (13.76) had the usual two platforms, the station buildings being on the down side, the signal cabin on the up. A goods siding trailed back on the down side beyond the platform to serve cattle pens and a goods store. A W&LR drawing dating from the early 1890s shows two cottages to the rear of the down platform and within the company's boundary. It would appear from this drawing that the signal cabin was originally on the Limerick side of the over-bridge carrying the Pallas to Doon road. Oola (18.35), another former block post, was a passing place with the signal cabin on the up platform, the station buildings being on the down side. A goods siding trailed back on the down side at the Limerick end. Following the singling of the line, a portion of the old up line was retained on either side of the platform to provide space for wagons. Approaching Limerick Junction, we come to Milltown level crossing, near which, on the down side, a direct connection was installed in 1967 to provide access to the Dublin-Cork main line for Limerick traffic.

Limerick Junction
Keane's Points Junction (21.50) is named after an early pointsman employed by the W&LR and is the divergence for trains serving Limerick Junction station (21.60). The latter was, for many years, the butt of jokes due to its most unusual layout. The celebrated railway writer, E. L. Ahrons in *Locomotive and Train Working in the Latter Part of the 19th Century*, devoted 3½ pages to the station and its immediate environs, which he described as 'one of the most extraordinary junction stations that ever existed, which may also be described as typically Irish. Limerick Junction is not really a place at all . . . one would be inclined to think that the railway people would at least have planted it in County Limerick, but they did not. Irish like, they selected a pleasant country spot in County Tipperary.' The main peculiarity of the station up until 1967, was that all trains, whether using either the former GS&WR or W&LR routes, had to reverse in the course of arriving and/or departing. Up and down Dublin-Cork main line trains ran past the platform and then reversed through a scissors crossover to reach the GS&WR platform. Frequently the two trains crossed here and when both had arrived at their respective stretch of platform, the two locomotives were facing each other, 'looking like a couple of cats —

Kilkenny brand — which, had they been able to waggle their trains, would very likely have sprung at each other'. Both trains departed through their respective cross-overs in the normal manner.

W&LR trains bound for Limerick crossed the GS&WR main line and ran past Keane's Points Junction, and then reversed into a bay platform behind the Dublin end of the main line platform. Departure was once again straightforward. Trains heading for Waterford however performed the most convoluted movements of all. Diverging from the main line at Keane's Points Junction, they came around the curve, passed behind the rear of the station and then reversed into a bay behind the Cork end of the main line platform. On departing, they pulled

Above: **At Limerick Junction on 30 June 1938 a Waterford to Limerick excursion is seen at the main platform used by services on the Dublin to Cork main line. Trains using the former WL&WR route normally used the bay platform just out of sight to the right of the picture. 'J15' No 106 is piloting an authentic WL&WR survivor in the form of GSR No 239. The locomotive was built by Kitson in 1897 as WL&WR No 58 Goliath. This 0-6-0 was finally withdrawn by CIE, its fourth owner, in 1949.** H. C. Casserley

Limerick Junction North signal cabin adjoining the diamond crossing in the foreground. Note the raised platform on the right-hand side for exchanging staff. A 'J15' approaches on a northbound main line goods, 23 April 1955. H. C. Casserley

forward out of the bay until clear of the points, from whence they had to reverse all the way back to the junction before going on their way towards Tipperary. These various manoeuvres meant that even the limited mails and boat trains spent between 15 and 20 minutes at the Junction. In early W&LR days it was referred to simply as 'Junction'. The accompanying diagram should enable readers unfamiliar with its layout to understand the foregoing description.

The remodelling of the station layout in 1967 benefited Dublin-Cork main line trains by the installation of new facing crossovers giving direct access to the platform road. However, Waterford line trains still perform their ritual manoeuvres to this day. Leaving Limerick Junction, the W&LR single line crosses the GS&WR main lines on the level. Just beyond the crossing is a short trailing spur which prevents runaways from the Waterford direction fouling the main line. Now climbing at a gentle 1 in 828 the line reaches a summit just before milepost 23 and then begins a gradual fall to Tipperary.

Tipperary (24.63) was the terminus of the line for four years after its opening in April 1848. There is only one passenger platform

on the down side with the large two-storey station building. The 21-lever signal cabin is at the Waterford end of the platform beside the level crossing. A pair of sidings existed on the down side at the Limerick end of the station, one of which served a cattle dock, the other a loading bank. The main goods facilities, including a store, were situated on the up side.

Shortly after leaving Tipperary, the line begins falling on generally easy gradients for the next 11 miles. On the down side, two miles beyond Tipperary was one of the company's ballast pits, at Puddingfield (26.40) in the parish of Killshane. It is not entirely clear when this pit was originally opened. A board minute of 16 February 1859 refers to the company being threatened with legal proceedings over the pit, the solicitor being urgently requested to obtain Counsel's Opinion. Although powers were taken under Section 9 of the company's Act of 1860, more than two years were to elapse before Joseph Fishbourne, the Government arbitrator, issued an award for more than five acres. In August 1861, however, it was reported that the company were only obtaining control over lot No 4, comprising a little more than

one acre due to the landlord's requirements being too stringent. Later, four more acres were taken over, the company paying £236 1s 6d in compensation. It is not known when the pit closed, there being few references to it in the company's records.

Bansha (29.49), situated on a falling gradient of 1 in 225, had a level crossing on the approach to the station, which had but one 412ft-long platform on the up side on which were the station building and signal cabin, the latter beside the crossing. A loop on the down side served a goods store and loading bank. Nearby was Bansha Castle, a Gothic folly fortress fashioned out of an earlier Georgian house for the Lord Lieutenant of the county.

Wayside sidings

Between Bansha and Cahir, at least two sets of sidings existed, possibly three. The exact position is unclear as there are various references to sidings at both Cappagh (also spelt Cappa) and Toureen level crossings, located respectively at 33m 60yd and 33m 1,685yd. Another source states that there was a ballast pit at Cappagh (33.03) for a short period after the opening of the line, this possibly being the siding reopened to handle timber traffic in 1864.

There were sidings on both sides of the line at Caher Abbey (37.60), named after nearby St Mary's Abbey. One siding was in existence in September 1856 as instructions were given for the engineer, J. C. Smith, to 'have the Mill siding widened', 500 sleepers being prepared. Complaints of obstruction to traffic were received in January 1862 as a portion of the loading bank walls was incomplete. An auxiliary signal was ordered in December 1862, another such being ordered in 1869 for the Clonmel side of the siding. The siding's removal was recommended in April 1885 as it was no longer in use, the board agreeing to this course of action. It is not known whether it was in fact removed at that time, but, if so it was later restored. Two sidings were installed here by the GSR in May 1927 to handle cattle traffic, while that on the down side was occasionally used for tar traffic in CIE days. The sidings on both sides of the line at this location were finally closed in 1979.

The line approaches Cahir on a rising gradient of 1 in 330 and crosses the River

Tipperary station looking towards Waterford with Railway Signal Co 15-lever signal cabin on single down-side platform, 30 June 1938. H. C. Casserley

Suir on an impressive viaduct. This was the scene of two accidents in CIE/IE days as related in Chapter Twelve. The deaths of the engine crew in the December 1955 tragedy are commemorated by a plaque on the station building. Cahir station (38.26) has both up and down platforms, only the former now being rail connected. The station building, designed by W. G. Murray, is architecturally interesting, and is on the up platform, the 16-lever signal cabin being at the Waterford end of the down platform. A footbridge connects the two platforms but now has gates preventing passenger access. The goods store, cattle bank and sidings, all on the up side at the Waterford end, are now out of use.

Another junction

Leaving Cahir, the line climbs, mainly at 1 in 150, to a summit near MP43½. Nicholastown level crossing (43.19) was the subject of several requests for a flag station, these requests all being declined on the grounds that the location was inconvenient and the extra station was considered inexpedient. Once over the summit, the line begins a long fall to Clonmel, much of it at 1 in 132. Clonmel station (49.20) has two passenger platforms and was until 1967 the junction for the former SR branch to Thurles. The main station building and the goods facilities, consisting of a goods store, loading bank and sidings, are all on the up side, the 55-lever signal cabin being at the Waterford end of the down platform. At one time, three cabins existed at Clonmel. Cabin 'A' was situated on the down side to the west of the station and controlled a loop and siding at this end; it was closed in 1909. Cabin 'B' was on the down platform, while Clonmel Junction cabin was in the vee between the main line and the branch. It was opened in 1879 and closed in 1909, when the current cabin replaced all three. Beyond the end of the down platform, adjacent to the divergence of the Thurles line were a two-road engine shed of reinforced concrete and a turntable of 49ft 9in diameter. Engine watering facilities were provided on both platforms and at the engine shed.

The line rises at 1 in 150 for about a mile after leaving Clonmel, and then, apart from a short rise at 1 in 213, continues to fall into Kilsheelan. A little over a mile west of Kilsheelan there was a ballast pit at milepost 54 opened about 1874. Kilsheelan (55.33), closed to all traffic in 1963, had two platforms with the main buildings on the up side. It remained as a block post until 1984, the signal cabin also being on the up side adjoining the level crossing at the Limerick

Clonmel station looking towards Limerick with a 'J15' 0-6-0 on a Waterford train, 2 July 1938. Note the ornate station building. H. C. Casserley

end of the station. On the Limerick side of the crossing were a goods siding and loading bank. Kilsheelan became a halt under Clonmel as from 1 January 1952.

Malcomson's or Carrick Factory siding (62.35) was opened in 1863 at a cost of £106 1s 8d, at the request of Messrs Malcomson in connection with a cotton factory. Whilst a wall and footbridge were to be kept in repair by the proprietors, the siding remained the company's property. Following an officers' inspection in January 1871 it was decided to erect a signal and provide a signal house at an estimated cost of £120, but the work was deferred and it is unclear whether it was ever carried out. Following a further inspection in July 1877 it was agreed that the siding to the factory be removed (it was about this time that the Malcomson family fell on hard times), the engineer reporting in August that all but a small portion of the trackwork in an enclosed yard had been removed.

Carrick-on-Suir (63.06), known until 1925 simply as Carrick and presumably renamed to avoid confusion with Carrick-on-Shannon on the Midland section of the GSR, has two platforms, the main buildings being on the up side. The 15-lever signal cabin is at the Waterford end of the down platform, although there is a level crossing at the Limerick end of the station. A loop runs behind the down platform and runs through the goods store at the Limerick end to an end-loading dock. At the opposite end of this loop is a long siding. Fiddown, known in later years as Fiddown & Portlaw (67.28), also closed in 1963, was approached over a level crossing. The line between here and Waterford was doubled by the W&LR in 1883, the section from Fiddown to Grange being singled by the GSR in May 1929 and from the latter point to Waterford West in October 1929. Fiddown was of course the terminus of the line from Limerick between April and August 1853, pending opening of the extension to Dunkitt. Fiddown had the usual two platforms, all the facilities

including the station building and signal cabin being on the down side. A goods siding trailed back from the Waterford end of the down loop to serve a goods store behind the signal cabin, while part of the second running road formed a long siding towards Waterford in GSR days. The station ceased to be a block post in 1978.

Grange (70.03) once again had two platforms, that on the up side having the station accommodation, with the cabin at the Waterford end of the down platform adjoining the level crossing. At one time the down side also included a goods siding and loading bank. Grange became a halt under Fiddown in December 1930 and was closed in 1963. Dunkitt (75.44) was the point of junction between the W&LR and the W&KR, the latter having reached there on 21 May 1853, the Limerick company opening to this point on 23 August of the same year. The site of the original W&KR station is located on the up side between the railway and the road, while the site of the temporary W&LR station can be seen at the last road over-bridge before the line crosses the 'Black Pill' by a girder bridge. A junction existed for a short time here, but the W&KR seemed to have a penchant for upsetting its neighbours and it was not long before the junction was removed.

As we have already seen in Chapter Two, the line was extended from Dunkitt to a new terminus on the site of the present goods yard. This new section of line passes over Newrath level crossing where, on the up side, was Newrath Junction signal cabin, opened in 1883 when the W&LR line was doubled out to Fiddown. This box controlled the junction of the two companies' lines situated just to the west of the crossing. It was maliciously destroyed on 11 November 1922, a replacement being erected on the same site. Following the singling of the Limerick line in 1929, Newrath cabin was dispensed with and the section extended to Waterford West.

Waterford North station with a train for Wexford via Abbey Junction and Macmine Junction at the main platform. The train is in charge of ex GS&WR 4-4-0 No 3. On the right is Mount Misery which towers over the station. This photograph was taken on 21 April 1954. D. G. Coakham

Waterford's various stations

The first Waterford station (77.07) used material which came from the Dublin Exhibition of 1853. This new joint station opened to traffic on 11 September 1854, the two stations at Dunkitt being closed in the following year. A layout drawing prepared shortly after its opening shows the two companies' lines approaching in parallel, a crossover being provided about ¼ mile from the terminus to allow the Kilkenny company access to the goods yard on the river side. There was a 'checking' platform between the two main lines for the collecting of tickets. There were two two-road engine sheds on the north side, each about 100ft long, access to each being via a turntable of about 38ft diameter situated in between them. The outer shed served the W&LR, the inner the W&KR. In later years, the Limerick shed was converted to a through shed and the turntable was removed to the south side close to the Upper Wharf. Later, the W&CIR (successor to the W&KR) erected a carriage shed on the down side to the west of the check platform. Old habits die hard as the two engine sheds were still referred to in CIE days as the 'Kilkenny' and the 'Limerick'.

To the rear of the Kilkenny shed were a pump-house for drawing water from an adjoining well, a carpenter's workshop, gasometer, store and a forge. On the W&KR line (north side) on the approach to the platforms were a timber and goods platform and carriage dock, corresponding to horse loading and goods platform and carriage dock on the W&LR side. There were four platform faces, each 275ft in length, covered by a two-arched roof. The centre platform served both lines, with railings down the centre to segregate the two companies' passengers! To the rear of the platforms, each company had its own office accommodation. On the south side were various goods sidings running parallel with the river. These included

a short extension along a jetty, accessed by means of two small wagon turntables.

A 19½-chain extension was opened in 1864 to a new joint station beside the toll bridge, bringing the railway somewhat closer to the city. Before proceeding to review the facilities here, however, we must retrace our steps to the west, for some major alterations took place following the arrival of the F&RR&H company in 1906. Prior to this date, the WD&LR terminus was situated on the south side of the river. The completion of the Fishguard lines saw a new junction at Grace Dieu on the south side of the Suir, which was crossed by a 1,205ft-long bridge consisting of nine spans, including an 80ft Scherzer lifting span. The new line coming off the bridge joined the joint lines on the Kilkenny side of the river at Suir Bridge Junction (76.50), having run parallel with them for nearly quarter of a mile. The junction was in fact close to the site of Gouldings' sidings, almost opposite the W&CIR carriage shed and close to Waterford West signal cabin. (This was cabin 'C' at 76.54/75.00, the latter being the distance from Mallow via Fermoy.) The junction was moved further to the west in December 1941.

Just on the Limerick side of Waterford West cabin, Messrs W. & H. Goulding had set up a fertiliser works, this being served by two sidings, in turn connected to a trailing siding installed in 1915 for the storage of coal. Gouldings also had road access to the site via Newrath No. 2 occupation crossing. The main line from Waterford West through the 1864 and 1906 stations to Abbey Junction is double tracked. The area occupied by the original joint station later became a freight and locomotive stabling and servicing area. Two goods stores existed here, one owned by the GS&WR, the other by the DW&WR (later D&SER), along with two cattle docks. There were extensive freight sidings on the south side of the line with connections to

three wharves, known as Upper, Middle and Lower Jetties. Beside the Upper Jetty, where locomotive coal arrived in vessels up to about 1941, was a coaling area and 45ft diameter turntable. The Lower Jetty, also at one time used for coal storage, was out of use prior to the Second World War but was not finally demolished until 1959. A footbridge, erected in November 1912 and removed in 1958, gave access from here across the running lines to the goods stores on the down side.

The 1864 Waterford station (77.20) was inconveniently situated in the rather cramped space between the foot of Mount Misery to the north and the river to the south. There were two passenger platforms which terminated in a two-storeyed building used in later years to house the district offices of CIE. At the time of its construction, the Newrath (Clonmel) road ran on the north side of the station and did not gain access to the river here until 1906. The 1864-1906 station signal cabin (cabin 'B') was situated on the up side of the line on the Limerick side of the subsequent road over-bridge. The extension to the North Wharf, opened as a single track in May 1883 and doubled in January of the following year, left the main line on the approach to the 1864 station by a facing junction and passed under the Newrath road, which was raised to accommodate the line, and then through a cutting in the side of Mount Misery to a point just beyond the 36-lever framed East cabin (cabin 'A'). Two lines trailed back on to the wharf with a number of sidings fanning out to the east. A large goods store, 400ft by 95ft, was erected on the North Wharf beside the toll bridge. This store was demolished in 1951 and replaced by a new goods store close to the site of the D&SER one, west of the station. The line now continues east to Rosslare past Abbey Junction, the one-time connection for the D&SER branch to Macmine.

Following the take over of the WL&WR by the GS&WR and the construction of the F&RR&H line, major alterations were made in Waterford. The only portion of the 1864 station incorporated in the 1906 Waterford station was the red-bricked building used as office accommodation. The Newrath road was altered to pass over the railway, the crossing becoming known as Terminus Street Bridge. The 1906 station, built partly on the site of the wharf extension line and partly blasted out of Mount Misery, was contracted to Messrs Collen Bros of Dublin.

Three roads run through the new station, from the north respectively: down, up and platform. There were eight platforms, the largest number at any Irish station until the remodelling of Heuston, Dublin, in 2004. Nos 1 and 2 were east facing bays which were removed in 1967 to form car parking facilities, while Nos 5 to 8 were bays at the west end; Nos 7 and 8 were later converted to provide parking for buses, while Nos 5 and 6 were retained for carriage storage. Nos 3 and 4 comprised a 1,210ft long platform face, access to both ends being provided by a scissors crossing in the middle. Waiting rooms, booking office and refreshment facilities were located behind this platform. Waterford Central cabin, with its 64-lever frame, straddles the three lines at the west end of Platform 3. More recent alterations have seen the demolition, in 1967, of the 1906 station building and the construction of a modern reinforced concrete structure at a cost of £120,000. The main concourse of the 1967 station is rectangular in shape with a long glass frontage facing out on to the river. The concourse itself is finished in black and white floor tiles and the building includes waiting and refreshment rooms.

Limerick to Collooney

We now return to Limerick, where leaving Ennis Junction the line rises for about half a mile at 1 in 160, from which point it runs more or less level to Longpavement. From this point, the line rises and falls on a ruling gradient of 1 in 100 to Ennis, the end of the line as constructed by the L&ER. The Shannon Bridge (03.49) of today, consisting of five spans, dates from 1909/10, this structure replacing the infamous bridge of L&ER days described in Chapter Five. Just beyond the bridge on the up side was Power Station Junction (03.68), one-time junction for the 1¼-mile branch to the power station at Ardnacrusha, completed in connection with the Shannon electrification scheme in July 1929.

Longpavement (03.73), a former block post, originally had two passenger platforms; but these were removed in August 1942 and replaced by a new platform on the up side. The signal cabin was situated at the Sligo end of this platform, while there was a level crossing at the Limerick end of the station. Cratloe (09.60), the closest station to the world-famous Bunratty Castle and also Cratloe Wood (one of the longest inhabited houses in Ireland to survive without a change of ownership), had one platform on the up side and a level crossing at the Limerick end. Sixmilebridge (13.00) also had one platform on the up side, while at the Sligo end on the same side were a goods loop and a store. A signal cabin at this station closed in September 1931. The next station, Ballycar (16.58), is situated in rich pasture land, resulting from the exertions of

Sir Edward O'Brien of nearby Dromoland Castle. At one stage known as Ballycar & Newmarket, the main station buildings were on the single, down side platform, while on the same side was a goods siding. There was a passing loop on the up side, the signal cabin being on the same side at the Sligo end, next to a level crossing. Ardsollus & Quin (19.60) was yet another station with a single platform on the up side. A trailing siding on the up side served a goods store. Clarecastle (23.00) was a blockpost until June 1963 with two passenger platforms, footbridge, a signal cabin (at the south end of the down platform), goods siding and passing loop.

Ennis (24.60) was, from 1887 to 1961, the interchange point with the narrow-gauge West Clare Railway. The main line station has two platforms with the station buildings on the down side, while the goods yard, store and loading banks were on the up side. There were two signal cabins. The South cabin with 13 levers was on the down side in front of the two-road locomotive shed at the Limerick end, and North cabin, which closed in 1979, was on the up side at the Sligo end. A 45ft turntable was located behind the South cabin, this being replaced in July 1950 by one of 47ft diameter transferred from Naas. The narrow-gauge lines were on the down side and ran beside the standard-gauge line for a little over a mile towards Sligo before curving away to the left.

Leaving Ennis, the line begins a climb of nearly eight miles to a point beyond the next station at Crusheen (32.37). Closed in 1963, Crusheen had two passenger platforms, with a goods siding and store behind that on the down side; the signal cabin was at the Sligo end of the down platform. Near to Crusheen is an ancient burial ground, which includes the last resting place of Sir Theobald Butler, who framed the articles of the Treaty of Limerick. Tubber (36.64) had a single, 202ft-long platform on the down side with a loop on the up side, controlled by a three-lever ground frame. The next station, Gort (42.25), served an important market town set in magnificent scenery; included amongst its industries was a large flour mill. Nearby

was Loughcooter Castle, named after the adjacent Lough Cooter, the home of Viscount Gort, after whom the town was named. It had two platforms connected by a footbridge, with the station buildings on the down side, behind which were the goods sidings, store and loading bank. The signal cabin was at the Sligo end of the up platform.

Kiltartan level crossing at 44.60 had automatic barriers installed in 1967. Ardrahan (49.06), a former block post, had a single platform on the up side along with the associated goods facilities and a signal cabin. A goods loop was provided in November 1945 and a new level crossing was brought into use at the north end in October 1966. Craughwell, formerly Craughwell & Loughrea (55.13), another former block post, had its passenger platform on the up side with a signal cabin at the Limerick end. On the same side were sidings, a goods store and cattle bank. The loop was extended in June 1946, allowing trains to be crossed there.

Athenry station (59.69), opened in 1851, was originally the property of the MGWR and is situated on that company's former main line to Galway. The line from Ennis joins the Midland main line on the down side by a facing connection, passing goods facilities on the same side, and a level crossing by the station itself. On the Dublin side of the gates is a disused goods store adjoining the up platform. The signal cabin of 64 levers is on the down side at the Galway end of the platform, the main station buildings also being on this side of the line. Trains for Tuam pass through Athenry in the Dublin direction and diverge on the up side just beyond a road over-bridge. The station nameboards are unique in that the one on the down platform displays Athenry & Ennis Junction, whilst that on the up platform reads Athenry & Tuam Junction.

Belville siding (64.00) trailed in on the up side of the line and was used for beet traffic until 1977. It was lifted on 8 February 1977. Ballyglunin (69.76) was previously known as Brook Lodge and had two platforms connected by a footbridge. The station buildings, goods loop, sidings, goods store

Exterior view of Ballyglunin station, June 1964. The first station north of Athenry on the Athenry & Tuam Railway, it opened on 27 September 1860. It was about 10 miles north of the A&T's junction with the MGWR's Galway to Dublin line. The station closed in April 1976. R. M. Casserley

and loading bank were all on the down side; the signal cabin nearly opposite the goods store closed in July 1967. Tuam, the one-time terminus of the A&TR, was formerly a parliamentary borough, founded by a religious establishment in the sixth century. Shortly afterwards, its church was made a cathedral for the diocese. Tuam had an extensive trade, including a large brewery and flour mills.

At Tuam (76.15/00.00), the mileposts start again from zero towards Claremorris, denoting the commencement of the extension railway. The station has two platforms with the station buildings on the up side. The signal cabin is on the down side, sidings for goods traffic being situated on both sides of the line. At the Limerick end of the up platform were a water tank, goods store and loading bank. There was a long loop on the down side and at the Limerick end of the down platform were four sidings, two of which served the engine shed, one with a turntable of 44ft 6in diameter. There is a level crossing at the Collooney end of the station. Leaving Tuam, we next come to Tuam Sugar Factory Junction (01.50), diverging on the up side and connecting into eight sidings in the sugar factory complex. Here, on the down side was a 22-lever signal cabin. The factory was opened in 1934 and closed in 1985.

Moving on, we come to Castlegrove (04.37), which had only one platform, on the down side, with a trailing siding on the up side which served a goods store and loading bank. There is a level crossing at the Limerick end. The next station is Milltown (08.49), a former blockpost, which at one time boasted two platforms. A siding off the loop on the up side served a small goods store. The signal cabin was also on the up side adjoining the level crossing at the Limerick end. Ballindine (12.44), another former block post, had a single platform on the up side, at the Limerick end of which was the signal cabin; there was a siding on the down side with a small store.

Claremorris Southern yard (16.50) was the terminus of the line from its opening in

1894 until extended to the MGWR station in the following year. It was the WL&WR and GS&WR goods station until 1925 and was still used until recent times for occasional goods traffic, all sidings and buildings being on the up side. There is a level crossing at the Sligo end and there was a signal cabin here until 1941. The most important intermediate station on the line was undoubtedly Claremorris Midland (17.00 from Tuam, 135.00 from Dublin, Broadstone and 00.00 at the start of the line to Collooney). The station here is quite extensive, and full details of the layout can be found in the companion volume on the MGWR. Suffice to say that over the years the station handled considerable pilgrimage traffic bound for the nearby Knock shrine, and for that reason it was extensively remodelled by CIE in 1952.

Leaving Claremorris in the direction of Westport, the junction for the Burma Road is on the up side. The line initially begins climbing at 1 in 70 before easing to 1 in 100. The first station on the line is at Kiltimagh (09.31) which had two platforms, that on the down being served by a loop. The station buildings were on the down side with the signal cabin on the opposite side at the Limerick end; there were level crossings at both ends of this station. The principal goods facilities were located behind the down platform and included a store, carriage dock and loading banks. Behind the up platform was the grain siding with another loading bank.

Swinford (17.25) had two platforms, with the main buildings on the up side. The quite extensive siding accommodation, goods store and loading bank were on the same side, as also was the signal cabin at the Limerick end. Charlestown (24.10) had a single platform on the up side, opposite to which there was a loop with goods sidings, a store and a loading bank. The signal cabin was at the Limerick end of the platform, with level crossing gates at the opposite end. Curry (27.00) was a small station with its platform on the down side. At its Sligo end was a short siding serving a goods store.

Tubbercurry (30.63) was somewhat larger with two platforms, and the main buildings on the up side. The signal cabin was at the Sligo end of the up platform, curiously remotely located from the level crossing, which was at the Limerick end of the station. There was siding accommodation on both sides of the line, the goods store being located behind the up platform.

Carrowmore (35.66) had but one platform, on the up side. Opposite the platform was a siding serving a store and loading bank; there was a level crossing at the Sligo end. Leyny (41.18) was another single-platform station, this time on the down side. Also on this side were goods sidings and a store, while on the up side was a passing loop with the signal cabin. The last station on the branch was Collooney (45.76). It had two passenger platforms, with the station buildings on the up side, as were the goods store and sidings. The line continued on to join up with the MGWR's Sligo line at Collooney Junction (128.03 from Dublin, Broadstone) by a trailing connection on the down side. From here the six miles to Sligo, over which the WL&WR had running powers, was the property of the MGWR. Until the closure of the Sligo, Leitrim & Northern Counties Railway in 1957, there was a direct connection between the Claremorris and SL&NCR lines, which passed under the MGWR line. Near to Collooney, at Carrick-nagatt (Carrignagat), Col Vereker, with his Limerick militia, attacked French troops in September 1798, probably preventing a French attack on Sligo.

Clonmel to Thurles

The branch diverged from the WL&W main line at the east end of Clonmel station, passing the engine shed on the left-hand side before heading north. Trains ran in the down direction from Thurles to Clonmel, distances being measured from Thurles Junction, the junction at Clonmel therefore being at 24.08. About half a mile from Clonmel Junction on the down side was the site of a platform which served the adjoining Powerstown Park racecourse (23.60). This platform was erected by the GS&WR in 1916 to serve race specials. From here the line began climbing at 1 in 100 through the picturesque 'Wilderness' and the 'Furzy Glen'. The summit was reached some 3½ miles from Clonmel where the line began a switchback journey to Fethard. On this stretch of line, magnificent views could be obtained of Slievenamon Mountain (2,634ft) to the east, the subject of many songs, novels and poems by the celebrated Charles Kickham.

Fethard (15.60) was the only intermediate

'J15' 0-6-0 No 123 at Tuam station on the 15.10 to Galway on 21 April 1955.
R. M. Casserley

station on the branch with both up and down platforms, the station buildings and 11-lever (two spare) signal cabin being on the down side, while the up platform was on a loop. Fethard was also the only station on the branch where trains could cross without reversing. The goods store was on the down side at the Thurles end, while there was also a siding on the up side, which trailed back behind the platform. Fethard had a monthly fair which necessitated livestock specials on the branch. Leaving here, the line initially fell away at 1 in 100, but soon began a climb all the way to a point nearly nine miles away on the Thurles side of Laffan's Bridge.

Farranalleen (12.55) was situated on a very short stretch of level track and in CIE days was controlled by a female halt keeper. Here the platform and station house were situated on the up side, opposite to which was a short siding giving access to a small goods shed. From Farranalleen the line began a virtually unbroken climb on varying gradients to Laffan's Bridge, 4½ miles away.

Laffan's Bridge (8.12) was a staff station and had a single platform on the up side. Trains could be crossed here by running one of them into a long siding on the down side, this latter being used for storing coal (anthracite) wagons. The nameboard stated the station was Laffan's Bridge & Killenaule, the latter a village several miles away. (Timetables and tickets referred to it simply as Laffansbridge.) This was an important station on the branch as it handled a heavy traffic in anthracite from the nearby Slieveardagh coal mines. Anthracite was mined in small lumps or 'beans' and was brought in lorries from the colliery to the station for onward transportation to Waterford for export to South Wales.

Between Laffan's Bridge and Horse & Jockey the character of the line changed as bogland dominated the scene. The summit of the branch was reached near milepost 17 and the line then began a gradual fall towards Thurles Junction. Horse & Jockey station (4.21) had a layout exactly opposite to that at Laffan's Bridge, in that the platform and station building were both on the down side, with a trailing siding on the up side, which included a small goods store. The signal cabin was at the Thurles end of the station on the up side. Trains were regularly crossed here in CIE days, the morning goods taking refuge in the siding to allow the up passenger to run through. It is interesting to note that the name of the village derives from the Horse & Jockey Inn, sited at a crossroads which served stage coach travellers in the mid-18th century. Later, a cluster of cottages developed round the inn from which the new village took its name.

Land was taken from between Horse & Jockey and Thurles Junction to allow for double track, although the line remained single throughout its life. Approaching Thurles Junction (00.00) on a rising gradient of 1 in 105 the River Suir was crossed in its upper reaches. Just before the junction a single-track spur diverged on the down side to serve the Thurles beet factory (0.15) with its many sidings. The factory was opened in 1934 and closed in 1989. A short length of the branch remained open at the Thurles end to allow access to the factory. From the junction to Thurles station (1.12 from Thurles Junction and 86.40 from Dublin, Kingsbridge) the W&LR exercised running powers over the line of the GS&WR. The GS&WR station, which is still an important stopping point on the Dublin–Cork main line, has up and down platforms, with a bay at the Cork end of the former which was used by branch trains until the closure of the Thurles–Clonmel line to passenger traffic in 1963. The signal cabin of 32 levers was at the Cork end of the station on the up side, and behind it were sidings and the locomotive depot, the latter including a turntable. The former locomotive shed was converted into a bus and lorry depot by CIE.

The North Kerry line

The Limerick to Tralee line, otherwise known as the North Kerry, is single throughout, with mileposts on the down (left-hand) side as far as Newcastle West. The original Foynes line departed from Limerick by a junction near the Check cabin by means of a trailing connection to trains departing from the station. In W&LR days, Foynes and North Kerry line trains were propelled out of the station by the train engine. Later, these trains were generally brought to the Check cabin by the station pilot, the train engine then backing on there. This unusual arrangement was made to provide an easy approach to the station, although even this line, known as the Foynes Loop, was on a gradient of 1 in 100 and a curve of 30 chains. Initially, C&LDR trains used the Foynes Loop pending the expansion of the station. For their accommodation a fourth platform was provided (No 4) and a new direct line from the station, 750 yards in length, was constructed to a point on the original loop and known as Foynes Junction. This Cork Direct Curve is much more steeply graded with a ruling grade of 1 in 52 for part of its length. In addition to the extra passenger platform, new goods facilities, known as Carey's Road or the Cork Direct Yard, were provided on the west side of the new line. There was a signal cabin at Foynes Junction, which was closed in February 1932, control then being passed to Limerick Check.

As originally constructed, the three-mile-long Castlemungret cement factory branch diverged on the up side at 01.78. This was the point of junction between 1957 and 1966 when, due to the great increase in traffic on the branch, the latter was

extended back to Foynes Junction parallel to the main line and the original junction was removed. At Fort Etna level crossing (06.40), a halt existed for some six years from 23 July 1861. Traces of the short platform could be found until comparatively recent times.

The line has by now begun climbing, mainly at 1 in 113, to a summit at Patrickswell (07.26), also shown as Patrick's Well. Here was the junction for the C&LDR line coming in from Charleville, opened in 1862. The actual location of the junction was soon moved to the Limerick side of the station, with the two lines running parallel. At Patrickswell there were two passenger platforms, that on the east side serving the Charleville line only, following the moving of the junction, the west platform serving Tralee line trains in both directions. The station buildings and signal cabin were both on the west side platform. The original cabin was located on the down side close to the junction points, but this was destroyed in the 'Troubles' in 1923. The replacement, with 24 levers, six of which were spare, was brought into use on 14 October 1923. Two facing sidings served a loading bank on the up side at the Limerick end. With the closure of the Charleville branch in 1967, a section of this line was retained for a short period as a siding.

Leaving Patrickswell the line begins a descent at 1 in 100 for rather more than a mile and a half but this was only a brief respite as the gradient from here was almost all adverse to down trains as far as Barnagh, some 26 miles away. Kilgobbin Halt (09.63), with its single platform on the up side just before the level crossing, was opened in 1928 and closed in 1963. Adare (11.04), which became a halt in May 1952, had one passenger platform on the down side just beyond the level crossing. There was a short siding trailing on the down side serving the goods store as well as a facing siding on the up side with a cattle bank. The station building was on the platform, and at the Limerick end of the latter there was a six-lever ground frame, two levers of which had extension pieces. Close to the station was Adare Manor, the seat of the Earls of Dunraven; the celebrated architect, A. N. W. Pugin, was involved in the design of some features of this magnificent house.

Ballingrane (17.27) was originally known as Rathkeale, but was renamed with the opening of the extension to Newcastle West in 1867 when a new station was opened nearer to the town of Rathkeale. The station had two platforms, with the main station buildings on the down side. Also on this side a facing siding served a loading bank and goods store. The 28-lever signal cabin was on the up platform at the Foynes end adjacent to the level crossing, just beyond which the Foynes and Tralee lines diverged.

Also on the up side, but at the Limerick end, was a turntable of 40ft diameter.

From Ballingrane the line as far as Newcastle West was constructed by the R&NJR. Rathkeale (19.14) was a block post with its single, 221ft long platform with station building on the down side, beyond which were trailing sidings serving a loading bank and goods store. The signal cabin was on the up side. There was also a siding on the up side at the Limerick end of the platform. A short distance beyond Rathkeale was Enright's Siding (19.75) opened in 1868 and closed about 1917. Towards the end of its life it was known as Johnstone's Siding. Ardagh (24.51) had a single platform on the up side on the Limerick side of the level crossing. Beyond the platform, also on the up side, was a loop serving a store and loading bank. Ardagh became a halt under Rathkeale as from 16 December 1938.

Newcastle West (27.18 and 00.00) was an unusual station in that it was really two terminal stations side by side; the layout clearly shows its origins as being the product of two separate companies, precluding through running of trains in either direction, other than by reversal. There was a single platform, serving Tralee line trains on its south side and Rathkeale and Limerick trains on its north face. The station buildings were on the platform with the signal cabin just off its Limerick end. The R&NJR had its own goods sidings, loading bank, goods store and engine turntable on the down side; the L&KR also had its own turntable and sidings. The accompanying drawing, although dating from CIE days, will hopefully serve to clarify the layout here. Mileposts (zero at Newcastle West) were on the up (right-hand) side from here to Tralee.

Between Newcastle West and Barnagh the line was at its most difficult for down trains with two miles at 1 in 81, followed by a short respite at 1 in 247 and then 1 in 61 for more than two miles to the curved 110yd Barnagh Tunnel; this tunnel had the distinction of being the only one on the entire WL&WR system. The summit of the line, at 630ft above sea level, was reached just beyond

Above left: **Foynes station showing a mixed train under the overall roof on 22 April 1955. The passenger carriage is ex-MGWR six-wheeler No 36M designed by Martin Atock.** H. C. Casserley

Above right: **A typical branch train at Newcastle West with the 8.15 Tralee-Limerick service, in charge of an ex-GS&WR 'J15' 0-6-0, 16 April 1955.** R. M. Casserley

the tunnel and was the highest point attained on any standard-gauge line in Ireland.

Barnagh station (06.16) had a single platform with station buildings on the up side. The signal cabin was on the down side, immediately beyond the road over-bridge, and just beyond the cabin was a water tank. At the Tralee end, also on the up side, were goods sidings, with the goods store, cattle pens and loading bank behind the platform. Special instructions applied in respect of the shunting of goods trains at Barnagh due to the severe gradients on either side of the station. Various W&LR timetables ordered that trains descending the inclines at either side of the station should have sufficient wagon brakes pinned down to ensure adequate control, 'not less than 10 in fine weather and 15 when there is a bad rail', and was continued in force by the 1935 GSR Appendix to the working timetable. It was the responsibility of the stationmaster at Barnagh to ensure that this was carried out. Trains shunting here were required to perform such work on the siding and 'under no circumstances whatever on the Main Line'. The GSR Appendix also required the provision of a banking engine, when available, from either Abbeyfeale or Newcastle West as far as Barnagh, to operate in rear of any goods train of over 23 wagons and not exceeding 40. It was not permitted to cross a banked train with a passenger train at Barnagh. Such a train could, however, cross a goods train, provided the latter was in the siding there before the banked train was accepted from either side. The signal cabin at Barnagh was dispensed with in November 1932.

Devon Road (10.60) had a short platform on the up side. A goods siding giving access

to a coal bank, cattle pens, loading bank and a goods store was situated at the Limerick end, also on the up side. There was a signal cabin at Devon Road until 1908. It became a halt under Abbeyfeale as from 1 February 1937. Abbeyfeale (14.10) was a block post with two passenger platforms, the main buildings being on the down side, with the up platform served by a loop. Goods facilities, including a store, were provided on the down side. Beyond Abbeyfeale the gradients eased somewhat and the line ran through the valley of the River Feale through Kilmorna to Listowel. Kilmorna (18.10) was similar to Devon Road and Ardagh, with one platform on the up side, as also were the goods siding, loading bank and goods store.

The town of Listowel took its name from Lis Tuathal, the Castle of Tuathal, one of the ancient kings of Ireland. Listowel (23.29) was, from 1888 to 1924, the interchange point for the unique Listowel & Ballybunion Railway. There were two platforms connected by a footbridge, this latter provided at the opening of the Lartigue line. The station buildings were on the down platform, the signal cabin on the up side. Sidings serving a goods store and cattle bank were situated at the Tralee end of the station on the down side, while there was a 45ft turntable on the same side at the Limerick end. Even after the closure of the Lartigue railway, Listowel handled much holiday traffic for the nearby resort of Ballybunion. Ennismore (26.60), also referred to in the board minutes as Killacrim, was provided as a flag station in 1882 for the use of George Hewson, one of the company directors. Reference is made in Chapter Nine to difficulties with Hewson leading to the station's closure.

On 20 July 1955, a siding was installed on the down side between Ennismore and Lixnaw for Kerry County Council for the off-loading of tar products. In July 1884, it was reported that Mr Hewson was quarrying stone inside the fences at both sides of the line at Ballintogher, near Lixnaw, and that two months later, lime kilns were in course of erection. Subsequently, in August 1888, the L&KR gave permission for rail lines at the quarry to be connected with the company's siding at Lixnaw, and the siding to the latter was in place by January of the following year. It was finally closed in 1943 and was gone by 1945. Lixnaw (29.71) had only one platform on the down side, with a goods siding, loading bank and goods store on the same side at the Limerick end. Just beyond the platform was a level crossing. Lixnaw became a halt under Listowel as from 1 July 1957.

The town of Abbeydorney is named after an abbey founded there in 1154 for Cistercian monks; the remains of the abbey lie just to the north of the town. The station (34.60) was situated on a short horizontal stretch of line before the commencement of a five-mile climb, much of it at 1 in 90. There was one platform, on the down side, along with the usual goods facilities. The station building and signal cabin were both located on the platform. A new goods loop was installed there in August 1912.

Ardfert was described by Lewis in 1837 as 'a decayed borough and market town . . . without either trade or manufacture'. Once again, it owed its origins to the establishment of a monastery, by St Brendan in the sixth century; this monastery was destroyed by fire on several occasions and a new one, probably on the same site, was founded by Lord Kerry in 1253. The station at Ardfert (38.17) had its facilities on the up side. Approaching from Limerick there was a 197ft-long platform, beyond which was a siding serving a loading bank and goods store. It became a halt under the control of Tralee in January 1932, but was transferred to Abbeydorney as from 1 August 1936.

On the approach to Tralee, at 41.42, the Fenit line could be seen diverging on the up side, there being no physical connection here as the two lines ran parallel from Tralee. Tralee (42.65) was the terminus of the L&KR. The passenger platform and station house were situated on the up side, with Fenit Bay located behind at the Limerick end. Opposite, on the down side, were the goods facilities and engine shed. Following the amalgamation of the two companies in 1901 all trains used the GS&WR (Edward Street) station.

Killonan to Killaloe
The section of line between Killonan and Birdhill is today part of the alternative route from Limerick to Dublin via Ballybrophy. In early W&LR days, however, it was simply a branch from the main line. The branch diverges from the Limerick–Waterford line by a facing junction on the down side. As already stated, between November 1931 and October 1947, the lines to Ballybrophy and Waterford were operated as two separate single lines out of Limerick. Mileages are now calculated from Ballybrophy with mileposts on the down side (left-hand side from Ballybrophy).

The first stopping place on the branch, Annacotty Halt (50.44), had one platform on the down side. At only 30ft long, and built of stone, it was the shortest passenger platform in regular use in Ireland. Originally opened in 1859 as Grange, it was soon renamed Annacotty. The original halt was closed in 1861, the later one being opened in 1928 and closed in 1963. Lisnagry (48.58), originally known as Nenagh Road, also had one platform, on the up side. A goods siding and cattle bank were on the down side. Lisnagry also closed in 1963. Castleconnell (47.03) once again had one passenger platform on the up side, opposite to which were the goods siding and cattle bank. There was a level crossing at the Birdhill end of the station. Closed in 1963, Castleconnell was reopened to passenger traffic on 15 May 1989.

Birdhill (42.36) has two passenger platforms, with the station buildings on the down side. The signal cabin was on the up platform at the Limerick end, a goods siding and loading bank being on the down side. The Killaloe branch left Birdhill by a facing junction on the up side. The line from Birdhill to Killaloe was on generally easy gradients. Killaloe station should really have been named Ballina as the town of Killaloe was actually situated on the opposite side of the river. The station had only one platform on the up side, with a run-round loop and goods siding behind it. An overall roof covered the middle section of the platform and the running road. In later years, following the closure of the branch, the station building became a tourist office. There was no signal cabin, but a ground frame covered by a hut at the lake end of the platform. Leaving the station, the line ran for about quarter of a mile, passing a timber engine shed and terminating beside Lough Derg, where there was a small pier.

Fenit, Foynes and Castlemungret branches
The Fenit branch had but two intermediate stations, that at Spa (04.24) having one passenger platform with the station building on the down side. On the same side was a goods siding serving a loading bank. There was a signal cabin located here until about 1905. The summit of the line was reached at Spa station, following which it dropped at 1 in 90 for more than a mile. Kilfenora (06.20) also had only one platform on the down side, no goods facilities being provided there. The last mile into Fenit was on a falling gradient of 1 in 100, the final approach to the latter being through a rock cutting in which the locomotive shed was located on the down side, along with a 40ft turntable. The passenger platform at Fenit (07.77) was on the up side of the line, opposite to which were a goods store and sidings. At the end of the goods sidings the

line entered the property of the Fenit Harbour Commissioners, crossing a short viaduct to run on to the pier, which in plan view was in the shape of an inverted 'L'. Two lines ran the length of the pier to the berths. There was also a small wagon turntable on the pier. Fenit became a halt under Tralee on 1 April 1935 and the branch was operated on the principle of 'one engine in steam' as from May 1944.

The Foynes branch left the North Kerry at Ballingrane Junction and fell all the way to Foynes, initially on a 1 in 150 gradient for nearly 1½ miles, then on easier gradients. There was just the one intermediate station, at Askeaton (20.70), where there was only one passenger platform, on the up side, with a siding serving a goods store and loading bank on the same side. This station, with a level crossing at the Ballingrane end, retained the old arrangement of a single station signal post with two arms facing in opposite directions and sharing the same signal lamp. Askeaton was converted to a halt under the control of Ballingrane as from February 1932, being transferred to Foynes in October 1938 and to Rathkeale in June 1964.

The station at Foynes was built in cut-stone and designed as the focal point of the model village commissioned from Sir Reginald Bloomfield by Lord Monteagle c1910. Approaching Foynes (26.65), which was a block post, two connections trailed in on the down side to serve sidings for respectively the Irish BP Co and the Irish American Oil Co. Opposite these sidings was the locomotive area which originally had a locomotive shed and turntable. The branch continued into the former passenger station with its one platform on the down side and with an overall roof. The signal cabin was situated at the Ballingrane end of this platform. The goods store and loading bank were opposite the passenger station on the up side. An extension of the engine shed road continued out on to the quay where there were further sidings.

The Castlemungret branch turns north after leaving the main line and crosses the marshes of Dooradoyle and the Cork to Limerick road on the level near Ballinacurra. Another road is crossed on the level and then the line begins falling to cross the Limerick to Foynes road, once again on the level. Arriving at Castlemungret the line fans out into a three-track yard with a wagon weighbridge. Beyond the yard the line crosses a road on the level entering the factory premises where it splits into two roads, the down (left) side serving the loading shed where bagged cement is loaded on to wagons. The branch is worked by an Annett's lock opened by a key on either the Limerick station to Patrickswell, or the Limerick Check to Patrickswell staff, thus allowing a train to be locked in on the branch.

Chapter Eighteen

PERSONNEL

Apart from officers, the first staff appointment made by the W&LR was that of John Griffin to the position of clerk at the office in Limerick in September 1845. Griffin's salary was fixed at £80 per annum. A Mr George Rogers was appointed in October 1847 as Superintendent of Police. He was later given the power of suspending and reporting on the 36 'trustworthy men not exceeding the age of 40 years', who were to be selected and employed by the Limerick committee as policemen. They were to be paid according to the scale of the GS&WR and to be supplied with suits of linen and good topcoats of Irish manufacture. Later, it was ordered that the policemen 'instead of being kept congregated at the several stations' were to be spread over the whole line.

With the opening date of the line approaching, stationmasters were appointed in February 1848, including John Conran at Limerick (£80 per annum), James Molony at Killonan, M. Kelly at New Pallas and William Lee at Oola, all at £50 per annum. Shortly afterwards, Thomas Worsted was appointed as shunter at Limerick at 3s per day and Maurice Hall as stoker at 2s 6d. Hall was still a stoker in August 1856 when he applied for leave of absence. This was granted with pay for one month. Molony, who had apparently moved from Killonan to New Pallas as stationmaster, was dismissed in January 1849 for neglect of duty. William Molony, possibly a relative and described as being a ticket collector at Killonan, was also dismissed in August 1849 for having allowed a passenger to pass without paying a fare.

Rogers reported to the board regarding injuries sustained by the guard of an early morning train on the morning of 13 September 1849. The report stated that the driver of the engine *Glengall*, one by the name of McCarty, 'was conducting the train at a speed not authorised by the arrangements of the Directors'. McCarty was suspended immediately, instructions being given that all drivers and firemen involved in accidents etc were to be suspended forthwith. Following further investigation, and it having been established that the driver had been seen in a state of intoxication or apparent intoxication by

several staff members, it was decided to refer the matter to the magistrates. It was made clear that any man so found in future would be immediately put under arrest. A guard and a porter were dismissed for drunkenness in the following January. Later, in February 1851, Rogers reported O'Grady, the policeman at Moore's Gate, for being found in a state of intoxication. O'Grady was summoned and convicted before the magistrates and given two months' imprisonment with hard labour. Needless to state, he was dismissed from the company's service.

A stationmaster defaults

Conran, the Limerick stationmaster, came to the attention of the board in May 1850, he being informed that his presence was expected on the platform on the arrival and departure of every train, 'except the 2.08am mail train from Dublin, when Sgt Pennefather will attend'. Shortly afterwards he was granted a free pass to and from Tipperary. However, only five months later, the board was inquiring into allegations made by the secretary against Conran for defalcation in his accounts, Conran admitting that the accounts were entered in his handwriting. He was duly suspended pending a full investigation, which led to his dismissal in November. Conran's name continued to crop up for some time afterwards as he claimed for salary allegedly due to him. He even had the temerity, in November 1850, to apply for the position of superintendent of traffic just two weeks after his dismissal. His successor at Limerick was Mr J. B. Gill at £100 per annum.

With the extension of the line to Clonmel, further appointments of stationmasters were made in March 1852. These included Messrs G. Baker, Patrick Whitstone and T. Hanny. Whitstone had previously been appointed only in January of the previous year to Pallas. His place there was taken by the clerk at Tipperary, Nicholas Wilkinson. Baker, who went to Clonmel, later applied for and received a lodging allowance. Only eight months later, further changes were made, with Wilkinson moving from Pallas back to his old station, this time in charge. Lee, who had in the interim transferred from Oola to Tipperary, was moved from the latter station to Carrick-on-Suir, Messrs

Moore and Fitzgerald taking up positions at Pallas and Fiddown. Lee asked to remain at Tipperary, this request being declined.

In October 1852, Guard William Hogan was in the news when he found a sum of £50 on the platform at Limerick Junction. He handed this over and it was duly returned to its owner, a resident magistrate by the name of Goold. He had previously been granted a gratuity of £1 in June 1849 'for running (on foot!) into Limerick when the mail train was delayed'. On this occasion, however, Hogan received no more than an expression of satisfaction of the board at his conduct. At a time when wages were so low, the finding of such a large amount must have been a temptation and it is perhaps surprising that neither the directors nor Goold saw fit to reward Hogan in some small way.

Wages and working conditions

A request was made to the board in July 1853 by Winifred Butler, the widow of a porter, for assistance to enable her to emigrate. The secretary was instructed to inquire whether she was in fact the widow of Thomas Butler, and, if so, to have her passage to America paid. An engineman and a boilermaker had previously applied for assistance to return to England, being granted a sum of £3 each towards their expenses. Rogers, the superintendent of police, having applied for compensation in lieu of clothing for four years, was informed that the board would instead give him £10 as a voluntary gift when removing himself and his family to England. This payment was made in August 1853. These various transactions clearly indicate that many of the early staff came from England. This was particularly so in the case of drivers, fitters and the like, which were skills relatively unknown in the Ireland of the mid-19th century, and some of the fledgling companies had to induce men to come from England to fill such positions. Wages and conditions for other grades, however, proved not to be as good as expected and the parties concerned returned to their homeland.

Shortly after the line opened, drivers were paid 7s a day, a good wage in those far-off days. Guards were initially paid 15s per week, soon increased to 17s 6d and to 19s in July 1852. In return for the latter sum, no allowance was made for overtime. In March 1864, the pay of the guards working the night mail trains was reduced by 1s to 20s per week. Reference has already been made to the salaries of stationmasters, who were paid monthly after June 1849. In some instances, they were given a lodging allowance pending the completion of station houses. Later, however, they were expected to pay rent for accommodation or land.

In June 1850, a petition was received from the porters at Limerick station objecting to a reduction made in their pay. The directors expressed little sympathy for them and pointed out that they had taken into consideration the reduction in the price of provisions generally since the porters had originally been engaged. They had also taken cognisance of the average wage in the locality and the fact that the men were partly clothed at the company's expense. The directors went on to say that the porters had much reason to be thankful for now receiving 1s 4d a day. No doubt there were hundreds who would be willing to take employment on even lower terms. An interesting reference is made in April 1854 to a porter by the name of Richard Strong, who it was agreed should be allowed an additional 5s per week for four weeks to enable him to procure additional nourishment, 'it appearing he needs same'. Strong had been acting as a guard on the line in the previous January and had been provided with a great coat. By the 1890s, porters were being paid between 8s 6d and 11s 6d a week.

As regards permanent way staff, gangers received between 10s and 12s a week in November 1854, milesmen between 8s and 9s a week. When permanent way staff went on strike in July 1882, they were seeking an increase of 2s a week to bring them up to 14s. The engineer sought approval to increase the pay to 13s or 13s 6d, he being authorised to make the best arrangements he could. In 1864, signalmen in Waterford received sums ranging from 12s 6d to 15s a week. Almost 30 years later, in October 1893, signalmen's wages varied from 14s at Rathkeale to 18s at Limerick.

A new scale of wages was introduced by Atock in October 1861 for the locomotive men. Drivers and firemen in their first year were to receive respectively 4s and 2s 6d per day, increased in the second year to 5s and 2s 9d, in the third year to 5s 6d and 3s, and in the fourth year to 6s for drivers. Fourth-year firemen who held a certificate for occasional driving could receive 3s 6d. Reference is made later to wages introduced in 1890 for footplate crews.

Comparisons were made in July 1890 between staff in the works at Limerick and those employed at the GS&WR and MGWR workshops at Inchicore and Broadstone. This indicated that fitters, who were paid between 30s and 33s per week at Limerick, fell below their Dublin colleagues by between 2s and 5s. Thirty years previously, W&LR fitters received 3s 4d per day. Likewise, carpenters, who received from 24s to 26s at Limerick, were paid from 26s to 32s in Dublin. Robinson, however, stated that it was difficult to accurately compare the scales. Nevertheless, the men sought an all-round increase of 2s per week, this being declined due to increases in the cost of coal and other materials. Boys working in the fitting shop had their wages increased at that time from between 9s and 12s to 20s. It had been reported in April 1880 that one boy had been receiving 5s a week for the previous four years, a request for an increase being turned down.

It is not clear what, if any, payments were made for employees who fell ill, but it was ordered in September 1855 that for the future, servants of the company on the sick list were only to receive half pay. Six months later in March 1856, arrangements were announced whereby no allowances would be made during illness as from 1 May 1856, and all persons on the line were urged to join the Irish Railway Friendly Society.

It was another matter when staff were injured or killed during the course of their employment. Compensation, if one could call it that, varied considerably from case to case and appeared to have little relevance to the extent of the injuries. In January 1854, it was agreed to give the widow of Driver John Smith a sum of £60 following his death as a result of the Anner Bridge derailment. On the other hand, when Fireman Walsh was killed at Castleconnell in February 1861, his widow received the sum of £5, while the widow of Donovan, a ganger killed between

Decorated with flags and greenery, one of the company's 4-4-0s heads a Waterford Young Men's Christian Association special train. Note the tallow on the tender side. It is interesting to contrast the dress styles of the two children in the photograph and to speculate as to who are the two individuals with the child in the foreground. Are they railway officials?
Photographer unknown/Green Studios collection

Fiddown and Carrick-on-Suir in July 1878 received an allowance of 6s a week for one year. John Maher was run over by a train on 7 December 1881 at Kilsheelan ballast pit, his widow being given the sum of £10 'as Charity to the family'. When Denis McCarthy was killed near Lixnaw station in February 1889, his sister requested an allowance for the removal of his remains from Listowel to Tralee, a request which was endorsed by a number of merchants of Tralee. This was declined as the board were of the view that Miss McCarthy was not dependent on the deceased.

In later years, it became the practice to take the sons of victims into the service of the company. For example, when Guard Linegar was killed at Tipperary in July 1888, his widow was granted £10 and his son was taken on at 5s a week. In another instance, after Guard Hickey was killed at Charlestown in 1896, it was reported that there was a 13-year old-son living at home who was attending school and was delicate. The company expressed its inability to afford assistance unless employment could be found for the boy. Also in this case, the company was threatened with proceedings when it refused to pay a sum of three guineas to a doctor.

William Mills lost a foot in an accident in February 1859 and was awarded an allowance of 3s 4d a week. He applied in

September of the following year for an artificial foot, it being agreed to pay for one if the cost was moderate. As the result of a shunting accident in Clonmel yard on 10 September 1883, Milesman James Daniel had a leg amputated and it was agreed to have a cork leg supplied. This latter was estimated to cost between 10 and 20 guineas, a sum of £10 being allowed; in the same accident, Ganger John Clancy was killed and his widow received £40 in compensation and permission to remain in the company's house so long as she attended to the gates. A signalman who lost a leg in an accident at Limerick yard in August 1896 was supplied with an artificial limb by Messrs Fannin of Dublin at a cost of £15. In his case, however, he was required to pay a sum of 2s 6d weekly until this amount was paid off.

Foreman Waddams at Limerick lost two fingers when a screw jack slipped on engine No 12, but there is no reference to any compensation being paid to him. However, it was agreed to pay half wages for three months to John Denihan, a carriage body maker, who lost three fingers in an accident in the works in June 1890, although it was initially ordered that he receive no payment as the accident was due to a breach of rules.

In March 1892, it was reported that Ganger E. Walsh had been found 'insensible' in a snowstorm at the end of the previous month. A letter was received from the Rev P. Keating drawing attention to the exertions of Dr Tuthill of Porthall, 'used to restore animation'. It was reluctantly agreed to pay Dr Tuthill the sum of £1 for his troubles. We will finalise this section with a reference to two elderly employees. In July 1891, a memorial was received from Mr E. Fitzgerald for an allowance after 38 years of service. He had just been paid-off through old age; this request was declined. A William Gleeson was reported to be incapacitated from work in the locomotive department at Waterford, being over 80 years of age; on this occasion a sum of £5 was granted.

Discipline

There are many instances cited in the board minutes of the breaching of rules, carelessness, disobedience and insubordination. It would be impossible to deal with more than a small selection of these and what follows will hopefully give a flavour of the day-to-day events which occurred on the railway and the manner in which these incidents were handled by the management.

Nicholas Wilkinson, who as we have already noted above, had been appointed stationmaster at Tipperary in November 1852, was brought up before the board in July 1855 after it was discovered he was in the habit of carting butter to the Junction. He was informed that the board did not wish its stationmasters to use carts for traffic

and he was informed that he should 'put away his cart'. Four months later, he received a fine of 5s for neglecting to forward a message to the Junction, thereby delaying a train for nearly an hour. A more serious misdemeanour came to light in August of the following year when he apparently allowed an officer of the GS&WR to see his books. This drew a strong reprimand and a letter was sent to the GS&WR traffic manager expressing surprise at his actions. Two years later, following further complaints regarding security in the discharge of his duties, Wilkinson's services were dispensed with, it appearing that his accounts were in arrears to the extent of £22 5s 0d.

Fitzgerald, who had moved from Cahir to Waterford as stationmaster in October 1856, received a fine of £1 in August 1859 for irregularities in his returns. In April of the following year his absence from the station on Good Friday was noted, for which he received a reprimand. His colleague at Clonmel (not mentioned by name) was fined the cost of the return ticket for having allowed Fitzgerald to leave the station at Clonmel without a pass or ticket. Fitzgerald was allowed to 'resign' (in those days an oft-used euphemism for being dismissed) in July 1860 after he had satisfactorily squared up his accounts, and he was even granted a gratuity of £10.

In May 1861 Payne, the traffic manager, referred to a source of complaint, when he reported that some of the stationmasters were in the habit of keeping fowl and pigeons, which were complained of by the public. An order was issued that any such fowls found after a fortnight would be killed forthwith and a heavy fine imposed. The order was extended to include goats along the line or at stations.

A Driver Sneyd was fined £1 and severely cautioned in November 1878 following an altercation between himself and a shunter by the name of Lambert. In November 1882 it was reported that Sneyd had been dismissed for having been found drunk on his engine at Limerick Junction. However, a Driver Sneyd is again mentioned four years later, and we shall deal with that anon. The only reason for mentioning this minor matter is that in the companion volume on the history of the MGWR, reference is made to the murder in 1869 of Thomas Anketell, the stationmaster at Mullingar. A rather more lengthy description of this event appears in Volume 18 of the *Journal of the Irish Railway Record Society*. During the course of the investigation into Anketell's murder, it came to light that two MGWR footplate men, Fireman Tom Sneyd and Driver John Sneyd, were suspected of some involvement in the foul deed. Tom was reported to have become a driver with the GS&WR, while John completed his service

on either the Blessington or Lucan steam tramway systems. It is an unusual name and one wonders if the W&LR man might have been related to, if not one of those supposedly involved in the Anketell murder.

The reference above to Driver Sneyd involved the misconduct of himself and another driver in November 1886. This event was to lead to the suspension of the locomotive foreman at Waterford, a Mr Graves, apparently resulting from the tone of his report to Appleby, the locomotive superintendent. Graves appealed to the board in August 1887, the latter also strongly disapproving of the tone of some of Graves's letters, in particular his threat to use force in resisting Appleby's orders. Pending further investigation it was agreed he be paid his salary and a committee of investigation, including the chairman amongst its number, was set up. In the interim, Graves had made serious allegations against his superior, accusations which he failed to substantiate. It was unanimously resolved that Graves be dismissed and he was ordered to give up possession of the company's house at Waterford. In response he said that he could not remove his family during the inclement season, the board relenting and allowing him to remain as a weekly tenant until the end of the following March. Even this was extended due to his daughter's ill health.

Problems arose in 1878/79 when it was reported that stores were being pilfered at Limerick Works. Orders were given for the provision of a central, securely locked store. Around the same time, tallow was stolen by an engineman at Waterford. It was decided not to appoint additional watchmen, but the engineer was instructed to secure the tallow and oil store. It also transpired that a wagon containing a consignment of brandy was tampered with, the watchman being fined 5s.

In May 1881, drivers were instructed to discontinue the practice of 'blowing off smoke in covered stations such as Waterford and Limerick, under (pain of) instant dismissal'. There is no record of any dismissals as a result of this instruction. Two months earlier, following an investigation by a sub-committee, an order was issued that no person employed in the locomotive department at Limerick should in future be owners of public houses, but it is not entirely clear how this matter came to light. In the following August, an extension of time was allowed to 1 September to enable the men concerned to comply with this order, in default of which they were to be dismissed.

In October 1894, a public house was in the news again, not however one in the ownership of a member of staff. On this occasion a Mr Griffiths had complained of the 11.00 down goods train being delayed at

Fiddown, it transpiring that Driver Montgomery and Guard Moore had decided to visit the local hostelry there. Both men were duly dismissed, although Montgomery later sought reinstatement, a request strangely enough supported by Griffiths. Montgomery was in fact reinstated but in a subordinate post.

Finally, we will conclude this section by referring to a report in August 1900 from the traffic manager as to the conviction of the stationmaster at Spa on the Fenit branch for having assaulted his wife. It was stated that 'Murphy's mind is somewhat unhinged lately'. It was ordered that his wife be allowed to continue the working of the station, and as such perhaps she became the first female stationmaster in Ireland!

Reductions in staff numbers and strikes

In February 1858, a letter was read from the secretary stating that he was willing to have his salary reduced by 20% until the company's finances allowed of an improvement. At this time, the directors had agreed to give up their remuneration as an example. By 1862, matters had become serious and the various departments were requested to see how savings could be achieved. In February, Atock reported that he had dispensed with five men, Payne had let seven porters go, while Tighe had replaced three men with boys during the previous three months. Details were given of staff in the locomotive department. As of June 1862, there were 119 men employed in the locomotive department at Limerick, 26 in the carriage and wagon department, with a further 38 employed at other locations, making a total of 183. This compared with 192 a year earlier. Atock reckoned that he could dispense with a further 11, making an annual saving of £420. The half-year wage bill for the department for the period ended June 1862 amounted to £4,545. At the same time, the traffic department was urged to reduce expenditure, 'which is the cause of extreme anxiety to the Directors'. Later, in January 1865, various drivers and firemen received bonuses, £3 for drivers and £1 for the latter, for time-keeping and lowest consumption of coal and oil.

It was reported in July 1866, that 10 or 12 porters had gone on strike, but had returned to work on being promised a fair hearing by the directors. Jacob, in their defence, stated that they were hard-worked and had long hours. The GS&WR paid its porters 12s a week at this stage, and the board agreed to an increase of 2s per week, but expected fewer hands to do the work.

Atock confirmed in November 1869 that he had given notice to nine carpenters, two smiths and two strikers, leaving barely enough men at Limerick for ordinary carriage and wagon repairs. Following this move, it was agreed to send some wagon

Two W&LR employees are seen at an unknown location. There appears to be a goods shed on the left beyond the bridge and a raised loading bank on the right.
Courtesy Green Studios, Dublin.

repairs to England, although it is doubtful whether this could have effected any real economies. In December it was agreed to 'let go' Foreman Carpenter Thomas Noonan at 35s a week. Noonan asked for some assistance on the grounds of his long service. He was granted £5 to help to move his family to Dublin. In December 1871, shortly before his resignation, Atock brought up the subject of the nine-hour day being conceded to the workmen. At that time, the men at Limerick were working a 58½-hour week compared with the 54 recommended. Atock was given leave to take any action he judged for the best. The 54-hour week was conceded, resulting in a resolution from the men thanking the directors most warmly for the generous manner in which they had been treated.

Yet another review of staff in the locomotive, carriage and wagon departments was carried out in November 1878. It was reported that 28 additional hands had been taken on in the previous 18 months at a cost of £75 a fortnight, or £1,950 per annum. A committee was appointed to inspect the works at Limerick and come up with suggestions for a reduction in expenditure. It was decided to dispense with the services of 11 men in the carriage department, giving an immediate reduction of £504 a year. The locomotive superintendent later agreed to dispense with a further 11 men in the locomotive department, bringing about a further saving of £525. The committee then turned its attention to train working, and instructed the traffic manager to make a reduction of 204 miles a day in running, adding a further saving of between £4,000 and £5,000 a year. Within a year, however, it became necessary to hire additional fitters and turners to cope with a backlog of repairs, and the opening of the L&KR two

years later made necessary the appointment of further staff. Attention was also turned to the permanent way and traffic departments. In the case of the latter, there had been a considerable increase in expenditure, due to the necessity for cleaning and disinfecting cattle wagons following on BoT regulations, and the appointment of additional staff.

Labour disputes

Three potentially serious labour disputes occurred during 1890 and 1891. It had been clear for some time that the men were actively being represented by trade unions. As an example, it was noted in December 1886 that representations had been made to the company on behalf of the enginemen and firemen in regard to their rates of pay. The locomotive superintendent was directed to interview the men to ascertain the nature of their grievances, following which the chairman was to meet them and, if possible, come to an amicable arrangement. It was made quite clear that negotiations were to be conducted directly with the men rather than through intermediaries, this being the stance adopted by all railway managements at that time.

A demand for a revision of hours and an increase of wages was made by the traffic department staff in December 1889. In January 1890, a settlement was reported, whereby all country uniform staff were to receive an increase of 1s per week. This increase was not to apply to staff at Clonmel,

Tipperary, Ennis, Listowel, Newcastle and Tralee, which were classified as second class stations, where the increase was to be at the rate of 1s 6d per week. Additionally, head porters, shunters and signalmen at these stations were to receive an increase of 2s per week, Sunday working to be paid for at the rate of 3d per hour for time of work. At Limerick and Waterford passenger and goods staff were to receive increases of 1s 6d and 2s respectively, the latter also to be paid 3d per hour for overtime after 12 hours per day, including meals. Men out at night from home were to be paid an allowance of 1s 6d. The head porter at Limerick was in future to be paid 23s per week, his assistant 18s. Despite this apparent agreement, the men went on strike at Limerick on 7 January, the matter being resolved only after the chairman personally met the workers. By the end of January, the enginemen and firemen agreed a settlement of their claim, with increases to date from 1 March 1890. It is interesting to note that the negotiations with these men were carried out by Robinson rather than by the directors, as had been the case previously, indicating the high regard they had for their locomotive superintendent.

Work was grouped into three classes: third class constituted work on the branch lines, goods, special goods, ballast working, shunting, banking and piloting; second class consisted of working of mixed trains between Limerick, Waterford, Tuam and Tralee; while first class referred to all main line passenger work between Limerick, Waterford, Tuam and Tralee. The published times were to be considered as the hours of duty, except in extreme cases, which would be dealt with separately on their merits. An allowance of one hour per day was made for preparing and disposing of engines.

Firemen's wages varied from 2s 3d per day for those engaged on shunting during their first year to 3s 6d per day after a year as a first class fireman, increased by 6d a day if acting as a passed fireman on shunting duties. Drivers received 4s a day on shunting duties, while first class drivers received 7s 6d a day after three years in the first class grade. Lodging allowance was to be 1s 6d per night, but in exceptional circumstances this might be increased to 2s. All advances in pay were dependent on the good conduct of each man, a fine of 2s 6d per day and upwards delaying an advance for 12 months from the date of the fine. They were also dependent on economy exercised in fuel and oil consumption. In the case of firemen, their advance depended on the state of cleanliness in which the footplate and backplate of their engines were maintained.

Next to seek an increase in their rate of pay were the men of the permanent way department, followed by the locomotive

department staff at Limerick Works. This latter dispute proved to be difficult to resolve. As far back as 1879 their wages had been reduced by 10% as an economy measure and they now felt that they were at least entitled to be paid on a par with their colleagues at Broadstone and Inchicore, the respective works of the MGWR and the GS&WR. They sought an increase of 2s per week and advised that, 'having given due deliberation to the grave consequences that may follow a board refusal to redress a grievance of 11 years standing, notice is given that on 26 July 1890, they will cease work and not return until the company accede to their demands'. This demand was signed by some 260 men, but the board refused to accede to threats of this nature, and the men, as noticed, went on strike on 26 July.

Within a week, the strike committee issued a circular to the citizens of Limerick seeking a subscription. A deputation from Limerick Corporation met with the board on 18 September urging a settlement of the dispute, which was having serious consequences for the city. The mayor led the deputation and advised that he had had long discussions with the strike committee, resulting in a modified demand being made. The board, however, explained its objections to such a proposal and advised that they in turn had agreed to recast the wages according to the qualification and value of the workmen, as estimated by the locomotive superintendent. The men were strongly urged to cease the strike and return to work on the following Monday. It was agreed that those who had remained loyal to the company should receive a gratuity of £1 each, while the fitter at Tuam was to receive £3 and the five foremen £5 each. In contrast, Robinson, in consideration of his energy and zealous devotion to duty, was rewarded with an additional £50 per annum to his salary.

Further difficulties occurred with the traffic staff, objections being made to a notice issued by the traffic manager in December 1890 relating to the system of work at Limerick stores and yard. A letter was penned to the chairman by Mr Flynn, described as the secretary to the W&LR Servants Trade Union, requesting a reply to a former letter detailing a list of the porters' complaints and requirements, by 17 December. Despite this official request, the men went on strike two days before the deadline and the Mayor of Limerick once again approached the board with a deputation. Before returning to work, the men insisted on the withdrawal of the notice. The discussions were described as being 'rather heated', Alderman O'Mara stating that he considered the men's demands reasonable. The directors however deplored the men's actions and they stressed that it

would be impossible to conduct their business 'unless a final stop can be put to the unreasonable dictation of their servants'. This said, they had now advertised for porters and guards and would use every means in their power to crush the combination of their employees. It became clear that these men were unlikely to be reinstated, and this proved to be so in the majority of cases.

An intervention by the Bishop of Limerick, the Most Rev Dr O'Dwyer, had little effect. Many other memorials were received from shopkeepers, the Limerick Harbour Board, and the Limerick Chamber of Commerce, all of which fell on deaf ears. It was made abundantly clear that any men who had gone on strike, and who had been replaced, would not be reinstated. It was reported that G. F. Quinton, the secretary and receiver of the SR, had acted as guard on that line during the dispute, a cheque for £10 being issued to him at the end of January 1891 in recognition of his services. A public meeting was held in Limerick on 13 March protesting at the manner in which traffic was currently being worked and the attitude of the directors towards the representations from Dr O'Dwyer. Those present pledged to use every means to divert traffic from the company. Eventually, a limited number of those men who went on strike were taken back.

Staff clothing

In November 1850 it was resolved that nine topcoats be obtained for stokers, turners and assistants. At the same time, tenders were sought for appropriate clothing for the police, guards, ticket collectors and porters, Mr E. Acheson being requested to send in a sample garment; hats and caps were also provided. The porter in the Limerick booking office was frequently required to go out as a guard of a train and it was therefore decided to provide him with a blue jacket and trowsers (sic) instead of corduroy. Further clothing for the locomotive department was sought in August 1853, viz 12 topcoats for enginemen (drivers), 12 for stokers and additional uniforms for nightmen and the foremen. By May 1860, Messrs Tobin of Waterford were supplying the necessities, at which time there were 72 porters, 15 switchmen (pointsmen), five passenger guards, seven goods guards, three ticket collectors and two policemen. Although the traffic manager reported in August 1864 that the men were 'getting very ragged', it was decided not to obtain new overcoats. In the following year, however, it was decided to provide blouses (shirts) for guards along with linen overcoats, the latter supplied for 7s 6d each.

Also in 1865, Malcomson returned from a trip to Brussels and persuaded the board that stationmasters should wear caps. These were of two types, red with gold braiding for the stationmasters at Waterford and Limerick; in addition, the station inspectors at these locations were to wear similar caps. At the second class stations, viz Tipperary, Clonmel, Carrick-on-Suir and Fiddown, as well as Captain Weir, master of the steamer *Rosa*, they were to have blue caps with a plain gold band.

In November of that same year, tenders were opened for the supply of 46 suits for enginemen (22 drivers, 22 firemen and 2 watchmen), it being decided to accept that of Messrs Tobin & Sons of Waterford at 35s each. The men were expected to pay for their clothing 'at the same scale as Mr Jacob's men'. This meant that they paid half the cost, the drivers in fortnightly instalments over six months, the firemen over 12 months; as the watchmen's wages were considered to be too low, they were to be supplied free. Atock had unsuccessfully endeavoured to have the uniforms supplied free on this occasion, his argument being that it was over three years since they had last had them. It transpired, in February 1866, that these uniforms were in fact coats rather than suits, it being reported that they had been rejected as being inferior. Following correspondence between Atock and the suppliers, it was reluctantly agreed to accept those already made up at a 10% reduction, the company declining to take any more except at a 20% reduction.

A minute of 29 June 1867 lists four tenders for further clothing supplies, it appearing that the company favoured local suppliers. These were Messrs Cannock, Tait & Co and Kearse of Limerick, Messrs Tobin & Sons of Waterford and Sparrow of Clonmel. On this occasion, Cannock & Co was successful, the order being quite sizeable from their point of view, viz three inspectors' suits comprised of cloth coat, vest, trousers and best-quality cap at £4 7s 6d each, 16 somewhat similar suits for guards at £3 17s 6d each, 58 suits for head porters at £2 9s 6d and finally, 131 porters' uniforms of cord jacket, vest, trousers and cloth cap, at £1 13s 3d each. In order to protect their uniforms, it was agreed to obtain white lawn coats for the guards. No doubt Tobin's previous poor performance weighed against them in this instance. When the subject of enginemen's coats arose in December 1870, Tait & Co declined to tender as they considered they had been 'unfairly treated' in February 1868, they having supplied samples of thick German cloth at 59s and fine blue cloth at 49s. The reason for the unfair treatment is not indicated. Once again, this contract went to Cannock & Co.

Whilst it had been agreed in 1865 that stationmasters should wear caps to distinguish them from other staff, the practice appears to have fallen into decline.

So we find a resolution being passed in June 1877, again calling on them to be worn. On this occasion, the order went to Messrs Ireland of Dublin, who were suppliers to many of the country's railway companies. The contract cap was to have the centre ornament removed and the letters 'W&LR' inserted instead. The question of caps and uniforms for stationmasters arose again in 1885 and 1888. In the former year, the directors decided to procure uniforms similar to that worn by the Limerick Junction agent, presumably that of the GS&WR, the agents to pay half the cost of same. In August 1888, in response to an instruction from the board, the traffic manager submitted a list of agents (stationmasters) who did not wear uniforms. Uniforms were in due course ordered from Messrs Todd & Co at £3 3s 9d each, plus caps at 5s 9d.

Complaints were made from time to time of bad workmanship, reductions generally being made on contract prices. Uniform colours were mentioned in April 1886, it being agreed that passenger and goods guards, head porters and policemen should wear blue, ordinary porters having a darker shade. Various materials were considered, including Devon wool, Irish frieze and dark kersey, the latter being recommended for cheapness and durability. Station agents' suits were to be of finer material.

In November 1890, following a request from the engineer, 40 coats and 46 capes or shawls were ordered respectively for gatemen and gatewomen. At about the same time, it was agreed to substitute 'monkey coats' and a pair of pants in lieu of the long overcoats previously supplied to the enginemen.

Officers

What follows is an attempt to collate a brief description of the careers of some of the principal officers who served the company through the years. It is not intended as an in-depth biography of the various individuals, and additional information may be found in some of the historical chapters. The first company secretary was William Septimus Saunders, brother of Charles Saunders secretary of the GWR, appointed in August 1845 at a salary of £600. Saunders remained in office for only five years, making the decision to step down in 1850 following a meeting of the board when it was decided to halve his salary. Saunders resigned but did not live to enjoy his retirement. When returning home to England, he slipped as he came down the gangplank at Holyhead on the morning of 1 December 1850 and was drowned. He was only 48 years of age.

Saunders' replacement, John O'Connor, was appointed as from 1 October 1850 at the reduced salary of £300. He does not appear to have made much of an impression on the affairs of the company and his

services were dispensed with in June 1858, his assistant John G. Davis being appointed secretary *pro tem*. However, there was some dissension amongst the directors, a Mr Galwey declaring that he believed the decision to remove O'Connor was illegal. O'Connor meanwhile wrote at some length regarding the alleged reasons for his dismissal, including the fact that he had been taking a prominent part in the establishment of the Milford steamers. The affair was raised in both the *Waterford Mail* and the *Waterford News*, the company denying this was the reason for his dismissal. In fact, they asserted that the W&LR was determined to encourage this or any other line of steamers serving Waterford. The order was duly rescinded and O'Connor was requested to perform the duties of secretary pending the outcome of advertisements placed for the position. O'Connor had also brought charges against Davis, which were proved to be unfounded, and this is most likely the reason for O'Connor's departure.

Thomas Ainsworth was appointed company secretary in September 1858. He also had a difficult period during his term of office. Charges were levelled against him in September 1866, when it was alleged that he had taken £4,000 of the company's money. He was completely exonerated following a detailed investigation, and he subsequently served both as secretary and traffic manager from 1868 to 1872. In March of the latter year he announced his resignation, it being decided to separate the two positions. Pending the appointment of a successor, Joseph Ambrose, the company's solicitor, was requested to act as temporary secretary. The next company secretary was John Fowler Nicoll, appointed in June 1872 at a salary of £400 per annum, M. J. Kennedy being given the position of assistant secretary. Fowler had previously made a name for himself on the Shrewsbury & Chester Railway and had been very much involved in the early years of the A&TR and the A&EJR; he proved to be a very capable holder of the office. Reference is made in Chapter Seven to the difficulties he encountered during the upheaval of the mid-1870s. Nicoll resigned in June 1877 due to continuing ill health and was replaced by his assistant, he being paid his salary to February 1878, the date of the termination of his engagement. He was also presented with 100 guineas in recognition of his zeal and integrity.

Kennedy's health also suffered and, after a lengthy spell at Vyon in Switzerland, he announced his resignation in August 1883. He was granted a pension of £300 per annum for life in consideration of his long and faithful service over a period of 26 years. John J. Murphy, the company accountant, was requested to take on the additional responsibility of company secretary as from August 1883 at a salary of £350. Murphy was to remain as secretary for the remaining years of the company's independence.

Traffic superintendents

The question of appointing a traffic superintendent was first raised in March 1847, when the secretary was instructed to inquire after a competent person. It was not, however, until 9 February 1848 that Thomas Mackie of Clonmel was appointed to the post at a salary of £200 per annum; this latter sum was to be reviewed when the board were 'better able to judge of the extent and value of the services' (of Mackie). In October 1849, it was decided to dispense with Mackie's services, his salary being paid up to the end of the year 'to give him an opportunity of seeking other employment'.

The post of traffic superintendent remained vacant for almost 2½ years, Charles Bagnell being appointed as from 1 April 1852, and who was informed that his duties were to be the same as those of George Ilberry on the GS&WR. Bagnell was called before the board in August 1853 in connection with an incident involving the stationmaster at Bansha. No details of the incident are recorded but Bagnell was severely censured for not taking more decisive action against the stationmaster. Possibly arising from this and an incidence of train delays, Bagnell's contract was not renewed when it expired in December 1853. Lewis DeMay was appointed traffic superintendent as from 1 January 1854. However, by the end of that year, with traffic not coming up to expectations, it was decided to dispense with DeMay's services. The secretary, John O'Connor, agreed to take on the joint responsibilities of secretary and traffic manager, the first occasion on which the latter title was used; John Davis was appointed to act as his assistant.

By May of the following year, however, the directors were once again giving consideration to the appointment of a traffic superintendent, and it was announced on 12 June 1855 that William Labatt Payne had been appointed to the position at a salary of £250. Payne also served in a similar capacity with the L&CR, L&ER and L&FR. He handed in his resignation in October 1862, to take effect from the end of the year. He then moved to a more lucrative position as traffic manager of the DW&WR, a post which he held until 1894. The vacant post on the W&LR was offered to Henry Jacob at an increased salary of £300 per annum, to include all the subsidiary companies.

Some, unspecified, difficulties arose in August 1867 involving Jacob and he was given a week to submit his resignation. Thomas Ainsworth was given the joint positions of secretary and traffic manager,

this taking effect from 1 January 1863, Isaac Banks being appointed assistant traffic superintendent at the same time. Ainsworth in due course submitted his resignation in January 1872, following complaints and allegations against him. Isaac Banks became traffic manager two months later, his salary being fixed at £400. Also in March, Ainsworth asked for a testimonial, it being agreed in June that he should receive a sum of £500 in consideration of his long service, viz 13½ years as secretary and 4½ as traffic manager. Consideration was also given to appointing him a director, this course of action being supported by Sir Daniel Gooch of the GWR. A large majority of the board were opposed to this move, unsuccessful attempts being made to rescind the June motion to grant the testimonial.

Isaac Banks had a short tenure as traffic manager, charges also being brought against him in September 1873, which were referred to in more detail in Chapter Seven. His successor, John Roberts, who took up the position on 1 May 1875, remained in office for almost 16 years. In November 1891 the chairman wrote to him advising that the directors had in mind doing away with the position, and retaining him in a consultative capacity. Roberts expressed great surprise at the proposed move after his long service, 'embracing the best years of his life'. He expressed the hope that the directors would not leave him and his family unprovided for. On further consideration, it was agreed to appoint Roberts as a consultant at £200 per annum, one-third of his previous salary.

With Roberts in this latter position, S. G. Glynn was appointed traffic superintendent, a position he held for only nine months, at which time Roberts also appears to have parted company with the W&LR. In November 1892 Frederick Vaughan from the Cambrian Railways was appointed as traffic manager at a salary of £400. Vaughan remained as the company's last traffic manager, Glynn being removed to Sligo as district superintendent.

Engineers

Charles Blacker Vignoles was appointed chief engineer in 1845 at a fixed salary of £1,000, payable quarterly. Vignoles, born in Co Wexford in May 1793, was an eminent engineer of his day and had served as engineer-in-chief to Ireland's first railway, the Dublin & Kingstown Railway. He was also one of the engineers involved in the Royal Commission of 1836-38. He remained only a short while with the W&LR, as in March 1846 the directors expressed themselves unhappy that Vignoles could not, due to his numerous other engagements, devote his constant and personal superintendence over the works. They then appointed Richard Boyse Osborne, Vignoles's

resident engineer, to take charge. Osborne was the eldest son of R. B. Osborne, another Wexford man, and as related in Chapter One, he had spent some time in America before coming to Waterford. Reference has also been made to some of his American ideas introduced to the W&LR. Osborne also had some differences with the board in relation to his commitment. The directors were moved in April 1847 to comment that 'Mr Osborne by no means evinces the same liberality towards the Company as he appears to expect from the Directors and which they would wish to show to him were they not acting in trust for others'. He left the W&LR in August 1848. Andrew Stewart, who had been working under Osborne, being appointed resident engineer in May of that year, now took over from Osborne.

Two years later, George Willoughby Hemans was appointed engineer-in-chief. He had served as a pupil under the great Sir John Macneill, becoming resident engineer on the Dublin & Drogheda Railway and later taking up a similar position on part of the GS&WR main line. Hemans had been appointed engineer-in-chief to the MGWR in August 1845. He also was involved with the two Athenry companies, and remained as engineer-in-chief to the W&LR until 1854, when he moved to England, later going to New Zealand.

Three months' notice was given to Stewart in February 1853, but he in fact remained on until 1 April 1854. Stewart was succeeded by John Challoner Smith, who was born in Dublin in August 1827 and was educated at Trinity College, Dublin. In June 1857, Smith sought permission from the board to accept a similar post on the W&KR. He remained with the W&LR until June 1861 when he submitted his resignation. Following his resignation, Smith went into partnership with John Bagnell and they constructed a number of lines, including Borris to Ballywilliam, Clara to Streamstown and Roscrea to Birdhill. He was appointed engineer to the DW&WR in February 1868. He was elected honorary secretary to the Institution of Civil Engineers in Ireland in 1873, a post which he held for 14 years until failing eyesight caused his resignation. Smith died of angina on 13 March 1895.

John Long, who had been acting as engineer to the L&FR under William Barrington, was requested in April 1861 to take charge of the W&LR line as far as Tipperary along with the various lines terminating at Limerick. James Tighe, who had worked under Smith, was put in charge of the lines from Tipperary to Kilkenny via Waterford. Long submitted his resignation in October 1864 and the entire system was placed under Tighe's control as from 1 January 1865. He remained in charge of engineering matters until his death on 27 December 1899, Mr R. H. Good being appointed to the position as acting engineer for the 12 months until the end of the company's independent existence.

Locomotive superintendents

As we have seen, the secretarial and civil engineering positions were reasonably stable. When we come to look at the locomotive superintendents we find that it was not so, with no fewer than 16 officers being responsible for the locomotive department in total. Initially, Vignoles took charge, but it is likely that he did little more than lay down broad outlines of what was required, detailed designs being prepared by the manufacturers, as was normal practice at that time. With Vignoles's departure in 1846, Osborne took over responsibility for rolling stock matters, his hand being seen in the carriage and wagon building programme, particularly in regard to the early bogie vehicles. William Martley, who had been Daniel Gooch's chief assistant on the GWR during the Gauge Commission's trials in 1845, and travelled on the 'narrow gauge' (4ft 8½in) engine trials, was appointed locomotive superintendent in April 1847.

As part of the economy measures in May 1848, the board announced that they alone were 'compelled to deny themselves (of) the continued advantage of his services in consequence of the necessity by which they are led to diminish the expenses of working the line'. Martley initially returned to the GWR, and later, in 1860, became locomotive superintendent of the London, Chatham & Dover Railway. Abraham Khlos, who had come over from America with Richard Osborne, and was described as the 'master mechanic', was instructed to take under his charge the superintendence of locomotives, carriages and workshops for 'one year certain'. Khlos did not remain long, as he resigned in May 1849 when the directors endeavoured to reduce his salary from £400 to £300 per annum. The only mention of note regarding his period in office was in January 1849 when he was asked to explain an apparent disparity in locomotive expenses. These varied from 7.264d per mile for *Waterford* to 12.825d for *Glengall*.

As already mentioned, Hemans was appointed engineer-in-chief in 1850 and he appears to have been in overall charge of locomotive matters, including the period of the haulage contract with Dargan. Charles Bagnell was appointed traffic superintendent in April 1852 and was requested to extend his duties to include the locomotive department on the termination of the haulage contract, his salary being increased by £20 a year to compensate. By the end of 1852 it was realised that a separate locomotive superintendent would, once again, be more advantageous and one of the directors, Col Snow, who was going to

Manchester in December 1852 to expedite the completion of locomotives by Messrs Sharp and Fairbairn, was requested to make inquiries regarding a suitable person.

In due course, Thomas Lunt of the Liverpool & Manchester Railway was interviewed by the board at Clonmel on 2 February 1853, his travelling expenses from and to Liverpool being reimbursed. He was appointed to the position of general locomotive, carriage and motive superintendent as from 1 March at a salary of 20 guineas per month. Later, in May 1854, the board agreed to pay £75 for the removal of Lunt and his family from Liverpool. His salary was increased in July 1856 to £280, to include all claims for services and travelling expenses over the line. Problems began to emerge towards the end of 1856 when complaints were made of a great number of failures and breakages in the locomotives, Lunt being instructed to prepare a detailed report. He was also censured for having, on his own responsibility, returned a cylinder from locomotive No 13 to Sharp, Stewart & Co.

Lunt was given three months' notice in December to discontinue his services. In January 1857 he was once again called on to report on the locomotives. When a driving wheel came off an engine in February, Lunt was informed that he would have received the 'severe censure of the Board were he not now leaving the line'. On his departure, and despite the criticisms recently levelled against him, Lunt was presented with a silver breakfast plate set as a testimony of 'the directors' high appreciation of his skill, ability and unassuming upright character'. In March, he requested a testimonial and six months' salary; he was given the testimonial and a sum of £30 to enable him to remove his family.

Jonathan Pim, the son of the late James Pim, secretary of the D&KR, was appointed locomotive superintendent in January 1857.

0-6-0 No 226, ex No 7 *Wasp*. Delivered from Kitson in July 1888 and named *Progress*, she was rebuilt from an 0-4-2 in 1893, receiving her new name at the same time. Ian Allan Library

Pim does not appear to have distinguished himself and during his tenure complaints were again made regarding the state of the motive power. Pim departed in October 1861, his replacement, Martin Atock, being appointed as from 1 November at a salary of £300, to include travelling expenses, a cottage also being provided for him at Limerick at a nominal rent of £1 per month. On his appointment, he was informed that the whole of his time was to be devoted to the company's service. Atock was born in Preston on 3 May 1834, his family later moving to Stratford where his father, George, whose surname was spelt Attock, became carriage and wagon superintendent of the Eastern Counties Railway, which became a constituent part of the Great Eastern Railway in 1862. Martin in due course, also joined the ECR, and served two years as a draughtsman with Messrs Mather & Platt of Manchester. He married on 16 August 1859 and moved to Limerick two years later, apparently as the result of a recommendation from Joseph Armstrong of the GWR.

Although Atock is better known for his long association with the MGWR between 1872 and 1900, where he introduced the principles of standardisation and regular replacement of locomotives and rolling stock, he did introduce a period of 11 years' stability to the Waterford company. During his tenure a reading room was provided for locomotive staff at Limerick. Atock resigned at the end of March 1872. It was reported that the men of the locomotive department had got up a present for Atock, an action, which for some unknown reason, was resented by the board, who stopped the men's wages.

Advertisements were placed in various newspapers and trade journals offering a salary of £400 per annum. In May, Mark Wardle was appointed on six months' trial, but when he officially became locomotive superintendent in November 1872 his salary was fixed at £300! Wardle did not remain long, the board agreeing in February 1873 to accept his resignation owing to ill health. Robert Andrews was duly appointed in March 1873 but his stay was little longer and no more distinguished. Robert Armitage, late of the Dublin & Meath Railway, became locomotive superintendent in June 1875; again he remained for only a short while, just two and a half years. Armitage was cautioned in November 1877 for his general inattention to his duties and was informed that any future dereliction would not be passed over. He was also informed that he was expected to attend the works at the same hours as his men. Some consideration was given to the appointment of a superintendent to take charge of carriage and wagon matters, the subject being discussed at some length and various names selected for further consideration. It also appeared that Armitage may have had a hand in the removal of Joseph Myles, the works foreman, it being ordered that he be at once reinstated. Armitage, obviously smarting at being taken to task, announced his resignation in December 1877, this being accepted and he was given a cheque in respect of his salary to 31 March 1878. Myles was now instructed to take temporary charge of the locomotive department, Thomas Nunan taking over the wagon shop 'pending a permanent appointment of a Superintendent of the Wagon Department'.

Edward Barry was appointed locomotive superintendent in March 1878 at a salary of £18 4s 0d per month, with house, coal and light. Myles was censured in May 1878 for the dirty and dangerous state of engine No 4 under repairs and informed that if this occurred again he would be instantly dismissed; however, at the same meeting it was decided to dispense with his services at once, he being paid four weeks' wages (£12) in lieu of notice. Another victim about this time was Mr Kelly, the chief clerk in the locomotive department, who resigned when he was refused an increase in pay. Nunan's position in charge of the wagon department seems to have come to an end with Barry's arrival.

Barry's stay at Limerick was also short-lived as advertisements were placed early in 1882 seeking the services of a qualified locomotive superintendent. Four applicants were considered early in July, viz Henry Appleby, John J. Johnstone locomotive superintendent of the Cork & Bandon Railway, Charles Clifford, district locomotive superintendent of the GNR(I) at Dublin and a Mr Raven. It was originally thought that this might have been Vincent Litchfield Raven, later to become the chief mechanical engineer of the North Eastern Railway in June 1910. Following interviews, Appleby was offered the appointment at a salary of £500 per annum, plus firing, gas and water and travelling expenses. Barry was offered the choice of three months' pay in lieu of notice or the position of locomotive foreman at Waterford at £2 per week. He chose the former option.

Henry Appleby was born in Sunderland in 1837 and appears to have commenced his career with Robert Stephenson & Co in Newcastle as it is reported that he accompanied *North Star* to Swindon, with a reputation for being able 'to eat a duck at one sitting'. At Swindon he became apprenticed to Daniel Gooch and was soon put in charge of locomotive matters at Chippenham. He was for a time locomotive superintendent (and general manager) of the West Cornwall Railway, moving from there to become divisional superintendent of the Manchester Sheffield & Lincolnshire Railway at Sheffield. Finally, before moving to Limerick, he went to the Monmouthshire Railway & Canal Co. Appleby's career at Limerick effectively came to an end in July 1888 when he was thrown from a jaunting car in the course of a directors' inspection of their line, receiving serious injuries. As a result, he spent lengthy periods off work, his place being increasingly taken by his assistant, John George Robinson. Appleby retired early in 1889 and died in England in December of that year at the early age of 52, leaving a wife and eight children.

Robinson's career has been well documented elsewhere (see Bibliography) and does not require repeating here. Suffice to say that he had been persuaded to come to Limerick from the GWR at Bristol by Appleby in 1884. He remained in charge of locomotive matters until he tendered his resignation in June 1900 to take up an appointment as chief mechanical engineer of the Great Central Railway and an even more successful career. His place at Limerick was taken on a temporary basis to the end of 1900 by his assistant William Gadd, who had also come from Swindon, where he had been a draughtsman. It is not known exactly when Gadd came to Limerick, but he was certainly there in June 1886 as works manager, when Appleby sought an increase in his salary.

Richard Keane and Thomas Sexton

Although not in the category of officers of the company, it is worth mentioning two particular individuals: one who left a legacy of his employment on the W&LR, the other a young boy employed in the office at Waterford and who later went on to greater things. The former gentleman is of course none other than Richard Keane, who was first employed in 1848. In March 1854 it was ordered that Richard Keane Snr be fined the amount of his suspended wages and moved to another station; it was also ordered that Richard Keane Jnr be dismissed. The minute makes no reference as to where Keane was employed at that time or whether this sanction resulted in a move to Limerick Junction. To this day, however, the name of Keane's Points Junction just outside Limerick Junction, is a lasting reminder of this employee.

Keane had two daughters and he applied to the board for cloaks for them, which were granted; he also applied for and obtained free passes to enable them to travel to and from the Tipperary market. Jacob, the traffic manager, suggested to the board in April 1863 that as Keane was working an 18-hour day, he was entitled to a rate of 20s a week. He queried, however, whether in the event of an accident occurring, this long day would be prejudicial. The alternative was to employ two men, day and night, at 12s 6d per week each. The board deferred a decision. Later, in March 1871, Keane's wages were increased by 1s to 18s 6d. The new traffic manager, Isaac Banks, proposed in March 1874 that Keane be allowed his new cottage at Limerick Junction free of rent, as being an old servant. This argument did not impress the directors who ordered that he pay the same as the other men. Banks tried again in February of the following year, suggesting Keane pay 1s a week, the board asking double this amount. Richard Keane died on 26 December 1877.

Thomas Sexton was born in 1848 and received his education at Mount Sion Schools in Waterford. He was only 12 years of age when he applied for a position as clerk in the secretary's office of the W&LR. Of 30 youths who had applied, Sexton was by far the youngest, yet he obtained first place and he remained with the company until 1867. He subsequently established a debating society in the city and worked for the *Waterford News* and other local papers. He then moved to Dublin where he joined the staff of *The Nation*, becoming a leader writer for that paper. In 1879, Sexton became involved in the Land League movement and in time he stood for Parliament, serving Co Sligo from 1880 to 1886 and North Kerry from 1892 to 1896. He was voted an honorary freedom of Waterford, later becoming Lord Mayor of Dublin in 1888. He was chairman of *Freemans Journal* from 1892 to 1912 and also of Boland's Ltd and other companies. He served on the Irish Railways Commission between 1906 and 1910. One can but wonder where Sexton's career might have gone had he remained with the W&LR!

Chapter Nineteen

CATERING, BOOKSTALLS AND STEAMER SERVICES

Although the company did not provide catering facilities on its trains, it did operate a number of refreshment rooms at various stations. Clonmel appears to have been the first such, with a plan for the proposed premises being submitted to the board in March 1852. Some discussion ensued as to its location, six months elapsing before it was decided that it should be erected on the town (up) side. The refreshment room at Clonmel was opened in August of the following year, the rent being fixed at £30 per annum; it was stipulated that it was to be closed following the arrival of the last train at night, and was not to be opened until the arrival of the first morning train. No mention is made of the identity of the first tenant, although it was most likely a Miss Brennan who was in charge in February 1855, at which date she was approached regarding the provision of hot tea for enginemen and guards at Clonmel, a suggestion put forward by the locomotive superintendent, Thomas Lunt.

A year later, the rent was reduced to £20 a year, to include gas lighting, this alteration to take effect from 25 March. It seems to have been assumed that Miss Brennan might not consent to this figure as provision was made to advertise for another party to have charge of the refreshment room, which from then on was to be closed each night at 21.00, and the gas shut off at the same hour. Miss Brennan remained in charge, but in July 1858 Abraham Stephens introduced notice of a motion to terminate her tenancy of the refreshment rooms at Clonmel and Waterford. In December, the subject was raised again but the secretary reported that he was unable to trace any copy of the notice in question. Miss Brennan herself advised early in January 1859 that she had never received notice to quit, but agreed to put herself in the company's hands. At a meeting on 26 January, it was resolved that Miss Brennan be informed that the privilege of selling books at the company's stations be surrendered, and also that the board was willing to receive proposals for the two refreshment rooms. We shall return to the question of book sales a little later.

The refreshment room at Waterford was short-lived. A Mr Wade wrote in March 1857 offering to erect or rent a refreshment room

there, Smith being requested to carry out plans dated January 1855 for such a room. January 1859 found Miss Brennan in charge, she being removed at the end of April 1861. The decision had been taken in July 1860 to dispense with these rooms, and it was not until January 1896 that a Mr C. Devane proposed the establishment of refreshment rooms at Waterford once again, it being stated in response that no room could be found. While on the subject of catering at Waterford, it should be mentioned that a Mrs Hurley applied in August 1866 for some remuneration for providing luncheon to the directors on the days of meetings, this being declined. She raised the matter again in the following January and it was agreed to give her a gratuity of £1 and to allow her a sum of 1s per week in future.

Reverting to the Clonmel refreshment room we find that Miss Brennan actually remained in charge for the next 20 years. In January 1861, the board made a general order prohibiting the sale of intoxicating liquor, except for wine. This order was apparently ignored and three months' notice was issued for the giving up of the various rooms. It was agreed, however, that Miss Brennan might remain at Clonmel until the licence ran out on 10 October, but she appears to have agreed not to sell spirits in the interim. Although she lost the tenancy of the Waterford premises in April 1861, a new agreement was signed for Clonmel in September, the rent remaining at £20 per annum, but the tenant was obliged to find her own gas and coal; two months later the rent was reduced to £15 per annum. Miss Brennan finally gave up possession of the Clonmel refreshment room in March 1881, the new tenant, a Miss Clancy, taking charge in the following September. Interestingly, and notwithstanding the arrival on the scene of Messrs W. H. Smith & Son in 1860, reference was made as late as March 1880 to bookselling at the Clonmel refreshment rooms. We find Miss Brennan asking for an extension of time for the disposal of books, and, whilst the board advised it could not interfere in the matter, it took it upon itself to allow her up to 1 May to do so.

Limerick refreshment rooms
It is not entirely clear from the company's records when the first refreshment room at

Limerick was opened, but it may well only have dated from the opening of the new terminus in 1858. It was certainly in existence in February 1859 when written proposals from a Miss Tidball were accepted for one year. Complaints were made in the following December that the refreshment room was situated in an 'out of the way' location. The engineer was requested to fit up the existing cloakroom and lost luggage room as refreshment rooms. Mr Jacob suggested to the board in February 1866 that the third class refreshment rooms should be converted into a ladies' waiting room. This alteration, it was stated, would leave another room for the telegraph company and also space for a third class waiting room. The engineer, Tighe, reporting in the following month, suggested that the directors should view the premises and thereafter decide, but nothing further was done in this context.

A Mrs Ward was the tenant at Limerick in September 1868, at which time she offered a rent of £15 per annum, finding coal and gas and excluding the sale of spirituous liquor. The board decided to seek £20 which was accepted, the new term to commence on 1 January 1869. We do not know when Mrs Ward vacated the position, but in December 1881 the engineer was instructed to submit plans for alterations, and arrangements were to be made for the signing of a caretaker's agreement. The annual rent was increased about this time to £40. It was reported in August 1883 that Patrick Fitzgerald, a guard on the line, had applied for the tenancy, but it was decided not to disturb the existing tenant, whose name was not recorded.

What we do know is that the secretary drew attention to 'the present tenancy' being terminated on 16 May 1885 and orders were given for an advertisement to be placed for a replacement. However, in the same month it was stated that Mrs Moloney had applied to be continued as the tenant of the third class refreshment room during the alteration of the other room, this request being declined. She later sought compensation for the termination of her tenancy, but this also was declined. By the end of May 1885, Charles McKern had been appointed to the position at a rent of £100 per annum — it is not made clear whether he was to be responsible for both refreshment rooms or simply the 'other room', presumably the first and second class one. It was made clear to McKern that the company's servants were not to be supplied with refreshments. It was also noted that the rooms had been painted and decorated and a new oven provided.

It was reported in June 1887 that an amount of £25 was owing from McKern (also occasionally spelt Mackern) in respect of rent due to 30 June. There were public rumours circulating that he had left the country but the business was still being carried on. It is not clear what happened to him, but in November of that year we find Mrs McKern being allowed a rebate of £20 on the current year's rent owing to the state of the business, a similar reduction being made to her in respect of each of the following three years. She wrote to the board in August 1891 intimating her intention to surrender the tenancy; at the same time an application was received from Miss Clancy, already mentioned in connection with Clonmel refreshment room. Miss Clancy in turn sought a reduction of the rent in April 1892, but this was declined.

Miss Clancy appears to have resigned the position following this as it was noted in February 1893 that the tenant, Mrs Hanratty, had died, the position being granted to her husband. The last reference to the refreshment rooms at Limerick was in October 1898 when a letter was submitted from Mrs Hanratty (one assumes that Mr Hanratty had married again!) asking that the premises be leased to her, but this was turned down.

Foynes and Ennis

Two refreshment rooms were inherited from worked companies, those at Foynes and Ennis. The former was in existence in September 1858 when a Mr Michael Walsh applied to be the named tenant there without rent. He was awarded the tenancy later in the month, but he had to agree to pay £20 per annum for the privilege. An application in the following January for a free pass over the L&FR system was turned down and, in fact, led to all other free tickets being withdrawn. A Mr Blackwell is briefly mentioned as tenant in July 1877, but efforts were made two months later to buy him out with a goodwill offer of £10. This was declined, and Blackwell wrote in October stating he would 'hold to his rights in respect of the rooms held by him at Foynes, and claiming £4 per annum for nine years for room occupancy by Guard'. This latter is an apparent reference to the provision of accommodation for the guard based at Foynes, this being a Mr Shanahan in July 1877.

Blackwell was issued with a notice to quit in January 1878, but he was still there in April of the following year when a decree for ejectment was obtained against him. At the same time, Blackwell made a counter-claim

for £30 for the accommodation already referred to above. A Miss Ellen O'Connell took over in May 1879 at a rent of £25 per annum. She remained at Foynes until her death in October 1897, her replacement being a Mrs Elizabeth O'Meara, who sought an improvement in the sanitary arrangements, but the directors declined to spend money in the absence of an increased rent.

As regards Ennis, there is a brief reference in the L&ER minutes to an application being made for the tenancy of the refreshment room there from a Miss Jane Molloy, but there the matter rests and it was not until 10 years later that Miss K. Tidball made a further application. In making this, Miss Tidball commented that 'it is the usual custom to give a refreshment room free for the first year'. This did not cut any ice with the directors. A reference in the works committee minutes for April 1873 refers to the establishment of refreshment rooms there, suggesting either that the previous rooms had been closed or converted into other use. A Mr Wardle took the tenancy in August 1874, being followed by his wife's niece, Mrs Shaw, in November 1879. At this time, she was paying a monthly rent of £2 10s 0d.

In September 1881 the aforementioned Miss Clancy applied for the tenancy, it being agreed that she occupy the rooms at the same weekly rent as Miss Brennan — presumably the same person who had given up the tenancy at Clonmel earlier in the same year. It is not clear when the latter took over these rooms from Mrs Shaw. It would appear that tenants did not generally remain long at Ennis as only two and a half years later, a Mrs T. O'Hanlon was in charge. However, she and her husband remained there for some time, a reference being made in October 1891 to a notice posted on the door of the rooms by O'Hanlon to the effect that the company had prevented him from selling drink. This led to O'Hanlon's departure; his place was taken by a Mrs Sarah Reade, who was still there in May 1893, when her rent was reduced from £70 to £50 per annum. It would seem by this time that refreshment rooms generally were not attracting a great deal of custom.

Listowel, Kilkenny and aspirations

Refreshment rooms were in use at Listowel from the opening of the North Kerry line, but in February 1886 there was a memorial from the pig buyers of Limerick asking for their continuance. This was at the period when the two companies were at odds over virtually every item conceivable, and the board replied to the effect that it would endeavour to induce the joint committee to continue the rooms. This appears to have had some success as the traffic manager was instructed to re-admit the tenant, a Mrs Lehane, as a weekly caretaker. She however declined in the following December to sign

an agreement unless the rent for the period from 1 May was cancelled. This led, in late 1887, to the rooms being again closed and further memorials from the pig, cattle and butter buyers in Limerick to the company. On this occasion, the board refused to alter its decision, a request from a Mr Potter in July 1897 for a room to supply refreshments to tourists also being turned down as the facility was considered unnecessary.

The only involvement the company had with refreshment rooms at Kilkenny was during the period of the lease of the W&KR between 1860 and 1867. During part of this period the refreshment rooms were in the charge of a Mr Wade, who in November 1866 sought the customary reduction in rent, due to a falling off in receipts resulting from alterations to the station. It was noted that 'Mr Wade always complains of excessive rent', and it was agreed that if he paid arrears due, then the rent might be reduced, otherwise the secretary was to make arrangements to take up possession. At different periods, requests were made for refreshment facilities to be provided at various other locations around the system. These included Birdhill in 1889, and Newcastle West in 1895, both being declined.

Advertising and bookstalls

As early as September 1857, Messrs W. H. Smith & Son made an approach offering to rent book stands at different stations along with the right of advertising for five years at £80 per annum. This correspondence appears to have been drawn out and it was not until July 1860 that a five-year agreement was signed, payment, however, to be at the rate of £100 per annum. This agreement was renewed in 1865, but by January 1869 Smith's protested strongly at any suggestion that it should increase the rent. This refusal to pay was renewed in January 1870 on the grounds that the business had 'been going back recently'. No doubt realising that there might not be too many offers, it was decided to renew the agreement for a further 12 months at the existing rent, instructions being given for advertisements to be placed three months before its expiry. In the event, a fresh agreement for five years was concluded in January 1871 at £110 per annum, and apparently extended for a further three years.

When Smith's refused to pay an increased rent in January 1878, it was granted a period of three months to remove their property. A Mr J. W. Cooper of Clonmel tendered in May, offering a three-year contract, which was accepted. It was agreed that any parcels in connection with his business would be carried free, and following further correspondence, the lease was extended to five years and a free pass was granted for 12 months to one of Cooper's workmen in connection with the erection and adjustment of show-frames. W. H. Smith & Sons was threatened with legal action about this time, when it was reported that it had erected a bookstall on the Cork platform at Limerick. It responded by stating that it had entered into a new agreement with the GS&WR. Whilst the chairmen of the two companies met in October 1878, this is the last reference to the matter and it is unclear whether the W&LR view prevailed that the entire station was its property.

Cooper sought a reduction in his rent in July 1880, his request being declined. He continued on until May 1884 when it was ordered that vacant possession be taken and communications opened with Smith's. The latter agreed to pay £100 per annum for the Waterford company's own lines, plus £25 for Waterford station. The question of the branch lines was left open for the approval of the individual companies. Agreements were in due course concluded with the A&EJR, A&TR, L&KR and the R&NJR.

W. H. Smith & Sons made arrangements early in 1886 for the transfer of their entire Irish operation and liabilities to Charles Eason & Sons and it was agreed to the transfer of seven contracts. Eason had previously been Smith's manager in Ireland. Arrangements were made for the renewal of these various agreements in 1890, but in the interim the company received an offer from the Automatic Library Co, which the directors considered most reasonable. They therefore approached Messrs Eason in September 1891 advising of this increased offer. They were reluctant to substantially increase their offer and sought an agreement for a minimum of three years, the company responding to the effect that it was unhappy with the service provided, which was described as being conducted in an inefficient manner. Despite this, Eason & Sons made an offer in December 1892 of £200 for all advertising spaces on the system for five years as from 1 January 1893. When the contract came up for reconsideration in December 1897 only one tender was received in response to the advertisement, that from Eason's. The tender, at £400 per annum for the entire system, was accepted for five further years, and this contract still being in force in January 1901 was therefore assigned to the GS&WR.

Steamer services

Steamer services can be categorised under three distinct headings, viz cross-channel, the River Suir and the River Shannon, the latter subdivided into river and estuary services. The cross-channel services were, of course, never operated by the W&LR, but as they formed an important part of the system's traffic arrangements and, more importantly, were the principal reason why the GWR maintained a long-standing alliance with the company, some discussion of the subject is warranted.

On 30 June 1938 'J15' No 118 is seen shunting vacuum braked vans, on the Limerick-bound curve at Limerick Junction. This locomotive, built in 1891, was one of the very last of this class to survive, being withdrawn in the mid-1960s. By then it had been rebuilt with a superheated boiler but was paired with an older type of tender with outside springs.
H. C. Casserley

Cross-channel services from the port of Waterford served Bristol, Liverpool, Fishguard (from 1906), Aberdovey (in 1887/88 only) and Milford Haven. The latter port was known as Milford Haven until 1859 when it was briefly altered to its more correct name of Neyland. By the end of 1859, the GWR/ South Wales Railway had decided to rename it New Milford, a title it retained until after Fishguard was opened in 1906. Although Waterford services to and from Bristol operated for more than 100 years they did not have any connection with the railway.

Passenger services between Waterford and Milford Haven appear to have commenced in the mid-18th century. Arthur Young, writing in 1780, referred to a rather unpleasant experience in 1776 on the mail packet brig *Countess of Tyrone*, and again two years later when he and his family had to wait 24 days before they set sail for Milford. At that time, the vessels were using the port of Passage East. Bill Irish (see Bibliography) reports that seven sailing packets operated on the route in 1815. The Waterford packet station was moved to Dunmore East about 1818 and five years later the Post Office took control of the mail packet service. The first paddle steamers entered service in 1824 with the arrival from the Holyhead–Howth service of the PS *Ivanhoe*. Built in Greenock in 1820, she was purchased by the Postmaster General in late 1823, and was soon joined by three other vessels. PS *Ivanhoe* was returned to the Holyhead service in 1827. Her replacement, the PS *Sybil*, is reputed to have made the crossing in a record time of 8hr 13min.

Between 1837 and 1848 the Admiralty operated the mail packet service on the Waterford route on behalf of the Postmaster General. Operations ceased in the latter year and were resumed only in 1856 with the completion and opening of the SWR to Neyland on 15 April. This new service was initially operated twice weekly by the PS *Malakhoff*, a 194ft-long iron paddle steamer built in Millwall in 1851 as the *Baron Osy*; she was renamed *Malakhoff* to commem-

orate her service carrying troops and materials in connection with the Crimean War. By August 1856, a second vessel had been put on the route, enabling a thrice-weekly service. This was the SS *City of Paris* built in Greenwich in 1850. Journey time was about nine hours each way, and the service was operated by Messrs Ford & Jackson of London on behalf of the SWR.

It is interesting to note that as late as November 1853, the W&LR directors were advocating the revival of the mail packet service between Waterford and Milford, and to further this aim they were prepared to assist in the provision of a line of railway to Dunmore. Within two months of this, however, the secretary of the SWR was in correspondence with the company regarding a proposed service between Waterford and Milford. In April 1854, a report was received from the London committee of the W&LR in which it was pointed out that three steamers would be required. Annual working expenses were to be in the region of £40,000, of which the company's proportion would be one-fifth, or £8,000, per annum.

At the end of January 1859 it was reported that the PS *Malakhoff* had taken 36 hours in making a passage, having been detained for 24 hours off Milford. It was stated that the ship was under repair, presumably having incurred sea damage during the crossing. The charges levied by Ford & Jackson were 12s 6d cabin and 7s 6d steerage, while the Admiralty had charged 30s single saloon and 5s steerage; the reason for the discrepancy in the cabin/saloon fares is not known. Passengers normally left London at 09.15, the steamer leaving Milford at 19.45 with a scheduled arrival in Waterford at 05.00 the next morning. As third class passengers were not accommodated on the 09.15 from London, they were forced to leave the capital at 06.00. On the Irish side, the Limerick train departed at 06.00 and arrived at its destination four hours later. Only those who had a necessity to travel would have made such a journey!

Opposition from Cork

The W&LR directors learned with some distress in June 1859 that the service of steamers which operated between Milford and Cork was to be increased to a daily frequency without prior consultation with them. This service had opened in September 1856 with a twice-weekly service and was also being operated by Ford & Jackson on behalf of the GWR/SWR. The secretary was authorised to obtain an explanation, the SWR secretary simply confirming the commencement of the daily service as from 15 June. In response the W&LR threatened to withdraw from the guarantee on the Waterford service. When the SWR wrote in April 1860 claiming £266 7s 0d as the Waterford company's proportion of the deficiency on the boats for the half-year ended December 1859, the W&LR protested as it considered the deficiency was caused by the running of the rival Cork boats. A further shock came in September 1860 when it was announced that the SWR intended to put boats of superior power and accommodation on the Cork station. However, a W&LR traffic committee minute of 1 July 1861 states that the Cork opposition boats had been taken off, as confirmed by Captain Jackson.

The operation of the Milford service appears to have run fairly smoothly from this time, the W&LR being called upon to pay its proportion of the operating deficit in each half-year. In February 1872, the GWR took over the steamers from Ford & Jackson and continued the working itself. By this time the latter firm had added three more paddle steamers to its fleet, namely the PS *Vulture*, PS *South of Ireland* and the PS *Great Western*. The *Vulture* had been built in 1864 and purchased by the firm in 1870. These three vessels together with the PS *Malakhoff* were acquired by the GWR, the latter vessel being withdrawn in 1874. Through fares between London and Waterford were 46s, 35s 6d and 20s single, respectively for first, second and third classes. The vessels departed Milford immediately on the arrival of the 16.50 train from London, Paddington, and arrived in Waterford to connect with the 10.00 departure for Limerick. In the opposite direction, the boat departed from Adelphi Wharf at 16.00 daily, Sundays excepted.

The traffic manager reported in August 1875 that an opposition steamer, the *Edith*, had commenced running fortnightly between Limerick and Liverpool and was diverting traffic. He was authorised to allow a rebate of 5s per wagon of livestock to meet the opposition. In April of the following year a prospectus was issued for a new company which proposed to open a service between Waterford and Holyhead. One might have thought that loyalty to the GWR, with whom a traffic agreement had been finalised in

April 1872, would have seen this scheme opposed. On the contrary, the traffic manager was instructed to meet with the L&NWR to obtain its views. Following this meeting, arrangements were made to give every facility and assistance to develop traffic by the new route. The scheme was however short-lived as the L&NWR announced in August 1876 that, bearing in mind the state of the accommodation in Holyhead Harbour, it did not feel able to cater for any additional sailings to or from that port.

A new wharf

Details of the extension of the railway to the east of the bridge and the construction of the new North Wharf have already been related in Chapter Seven. It was proposed in March 1878 that one-third of the new quay should be made public and be subject to the control and management of the Corporation. When the latter body came to inspect the facilities, it declined to take them over, alleging that it never contemplated it would be a wooden jetty, apart from the fact that there appeared to be several defects in the construction of the quay. In March 1879, the traffic manager, Roberts, was authorised to carry out the needful arrangements for the conduct of traffic in conjunction with the GWR, while Tighe was instructed to erect suitable offices for that company's accommodation and to provide gas lighting. It was reported about this time that James Connington had been appointed piermaster. Agreement was eventually reached with the GWR that as from 1 April 1879 the Milford steamer reaching Waterford on Fridays would, after discharging her cargo at Adelphi Wharf (on the south side of the river, at the east end of Custom House Quay), go over to the Railway Wharf and start from there on Sundays. In addition, on one day per week, a cattle steamer would sail from the Railway Wharf. The W&LR undertook to pay the relevant bridge tolls, and advised both the Harbour Board and the Corporation of the revised arrangements.

By January 1882, there were two morning sailings from the North Wharf, on Tuesdays and Thursdays, the GWR agreeing to the Waterford company's proposals for an equitable division of the traffic carried by these boats. It would appear that approaches had been made to the GWR towards the end of 1883 for the provision of a daily steamer service from the north side of the river. In May 1884 the W&LR secretary was instructed to place an advertisement seeking tenders for such a service. Initially, only one reply was received, from Messrs James Hay & Sons of Glasgow, seeking further information. The GWR took exception to the advertisement and advised that it was 'postponing arrangements for sending daily steamers to the 'North Wharf'. Later in June, Hay & Sons advised they could not make a proposal on

the information given them, while Messrs McIver & Co said they had arranged other employment for their boats.

Sir Daniel Gooch wrote in November 1884 advising that the GWR had agreed to send daily steamers to the new wharf to load and discharge through traffic. It was prepared to experiment for three months whereby its steamers, after discharging local Waterford traffic at Adelphi Wharf, would then proceed to the North Wharf to discharge and load through traffic by the railway, and return on the following morning to load local traffic at Adelphi Wharf, from whence they would sail for Milford. Despite this apparent agreement on the matter, daily sailings to and from the North Wharf did not commence operating until 31 May 1893.

In the interim, the GWR proposed in January 1886, that the Sunday morning sailing should be discontinued, an action strongly deplored by the W&LR. The protests were to no avail and the service was withdrawn, the GWR still declining to resume it as late as May 1891. As a consequence, the traffic manager reported that arrangements had been made with the Waterford Steamship Co to commence a sailing from Waterford to Liverpool on the first Sunday in June, the W&LR giving a modest subsidy of £5 per trip for three months.

Cambrian intervention

It was reported in August 1886 that the secretary and engineer of the Cambrian Railways had had an interview with the Waterford board with a view to introducing a morning steamer service between Waterford and Aberdovey. This would be of some advantage to the W&LR as it could provide it with better and faster access to the Midland markets. An agreement was reached with the Cambrian early in 1887, drawing an angry response from the GWR at admitting 'the new company to the South of Ireland'. Despite this rebuke, a twice-weekly service for passengers, livestock and goods commenced on 19 April 1887, being operated by the SS *Liverpool*. This was a Sligo-based steamer originally built in Glasgow in 1864, and had been chartered in 1877 to work between Dublin and Barrow, on which service she remained for about a year.

After some six months, the SS *Liverpool* was replaced by the former Belfast Steamship Company's SS *Magnetic*. The service, which was sponsored by the Cambrian, was actually operated by the Waterford & Aberdovey Steamship Co. The main thrust of the operation was to carry livestock, it being reported that the cattle space on the *Magnetic* was lit by electric light. The saloon fare was 10s single, while for 5s intending passengers could travel steerage on the *Liverpool* or second cabin on the *Magnetic*. The GWR continued to object to the service, claiming it was in contravention of the terms

Limerick Junction station showing a Limerick train in the bay platform at right headed by GSR No 306, 23 April 1955. On the left are main lines to and from Dublin and Cork. R. M. Casserley

of the 1872 agreement. Nevertheless it continued to operate until 1 December 1888.

A further opposition service was reported in June 1894 when the traffic manager submitted a letter from the Manchester Ship Canal Co regarding the use of a berth at the North Wharf. The service apparently started up about this time as two months later the BoT submitted complaints from Manchester traders as to through rates and diversion of traffic. It is not known how long this service operated but it appears to have been short-lived.

Reference has already been made to the steamers which operated the Milford service in the early days. Following the take-over of the service by the GWR in 1872, three iron paddle steamers of identical design were put in hand at Renfrew. These were the PS *Milford* (1873), PS *Limerick* (1874) and the PS *Waterford* (1874), which were described as being good sea boats, remaining on the station until the turn of the century. The *Milford* was badly damaged following an epic 40-hour crossing in December 1900 and was withdrawn shortly afterwards and broken up. The last to go was the *Waterford*, which was withdrawn in 1905.

Brief details have been quoted of journey times in the 1860s. By the end of the WL&WR era, trains departed from Paddington at 18.10, arriving in New Milford at 01.50 with the boat leaving at 02.25 and arrival in Waterford at 08.10. The eastbound sailing departed Waterford at 21.00, the London train leaving New Milford at 06.00. The opening of the Rosslare route in 1906 saw the Waterford steamer service transfer to Fishguard on the Welsh side. Overall, a saving of about four hours could be made by using the Rosslare boat and, of course, the sea crossing was considerably shorter.

River Suir services at Waterford

The opening of the railway brought the problem of transferring goods and passengers across the river at Waterford, where the toll bridge had been opened in 1793. The Bridge Commissioners suggested in December 1855 that the railway company should pay £200 per annum for working its boats under the bridge. The W&LR response was to authorise its solicitor to take Counsel's Opinion on whether the Bridge Commissioners had authority to enforce a payment for the company's boats taking goods across the river and under the bridge for loading vessels going to England. Supposing the commissioners did once have the right, had they not lost it by their failure to exercise it for the past 20 years? In addition to goods, the W&LR had been using the PS *Undine* to carry passengers free of charge across the river. This latter service was short-lived as the bridge owners successfully sued the company for interfering with their right to levy tolls. The *Undine*, which had originally been built in London in 1847, was in fact sold to a Mr Moore for £750 in June 1856.

The conveyance of goods across the river continued, however, for some time after this. In September 1857, Mr T. C. Grubb of Carrick offered three lighters at £45 each, this offer being declined. In June of the following year, the whole question of carrying goods across the river was further considered when the traffic manager suggested that such an arrangement be stopped as, in his view, it was a far from efficient way of dealing with it. Delays were frequently experienced waiting for tides, and the operation was largely dependent on the boatmen for their services. Neither the company nor the public were happy with the existing arrangements. Payne recommended advertising for a party who would convey the goods with a steamer or carts at a rate not exceeding 1s per ton. Such an arrangement would bring about savings in wages of almost £14 per week. Payne's suggestion was acceded to and it was agreed to seek a competent person.

It would appear that nobody was found to undertake the work as in November 1858 the engineer, Smith, recommended the use of a steam tug in lieu of a boat service, he being requested to obtain an estimate for such a boat to replace the lighters then in use. In December, Smith was authorised to treat for the hire of a likely boat, reserving an option to purchase same if found satisfactory. In February 1859, a Mr Whyte of Glasgow was asked if he would send his tugboat to Waterford for a three months' trial, he to provide a crew. The terms offered by Whyte proved to be too high — £28 per week for four months guaranteed — and the offer was declined. In May, it was reported that of the six river boats at Waterford, one was condemned while the remaining five were in bad order. Smith was ordered to repair five and to sell the sixth. Pim, the locomotive superintendent, visited Glasgow on several occasions over the following six months and inspected various vessels on offer, none proving suitable.

In November 1860, it was decided to advertise for boats to carry about 60 tons. Messrs Penrose of Waterford offered a new 45ton lighter for £120, while a Mr Doherty offered two for £180. Mr Robinson reported on iron boats likely to be had cheap and it was ordered that they be inspected by John Horn, who was the manager (and a marine engineer) of the Neptune Ironworks. There is no reference to any of the boats actually being purchased or of Horn's report. By October 1865, the traffic manager was advocating that the three iron and two wooden boats should receive a complete overhaul. As one or two new boats were by now required, Jacob also suggested purchasing at least one from Messrs Malcomson. Instead, it was decided to hire one new boat and have the iron boats repaired one at a time at the Neptune Works.

A tug is obtained

In October 1870 Horn (whether senior or junior we do not know, for John Horn retired some time during 1870 and was replaced by his son Andrew) offered the services of the steam tug *Seagull* free if the company would maintain her in repair and allow her to be used for towing coal ships and boats to and from Portlaw. The board decided instead to try to arrange a purchase of the vessel. The SS *Seagull* had been constructed in Waterford in the Neptune Ironworks shipyard in 1861. She was 60ft long, had a 10ft beam, and drew a 7ft draught. It was reported in November that the company's new tug had collided with and damaged the schooner *Victory*, compensation being paid to the latter's captain. A sum of £500 was paid for the *Seagull* in December 1870. Two iron boats, costing £154 15s 0d, were obtained from Malcomson in the following March. The *Seagull* was in the news again in April 1871 when it was reported that damage had occurred to two vessels while being towed; orders were then given to discontinue towing.

The Harbour Commissioners were approached in January 1877 with a request for additional mooring chains and a hulk at the Railway Wharf. The commissioners did not consider it needful to supply any hulk and fixed stage except the hulk *Concordia* as she was deemed sufficient for foreign traders going to and from the wharf. Apart from this, the commissioners advised that the cost of keeping that part of the port in fair working order was far in excess of dues derived from it. They had just completed dredging the Railway Wharf at a cost of £800, which was more than they had received in tonnage dues in the previous two years.

Andrew Horn prepared a detailed report on the condition of the company's barges at Waterford in June 1877. There were seven in all, four iron and three wooden vessels. Only one of the iron boats was reported to be in sound condition, the other three being fair but rather thin in places. One of the wooden barges was in fair condition, another was in a shaky, worn state, while the third was in danger of losing its rudder. Instructions were given for the necessary repairs to be carried out. An additional barge was obtained from Malcomson in October, at which time a replacement hulk, *Orlando*, was put in place. The GWR quickly pointed out that the *Orlando* was not only unfit for its steamers to go alongside, but it was positively dangerous. The Harbour Commissioners were instructed to remove and replace it. In August 1878, the W&LR purchased the hulk *Hibernia* for £750 and it was placed in position two months later. *Hibernia* was one of four paddle steamers built in Liverpool in 1847/8 for the Chester & Holyhead Railway and operated between Holyhead and Dublin. Her plates were reported in August 1896 to be very worn at the water line and, following an inspection, she was sold to a Mr J. Hurley for £255.

The *Seagull* was reported to have sunk in December 1881, apparently following a collision in the river. She was raised in the following month by the contractors for the railway extension, Messrs Stanford & Falkner, for £45 and beached near the Neptune Ironworks. She was repaired and was still in service in 1915 when a photograph was taken of her. Another tug, the *Kestrel*, was advertised for sale by auction in October 1890 and she was purchased by the W&LR for £120, although boiler repairs costing £95 were necessary within three months of

purchase. In June 1891, hull repairs costing £120 were also necessary. Originally built at Deptford in 1857, *Kestrel* passed into GS&WR ownership and was withdrawn in 1914. Finally, in 1893, the secretary reported the purchase of seven lighters, second-hand, for £533 plus 5% auctioneers' fees.

Shannon services

For about 100 years from 1829, various inshore steamers operated on the Shannon, the longest river in Britain and Ireland. Initially these were operated by the City of Dublin Steam Packet Co but in 1854, William Dargan, who was shortly to become the contractor and a major financial contributor to the L&FR, began operating a rival service. In 1854, Dargan chartered the PS *Koh-I-Norr* to operate on the Shannon estuary. The experiment was however unsuccessful and the vessel foundered off the southwest coast on her return voyage to the Clyde in March 1855. Even before the opening of the L&FR, correspondence was entered into with the CofDSP regarding steam communication between Foynes and Kilrush on the Clare side of the estuary. The Steam Packet Co offered to put its PS *Garryowen* on, but the railway directors were of the opinion that a faster and more commodious boat was required. Her owners advised in August 1857 that they had carried out improvements and this seems to have made her more acceptable to the L&FR. Arrangements were made for her operations to commence as soon as the railway was opened for traffic, hopefully early in October. When the latter was delayed, the CofDSP withdrew its offer, stating that it was not prepared to put her on station at its own risk. If, however, the L&FR would guarantee a fair remuneration, then it would do so.

At the half-yearly meeting in March 1858, the shareholders were told that it was of the utmost importance to the well-working of the railway that a fast and suitable steamer be employed between Foynes and Kilrush. If the CofDSP would not provide one, then advertisements must be placed seeking a suitable vessel. The Steam Packet Co advised in the following month that it was prepared to put the PS *Albert* on at the terms agreed the previous year for the *Garryowen*. It declined to run the latter vessel twice a day as suggested. The directors then inquired if instead of the *Albert*, the Steam Packet Co would put on the PS *Erin-go-bragh*, but this request was also declined. This effectively was the end of contact with the CofDSP which withdrew from the river shortly afterwards.

In the interim, instructions were given to the secretary to arrange to charter a small steam barge belonging to the Grand Canal Co which the previous year had plied between Limerick and Clarecastle. Dargan was approached in May 1858 to see what

might be done to counter the opposition created by the entry to the river trade of the PS *Cardiff Castle*. The CofDSP was now once again asked to place the *Garryowen* on the estuary at an opposition rate of 1s for first class rail and cabin from Limerick to Kilrush, the whole fare to go to the steamer. Otherwise, the railway company would be prepared to charter the *Garryowen* at £10 per week if given over entirely to the company's management. The Steam Packet Co now advised that it could not spare a boat so it was therefore decided to raise a sum of £7,000 to provide a suitable vessel, various people agreeing to subscribe — Dargan himself offering £2,000.

Towards the end of June 1858 the secretary reported that a small steam barge belonging to the MGWR had been chartered for a Foynes to Kildysart service. Barrington, the engineer, was requested to put seats for passengers on deck, the vessel to be placed on station as soon as possible. Patrick O'Driscoll was appointed the company's agent at Kildysart. Within a week, however, Dargan announced that he had purchased the fine steamer PS *Kelpie* to ply between Foynes and Kilrush. Mr Mackie, on behalf of Dargan, submitted a proposed timetable for the steamer, including arrangements for through ticketing (first class only) between Limerick and Kilkee. Conveyance between Kilrush and Kilkee was to be by omnibus or car, the service to commence on Wednesday, 14 July. Application was made to the Board of Public Works for the provision of a barge to be placed as a floating stage at Foynes.

Within a short while of the commencement of the service, Mackie was suggesting that the steamer might run in connection with the 10.30 train from Limerick, rather than that leaving at 06.00 which was not attracting much traffic. This was agreed to, and at the same time it was decided to cease through booking as there were many complaints due to more passengers booking than could be accommodated on the cars.

The L&FR approached the W&LR in August 1858 asking it to remit a sum of £100 per week out of traffic receipts to enable it to meet the expenses of working to Kilrush, the W&LR declining to meet this request. A month later it was agreed to make fortnightly payments, but only against actual expenses. When the MGWR steam barge No 2 was returned in October following 12 weeks' hire, and as she had not actually operated for more than five weeks, the company asked the Midland to reduce the account to six weeks' charter. It is not known how successful it was in this quest. It was suggested to Dargan that *Kelpie* should be taken off at the end of October, but he persuaded the company that she should be retained until the end of November. In future years, she was generally withdrawn to Limerick at the end of November.

October 1858 saw the first of many complaints to the Board of Public Works as to the accumulation of mud in the harbour at Foynes. At one stage, the company went so far as to request the local MP to take up the matter in Parliament so that the Government might be aware of the difficulties being encountered. Another complaint related to the difficulties experienced in berthing at Cappa Pier, the harbour for Kilrush, due to the irregular manner in which that pier was allowed to be occupied by the CofDSP vessels. The Board of Public Works stated, however, that it was not possible to advantageously alter the arrangements.

Malcomson takes over

Kelpie resumed the Foynes to Kilrush service on 1 June 1859. For the summer of 1861, Dargan agreed to operate two services, from Foynes to Kilrush and from the latter point to Tarbert, the board agreeing to give him one-quarter of all receipts from through traffic. In 1861, Dargan disposed of his financial holding in the L&FR, amounting to £33,000, to William Malcomson. Malcomson at this time was chairman of the W&LR and was also proprietor of the Waterford Steamship Co. Malcomson became chairman of the L&FR in 1862 and, shortly afterwards, *Kelpie* was sold, and became a blockade runner in the American Civil War, being replaced by Malcomson's own vessels. Malcomson operated this service under the title of the Lower Shannon Steamship Co. Initially, the SS *Erin* was purchased by Malcomson from the Citizens River Steamer Co of Cork to replace *Kelpie*. She remained on the Shannon for about 12 years before going to Waterford. Then, in July 1863, Malcomson announced that a new steamer, the PS *Rosa*, had commenced operations on 19 June. The 130ft long *Rosa* had been launched from Malcomson's Neptune Ironworks at Waterford in the previous May, having cost £4,561. Her engine had come from the old steamer *Duncannon* and had been reconditioned.

In October 1863, the W&LR traffic manager suggested continuing the steamer service through the winter months, running on alternate days to Kilrush. Malcomson advised, however, that other arrangements had been made for the *Rosa* but it was agreed that she should be replaced by the SS *Erin*. In August 1865 it was ordered that Captain Weir of the *Rosa* should wear a blue cap while on duty. This was an idea brought back from one of Malcomson's trips abroad, stationmasters also being obliged to wear special caps as detailed in Chapter Eighteen. Weir had previously captained the *Kelpie*.

Malcomson announced in March 1866 that yet another vessel was to go on the Kilrush service during the summer. This was the PS *Vandaleur*, which had also been built at the Neptune yard. The 156-ton *Vandaleur*, also 130ft in length, was named after a Quaker who introduced the social experiment of co-operative communities into Co Clare in the 1820s. Alongside the *Vandaleur*, the *Rosa* was to operate quay-to-quay from Limerick to Kilrush on alternate days, to help relieve the *Vandaleur*, the inconvenience of the goods traffic. Fares from Limerick to Kilrush were agreed at 4s 6d, 3s 6d and 2s 6d, first, second and third class rail and steamer, and 4s 6d cabin and 2s 6d deck by the direct river steamer. Malcomson agreed to pay the company an additional one-eighth of receipts from the direct service in consequence of its competition with the rail/steamer service.

It would appear that complaints were made about the poor level of service provided by Malcomson's steamers, which led to the Mayor of Limerick, a Mr P. Tait, chartering the PS *Elwy* to run the Limerick to Kilrush route. The competition was short-lived, however, as fares were slashed by the Lower Shannon Steamship Co, in the case of the *Rosa* to 1s cabin and 6d deck. It is hardly surprising that the *Elwy* was gone within weeks! The *Vandaleur* remained on the Shannon estuary until the mid-1870s when she returned to Waterford and was placed on the Waterford to Duncannon run. She was lengthened to 146ft in 1893 and was finally broken up in 1907. The *Rosa* was broken up at Bristol in 1892, having spent 29 years on the Shannon.

Upper Shannon services

It was reported in April 1874 that the secretary of the W&LR and one of the directors, Henry Slattery, had attended a meeting at Killaloe, of proprietors bordering Lough Derg with the object of preventing the navigable waters of the lough being reduced below summer level. The intention of those present was to place steamers on the lake in connection with the W&LR to and from Killaloe. The proprietors agreed to give their cordial support by becoming shareholders in any company formed for the purpose. The hope was that steamers would connect the two railway towns of Killaloe and Banagher.

Shortly after the opening of the Killaloe extension in August 1863 the company had purchased the SS *Lord Lorton*, an ex-MGWR steamer. This vessel was one of four which had been operated between Killaloe and Athlone as part of the rivalry between the MGWR and the GS&WR in the late 1850s. Following the 1860 arbitration between the two companies, the *Lord Lorton* had been transferred briefly to the GS&WR. The W&LR set up a separate company, the Shannon Inland Navigation Co, to operate its shipping services on the River Shannon.

The W&LR ordered a new vessel in May 1880 from Messrs Grendon & Co of Drogheda, the SS *Lady of the Lake* being launched in December of that year. Ownership was immediately transferred to the Shannon Inland Navigation Co. The vessel was scheduled to make a weekly round trip between Killaloe and Portumna and two to Scariff. During the 1880s she was timed to sail shortly after the arrival of the 11.35 train from Limerick and returned to connect with the 15.15 departure from Killaloe landing stage. Single fares from Killaloe to Portumna and Scariff were 2s and 1s respectively. By October 1882, the locomotive superintendent was requesting that the vessel and her engineer be placed under his charge. Appleby reported that *Lady of the Lake* was by then in a bad state of repair, after only two years in service. When further repairs became necessary in July 1886, it was ordered that a full estimate of repairs be submitted before her passenger certificate was renewed. At this time also, a request was made for the provision of three beds and bed clothing for the crew, a request which was granted.

Although questions were raised about disposing of *Lady of the Lake* in 1898, when she was valued by Andrew Horn at £395, she was still in operation during the summer of 1899 and was not finally scrapped until 1910, thus bringing to an end the railway-operated steamer services on Lough Derg.

The coaling stage and jetty beside the River Suir at Waterford on 18 June 1939. On the opposite side of the river is the old Waterford, Dungarvan & Lismore Railway terminus. The vessel at the stage is believed to be the SS *Carrickmore*.
W. A. Camwell/IRRS collection

Appendix A

STATIONS, JUNCTIONS AND SIDINGS

Limerick to Waterford

Miles	Station	Opened	Closed	Water tank gallons	Turn-table ft in	Remarks
0.00	Limerick 2	1858	Open	37,000	45'0"	
0.25	Limerick 1	1848	1858			
0.13	Market Tramway	1864	c1940			
0.37	Denny's Factory	1873	c1931			
0.40	Check Platform	1910	1963			
0.70	Ennis Jct	1859	Open			Munster Fair Siding.
4.17	Killonan	1848	1963			
7.50	Boher	1852	1963			
11.46	Dromkeen	1852	1976			
13.76	Pallas	1848	1963	4,750		
18.35	Oola	1848	1963			
21.33	Milltown Curve	1967	Open			
21.50	Keane's Points	1848	Open			
21.60	Limerick Jct	1848	Open			
24.63	Tipperary	1848	Open	3,550		
26.40	Puddingfield Pit					
29.49	Bansha	1852	1963			
33.15	Cappagh Siding	c1860				
37.60	Caher Abbey Sdg	c1865	1979			Cattle sidings added 1927.
38.26	Cahir	1852	Open	13,400		
49.20	Clonmel	1852	Open	12,850	45'0"	
24.22	Clonmel Jct	1879	1967			
54.00	Ballast Pit	1874				
55.33	Kilsheelan	1873	1963			
62.35	Malcomson's Sdg	c1865	1877			Cotton factory.
63.06	Carrick-on-Suir	1853		13,390		Carrick until 1925.
64.14	Carrick Ballast Pit	c1894				
67.28	Fiddown	1853	1963			
70.03	Grange	1853	1963			
	Rathcurby		1862			Also spelt Rathkirby.
75.44	Dunkitt	1853	1854			
75.78	Newrath Jct	1906	1929			Dates for signal cabin.
76.00	Waterford Newrath	1854	1869			
77.09	Waterford	1864	1906			
77.22	Waterford	1906	Open	23,350	40'0"	Also 36' T.T. between two engine sheds.
	North Wharf	1883	1985			

Limerick to Tralee

Miles	Station	Opened	Closed	Water tank gallons	Turn-table ft in	Remarks
0.45	Check Cabin	1910	Open			
1.00	Foynes Jct	1862	Open			
1.78	Cement Factory Jct	1957	1966			Junction moved to Foynes Jct.
3.00	Cement Factory	1957	Open			
6.40	Fort Etna	1861	1867			
7.26	Patrickswell	c1856	1974			Also spelt Patricks Well.
9.63	Kilgobbin	1917?	1963?			
11.04	Adare	1856	1974			Closed to passengers 1963.
17.27	Ballingrane Jct	1856	1974			Originally named Rathkeale.
19.14	Rathkeale	1866	1963	5,500		
19.75	Enright's Siding	1868	c1917			Renamed Johnstone's Siding.
24.51	Ardagh	1867	1963			
27.26	Newcastle West (R&NJR)	1867	1963		40'0"	
0.00	Newcastle West (L&KR)	1880	1977	9,800	44'0"	Closed to passengers 1963.
6.16	Barnagh	1880	1963	3,630		
10.58	Devon Road	1880	1963			
14.10	Abbeyfeale	1880	1963	3,630		
18.10	Kilmorna	1880	1963			
23.29	Listowel	1880	1977	3,550	40'0"	Closed to passengers 1963.
26.60	Ennismore	1882	1889			Flag station for G. Hewson.
29.18	Ballintogher Sdg		1943			
29.30	County Council Tar Sdg	1955				
29.76	Lixnaw	1880	1974			Closed to passengers 1963.
34.60	Abbeydorney	1880	1974			Closed to passengers 1963.

Miles	Station	Opened	Closed	Water tank gallons	Turn-table ft in	Remarks
38.17	Ardfert	1880	1974			Closed to passengers 1963.
42.58	Kingdom Tubes	1936				
43.01	Tralee (L&KR)	1880	1901	4,790	40'0"	
43.07	End-on Jct with GS&WR	1883				
43.10	Tralee (GS&WR).	1883	Open			Passenger traffic used this stn. From 1901.

Limerick to Sligo

Miles	Station	Opened	Closed	Water tank gallons	Turn-table ft in	Remarks
0.00	Ennis Jct	1859	Open			
3.58	Ardnacrusha Sdg	1928	1980			Refuse siding 1975.
3.73	Longpavement	1859	1963			
6.32	Meelick	1859	1862			
9.60	Cratloe	1859	1963			
12.71	Sixmilebridge	1859	1963			
16.51	Ballycar	1859	1963	930		Also Ballycar & Newmarket.
19.60	Ardsollus & Quin	1859	1963			
23.00	Clarecastle	1859	1963			
24.49	Ennis	1859	Open	17,500	45'0"	T.T. supplied by Isca.
32.37	Crusheen	1869	1963			
36.64	Tubber	1870	1963			
42.20	Gort	1869	1963	4,660		
48.70	Ardrahan	1869	1963			
55.05	Craughwell	1869	1963			
59.69	Athenry (A&EJ Jct)	1869	Open			
60.01	Athenry MGWR	1869	Open			MGWR
60.14	Athenry (A&T Jct)	1860				
61.21	Athenry Ballast Pit	c1907	c1914			
64.00	Belville Sdg	c1935	1977			
69.76	Ballyglunin	1860	1976			
73.58	Cloonascragh Pit					Re-opened 1915.
76.11	Tuam	1860	1976	24,750	45'6"	Mileposts zero from here.
1.50	Sugar Factory Sdgs.	1934	1986			
3.35	Pollacorragaune Pit	c1904	c1910			
4.37	Castlegrove	1894	1963			
8.49	Milltown	1894	1963			
12.44	Ballindine	1894	1963			
16.50	Claremorris (W&LR)	1894	1895	8,120	45'0"	Closed 1925 for goods.
17.02	Claremorris MGWR	1895	1963			Open for MGW section traffic.
0.20	Claremorris (Coll.Jct)	1895	1975			
9.31	Kiltimagh	1895	1963			
16.20	Ballast Pit					
17.25	Swinford	1895	1963	8,120		
20.40	Drumshinagh Pit					
24.10	Charlestown	1895	1963			
27.00	Curry	1895	1963			
30.63	Tubbercurry	1895	1963	8,120	45'0"	
35.66	Carrowmore	1895	1963			
41.18	Leyny	1895	1963			
42.41	West of Ireland Brick Sdg	c1906	c1918			
43.60	Ballast Pit					
45.76	Collooney Southern	1895	1963	8,120		
46.38	SL&NCR Jct	1895	1957			End-on junction.
46.14	Collooney Jct	1895	1975			
52.33	Sligo	1895	Open			Running powers from Collooney Jct
52.61	Sligo Goods	1895	Open			

Killonan to Killaloe

Miles	Station	Opened	Closed	Water tank gallons	Turn-table ft in	Remarks
4.17	Killonan	1858	1963			
6.25	Annacotty	1858	1963			Previously known as Grange.
7.00	Thornhill Peat	c1866				
8.00	Lisnagry	1858	1963			Previously known as Nenagh Road.
9.60	Castleconnell	1858	Open			
12.70	Annaholty Peat	c1869	c1884			
14.32	Birdhill	1860	Open			
	Coolnadorny Ballast Pit	c1861				
17.17	Killaloe 1	1862	1894			
17.51	Killaloe 2	1894	1931	3,700	45'0"	
18.02	Killaloe Pier/Lakeside	1867				

Miles	Station	Opened	Closed	Water tank gallons	Turn-table ft in	Remarks

Clonmel to Thurles

Miles	Station	Opened	Closed	Water tank gallons	Turn-table ft in	Remarks
23.60	Powerstown Park	1916	c1941			
15.60	Fethard	1879	1963			
12.55	Farranaleen	1880	1963			
8.12	Laffansbridge	1880	1963	3,980		Also Laffan's Bridge & Killenaule.
4.21	Horse & Jockey	1879	1963			
0.15	Sugar Factory Jct	1934				
0.00	Thurles Jct	1879	1963			
1.12	Thurles GS&WR	1879	Open			

Ballingrane Jct to Foynes

17.27	Ballingrane Jct	1856	1974			
20.70	Askeaton	1857	1974			
26.69	Foynes	1858	Open	2,570	45'0"	
	Foynes Pier	1858				

Tralee to Fenit

0.00	Tralee (L&KR)	1887	1901			
4.40	Spa	1887	1934			
6.20	Kilfenora	1887	1934			
8.00	Fenit	1887	1934	3,750	40'0"	
8.48	Fenit Pier	1887	1973			

Appendix B

LOCOMOTIVES

No.	Name.	GS&WR No.	Type	GSR Class	Wheels	Built	Builder	Maker's No.	Wdn.	Remarks
1	*Glengall*		I		2-2-2	1846	Stothert		1861	
2	*Bessborough*		I		2-2-2	1846	Stothert		1862	
3	*Waterford*		I		2-2-2	1846	Stothert		1861	Probably rebuilt as a tank engine.
4	*Limerick*		I		2-2-2	1846	Stothert		1861	
5	*Suir*		I		2-2-2	1846	Stothert		1862	
6	*Shannon*		I		2-2-2	1846	Stothert		1862	
7			II		2-2-2	1851	Grendon		c1867	Ex Dargan 1853
8			III		2-2-2	1848	Bury		c1880	Ex Dargan 1853; originally NW&RR No.3.
9			III		2-2-2	1848	Bury		1886	Ex Dargan 1853; originally NW&RR No.1 or 2.
10			III		2-2-2	1848	Bury		1888	Ex Dargan 1853; originally NW&RR No.1 or 2.
11		264	IV		2-4-0	1853	Fairbairn		1904	
12			IV		2-4-0	1853	Fairbairn		c1885	
13			V		0-4-2	1853	Sharp Stewart	736	1891	
14			V		0-4-2	1853	Sharp Stewart	737	1891	
15			V		0-4-2	1853	Sharp Stewart	740	1894	Reconstructed as Type XXX in 1894.
16			V		0-4-2	1854	Sharp Stewart	764	1896	
17			VI		2-4-0	1854	Fairbairn		1896	
18			VI		2-4-0	1854	Fairbairn		1897	
19			VI		2-4-0	1854	Fairbairn		c1875	
20			VI		2-4-0	1854	Fairbairn		1892	
21			VI		2-4-0	1855	Fairbairn		1897	
22					0-4-2	1857	Wilson			Ex W&KR No.2; returned in 1867 as No.1.
23					2-4-0	1852	Stothert			Ex W&KR No.4; returned in 1867 as No.2.
24					2-4-0	1852	Stothert			Ex W&KR No.5; returned in 1867 as No.3.
25					2-2-2	1853	Kitson	320		Ex W&KR No.6; returned in 1867 as No.4.
26			VI		2-4-0	1855	Fairbairn		1875	Ex W&KR No.1.
27					2-2-2	1853	Kitson	321		Ex W&KR No.7; returned in 1867 as No.5.
1			XII		0-4-2	1859	Fairbairn		1883	Ex L&ER No. 1.
2			XII		0-4-2	1856	Fairbairn		1900	Ex L&ER No. 2.
3	*Pioneer*		XIII		0-4-2	1845	Sharp Bros.	279	c1873	Ex L&ER No. 3 *Pioneer*; originally *Lady McNeill*
4		(223)	XIV		0-4-2	1862	Sharp Stewart	1345	1901	
5			XIV		0-4-2	1862	Sharp Stewart	1346	1909	Rebuilt as Type XIVa in 1893.
6			XIV		0-4-2	1864	Sharp Stewart	1529	1890	Rebuilt as Type XIVa in 1890.
28	*South of Ireland*	280	XV		2-2-2	1864	Kitson	1213	1902	

No.	Name.	GS&WR No.	Type	GSR Class	Wheels	Built	Builder	Maker's No.	Wdn.	Remarks
29		228	XVI		0-4-0ST	1865	Sharp Stewart	1653	1924	Unofficially named *Darkie*
3			XVII		0-4-2	1872	Kitson	1783	1892	Rebuilt as Type XVIIa in 1892.
7			XVII		0-4-2	1872	Kitson	1784	1888	Rebuilt asType XIVa in 1888.
22			XVIII		0-4-2	1862	Fossick		1890	Ex A&TR No.1; originally D&MR No.1.
23			XVIII		0-4-2	1862	Fossick		1892	Ex A&TR No.2; originally D&MR No.2.
24	*Gort*		XVIII		0-4-2	1862	Fossick	187	1886	Ex A&EJR No.3; originally D&MR No.5.
25					0-4-2	1847	Bury		c1874	Ex A&TR No.3; originally GS&WR No.102
30	*Drumconora*				2-2-2	1847	Grendon		1873	Ex A&EJR No.1; originally MGWR No.8.
31	*Lough Cutra*				2-2-2	1847	Grendon		c1873	Ex A&EJR No.2; originally MGWR No.9 or 10.
25	*Verbena*	277	XIX		2-4-0	1874	Vulcan Foundry	706	1902	Originally named *Limerick*.
30	*Lily*	281	XIX		2-4-0	1874	Vulcan Foundry	707	1904	
31	*Myrtle*	282	XIX		2-4-0	1874	Vulcan Foundry	708	1910	Originally named *Ennis*.
32	*Dahlia*	283	XIX		2-4-0	1874	Vulcan Foundry	709	1910	
19	*Kincora*	272	XX		0-4-2	1876	Avonside	1126	1901	
26		278	XX		0-4-2	1876	Avonside	1125	1910	
27			XX		0-4-2	1876	Avonside	1127	1899	Rebuilt as Type XXa in 1899.
33		284	XX		0-4-2	1876	Avonside	1128	1902	
34		(229)	XXI		0-6-0T	1878	Avonside		1901	
8	*Primrose*	261	XIX		2-4-0	1881	Vulcan Foundry	910	1902	
35	*Duncannon*	285	XIX		2-4-0	1881	Vulcan Foundry	911	1911	
36	*Violet*	286	XIX		2-4-0	1881	Vulcan Foundry	913	1904	
37	*Camelia*	287	XIX		2-4-0	1881	Vulcan Foundry	912	1909	
38	*Hyacinth*	288	XIX		2-4-0	1882	Vulcan Foundry	990	1907	
39	*Shamrock*	289	XIX		2-4-0	1882	Vulcan Foundry	991	1905	Originally named *North Star*.
40	*Vulcan*	230	XXII		0-6-0	1883	Vulcan Foundry	1010	1909	
41	*Titan*	231	XXII		0-6-0	1883	Vulcan Foundry	1011	1910	
1		221	XXIII		0-6-0	1884	R. Stephenson	2379	1909	Rebuilt as 0-6-0ST in 1899.
12	*Earl of Bessborough*	265	XXVI		4-4-0	1886	Vulcan Foundry	1162	1907	Rebuilt as 2-4-0 in 1894.
9	*Garryowen*	262	XXV		4-4-0	1886	Dübs	2194	1912	
24	*Sarsfield*	227	XXVII		0-6-0	1886	Dübs	2195	1910	
42		232	XXIV		0-6-0T	1862	Hawthorn (Leith)	284	1901	Purchased secondhand in 1886.
7	*Progress / Wasp*	226	XIVa		0-6-0	1888	Limerick	7	1905	Rebuilt from Type XVII; renamed *Wasp* in 1893.
10	*Sir James*	263	XXVIII		2-4-0	1889	Dübs	2477	1906	
22	*Era*	275	XXVIII		2-4-0	1890	Dübs	2662	1913	
6	*Ant*	225	XIVa		0-6-0	1890	Limerick	6	1907	Rebuilt from Type XIV.
13	*Derry Castle*	266	XXIX	F5	2-4-2T	1891	Vulcan Foundry	1315	1934	To C&MDR as No. 6, 1914. GSR No.491
14	*Lough Derg*	267	XXIX	F4	2-4-2T	1891	Vulcan Foundry	1316	1935	
3	*Zetland*	260	XVIIa		0-4-2T	1892	Limerick	3	1914	Rebuilt from Type XVII.
20	*Galtee More*	273	XXVIII		2-4-0	1892	Dübs	2880	1909	
23	*Slieve-na-Mon*	276	XXVIII	G3	2-4-0	1892	Dübs	2881	1949	
5	*Bee*	224	XIVa		0-6-0	1893	Limerick	5	1909	Rebuilt from Type XIV.
43	*Knockma*	290	XXVIII	G3	2-4-0	1893	Dübs	3025	1951	
44	*Nephin*	291	XXVIII	G3	2-4-0	1893	Dübs	3026	1959	
45	*Colleen Bawn*	233	XXXI		0-6-0	1893	Dübs	3042	1919	
46	*Erin-go-Bragh*	234	XXXI		0-6-0	1893	Dübs	3043	1911	
47	*Carrick Castle*	292	XXVIII		2-4-0	1894	Dübs	3109	1913	
48	*Granston*	293	XXVIII	G3	2-4-0	1894	Dübs	3110	1954	
15	*Roxborough*	268	XXX		0-4-4T	1894	Limerick	15	1912	Reconstructed from Type V.
49	*Dreadnaught*	235	XXXI	J22	0-6-0	1895	Dübs	3222	1927	
50	*Hercules*	236	XXXI	J22	0-6-0	1895	Dübs	3223	1951	
51	*Castle Hackett*	294	XXXII		0-4-4T	1895	Kitson	3587	1910	
52	*Brian Boru*	295	XXXII	E2	0-4-4T	1895	Kitson	3588	1954	
16	*Rocklands*	269	XXXIII	C5	4-4-2T	1896	Kitson	3616	1957	
17	*Faugh-a-Ballagh*	270	XXXIII	C5	4-4-2T	1896	Kitson	3617	1949	
53	*Jubilee*	296	XXXIV	D15	4-4-0	1896	Kitson	3618	1950	
54	*Killennee*	297	XXXIV	D15	4-4-0	1896	Kitson	3619	1928	
18	*Geraldine*	271	XXXIII	C5	4-4-2T	1897	Kitson	3689	1949	
21	*Castle Blarney*	274	XXXIII	C5	4-4-2T	1897	Kitson	3690	1949	
56	*Thunderer*	237	XXXI	J25	0-6-0	1897	Kitson	3691	1951	
57	*Cyclops*	238	XXXI	J25	0-6-0	1897	Kitson	3692	1934	
58	*Goliath*	239	XXXI	J25	0-6-0	1897	Kitson	3693	1949	
55	*Bernard*	298	XXXIV	D15	4-4-0	1897	Kitson	3694	1950	
27	*Thomond*	279	XXa	E1	0-4-4T	1899	Limerick	27	1953	Rebuilt from Type XX.
2	*Shannon*	222	XXXV	J25	0-6-0	1899	Kitson	3908	1949	
(4)	(*Samson*)		XXXV	J17	0-6-0	1901	Kitson	3974	1929	Sold to MGWR as No.141 *Limerick*; GSR No.233.
(11)	(*Dragon*)		XXXV	J17	0-6-0	1901	Kitson	3975	1950	Sold to MGWR as No. 142 *Athenry*; GSR No.234.

Note: As the W&LR did not have an official classification system for engines, the late Bob Clements used the above type numbers to differentiate between engine classes. The present author has continued its use for clarity.

Appendix C

LOCOMOTIVE DIMENSIONS

Type	Wheels	Cylinders	D.W. ft. in.	B.P. p.s.i	H.S. sq. ft.	G.A. sq. ft.	Weight. t. cwt.	Remarks	
I	2-2-2	15"x22"	5'9"				32-00	See Note 1.	1, 2, 3, 4, 5, 6
II	2-2-2	13"x18"	4'10"	80				See Note 2.	7
III	2-2-2	15"x20"	5'6"	80		11.59	19.10		8, 9, 10
IV	2-4-0	15"x21"	5'0"	95		14.31			11, 12
V	0-4-2	16"x24"	4'6"	95	1178				13, 14, 15, 16
VI	2-4-0	15"x21"	5'6"	95					17, 18, 19, 20, 21, 26
XII	0-4-2	15½"x22"	5'0"			14.40			1, 2
XIII	0-4-2	13½"x20"	4'6"						3
XIV	0-4-2	16"x24"	4'6"		1135.8				4, 5, 6
XV	2-2-2	15"x22"	5'9"	140	882	14.58	28-00		28
XVI	0-4-0ST	12"x17"	4'0"	120	344.5	8.7	20-00		29
XVII	0-4-2	16"x24"	4'6"	140	1010.6	13.00	26-17		3, 7
XVIII	0-4-2	15"x20"	4'8"			11.37			22, 23, 24
XIX	2-4-0	16"x24"	5'6"		816	15.00			8, 25, 30, 31, 32, 35, 36, 37, 38, 39
XX	0-4-2	16"x24"	5'4"		896	15.40	30-00		19, 26, 27, 33
XXI	0-6-0T	15"x18"	4'0"						34
XXII	0-6-0	17½"x26"	5'2"		1027	19.50		See Note 3.	40, 41
XXIII	0-6-0ST	17"x24"	4'6"		1027	19.50		As rebuilt in 1899	1
XXIV	0-6-0WT	15"x21"	3'6"		612				42
XXV	4-4-0	17½"x26"	5'6"	150	1098	15.50	38-10		12
XXVI	4-4-0	16½"x24"	5'1"	160	1098	15.50	32-16		9
XXVII	0-6-0	17"x24"	4'6"	150	1098	15.00	33-02		24
XIVa	0-6-0	16"x24"	4'7"		1135.8		35-15		5, 6, 7
XXVIII	2-4-0	17"x24"	6'0"	150	1110	18.00	36-09		10, 20, 22, 23, 43, 44, 46, 47
XXIX	2-4-2T	16"x24"	5'6"	150	868	15.80	45-00		13, 14
XVIIa	0-4-2T	16"x24"	4'7"	150			41-06		3
XXXI	0-6-0	17"x24"	5'2"	150	1098	19.84	37-00		45, 46
XXX	0-4-4T	16"x24"	4'7"	150	800	14.00			15
XXXIa	0-6-0	17½"x24"	5'2"	150	1098	19.84	33-13		49, 50
XXXII	0-4-4T	16"x24"	5'6"	150	868	15.00	43-00		51, 52
XXXIII	4-4-2T	16"x24"	5'6"	150	868	15.00	46-19		16, 17, 18, 21
XXXIV	4-4-0	17"x24"	6'0"	150	994.36	17.84	40-12		53, 54, 55
XXXV	0-6-0	17"x24"	5'2"	150	981.2	17.84	39-16		56, 57, 58
XXa	0-4-4T	16"x24"	5'3"	150	945	15.8	49-19		27
XXXVa	0-6-0	17"x24"	5'2"	150	981.2	19.8	40-13	Belpaire fireboxes	2, 4, 11

Notes:
1	Total weight including tender.
2	Reduced boiler pressure as in 1861.
3	Cylinders may have originally been 18" diameter as Robinson stated he reduced them.

Appendix D

CARRIAGE STOCK

No.	Type	Built	Builder	Wheels	Length	Compartments 1st 2nd 3rd Lavatory Luggage Guard						Seats 1st 2nd 3rd			GS&WR number	W/drawn	Notes
1	First	1846	Dawson	8								50				1851	
2	First	1846	Dawson	8								50				1851	
3	Second	1846	LMK	8									60			1851	
4	Second	1846	LMK	8									60			1849	Cut in two to form a separate First and Second
5	Second	1847	LMK	8									60			1849	Cut in two to form a separate First and Second
6	Second	1847	LMK	8									60			1851	
7	Third	1847	LMK	8										72		1849	Cut in two to form two separate Thirds
8	Third	1847	LMK	8										72		1849	Temporary Booking Office Boher
9	Third	1847	LMK	8										72		1851	
10	Third	1847	LMK	8										72		1851	Temporary Booking Office Bansha
11	Third	1847	LMK	8										72		1851	
12	Third	1847	LMK	8										72		1851	

No.	Type	Built	Builder	Wheels	Length	1st	2nd	3rd	Lavatory	Luggage	Guard	1st	2nd	3rd	GS&WR number	W/drawn	Notes
4	Second	1849	LMK	4												1854	
5	Second	1849	LMK	4												1854	
7	Third	1849	LMK	4	25' 0"			2								1865	
8	Third	1849	LMK	4	25' 0"			2								1865	
13	First	1849	LMK	4												1854	
14	First	1849	LMK	4												1854	
1	Second	1851	Fagan	6	25' 0"		5									1885	Ex-Dargan; To Third No. 45, 1872
2	Second	1851	Fagan	6	25' 0"		5									1885	Ex-Dargan; To Third No. 46, 1872
3	Third	1851	Fagan	6	25' 0"			2								1872	Ex-Dargan
6	Third	1851	Fagan	6	25' 0"			2								1887	Ex-Dargan
9	Third	1851	Fagan	6	25' 0"			2								1888	Ex-Dargan
11	First	1851	Fagan	6	25' 0"	4										1892	Ex-Dargan
12	First	1851	Fagan	6	25' 0"	4										1896	Ex-Dargan
15	Compo	1848	Fagan	6	25' 0"	1	2	2								1889	Ex-Hutton 1852
16	First	1849	Hutton	6	25' 0"	2									903	1902	Rebuilt as Saloon in 1867; to Compo 1898
17	Compo	1848	Fagan	6	25' 0"		2	3								1892	Ex-GS&WR 1852
18	Compo	1848	Fagan	6	25' 0"		2	3								1895	Ex-GS&WR 1852
10	Coupé Compo	1848	Fagan	6	27' 0"			2		1						1874	Ex-GS&WR 1852; To Third Brake, 1861
19	Third	1848	Fagan	6	25' 0"			2								1887	Ex-GS&WR 1852
20	Third	1848	Fagan	6	25' 0"			2								1877	Ex-GS&WR 1852
21	Third	1848	Fagan	6	25' 0"			2								1888	Ex-GS&WR 1852
22	Third	1848	Fagan	6	25' 0"			2								1889	Ex-GS&WR 1852. New First class body 1859
23	Compo	1852	RCC	6	27' 0"	2	2	2								1897	
24	Compo	1852	RCC	6	27' 0"	2	2	2								1889	
25	Compo	1852	RCC	6	27' 0"	2	2	2							903	1889	
26	Compo	1855	Dawson	6		1	2	1								1896	
27	Compo	1855	Dawson	6		1	2	1								1893	
4	Second	1856	Wright	6	25' 0"		5										901
5	Second	1856	Wright	6	25' 0"		5										
13	First	1856	Wright	6	25' 0"	4						32			946	1916	
14	First	1856	Wright	6	25' 0"	4						32			947	1908	
28	Third	1855	Dawson	6	25' 0"			2								1890	
29	Third	1855	Dawson	6	25' 0"			2								1888	
30	Third Bke	1856	Dawson	6	27' 0"			2			1					1890	Brake Compt. in centre
31	Third Bke	1856	Dawson	6	27' 0"			2			1					1889	Brake Compt. in centre
32	Compo	1856	Dawson	6	27' 0"	2	4									1890	
33	Compo	1856	Dawson	6	27' 0"	2	4									1890	
34	Third	1857	Dawson	6	25' 0"			2								1892	
35	Third	1857	Dawson	6	25' 0"			2								1891	
36	Third	1857	Dawson	6	27' 0"			2								1893	
37	Third	1857	Dawson	6	25' 0"			2						48	958	1901	
38	Third Bke	1857	Dawson	6	27' 0"			2			1			24		1898	Brake Compt. at end. Converted into Accident van No. 38 for Tuam
39	Third	1857	Dawson	6	25' 0"			2								1894	
40	Third	1860	Dawson	6	25' 0"			2								1890	Ex-L&ER 1861
41	Third	1859	Dawson	6	25' 0"		5									1890	Ex-L&ER 1861
42	Second	1859	Dawson	6	25' 0"		5									1894	Ex-L&ER 1861
43	First	1859	Dawson	4	24' 0"	4						31			962	1906	Ex-L&ER 1861 To Compo c1887 and Third 1896
44	Compo	1859	Dawson	6	24' 0"	2	2									1891	Ex-L&ER 1861
47	Compo	1859	Dawson	6	25' 0"	2	3									1895	Ex-L&ER 1861
48	Third	1859	Dawson	6				2								1886	Ex-L&ER 1861
53	Third Bke	1859	Dawson	6				2			1					1892	Ex-L&ER 1861. Brake Compt. in centre c1872
7	Third	1865	LMK	6				2								1891	
8	Third	1866	LMK	6				2								1889	
49	Third	1859	Bristol	4				2								1886	Ex-A&E 1872
50	Compo	1869	Bristol	4	24' 0"	2	2									1892	Ex-A&E or A&T 1872
51	Second	1869	Bristol	4	24' 0"	1	2									1891	Ex-A&E 1872
52	Compo	1869	Bristol	4	24' 0"	2	2									1893	Ex-A&E or A&T 1872
54	Compo	1869	Bristol	4	24' 0"	2	2									1893	Ex-A&E or A&T 1872
55	Second	1869	Bristol	4	24' 0"	1	2									1891	Ex-A&E 1872
56	Compo	1869	Bristol	4	24' 0"	2	2									1897	Ex-A&E or A&T 1872
57	Third	1869	Bristol	4	24' 0"			2								1897	Ex-A&E 1872
(58)	Third	1869	Bristol	4	23' 4"			5								1897	Ex-A&E No. 1, 1872
(59)	Third	1869	Bristol	4	23' 4"			5								1891	Ex-A&E No. 7, 1872
(60)	Third	1869	Bristol	4	23' 4"			5								1891	Ex-A&T No. 4, 1872
1	Second	1872	Ashbury	4	21' 6"		4						40		939	1907	To Third 1888/9
2	Second	1872	Ashbury	4	21' 6"		4						40		940	1907	To Third 1888/9
3	Second	1872	Ashbury	4	21' 6"		4						40		941	1908	To Third 1888/9
10	Compo	1874	WLW	6	25' 0"	2	2					16	20			1898	Converted into Accident van No. 1 for Limerick
20	Compo	1877	MCW	6	30' 0"	2	2			1		16	20		904	1905	
61	Third	1877	MCW	6	28' 0"			6						72		1959	Body rebuilt as Post Office van No. 61, 1900
62	Third	1877	MCW	6	28' 0"			6						72	973	1909	
63	Third	1877	MCW	6	28' 0"			6						72	974	1907	To 26A broken up 1909

No.	Type	Built	Builder	Wheels	Length	Compartments						Seats			GS&WR number	W/drawn	Notes
						1st	2nd	3rd	Lavatory	Luggage	Guard	1st	2nd	3rd			
64	Third	1877	MCW	6	28' 0"			6						72	975	1908	
65	Third	1877	MCW	6	28' 0"			6						72	976	1920	
66	Compo	1877	MCW	6	28' 0"			6						72		1959	Body rebuilt as brake and mail van No. 50, 1899
67	Compo	1877	MCW	6	30' 0"	2	2		1			16	20		917	1905	
68	Compo	1877	MCW	6	30' 0"	2	2		1			16	20		918	1910	To Tool van
69	Compo	1881	BCW	6	30' 0"	2	2		1			16	20		919	1949	To First/Third Compo in 1930
70	Compo	1881	BCW	6	30' 0"	2	2		1			16	20		920	1917	
71	Compo	1881	BCW	6	30' 0"	2	2		1			16	20		921	1905	
72	Compo	1881	BCW	6	30' 0"	2	2		1			16	20		922	1920	
73	Compo	1881	BCW	6	30' 0"	2	2		1			16	20		923	1953	To First/Third Compo in 1930
74	Compo	1881	BCW	6	30' 0"	2	2		1			16	20		924	1923	Maliciously destroyed
75	Compo	1881	BCW	6	30' 0"	2	2		1			16	20		925	1949	To First/Third Compo in 1930
76	Compo	1881	BCW	6	30' 0"	2	2		1			16	20		926	1947	To First/Third Compo in 1930; renumbered 239A 1947
46	Third	1885	LMK	6	26' 0"			6						72	964	1909	
48	Third	1886	LMK	4	24' 0"			4						48	965	1909	Originally Composite, altered to Third
49	Third	1886	LMK	4	24' 0"			4						48	966	1911	Originally Composite, altered to Third 1898
6	Third	1887	LMK	6	30' 0"			5						60	943	1920	
19	Third	1887	LMK	6	30' 0"			5						60	950	1920	
9	Third	1888	LMK	6	24' 0"			4						48	945	1919	To Stores van 1055, broken up 1958
21	Third	1888	LMK	6	30' 0"			5						60	951	1920	Electric light (Double-battery) 08/04/98
29	Third	1888	LMK	6	30' 0"			5						60	953	1941	To Turf wagon, broken up 1955
45	Third	1888	LMK	6	30' 0"			5						60	963	1907	
8	Third	1889	LMK	6	30' 0"			5						60	944	1932	
15	Third	1889	LMK	6	30' 0"			5						60	948	1920	Body to dormitory at Limerick Junction
24	Compo	1889	LMK	6	30' 0"	2	2		1			16	20		906	1946	To First/Third Compo in 1930 and 233A in 1946
25	Compo	1889	LMK	6	30' 0"	2	2		1			16	20		907	1947	To First/Third Compo in 1929 and 234A in 1947
31	Third	1889	LMK	6	30' 0"			5						60	954	1927	To 125A
28	Third	1890	LMK	6	30' 0"			5						60	952	1949	
30	Third Bke	1890	LMK	6	30' 0"			2						24	994	1948	
32	Compo	1890	LMK	6	30' 0"	2	2		1			16	20		910	1919	Electric light (Double-battery) 13/09/98
33	Compo	1890	LMK	6	30' 0"	2	2		1			16	20		911	1954	To First/Third Compo in 1930
40	Third	1890	LMK	6	30' 0"			5						60	960	1941	To 209A, broken up 1955
41	Third	1890	LMK	6	30' 0"			5						60	961	1907	
7	Third Bke	1891	LMK	6	30' 0"			2			1			24	991	1920	Slip coach
35	Third	1891	LMK	6	30' 0"			5						60	956	1941	To Turf wagon, broken up 1955
44	Compo	1891	LMK	6	30' 0"	2	2		1			16	20		912	1923	Maliciously destroyed
51	Third	1891	LMK	4	24' 0"			4						48	967	1909	To 45A
55	Third	1891	LMK	4	24' 0"			4						48	969	1912	To 18A, broken up 1929
59	Third	1891	LMK	6	30' 0"			5						60	972	1916	To 44A, broken up 1940
77	Saloon	1891	LMK	6	30' 5"	2		1				22			900	1963	Spencer's Auxiliary bearing springs. Electric light (Double-battery) 10/01/98 Ambulance coach 1954 Renumbered 465A in 1963. To RPSI 1976.
11	Compo	1892	LMK	6	30' 0"	2	2					16	20		901	1905	
17	Third	1892	LMK	6	30' 0"			5						60	949	1928	
34	Third	1892	LMK	6	30' 0"			5						60	955	1958	Electric light (Double-battery) 28/12/97
50	Compo	1892	LMK	6	30' 0"	2	2					16	20		914	1954	To First/Third Compo in 1930
53	Third Bke	1892	LMK	6	30' 0"			2			1			24	996	1910	
78	Compo	1892	LMK	6	30' 0"	2	2					16	20		927	1958	To First/Third Compo in 1930
27	Compo	1893	LMK	6	30' 0"	2	2					16	20		909	1960	Fitted with Spencer's Auxiliary bearing springs. To First/Third Compo in 1930
36	Third	1893	LMK	6	30' 0"			5						60	957	1923	Electric light (Double-battery) 28/12/97. Maliciously destroyed
52	Compo	1893	LMK	6	30' 0"	2	2					16	20		915	1958	To First/Third Compo in 1930
54	Third	1893	LMK	6	30' 0"			5						60	968	1917	
79	Compo	1893	GCW	6	31' 0"	2	2	1				14	20		928	1958	Claremorris & Collooney Stock, First/Third Comp 1930
80	Compo	1893	GCW	6	31' 0"	2	2	1				14	20		929	1958	Claremorris & Collooney Stock. Electric light (Double-battery) 08/04/98. First/Third Compo 1930
81	Compo	1893	GCW	6	31' 0"	2	2	1				14	20		930	1955	Claremorris & Collooney Stock, First/Third Co 1930
82	Third	1893	Bristol	6	30' 0"			5						60	977	1923	Claremorris & Collooney Stock. To 91A, b/u 1940
83	Third	1893	Bristol	6	30' 0"			5						60	978	1951	Claremorris & Collooney Stock. To 298A, b/u 1951
84	Third	1893	Bristol	6	30' 0"			5						60	979	1942	Claremorris & Collooney Stock. To Loco Dept. Turf wagon 216A, broken up 1955
4	Third	1894	LMK	6	30' 0"			5						60	942	1923	To 101A, broken up 1962
39	Third	1894	LMK	6	30' 0"			5						60	959	1952	
42	Third Bke	1894	LMK	6	30' 0"			2			1			24	995	1958	Slip coach
5	Third Bke	1895	LMK	6	30' 0"			2			1			24	990	1948	
18	Third Bke	1895	LMK	6	30' 0"			2			1			24	992	1958	
47	Compo	1895	LMK	6	30' 0"	1	1	2				8	10	24	913	1917	To 31A
85	Third	1895	MCW	6	30' 0"			5						60	980	1942	To Turf wagon, broken up 1955

No.	Type	Built	Builder	Wheels	Length	1st	2nd	3rd	Lavatory	Luggage	Guard	1st	2nd	3rd	GS&WR number	W/drawn	Notes
								Compartments					**Seats**				
86	Third	1895	MCW	6	30' 0"			5						60	981	1950	To 249A
87	Third	1895	MCW	6	30' 0"			5						60	982	1923	To 90A, broken up 1940
88	Third	1895	MCW	6	30' 0"			5						60	983	1920	Electric light (Double-battery) 08/04/98
89	Third	1895	MCW	6	30' 0"			5						60	984	1949	Spencer's Auxiliary Bearing Springs
90	Third	1895	MCW	6	30' 0"			5						60	985	1941	To Turf wagon, broken up 1950
91	Compo	1895	MCW	6	30' 5"	1	1	2	1			7	9	24	931	1958	To First/Third Compo in 1930
92	Compo	1895	MCW	6	30' 5"	1	1	2	1			7	9	24	932	1955	Electric light (Double-battery) 08/04/98 To First/Third Compo 1930; Third 1948
93	Compo	1895	MCW	6	30' 5"	1	1	2	1			7	9	24	933	1954	Claremorris & Collooney Stock; First/Third in 1930
94	Third Bke	1895	LMK	6	30' 0"			2		1	1			24	998	1954	Claremorris & Collooney Stock
12	Coupé Compo	1896	LMK	6	30' 5"	2	2		1			11	14		902	1949	Electric Light 24/02/96, Double Battery 17/09/98 To First/Third Compo in 1930
26	Coupé Compo	1896	LMK	6	30' 5"	2	2		1			9	14		908	1949	Electric light 18/08/96, Double-battery 12/01/98 To First/Third Compo 1930
95	Third	1896	ASH	8	48' 0"			8						96	986	1960	Electric light 23/08/96, Double-battery 08/04/98
96	Third	1896	ASH	8	48' 0"			8						96	987	1959	Electric light 23/08/96, Double-battery 18/02/98
97	Compo	1896	MCW	8	48' 0"	3	3		1			21	27		934	1959	Electric light 23/08/96, Double-battery 08/04/98 First/Third Compo 1930; HC4 1959, and 526A 1967
98	Compo	1896	MCW	8	48' 0"	3	3		1			21	27		935	Prvd	Electric light 23/08/96, Double-battery 18/02/98 Invalid coach 1919; Radio Studio 1953; RS21 1964
99	Coupé Compo	1896	LMK	6	30' 5"	2	2		1			9	14		936	1958	Electric light 18/08/96, Double-battery 12/01/98 To First/Third Compo in 1930
100	Third	1896	ASH	6	30' 5"			5						60	988	1942	Electric Light 18/08/96, Double Battery 12/01/98 To Turf Wagon, broken up 1955
101	Third	1896	ASH	6	30' 5"			5						60	989	1923	Electric light 18/08/96, Double-battery 12/01/98 To 92A
23	Compo	1897	LMK	6	30' 5"	2	2					11	19		905	1960	Electric light (Double-battery) 28/12/97 To First/Third Compo in 1930
56	Coupé Compo	1897	LMK	6	30' 0"	2	2		1			11	19		916	1952	Electric light (Double-battery) 28/12/97 To First/Third Compo in 1930
57	Third	1897	LMK	6	30' 0"			5						60	970	1923	Maliciously destroyed
58	Third	1897	LMK	6	30' 0"			5						60	971	1942	To Turf wagon, broken up 1955
102	Compo Bke	1898	LMK	8	48' 0"	2	2			1	1	20	24		937	1955	Electric light (Double-battery) 12/01/99 To Third Brake 1930
103	Compo Bke	1898	LMK	8	48' 0"	2	2			1	1	20	24		938	1955	Electric light (Double-battery) 12/01/99 To Third Brake 1929
22	Third Bke	1899	LMK	6	30' 0"			2		1	1			24	993	1923	Maliciously destroyed
60	Third Bke	1899	LMK	6	30' 0"			2		1	1			24	997	1958	

Appendix E

WAGON STOCK

Capital acquisitions

Wagon Nos	Year built	Type	Builder	Remarks
1 to 68	1846-48		Limerick	Early stock – see text
69 to 118	1852	Open Cattle	B-M	
119 to 162	1852	Cov OC	B-M	
163 to 202	1855-56	Cov OC	Dawson	
203 to 232	1856	Cov OC	Limerick	
233 to 254	1859	Cov OC	Dawson	
255 to 258	1859	Open	Dawson	
259 to 263	1859	Cov OC	Dawson	
264 to 279	1859	Open	Dawson	
280 to 320	1860	Cov OC	Dawson	Last 11 to W&KR in 1867
321 to 353	1856	Cov OC	Ashbury	Ex-W&KR; 16 rebuilt as cattle wagons and returned to W&KR in 1867
354 to 383	1848	Open	Walshe	Ex-W&KR; all replaced 1862
384 to 396	1856	Open	Ashbury	Ex-W&KR; three rebuilt as cattle wagons and returned to W&KR in 1867
397 to 402				Two cattle and four Cov OC Ex-W&KR. All rebuilt as cattle wagons; returned 1867.
403 to 412		Ballast		Ex-W&KR; four rebuilt as cattle wagons, six renumbered 26 to 31, all returned 1867.
413 to 443	1862	Open	Limerick	All but last two to W&KR in 1867
444 to 449	1864	Open	Limerick	Rebuilt from Ballast wagons Ex-Dargan.
450 to 489	1861	Open		Purchased from Smith & Knight 1863

Wagon No.	Year Built	Type	Builder	Notes
490 to 529	1859	Cov OC	Dawson	Ex-L&ER 1861, renumbered 1863
530 to 533	1859	Open	Dawson	Ex-L&ER 1861, renumbered 1863
534 to 560	1866-67	Open	Limerick	
561 to 563	1872	Cov OC	MCW	
564 to 609	1870-71	Cov OC	Bristol	Ex-A&EJR/A&TR in 1872
610 to 612	1876	Cov OC	Limerick	
613 to 712	1876	Covered	Oldbury	
713 to 730	1877	Coal	SWC	
731 to 748		Timber		Renumbered from separate list c1879
749	1889	Timber	Limerick	
750 to 849	1880	Cov OC	SIW	
850	1888	Cov OC	Limerick	
851 to 950	1883	Cov OC	SWC	
951 to 1005	1891-92	Cov OC	SWC	
1006 to 1030	1891-92	Covered	SWC	
1031 to 1050	1892	Cov Cattle	SWC	
1051 to 1093		Loco Coal		43 wagons displaced by new SWC opens in 1891; rebuilt at Limerick from 1892.
1094 to 1113	1894	Cov Cattle	Limerick	
1114 to 1153	1895	Cattle	GCW	
1154 to 1167	1895	Open	GCW	
1168 to 1177	1894	Coal	MCW	Purchased from Fisher & LeFanu, 1896
1178 to 1179	1892	Covered	TFC	Rented prior to purchase in 1896
1180 to 1199	1896	Open	Limerick	
1200 to 1212	1888	Covered	Stableford	From W. J. Shaw & Sons, 1896
1213 to 1312	1896-97	Open	Limerick	Ashbury underframes
1313 to 1317	1897	Covered	Limerick	
1318 to 1342	1898	Open	Limerick	Metropolitan underframes
1343 to 1347	1898	Cov Cattle	Limerick	

Wagons provided by W&LR for working A&TECLR — 55-8, 61, 66-8, 144, 258, 264/9, 273/7/9, 355, 362, 378/9, 388, 506, 519, 522, 536, 542, 555/7, 560, 571, 715

Wagon replacements built at Limerick

Year	Open coal	Covered goods (Open centre)	Covered	Open cattle	Ballast	Timber
1861		151				
1862	16, 372				1, 2, 3, 4, 5, 6, 7, 8, 9, 10, 11, 12, 13, 14, 15	
1863	51, 52, 53, 62, 66.			80		
1864	18, 19, 20, 21, 22, 23, 24, 25, 26, 49, 54, 55, 56, 63, 68	124		82, 89, 99, 110		
1865	64	163, 407, 408, 409, 410, 411, 412		107, 113		
1866	59, 547, 554, 556, 558			72, 96, 111		
1867	57	223, 283, 285		69, 70, 71, 73, 74, 75, 76, 77, 78, 79, 81, 83, 84, 85, 86, 87, 88, 90, 91, 92, 93, 94, 95, 97, 98, 100, 101, 102, 103, 104, 105, 106, 108, 109, 112, 114, 115, 116, 117, 118		
1868	533	122, 123, 125, 128, 133, 134, 137, 139, 142, 150, 153, 155, 157, 158, 160				
1869	48	119, 120, 121, 126, 127, 129, 130, 132, 136, 138, 140, 141, 144, 145, 146, 147, 148, 149, 152, 154, 156, 159, 161, 162, 185, 301	135 (Gunpowder)			
1870	61, 67	187, 189, 198				
1871		164, 186, 564				
1872		131, 143				
1875		215				
1876	275		205, 565			
1879		524				
1880		241, 308, 511, 656				744, 748
1881		169, 216, 230, 235, 254, 392, 491, 501, 580		77, 315		
1882	52, 259, 374, 381, 541, 546	175, 206, 222, 243, 245, 253, 263, 281, 302, 514, 576, 586, 597, 602, 608		87, 89, 92, 104, 310, 311, 313, 316, 320, 322	14	
1883		223, 247, 582, 585, 607, 667	604	74, 106, 108, 110, 111, 319	17, 18, 19, 20	
1884	238, 612	286, 291, 391, 496, 515, 527, 575, 589, 605				739

Year	Open coal	Covered goods (Open centre)	Covered	Open cattle	Ballast	Timber
1885		210	583, 584, 587, 590, 592, 598, 606	312		730, 745
1886	287, 300	231, 232	566, 572, 573, 574, 609			737, 738
1887		309				731, 736, 743, 746
1888		577		71, 73, 79, 90, 96, 100, 101, 105, 107, 116, 118, 317, 323, 324, 325, 326, 327	1, 2, 3, 4, 5, 6, 7, 8, 9, 11, 12, 13, 15, 16	

Year	Open coal	Covered goods (Open centre)	Covered goods	Covered cattle	Open cattle	Ballast	Timber	Loco coal
1889	60, 377, 380, 531, 551	143, 201, 399, 492	632, 633, 668	334, 335, 336, 337, 338, 339	80, 82, 85, 93, 99, 103, 114		720, 721, 722, 723, 724, 725, 726, 727, 728, 729, 732, 733, 740, 741, 747	
1890	274, 552	126, 133, 138, 139, 162, 166, 179, 203, 214, 640	142, 151, 165, 180, 251, 294, 358, 397, 403, 406, 411, 493, 563, 581, 591, 634, 636, 648, 655, 660, 662, 689, 693, 695, 709, 710		69, 91, 115		718, 719	
1891		127, 140, 141, 146, 150, 155, 156, 157, 159, 160, 171, 174, 199, 211, 240, 246, 250, 284, 395, 401, 408, 410, 412, 502, 504, 513, 521, 526, 601, 603, 620, 628, 690, 711	191, 192, 296, 393, 499, 505, 562			21, 22, 23, 24		
1892	51	128, 134, 172, 182, 220, 283, 292, 298, 498	184, 209, 213, 218, 219, 224, 289, 394, 494, 518, 611		70, 72, 76, 94, 95, 97, 109, 117	25		1051, 1052, 1053, 1055, 1057, 1058, 1059, 1065, 1066, 1069, 1082, 1087, 1084
1893		132, 202	167, 190, 194, 197, 212, 226, 233, 500, 517, 528, 651	330, 331, 332, 333, 340, 341, 342, 343, 344, 345, 346, 347				
1894	193		163, 285, 503, 507, 625, 631, 639, 698	328, 348, 349, 350, 351, 352, 353, 354, 355, 356, 357		10		1060, 1061, 1074, 1088, 1091, 1093
1895	62, 147, 373, 530, 538, 544, 548, 599, 600		249, 295, 305, 508, 653, 684, 708	75, 102, 113, 318, 329				1077
1896	307		204, 569, 570, 578, 622, 623, 638, 641, 642, 644, 652, 659, 665, 672, 677, 683, 687, 704	81, 88, 112			734, 735 (Flats for Furniture vans)	
1897	535, 553, 716		181, 303, 561, 593, 613, 618, 619, 621, 624, 629, 643, 645, 646, 649, 654, 658, 663, 664, 666, 673, 675, 678, 679, 681, 685, 686, 694, 696, 702, 707, 712		78, 83, 84, 86, 98, 119, 120, 121, 122, 123, 124, 125		742	1054, 1072, 1073, 1076, 1090
1898	567		579, 697, 699, 705, 817, 821, 832, 840					368
1899	178, 300, 539, 541, 556, 558, 595, 612		393, 670, 692, 756, 766, 804, 846	126, 127, 128, 129, 130, 131				372, 1056, 1064, 1068, 1079, 1080, 1086
1900	59, 64, 65, 177, 265, 525, 545			132, 133, 134, 135, 136, 137, 138, 139, 140, 322				

Wagon replacements procured from outside builders

Year	Builder	Open coal/Covered goods (Open centre)	No
1860	Dawson	Covered goods (Open centre)	47, 50
1862	Dawson	Open Coal	354, 355, 356, 357, 358, 359, 360, 361, 362, 363, 364, 365, 366, 367, 368, 369, 370, 371, 372, 373
1870	MCW	Covered goods (Open centre)	166, 167, 171, 173, 176, 187, 189, 190, 195, 198, 201, 384
1870	MCW	Open cattle	310, 311, 321, 313, 314, 315, 316, 317, 318, 319, 320, 322, 323, 324, 326, 327, 328, 329, 331, 333
1870	MCW	Open coal	413, 414, 415, 416, 417, 418, 419, 420, 421, 422, 423, 424, 425, 426, 427, 428, 429, 430, 431, 432
1870-71	Bristol	Open coal (Ex-A&TR/A&EJR 1872)	17, 26, 27, 28, 29, 30, 31, and one other
1871	MCW	Covered goods (Open centre)	164, 172, 179, 181, 182, 184, 186, 188, 191, 192, 194, 197, 199, 203
1872	MCW	Open Coal	265, 433, 434, 435, 436, 437, 438, 439, 440, 441
1872	MCW	Covered goods (Open centre)	170, 221, 336, 337, 339, 340, 346, 349, 353, 393, 394, 397, 398, 399, 400, 401, 402, 403, 404, 405, 406, 407, 408, 409, 410, 411, 412
1877	MCW	Covered goods vans	200, 207, 225, 227, 236, 237, 239, 248, 252, 276, 280, 297, 304, 359, 389, 396, 490, 495, 497, 509, 512, 516, 520, 529, 568
1877	SWC	Open coal	63, 64, 65, 173, 177, 178, 183, 261, 262, 271, 278, 364, 365, 367, 369, 370, 371, 375, 488, 523, 525, 537, 539, 543, 545, 549, 550, 567, 568, 594, 595, and one other
1888	Stableford	Open coal	26, 27, 28, 29, 30, 31, 32, 33, 34, 35, 36, 37, 38, 39, 40, 41, 42, 43, 44, 45, 46, 47, 48, 49, 50
1888	Stableford	Covered goods (Open centre)	413, 414, 415, 416, 417, 418, 419, 420, 421, 422, 423, 424, 425, 426, 427, 428, 429, 430, 431, 432, 433, 434, 435, 436, 437, 438, 439, 440, 441, 442, 443, 444, 445, 446, 447, 448, 449, 450, 451, 452, 453, 454, 455, 456, 457, 458, 459, 460, 461, 462, 463, 464, 465, 466, 467, 468, 469, 470, 471, 472, 473, 474, 475, 476, 477, 478, 479, 480, 481, 482, 483, 484, 485, 486, 487
1880-81	SIW	Open coal	59, 270, 360, 363, 366, 540
1891	SWC	Open coal	53, 54, 55, 56, 57, 58, 61, 66, 67, 68, 137, 144, 152, 196, 228, 242, 255, 257, 258, 260, 264, 266, 267, 268, 269, 272, 273, 277, 279, 282, 362, 378, 379, 382, 383, 388, 489, 506, 519, 522, 532, 534, 536, 542, 555, 557, 560, 571, 715, 717
1893	Bristol	Open coal (Ex-Fisher & LeFanu 1896)	154, 207, 227, 276, 297, 304, 389, 490, 495, 497, 520, 559
1894	Bristol	Open coal (Ex-Fisher & LeFanu 1896)	129, 136, 402, 516, 280
1894	SWC	Open coal (Ex-Fisher & LeFanu 1896)	188, 200, 236, 237, 239, 248, 509, 512, 610

Rolling stock builders

BCW	Birmingham Railway Carriage & Wagon Co.		RCC	Railway Carriage Company, Bromsgrove
B-M	Brown Marshall & Co., Birmingham		SIW	South of Ireland Wagon Co., Cappoquin
GCW	Gloucester Railway Carriage & Wagon Co.		SWC	Swansea Wagon Co.
MCW	Metropolitan Railway Carriage & Wagon Co., Saltley		TFC	Tubular Frame Wagon Co., Barrow-in-Furness

Appendix F

CHAIRMEN AND PRINCIPAL OFFICERS

Chairmen

1848	Thomas Meagher
1850	Earl of Glengall
1856	Henry Massy
1859	John Connolly
1861	William Malcomson
1873	Abraham Stephens
1876	Thomas Synnott
1883	Abraham Stephens
1885	James Spaight
1892	Edmond R. Mahony
1893	Percy Bernard

Secretaries

1848	William Septimus Saunders
1851	John O'Connor
1858 [1]	Thomas Ainsworth
1873 [2]	John Fowler Nicoll
1878	M. J. Kennedy
1883 [3]	John J. Murphy

Traffic Superintendents/Managers [4]

1848	Thomas Mackie
1852	Charles Bagnell
1853	Lewis DeMay
1854 [5]	John O'Connor
1855	William Labatt Payne
1862	Henry Jacob
1867	Thomas Ainsworth
1872	Isaac Banks

1875	John Roberts
1892	S. J. Glynn [Acting]
1892	Frederick Vaughan

Engineers

1848	Richard B. Osborne
1850	Andrew Stewart
1855	John Challoner Smith
1864 [6]	James Tighe
1864 [7]	John Long
1900 [8]	R. H. Good

Consulting Engineers

1851-66 [8]	George W. Hemans

Locomotive Superintendents

1847	William Martley
1848	Abraham Khlos
1848-52	Vacant (haulage contract)
1852	Charles Bagnell
1853	Thomas Lunt
1857	Jonathan Pim
1861	Martin Atock
1872	Mark Wardle
1873 [9]	Robert Andrews
1875 [10]	Thomas Armitage
1879	Edward Barry
1883	Henry Appleby
1889 [11]	John George Robinson
1900 [12]	William Gadd

Notes

1. Ainsworth acted as Secretary & Traffic Superintendent from 1868 to 1872.
2. Nicoll was Secretary and General Manager in 1876/7.
3. Murphy was Secretary and Accountant between 1883 & 1889.
4. Titles changed at intervals for no apparent reason.
5. O'Connor acted jointly as Secretary and Traffic Superintendent from 1854 to 1855.
6. James Tighe was District Engineer at Waterford from 1864 to 1866, when he was appointed as Engineer for the entire line.
7. John Long was District Engineer at Limerick between 1864 and 1866.
8. R. H. Good was appointed Acting Engineer following the death of Tighe in 1900.
9. Robert Andrews later went to Belfast & Northern Counties Railway.
10. Armitage came from Dublin & Belfast Junction Railway and may have had connections with DN&GR/LNWR.
11. Robinson was appointed Assistant to Appleby in 1884.
12. Following Robinson's departure to GCR in 1900, Gadd was appointed Acting Superintendent. He remained with GS&WR until 1908. He later joined C&MDR as Locomotive Superintendent.

Appendix G

PRINCIPAL ACCIDENTS

Date	Location	Killed	Injured	Remarks
2 Dec.1852	Bansha	1	?	Poor Permanent way and use of outside-cylinder engine.
1 Jan. 1854	Nr Kilsheelan	1	3	Derailment. Engine and permanent way both defective.
27 May 1858	Nr Pallas	1	0	Passenger exited train on wrong side and fell off bridge.
6 Apr. 1859	Nr Bansha	0	3+	Collision. BoT condemned irregular working.
2 Aug. 1860	Nr Limerick	0	0	Derailment of engine. Use of outside-cylinder engine?
29 Mar. 1869	Nr Clonmel	0	17	Collision. Train left station without authority.
20 Oct. 1873	Ballyglunin	0	Several	Collision due to neglect of driver.
2 Nov. 1873	Tuam			Derailment. Engine PW defective. Interlocking suggested.
29 Nov. 1873	Limerick Jct	0	4	Collision due to neglect by driver.
21 Aug. 1875	Longpavement	1	1	Train derailed. Fracture of tyre on leading wheel of engine.
29 Sep. 1881	Patrickswell	0	56	Collision. Train failed to stop. Defective working arrangements.
7 Dec. 1882	Limerick Jct.	0	3	Collision. Non-observance of rules.
2 Apr. 1883	Fethard	0	8	Collision. Train failed to stop. Driver unfamiliar with road.
5 Dec. 1883	Carrick-on-Suir	0	0	Collision. Violation of rules.
2 Jan. 1884	Athenry	0	7	Collision between MGWR/W&LR trains. Driver passed signal.
19 July 1890	Limerick Jct.	0	1	Collision between passenger train and light engine.

INDEX